CompTIA Security+ (Exam SY
Objective lesson map

M000190899

	OBJECTIVE	CHAPTER
1.0	**NETWORK SECURITY (21 PERCENT)**	
1.1	Explain the security function and purpose of network devices and technologies: Firewalls; Routers; Switches; Load Balancers; Proxies; Web security gateways; VPN concentrators; NIDS and NIPS (Behavior based, signature based, anomaly based, heuristic); Protocol analyzers; Sniffers; Spam filter, all-in-one security appliances; Web application firewall vs. network firewall; URL filtering, content inspection, malware inspection	2
1.2	Apply and implement secure network administration principles: Rule-based management, Firewall rules, VLAN management, Secure router configuration, Access control lists, Port Security, 802.1x, Flood guards, Loop protection, Implicit deny, Prevent network bridging by network separation, Log analysis	2, 3
1.3	Distinguish and differentiate network design elements and compounds: DMZ, Subnetting, VLAN, NAT, Remote Access, Telephony, NAC, Virtualization, Cloud Computing (Platform as a Service, Software as a Service, Infrastructure as a Service)	3
1.4	Implement and use common protocols: IPSec, SNMP, SSH, DNS, TLS, SSL, TCP/IP, FTPS, HTTPS, SFTP, SCP, ICMP, IPv4 vs. IPv6	3
1.5	Identify commonly used default network ports: FTP, SFTP, FTPS, TFTP, TELNET, HTTP, HTTPS, SCP, SSH, NetBIOS	3
1.6	Implement wireless network in a secure manner: WPA, WPA2, WEP, EAP, PEAP, LEAP, MAC filter, SSID broadcast, TKIP, CCMP, Antenna Placement, Power level controls	3
2.0	**COMPLIANCE AND OPERATIONAL SECURITY (18 PERCENT)**	
2.1	Explain risk related concepts: Control types (Technical, Management, Operational); False positives; Importance of policies in reducing risk (Privacy policy, Acceptable use, Security policy, Mandatory vacations, Job rotation, Separation of duties, Least privilege); Risk calculation (Likelihood, ALE, Impact); Quantitative vs. qualitative; Risk-avoidance, transference, acceptance, mitigation, deterrence; Risks associated to Cloud Computing and Virtualization	1, 4
2.2	Carry out appropriate risk mitigation strategies: Implement security controls based on risk, Change management, Incident management, User rights and permissions reviews, Perform routine audits, Implement policies and procedures to prevent data loss or theft	1, 4
2.3	Execute appropriate incident response procedures: Basic forensic procedures (Order of volatility, Capture system image, Network traffic and logs, Capture video, Record time offset, Take hashes, Screenshots, Witnesses, Track man hours and expense), Damage and loss control, Chain of custody, Incident response: (first responder)	1
2.4	Explain the importance of security related awareness and training: Security policy training and procedures; Personally identifiable information; Information classification: Sensitivity of data (hard or soft); Data labeling, handling and disposal; Compliance with laws, best practices and standards; User habits (Password behaviors, Data handling, Clean desk policies, Prevent tailgating, Personally owned devices); Threat awareness, (New viruses, Phishing attacks, Zero-day exploits); Use of social networking and P2P	4
2.5	Compare and contrast aspects of business continuity: Business impact analysis, Removing single points of failure, Business continuity planning and testing, Continuity of operations, Disaster recovery, IT contingency planning, Succession planning	4

2.0	**COMPLIANCE AND OPERATIONAL SECURITY (18 PERCENT)**	
2.6	Explain the impact and proper use of environmental controls: HVAC, Fire suppression, EMI shielding, Hot and cold aisles, Environmental monitoring, Temperature and humidity controls, Video monitoring	4
2.7	Execute disaster recovery plans and procedures: Backup / backout contingency plans or policies; Backups, execution and Frequency; Redundancy and fault tolerance (Hardware, RAID, Clustering, Load balancing, Servers); High availability; Cold site, hot site, warm site; Mean time to restore, mean time between failures, recovery time objectives and recovery point objectives	4
2.8	Exemplify the concepts of confidentiality, integrity and availability (CIA)	1
3.0	**THREATS AND VULNERABILITIES (21 PERCENT)**	
3.1	Analyze and differentiate among types of malware: Adware, Virus, Worms, Spyware, Trojan, Rootkits, Backdoors, Logic bomb, Botnets	5
3.2	Analyze and differentiate among types of attacks: Man-in-the-middle, DDoS, DoS, Replay, Smurf attack, Spoofing, Spam, Phishing, Spim, Vishing, Spear phishing, Xmas attack, Pharming, Privilege escalation, Malicious insider threat, DNS poisoning and ARP poisoning, Transitive access, Client-side attacks	5
3.3	Analyze and differentiate among types of social engineering attacks: Shoulder surfing, Dumpster diving, Tailgating, Impersonation, Hoaxes, Whaling, Vishing	5
3.4	Analyze and differentiate among types of wireless attacks: Rogue access points, Interference, Evil twin, War driving, Bluejacking, Bluesnarfing, War chalking, IV attack, Packet sniffing	5
3.5	Analyze and differentiate among types of application attacks: Cross-site scripting, SQL injection, LDAP injection, XML injection, Directory traversal/command injection, Buffer overflow, Zero day, Cookies and attachments, Malicious add-ons, Session hijacking, Header manipulation	5
3.6	Analyze and differentiate among types of mitigation and deterrent techniques: Manual by-passing of electronic controls (Failsafe/secure versus failopen), Monitoring system logs (Event logs, Audit logs, Security logs, Access logs), Physical security (Hardware locks, Mantraps, Video surveillance, Fencing, Proximity readers, Access list), Hardening (Disabling unnecessary services, Protecting management interfaces and applications, Password protection, Disabling unnecessary accounts), Port security (MAC limiting and filtering, 802.1x, Disabling unused ports), Security posture (Initial baseline configuration, Continuous security monitoring, remediation), Reporting (Alarms, Alerts, Trends), Detection Controls vs. prevention controls (IDS vs. IPS, Camera vs. guard)	6
3.7	Implement assessment tools and techniques to discover security threats and vulnerabilities: Vulnerability scanning and interpret results, Tools (Protocol analyzer, Sniffer, Vulnerability scanner, Honeypots, Honeynets, Port scanner), Risk calculations (Threat vs. likelihood), Assessment types (Risk, Threat, Vulnerability), Assessment technique (Baseline reporting, Code review, Determine attack surface, Architecture, Design reviews)	7
3.8	Within the realm of vulnerability assessments, explain the proper use of penetration testing versus vulnerability scanning: Penetration testing (Verify a threat exists, Bypass security controls, Actively test security controls, Exploiting vulnerabilities), Vulnerability scanning (Passively testing security controls, Identify vulnerability, Identify lack of security controls, Identify common misconfiguration), Black box, White box, Gray box	7
4.0	**APPLICATION, DATA AND HOST SECURITY (16 PERCENT)**	
4.1	Explain the importance of application security: Fuzzing, Secure coding Concepts (Error and exception handling, Input validation), Cross-site scripting prevention, Cross-site Request Forgery (XSRF) prevention, Application configuration baseline (proper settings), Application hardening, Application patch management	8
4.2	Carry out appropriate procedures to establish host security: Operating system security and settings, Anti-malware (Anti-virus, Anti-spam, Anti-spyware, Pop-up blockers, Host-based firewalls), Patch management, Hardware security (Cable locks, Safe, Locking cabinets), Host software baselining, Mobile devices (Screen lock, Strong password, Device encryption, Remote wipe/sanitation, Voice encryption, GPS tracking), Virtualization	9
4.3	Explain the importance of data security: Data Loss Prevention (DLP), Data encryption (Full disk, Database, Individual files, Removable media, Mobile devices), Hardware based encryption devices (TPM, HSM, USB encryption, Hard drive), Cloud Computing	10

5.0	**ACCESS CONTROL AND IDENTITY MANAGEMENT (13 PERCENT)**	
5.1	Explain the function and purpose of authentication services: RADIUS, TACACS, TACACS+, Kerberos, LDAP, XTACACS	11
5.2	Explain the fundamental concepts and best practices related to authentication, authorization and access control: Identification vs. authentication, Authentication (single factor) and authorization, Multifactor authentication, Biometrics, Tokens, Common access card, Personal identification verification card, Smart card, Least privilege, Separation of duties, Single sign on, ACLs, Access control, Mandatory access control, Discretionary access control, Role/rule-based access control, Implicit deny, Time of day restrictions, Trusted OS, Mandatory vacations, Job rotation	
5.3	Implement appropriate security controls when performing account management: Mitigates issues associated with users with multiple account/roles, Account policy enforcement (Password complexity, Expiration, Recovery, Length, Disablement, Lockout), Group based privileges, User assigned privileges	11
6.0	**CRYPTOGRAPHY (11 PERCENT)**	
6.1	Summarize general cryptography concepts: Symmetric vs. asymmetric, Fundamental differences and encryption methods (Block vs. stream), Transport encryption, Non-repudiation, Hashing, Key escrow, Steganography, Digital signatures, Use of proven technologies, Elliptic curve and quantum cryptography	12
6.2	Use and apply appropriate cryptographic tools and products: WEP vs. WPA/WPA2 and pre-shared key, MD5, SHA, RIPEMD, AES, DES, 3DES, HMAC, RSA, RC4, One-time-pads, CHAP, PAP, NTLM, NTLMv2, Blowfish, PGP/GPG, Whole disk encryption, TwoFish, Comparative strengths of algorithms, Use of algorithms with transport encryption (SSL, TLS, IPSec, SSH, HTTPS)	12
6.3	Explain the core concepts of public key infrastructure: Certificate authorities and digital certificates (CA, CRLs), PKI, Recovery agent, Public key, Private key, Registration, Key escrow, Trust models	12
6.4	Implement PKI, certificate management and associated components: Certificate authorities and digital certificates (CA, CRLs), PKI, Recovery agent, Public key, Private keys, Registration, Key escrow, Trust models	12

CompTIA Security+ (Exam SYO-301)
Training Kit

David Seidl
Mike Chapple
James Michael Stewart

Published with the authorization of Microsoft Corporation by:

O'Reilly Media, Inc.
1005 Gravenstein Highway North
Sebastopol, California 95472

ISBN: 978-0-7356-6426-5

1 2 3 4 5 6 7 8 9 QG 8 7 6 5 4 3

Printed and bound in the United States of America.

Microsoft Press books are available through booksellers and distributors worldwide. If you need support related to this book, email Microsoft Press Book Support at mspinput@microsoft.com. Please tell us what you think of this book at *http://www.microsoft.com/learning/booksurvey*.

Acquisitions and Developmental Editor: Kenyon Brown

Production Editor: Melanie Yarbrough

Editorial Production: Online Training Solutions, Inc. (OTSI)

Technical Reviewer: Addam Schroll

Copyeditor: Online Training Solutions, Inc. (OTSI)

Indexer: BIM Publishing Services

Cover Design: Twist Creative • Seattle

Cover Composition: Ellie Volkhausen

Illustrator: Online Training Solutions, Inc. (OTSI)

Contents at a glance

Contents

What do you think of this book? We want to hear from you!

Microsoft is interested in hearing your feedback so we can continually improve our
books and learning resources for you. To participate in a brief online survey, please visit:

www.microsoft.com/learning/booksurvey/

Chapter 9   Establishing host security   317

What do you think of this book? We want to hear from you!

Microsoft is interested in hearing your feedback so we can continually improve our
books and learning resources for you. To participate in a brief online survey, please visit:

www.microsoft.com/learning/booksurvey/

Introduction

This training kit is designed for information technology (IT) professionals who want to earn the CompTIA Security+ certification. It is assumed that you have a basic understanding of computers and operating systems. However, the CompTIA Security+ certification is an entry-level certification, so you are not expected to have any in-depth knowledge to use this training kit.

To become a CompTIA Security+ certified technician, you must take and pass the SY0-301 exam. The primary goal of this training kit is to help you build a solid foundation of IT knowledge so that you can successfully pass the exam the first time you take it.

The materials covered in this training kit and on exam SY0-301 relate to the technologies a successful security professional is expected to understand. These include risk management, infrastructure security, application security, policy, and confidentiality/integrity/availability controls. You can download the objectives for the SY0-301 exam from the CompTIA website here:

http://certification.comptia.org/Training/testingcenters/examobjectives.aspx

By using this training kit, you will learn how to do the following:

- Conduct risk assessment and risk management activities.
- Respond to a security incident.
- Understand the risks associated with cloud computing and virtualization.
- Explain the various types of network security devices and technologies.
- Design a network with adequate security controls.
- Administer network security controls on an ongoing basis.
- Secure wireless networks with acceptable encryption.
- Provide adequate environmental and operational security controls.
- Understand the threats on the security landscape.
- Deploy defenses to prevent and mitigate attacks.
- Conduct vulnerability assessments and manage vulnerabilities.
- Secure applications against attack.
- Secure operating systems against common threats.
- Use encryption to protect information at rest and in motion.
- Deploy access controls to implement identification, authentication, and authorization.

Refer to the objective mapping page in the front of this book to see where in the book each exam objective is covered.

About the exam

The SY0-301 exam is focused on skills required to secure systems, applications, and networks. It includes objectives in the following six areas:

- Network security (21 percent of exam)
- Compliance and operational security (18 percent of exam)
- Threats and vulnerabilities (21 percent of exam)
- Application, data, and host security (16 percent of exam)
- Access control and identity management (13 percent of exam)
- Cryptography (11 percent of exam)

The current version of the exam became available in 2011. Over the years, more than 45,000 people around the world have earned the CompTIA Security+ certification. Information security professionals often start with the CompTIA Security+ certification to lay a solid foundation of information security knowledge and later move on to higher-level certifications and better-paying jobs. Among those test takers are those who are working to meet the US Department of Defense's Directive 8570.01-M, which lists the CompTIA Security+ exam as one of the required certifications for employees and contractors who perform information security work.

The CompTIA Security+ exam has a maximum of 100 questions, including both multiple-choice and performance-based questions. You will have 90 minutes in which to take the test, and a score of 750 on a scale of 100-900 is considered a passing score. You can find more information about the exam at:

http://certification.comptia.org/getCertified/certifications/security.aspx

Prerequisites

CompTIA recommends that test takers have the CompTIA Network+ certification as well as two years of technical networking experience with an emphasis on information security work.

Note that this is not a requirement to take the exams. Anyone can take the exams after paying for them, and if they pass, they earn the certification. However, you'll have the best chance of success if you have been studying and working with networks and information security professionally and are familiar with the material in the CompTIA Network+ exam.

Performance-based testing

A significant difference in the SY0-301 exam over previous versions is the introduction of performance-based testing. Instead of just using multiple-choice questions, CompTIA is introducing questions that will require you to perform a task. You should expect to see somewhere around three of these questions on the exam, so don't stress over them.

Imagine that you wanted to know if a person could ride a bike. You could ask some multiple-choice questions but you'll find that these questions aren't always reliable. A person might answer questions correctly but not be able to actually ride the bike. Put the person in front of a bike, ask them to ride it, and you'll quickly know whether they can or not. Performance-based testing uses this philosophy to see if the candidate has a skill.

Consider this multiple-choice question:

1. What TCP port is used for SMTP traffic by default?

    A. 21

    B. 23

    C. 25

    D. 80

The correct answer is port 25.

In a performance-based question, you might instead be asked to complete a set of firewall rules by filling in the missing information. This might include selecting the ports corresponding to several services and specifying which rules should be set to allow or deny traffic.

When it's a multiple-choice question, you have a 25-percent chance of getting it correct. In a performance-based question, there are an infinite number of possibilities, and the test designers are able to test you on multiple concepts or facts simultaneously.

Throughout the book, we've included steps and instructions on how to do many tasks with performance-based testing in mind. If you do these tasks as you work through the book, you'll be better prepared to answer these performance-based tests.

Study tips

There's no single study method that works for everyone, but there are some common techniques that many people use to successfully pass these exams. These include:

- **Setting a goal** Pick a date when you expect to take the exam, and set your goal to take it then. The date is dependent on how long it will take you to read the chapters and your current knowledge level. You might set a date two months from now, four months from now, or something else. However, pick a date and set a goal.

- **Taking notes**   If concepts aren't familiar to you, take the time to write them down. The process of transferring the words from the book, through your head, and down to your hand really helps to burn the knowledge into your brain.

- **Reading your notes**   Go back over your notes periodically to see what has stuck, and what you need to review more. You can't bring notes with you into the testing area, but you can use them to review key material before the exam.

- **Using flash cards**   Some people get a lot out of flash cards that provide a quick test of knowledge. These help you realize what you don't know and what you need to brush up on. Many practice test programs include flash cards, so you don't necessarily have to create them yourself.

- **Reviewing the objectives**   This is what CompTIA says they'll test you on. Sometimes just understanding the objective will help you predict a test question and answer it correctly.

- **Recording your notes**   Many people record their notes in an MP3 player and play them back regularly. You can listen while driving, while exercising, or just about any time. Some people have a partner read the notes, which can give an interesting twist to studying.

- **Taking the practice test questions on the CD**   The practice test questions on the CD are designed to test the objectives for the exam but at a deeper level than you'll have on the live exam. Each question includes detailed explanations on why the correct answer is correct, and why the incorrect answers are incorrect. Ideally, you should be able to look at the answers to any question and not just know the correct answer, but also why the incorrect answers are incorrect.

System requirements

The actual system requirements to use this book are minimal. The only requirement is a computer you can use to install the practice tests on the companion CD.

Many of the examples in the book use Windows 7 and Linux or Mac OS X. In most organizations, security staff work with a variety of operating systems, and we have attempted to reflect that in this book. You will find that most Windows commands remain the same whether you are using Windows XP, Windows Vista, Windows 7, or Windows 8, with most differences appearing in the menus used to get to settings. Thus, if you only have a Windows XP–based system to practice Windows commands with, you can still expect to successfully learn the critical practical techniques covered in the book.

Instead of having two or three separate computers to allow you to run Windows and Linux, you can use a single PC with virtualization software hosting these operating systems, or a Linux Live-CD or USB flash drive bootable system to work with. The next section provides suggested hardware requirements for running a virtualized workstation for practice. Booting into a LiveCD or portable Linux distribution can also be done on similar hardware.

Hardware requirements for virtualization

If you plan to use virtualization, your computer should have the following:

- A processor that includes hardware-assisted virtualization (AMD-V or Intel VT) that is enabled in the BIOS. (Note that you can run Windows Virtual PC without Intel-VT or AMD-V.) Ideally, the processor will be a 64-bit processor so that you can have more RAM.

- At least 2.0 GB of RAM, but more is strongly recommended, and 4 GB is often a more practical minimum.

- 20 GB of available hard disk space for a single VM, and at least 80 GB of total hard disk space for a system running virtual machines.

- Internet connectivity.

Software requirements

Most of the examples in this book use Windows 7, Linux, or Mac OS X. Virtualization allows you to use all three simultaneously, which can ease your learning experience. Fortunately, there are several free virtualization software packages available, including Windows Virtual PC, VirtualBox, and VMWare Player.

Oracle provides VirtualBox as a free download from *https://www.virtualbox.org/wiki/Downloads*, and you can download a free version of VMware Player from *http://www.vmware.com/products/player/overview.html*. Both VirtualBox and VMware Player support 64-bit host machines, but you can only run 32-bit hosts within Windows Virtual PC.

Linux virtual machines are commonly available, including BackTrack Linux, a security-focused distribution that combines an excellent collection of security tools into a downloadable virtual machine. You can download BackTrack Linux at *http://www.backtrack-linux.org/downloads/*. For the purposes of the examples in this book, most common Linux security distributions are also valid options.

Using the companion CD

A companion CD is included with this training kit. The companion CD contains the following:

- **Practice tests** You can reinforce your understanding of the topics covered in this training kit by using electronic practice tests that you customize to meet your needs. You can practice for the SY0-301 certification exam by using tests created from a pool of 200 realistic exam questions, which give you many practice exams to ensure that you are prepared.

- **An ebook download** Instructions to download the electronic version (eBook) of this book is included for when you do not want to carry the printed book with you.

> **NOTE COMPANION CONTENT FOR DIGITAL BOOK READERS**
>
> If you bought a digital-only edition of this book, you can enjoy select content from the print edition's companion CD. Visit *http://aka.ms/CompTIASecurityTK/files* to get your downloadable content.

How to install the practice tests

To install the practice test software from the companion CD to your hard disk, perform the following steps:

1. Insert the companion CD into your CD drive and accept the license agreement. A CD menu appears.

> **NOTE IF THE CD MENU DOES NOT APPEAR**
>
> If the CD menu or the license agreement does not appear, AutoRun might be disabled on your computer. Refer to the Readme.txt file on the CD for alternate installation instructions.

2. Click *Practice Tests* and follow the instructions on the screen.

How to use the practice tests

To start the practice test software, follow these steps:

1. Click Start, All Programs, and then select Microsoft Press Training Kit Exam Prep.

   A window appears that shows all the Microsoft Press training kit exam prep suites installed on your computer.

2. Double-click the practice test you want to use.

When you start a practice test, you choose whether to take the test in Certification Mode, Study Mode, or Custom Mode:

- **Certification Mode**   Closely resembles the experience of taking a certification exam. The test has a set number of questions. It is timed, and you cannot pause and restart the timer.

- **Study Mode**   Creates an untimed test during which you can review the correct answers and the explanations after you answer each question.

- **Custom Mode**   Gives you full control over the test options so that you can customize them as you like.

In all modes, the user interface when you are taking the test is basically the same but with different options enabled or disabled depending on the mode.

When you review your answer to an individual practice test question, a "References" section is provided that lists where in the training kit you can find the information that relates to that question and provides links to other sources of information. After you click Test Results to score your entire practice test, you can click the Learning Plan tab to see a list of references for every objective.

How to uninstall the practice tests

To uninstall the practice test software for a training kit, use the Program And Features option in Windows Control Panel.

CompTIA professional certification program

CompTIA.

CompTIA professional certifications cover the technical skills and knowledge needed to succeed in a specific IT career. Certification is a vendor-neutral credential. An exam is an internationally recognized validation of skills and knowledge and is used by organizations and professionals around the globe. CompTIA certification is ISO 17024 Accredited (Personnel Certification Accreditation) and, as such, undergoes regular reviews and updates to the exam objectives. CompTIA exam objectives reflect the subject areas in an edition of an exam and result from subject matter expert workshops and industry-wide survey results regarding the skills and knowledge required of a professional with a number of years of experience.

> **MORE INFO   COMPTIA CERTIFICATIONS**
>
> For a full list of CompTIA certifications, go to *http://certification.comptia.org/getCertified/certifications.aspx*.

 Training materials given the CAQC seal has gone through a rigorous approval process to confirm the content meets exam objectives, language standards, necessary hands-on exercises and labs and applicable Instructional Design standards.

How certification helps your career

Certification can help your Security career in the following ways:

- **Security is one of the highest demand job categories**   Growing in importance as the frequency and severity of security threats continues to be a major concern for organizations around the world.

- **Jobs for security administrators are expected to increase by 18%**   The skill set required for these types of jobs maps to the CompTIA Security+ certification.

- **Network Security Administrators**   Can earn as much as $106,000 per year.

- **CompTIA Security+ is the first step**   In starting your career as a Network Security Administrator or Systems Security Administrator.

- **More than ¼ million**   Individuals worldwide are CompTIA Security+ certified.

- **CompTIA Security+ is regularly used in organizations**   Such as Hitachi Systems, Fuji Xerox, HP, Dell, and a variety of major U.S. government contractors.
- **Approved by the U.S. Department of Defense (DoD)**   As one of the required certification options in the DoD 8570.01-M directive, for Information Assurance Technical Level II and Management Level I job roles.

It pays to get certified

In a digital world, digital literacy is an essential survival skill. Certification demonstrates that you have the knowledge and skill to solve technical or business problems in virtually any business environment. CompTIA certifications are highly- valued credentials that qualify you for jobs, increased compensation and promotion.

Some of the primary benefits individuals report from becoming Security+ certified are:

- More efficient troubleshooting
- Improved career advancement
- More insightful problem solving

Four steps to getting certified and staying certified

If you want to get certified and stay certified, follow these steps:

1. **Review Exam Objectives**   Review the Certification objectives to make sure you know what is covered in the exam. Visit *http://certification.comptia.org/examobjectives. aspx* for information.

2. **Practice for the Exam**   After you have studied for the certification, review and answer the sample questions to get an idea what type of questions might be on the exam. Go to *http://certification.comptia.org/samplequestions.aspx* for additional information.

3. **Purchase an Exam Voucher** Purchase exam vouchers on the CompTIA Marketplace, which is located at: *www.comptiastore.com*

4. **Take the Test** Go to the Pearson VUE website and schedule a time to take your exam. Visit *http://www.pearsonvue.com/comptia/* for information.

Stay certified! Take advantage of continuing education

Effective January 1, 2011, new CompTIA Security+ certifications are valid for three years from the date of certification. There are a number of ways the certification can be renewed. For more information, go to *http://certification.comptia.org/ce.*

How to obtain more information

You can obtain more information about CompTIA in several ways:

- Visit CompTIA online: At *http://certification.comptia.org/home.aspx* to learn more about getting CompTIA certified.
- Contact CompTIA: Call 866-835-8020 and choose Option 2 or email *questions@comptia.org.*
- Connect with us:
  - **LinkedIn** *http://www.linkedin.com/groups?home=&gid=83900*
  - **Facebook** *http://www.facebook.com/CompTIA*
  - **Twitter** *https://twitter.com/comptia*
  - **Flickr** *http://www.flickr.com/photos/comptia*
  - **YouTube** *http://www.youtube.com/user/CompTIATV*

Acknowledgments

I would like to thank Mike Chapple, who pulled me into the world of professional writing, and who is both a mentor and a friend. I'd also like to thank all of those involved in the creation of this book, including our co-author James Michael Stewart; our technical editor Addam Schroll, whose thoughtful analysis, useful comments, and deep knowledge helped make our content even better; my ever helpful agent Carole Jelen from Waterside Productions; Kenyon Brown, our awesome senior editor; and Melanie Yarbrough, Kathy Krause, and the other staff at O'Reilly, OTSI, and Microsoft Press for their great work in making this a polished work.

This book wouldn't have been possible without the information security team at the University of Notre Dame, and my students in MGTI 30640, who asked great questions and drove conversations that shaped how I wrote explanations and stories in this book. Thank you!

Finally, I'd like to thank Lauren for providing balance and care as I wrote, my many wonderful and supportive friends who cheered me on through this process, and my librarian parents, Jim and Kathleen Seidl, for raising me with a love of books and writing.

—DAVID SEIDL

I would like to thank the many people who contributed to this book. First, my co-authors, David Seidl and James Michael Stewart, without whom we never would have been able to complete this project. Ken Brown from O'Reilly Media was an invaluable resource who pitched the idea to us and then guided us through the editorial process. Addam Schroll provided valuable insight with detailed comments on each chapter, while Melanie Yarbrough, Kathy Krause, and Marlene Lambert kept us on track and ensured that we didn't mangle the English language too badly! Finally, Carole Jelen with Waterside Productions, my literary agent, has served as my advocate and coach for the past decade.

My deepest thanks go to my wife, Renee, and my boys, Richard, Matthew, and Christopher, for their patience over the past six months as Dad spent many evenings and weekends pecking away at the keyboard wrapping up this project.

—MIKE CHAPPLE

Thanks to Mike Chapple and David Seidl for inviting me to contribute to this book. Working with you guys is and always has been a pleasure. Thanks to the management and editors at O'Reilly for putting up with my bad grammar. Thanks to my wife, Cathy, and our wonderful kids, Slayde and Remi—you will never be able to comprehend my love for you. To my dad, you are missed. To my mom, thanks for your love and consistent support; we are always here for you. To my best friend Mark—now that I'm 42, I realize how important the answer is to the ultimate question. And as always, to Elvis—now I see the wisdom of deep-fried, battered bacon.

—JAMES MICHAEL STEWART

Support & feedback

The following sections provide information on errata, book support, feedback, and contact information.

Errata

We've made every effort to ensure the accuracy of this book and its companion content. Any errors that have been reported since this book was published are listed on our Microsoft Press site at oreilly.com:

http://aka.ms/CompTIASecurityTK/errata

If you find an error that is not already listed, you can report it to us through the same page.

If you need additional support, email Microsoft Press Book Support at:

mspinput@microsoft.com.

Please note that product support for Microsoft software is not offered through the addresses above.

We want to hear from you

At Microsoft Press, your satisfaction is our top priority, and your feedback our most valuable asset. Please tell us what you think of this book at:

http://www.microsoft.com/learning/booksurvey

The survey is short, and we read every one of your comments and ideas. Thanks in advance for your input!

Stay in touch

Let us keep the conversation going! We are on Twitter: *http://twitter.com/MicrosoftPress.*

Preparing for the exam

The CompTIA Security+ exam is a great way to build your resume, and to show potential employers that you have the knowledge you need for a career in information security. This book covers the CompTIA Security+ body of knowledge, and includes both real-world knowledge and practical explanations that will help you apply what you learn in the real world.

As you prepare for the exam, we recommend that you use the self-check questions in the book to help test your knowledge as your read each chapter. When you're ready to test your knowledge, use the included self-tests to take the next step to prepare for the exam. If you want more hands-on classroom experience, you might also choose to take the CompTIA Security+ professional certification course.

## CHAPTER 1

Risk management and incident response

I nformation security is the art and practice of managing the confidentiality, integrity, and availability risks associated with information. As you begin your exploration of the field, it is best to start with that in mind. In this chapter, we'll explore the process that security professionals use to identify, assess, and manage the risks facing their organizations. We will also review the incident response procedures used when a risk materializes.

> **IMPORTANT**
> ### Have you read page xxxi?
> It contains valuable information regarding the skills you need to pass the exam.

Exam objectives in this chapter:

Objective 2.1: Explain risk related concepts

- Control types
    - Technical
    - Management
    - Operational
- Risk calculation
    - Likelihood
    - ALE
    - Impact
- Quantitative vs. qualitative
- Risk-avoidance, transference, acceptance, mitigation, deterrence
- Risks associated to Cloud Computing and Virtualization

Objective 2.2: Carry out appropriate risk mitigation strategies

- Implement security controls based on risk
- Change management

- Incident management
- User rights and permissions reviews
- Perform routine audits

Objective 2.3: Execute appropriate incident response procedures

- Basic forensic procedures
  - Order of volatility
  - Capture system image
  - Network traffic and logs
  - Capture video
  - Record time offset
  - Take hashes
  - Screenshots
  - Witnesses
  - Track man hours and expense
- Damage and loss control
- Chain of custody
- Incident response: first responder

Objective 2.8: Exemplify the concepts of confidentiality, integrity and availability (CIA)

CIA and DAD triads

Security professionals, tasked with protecting the information assets of an organization, typically think of their responsibilities in three realms: confidentiality, integrity, and availability (CIA). Adversaries, seeking to disrupt an organization's security, have three corresponding goals in mind: disclosure, alteration, and denial (DAD). These models, shown in Figure 1-1, are known as the CIA and DAD triads and are the classic models embraced by security professionals around the world.

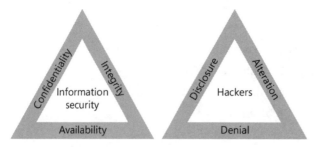

FIGURE 1-1 The CIA and DAD triads are the classic models of information security principles.

Confidentiality and disclosure

The goal of *confidentiality* is to prevent unauthorized access to sensitive information. Quite simply, it is to keep secrets secret. Achieving confidentiality first requires that an organization classify its data—identifying which information assets are worthy of protection and the appropriate level of protection for each. For example, an organization might consider design documents for an unreleased product highly sensitive due to their competitive value. On the other hand, the internal phone book might be considerably less sensitive. Organizing confidential information into different data classifications allows security professionals to design appropriate controls, focusing scarce resources on the most sensitive data.

Adversaries, on the other hand, pursue the goal of *disclosure*, gaining access to sensitive information without permission. They may want to use this information for personal gain, to embarrass the organization publicly, or to simply make information freely available.

Real world

WikiLeaks

The WikiLeaks website, made famous by disclosures of sensitive US government information by Bradley Manning in 2010 and Edward Snowden in 2013, is dedicated to the disclosure of information that governments and corporations may find embarrassing.

Integrity and alteration

Security professionals also pursue the goal of *integrity*, ensuring that information is only modified or deleted by authorized means. Protecting the integrity of information requires controls against deliberate *alteration* by adversaries—such as an employee seeking to modify his payroll information without permission. It also requires protection against unintentional alteration, such as the corruption of data due to a software or hardware failure.

> *MORE INFO* INTEGRITY CONTROLS
>
> Chapter 4, "Operational and environmental security," covers integrity controls in more detail and includes a discussion of disaster recovery and business continuity procedures.

Availability and denial

It's not sufficient for security professionals to provide confidentiality and integrity controls. These must be supplemented with *availability* protection that ensures that authorized individuals have access to information when needed. *Denial* attacks occur when an adversary is able to successfully interrupt the availability of information, such as through a denial of service (DoS) attack. Adversaries might also attempt to harness many systems around the world to simultaneously perform a denial attack by using a technique known as distributed denial of service (DDoS).

MORE INFO   DOS AND DDOS ATTACKS

Chapter 5, "Threats and attacks," includes a discussion of denial of service and distributed denial of service attacks.

 Quick check

1. What are the three goals of information security professionals?

2. What are the corresponding three goals of hackers?

Quick check answers

1. Confidentiality, integrity, and availability

2. Disclosure, alteration, and denial

Risk assessment and mitigation

In order to meet the three goals of confidentiality, integrity, and availability, security professionals must have a solid understanding of the specific risks facing their organization. These will vary, depending upon the organization's line of business, types of information handled, and even physical location. For example, an educational institution might consider the loss of student records, preventing grades from being issued, to be its greatest risk; whereas a military unit might believe that its greatest risk is the disclosure of secret plans that might lead to the death of personnel. Similarly, a business located in Florida might be very concerned about the risk posed by a hurricane, whereas a business in Nebraska would worry more about tornados.

To perform an assessment of risks, we first must have a common language. There are three important terms related to risk assessment:

- **Vulnerabilities**   Weaknesses in an organization's security controls that might allow a breach of confidentiality, integrity, or availability. Vulnerabilities are internal factors.

- **Threats**   External forces that might undermine the security controls of an organization.

- **Risks**   Situations that occur when there is an intersection of a vulnerability in an organization's security controls and a threat that seeks to exploit that vulnerability (see Figure 1-2).

FIGURE 1-2 This equation shows the relationship between threats, vulnerabilities, and risks.

Consider the example of a web server that contains sensitive, password-protected information that has limited distribution to the customers of an organization. An individual who seeks to gain access to this information without paying is a threat to the confidentiality of that data. A misconfiguration in the web server that allows unlimited attempts to guess the password is a vulnerability. The combination of this vulnerability with a corresponding threat seeking to exploit it presents the risk that the organization's information will be stolen.

A vulnerability without a corresponding threat does not pose a risk to the organization. For example, an organization's data center might be vulnerable to flooding. If the data center is in a desert environment where there is no threat of flooding, there is no risk to manage. Similarly, a threat without a corresponding vulnerability also does not pose a risk. If an intruder knows how to pick locks, he may pose a threat to your organization, but if you use locks that have keypads rather than keys, they are not vulnerable to this threat. (Of course, they remain vulnerable to an intruder who knows how to defeat the keypad!)

Organizations seeking to secure their information normally begin with a risk identification process that enumerates the threats facing the organization, the vulnerabilities in the organization's existing security controls, and the risks that result from intersections between these threats and vulnerabilities.

Likelihood and impact

After an organization identifies those threats and vulnerabilities that pose a risk to their information assets, the next step in the risk assessment process is to evaluate the priority of those risks based upon two factors:

- The *likelihood* that a risk will materialize. Some risks are simply more likely than others, depending upon the nature of the vulnerability or threat. For example, the threat of a physical break-in is much more likely to occur in a high-crime urban environment than it is on a military base located in a desert.

- The *impact* that a risk will have on the organization if it does materialize. Some breaches of confidentiality, integrity, or availability will have more disruptive impacts on an organization than others. For example, a successful website denial of service attack might have low impact on a construction firm, but the same attack would be disastrous for an e-commerce retailer that depends upon the website to generate revenue.

Organizations might perform this risk assessment by using techniques that fall into two different categories: qualitative techniques and quantitative techniques.

Qualitative risk assessment

Qualitative risk assessment uses the subjective judgment of experts to evaluate the likelihood and impact of risks facing the organization. The process used to create a qualitative risk assessment can range significantly, depending upon the sophistication of the organization. Some organizations with advanced risk assessment capabilities have standing executive committees that meet regularly to discuss and evaluate risks. In less formal approaches, several experts at lower levels in the organization might work together to develop a qualitative risk assessment.

Regardless of the approach, qualitative assessments rely upon the judgment and institutional knowledge of these individuals to rank risks based upon the likelihood that they will occur and the impact on the organization if they do. The most common approach is to assign each risk a rating of "high," "moderate," or "low" for both likelihood and impact. The results can then be visually portrayed in a matrix similar to the one shown in Figure 1-3.

	Low	Moderate	High
High	Power outage	Disclosure of employee SSNs	Website DoS
Moderate		Database corruption	
Low	Theft of encrypted laptop		Tornado

Likelihood (vertical axis) — Impact (horizontal axis)

FIGURE 1-3 A matrix such as this can be used for qualitative risk assessment.

Using this type of visual approach for a qualitative risk assessment allows decision-makers to easily grasp the priority of addressing each risk. In the matrix shown in Figure 1-3, it is apparent that the greatest risk facing the organization is a denial of service attack on the website (high likelihood, high impact). If the organization's chief information officer is trying to decide between investing in availability controls that will reduce the likelihood that the risk will materialize or purchasing anti-theft devices for encrypted laptops, she will be able to make the decision easily after reviewing the qualitative risk assessment. Improving the availability controls addresses a much more significant risk than protecting encrypted laptops against theft (low likelihood, low impact).

Quantitative risk assessment

Quantitative risk assessments take a more rigorous approach, using numeric data to perform risk calculations in terms of financial value. This requires the use of several factors and formulas:

- Organizations must first identify the *asset value (AV)* for each asset covered by the risk assessment. AV is normally expressed in terms of dollar value. This can be done by using a variety of valuation techniques, such as purchase price, replacement cost, or depreciated value. It's a good idea to consult your organization's financial division to ensure that the asset valuation technique used in your risk assessment process is consistent with organizational standards.

> **NOTE   DETERMINING ASSET VALUE**
>
> Identifying the value of an asset can be quite difficult, especially for information assets. It's easy to put a value on a server by using either the purchase price or replacement cost. But what is the value of a list of employee Social Security numbers (SSNs)? One way of valuing such intangible assets is to estimate the costs you would incur if the information were disclosed or lost.

- For each risk facing an asset, the risk assessment process next identifies the *exposure factor (EF)*. The exposure factor is the amount of damage that would occur to an asset if the risk were to materialize; this is normally expressed as a percentage. For example, if the risk of fire is likely to destroy half of a data center, the EF is 50 percent.

- The last input into the quantitative risk assessment process is the *annualized rate of occurrence (ARO)*. This is the likelihood that the risk will materialize, expressed as the number of times the risk is expected to occur in a typical year. The value may be less than one if the risk is expected less than once per year. For example, a business located in a 100-year flood plain expects flooding once every 100 years. The ARO for this risk would be 1 in 100, or 0.01.

- Next, the risk assessment process calculates the *single loss expectancy (SLE)*. This is the impact of the risk, expressed as the financial loss that occurs each time the risk materializes; it is calculated by using this formula:

    $SLE = AV \times EF$

- Finally, the risk is calculated as the product of likelihood (ARO) and impact (SLE) by using this formula:

    $ALE = SLE \times ARO$

This formula provides the *annualized loss expectancy (ALE)*, or the expected financial loss that will occur due to the risk in a typical year.

Let's work through an example of quantitative risk assessment. Consider a data center located in the San Francisco Bay Area. Risk managers for the firm owning the data center would certainly be interested in assessing the risk associated with an earthquake damaging the data center. Here's the process they would go through to do this by using quantitative techniques:

1. Identify the asset value (AV). They might do this by consulting data center construction experts and determining that the replacement cost of the data center would be $20 million. (AV = $20 million)

2. Determine the exposure factor (EF). Consulting with those same experts might identify that the data center would be half destroyed by a significant earthquake. (EF = 50 percent)

3. Identify the annualized rate of occurrence (ARO). This is the likelihood of an earthquake occurring in a particular year. The US Geological Survey estimates that the Bay Area is likely to suffer an earthquake causing extensive damage once every 30 years. (ARO = 0.03)

4. Calculate the single loss expectancy (SLE). This is the impact of an earthquake, expressed as the financial loss that a single earthquake would create, and is calculated as the product of the asset value and exposure factor:

    $SLE = AV \times EF$
    $SLE = \$20 \text{ million} \times 50 \text{ percent}$
    $SLE = \$10 \text{ million}$

5. Calculate the annualized loss expectancy (ALE). This is the risk, expressed as the financial loss from earthquakes expected in a typical year:

$ALE = SLE \times ARO$

$ALE = \$10\ million \times 0.03$

$ALE = \$300,000$

A risk manager can now use the annualized loss expectancy to make risk-based decisions. For example, an earthquake insurance policy with a $50,000 annual premium would be a good investment!

Managing risk

After an organization completes a risk assessment, it has a clear picture in quantitative and/or qualitative terms that allows it to prioritize the risks facing the organization. Security professionals must then take action to manage those risks. They have five options at their disposal: risk avoidance, risk transference, risk mitigation, risk deterrence, and risk acceptance. They can select one or more of these strategies for each risk identified in the risk assessment.

Risk avoidance

In a *risk avoidance* strategy, the organization changes its business activities to avoid the risk entirely. For example, an organization considering the earthquake risk described in the quantitative risk assessment section of this chapter might decide that the risk is simply too high to justify and decide to relocate the data center to an area that is not threatened by earthquakes. In other cases, an organization might be able to stop performing a particular activity that creates risk. For example, an organization concerned about the theft of Social Security numbers might decide to stop collecting them and purge them from its databases.

Risk avoidance is often a dramatic step that involves significant time and expense to implement. In many cases, business requirements prevent the use of this strategy because of the disruption of necessary business activity. For example, a credit card processing company cannot decide to entirely avoid the risk of handling highly sensitive credit card information without going out of business!

Risk transference

Risk transference moves the impact of a risk from one entity to another. The most common form of transferring risk is the purchase of an insurance policy where, in exchange for a periodic premium payment, an insurance company agrees to accept the financial risk associated with an asset or activity. Businesses often purchase insurance policies for fire, accident, theft, and other risks. It is also becoming more common to see organizations purchase insurance that protects against information security liabilities.

Another form of risk transference takes place when two entities sign a contract that contains an indemnification clause. When placed into a contract, an indemnification clause specifies the terms under which one entity will assume responsibility, especially financial responsibility, for a particular type of liability. For example, a company that provides you with cloud services might indemnify you against the risk that their software violates the intellectual property of a third party. In the event that a third party later attempted to sue you for damages, the indemnification clause of your contract would transfer liability for those damages to the cloud provider.

Risk mitigation

The most common risk management strategy followed by information security professionals is *risk mitigation*. In this strategy, security professionals use controls designed to reduce the likelihood that a risk will affect an organization and/or the impact that a risk will have on the organization if it materializes.

When an organization decides to adopt a risk mitigation approach, it designs and implements one or more security controls that can be directly mapped to that risk. For example, an organization seeking to reduce the risk of network intrusion might decide to install a network firewall, a network intrusion prevention system, and monitoring software. Each of these three controls can then be directly mapped to the risk of network intrusion.

> **NOTE** **VIRTUALIZATION RISKS**
>
> The increased use of virtualization to host multiple guest operating systems on a single hardware platform promises reduced costs and increased efficiencies, prompting many IT organizations to pursue virtualization strategies. Security professionals in organizations adopting virtualization have additional risks that they should consider mitigating. For example, they should take steps to ensure that it is not possible for someone working inside a guest operating system to gain access to the virtualization platform or other guest operating systems. This attack, known as a "VM escape," runs the risk of exposing unrelated, and potentially sensitive, data to unauthorized individuals.

Risk deterrence

In some cases, the organization might be able to adopt a strategy of *risk deterrence*. This approach uses measures designed to reduce the likelihood that a threat will surface. The most common example of deterrence is used to thwart criminal activity by counter-threatening with an aggressive reaction stance. For example, an organization might aggressively prosecute individuals who attempt to intrude into computer systems without permission. Similarly, the owners of a physical facility might have vicious guard dogs on site that threaten intruders with bodily harm. This strategy, used judiciously, can be highly effective, because criminals looking for a target of opportunity will simply go elsewhere.

Risk acceptance

In some cases, an organization might decide that *risk acceptance* is the most appropriate strategy for managing a particular risk. In this scenario, after careful evaluation, the organization decides that the most prudent course of action is to simply monitor the evolution of a risk. Cost or operational concerns dictate that the organization cannot or should not avoid, mitigate, transfer, or deter the risk, so no further action is taken.

NOTE   RISK ACCEPTANCE SHOULD BE ON AN EDUCATED BASIS

It's far too easy to look at a complex risk and simply utter the words "we accept that risk as a cost of doing business." This is not an acceptable risk management strategy, because it is more akin to *ignoring* a risk rather than accepting it. Risks should only be accepted after careful study and analysis reveals that there simply is no other acceptable strategy for managing the risk.

 Quick check

1. What are the five risk management strategies?

2. What risk management strategy is most commonly used by information security professionals?

Quick check answers

1. Risk avoidance, risk transference, risk mitigation, risk acceptance, and risk deterrence

2. Risk mitigation

Security controls

As mentioned in the previous section, security professionals spend a large amount of their time developing ways to mitigate risks facing an organization's information assets. The methods they develop to reduce risk are known as security controls and are grouped into three categories: technical controls, operational controls, and management controls. A balanced approach to information security combines controls from each of these categories to mitigate a wide variety of risks.

Technical controls

Technical controls, as the name implies, leverage technology to reduce the likelihood or impact of a risk on an organization. These controls are typically implemented with the advice and consultation of security professionals and are then maintained either by security professionals, system administrators, network engineers, database administrators, or other technical staff with the appropriate skillset.

Examples of technical controls abound in the security industry. Firewalls, intrusion detection systems, and wireless encryption are examples of technical controls used in network security. Antivirus software, full disk encryption, and user authentication are examples of technical controls for host security. Transport encryption, input validation, and role-based access are examples of application-oriented technical controls. Most organizations with a well-developed security program can likely list dozens of individual technical controls in place to mitigate various security risks.

Operational controls

Operational controls are similar to technical controls in that they directly impact information systems, but the job of carrying out an operational control is primarily done by individuals, rather than technology. For example, although implementing access control systems is a technical control, performing periodic reviews of user rights and permissions is an operational control. Similarly, the process of business continuity planning, which is discussed in Chapter 4, is an operational control. Other operational controls include conducting routine information security audits, implementing change and configuration management procedures, ensuring physical security, and conducting background checks and other personnel security measures.

Management controls

Management controls are those controls focused on the risk management process itself. They ensure that the risk management process is running effectively and, therefore, have an indirect impact on the security of an organization's information assets. Operational and technical controls, on the other hand, directly impact those assets.

Examples of management controls include conducting periodic risk assessments and security control assessments, following a security planning process, and protecting the security of the system and services acquisition life cycle.

MORE INFO **CONTROLS**

A large portion of this book is dedicated to describing security controls in more detail. For example, Chapters 2 and 3 describe technical controls for network security, Chapter 4 covers operational controls, and Chapters 6 and 7 cover a variety of management controls.

 Quick check

1. What are the three categories of controls discussed on the CompTIA Security+ exam?

2. Firewalls are an example of what type of control?

Quick check answers

1. Technical, operational, and management

2. Technical

Incident response

Though security professionals strive to ensure that risk management and control processes prevent breaches of confidentiality, integrity, and availability, it is simply impossible to build a completely secure system. A determined (or lucky) attacker can often find a way to bypass even the most sophisticated control systems. Therefore, security professionals must also develop, train on, and implement sound incident response procedures to activate in the event of an information security incident. In this section, you'll learn the building blocks of a solid incident response program.

Real world

Advanced persistent threats

If you're wondering whether it is really possible to breach your well-designed security controls, consider the risk posed by the advanced persistent threat (APT). In this scenario, a determined attacker with tremendous resources focuses on breaching the security controls of your organization in particular. Although you certainly may have designed your defenses in such a way that they will easily foil the determined attacker, would you be able to defend against someone who carefully studies your organization, perhaps with insider knowledge, and then dedicates a team of highly skilled individuals with advanced tools to penetrating your defenses? Though this might sound far-fetched, it's exactly what happened to a nuclear enrichment plant in Iran that was the victim of the Stuxnet attack. In the Stuxnet case, a group of dedicated programmers spent several months developing a worm with one purpose—to work its way into the central control systems of the plant to destroy the centrifuges. Although no government has publicly taken credit for the attack, it is widely assumed that the United States and/or Israel was behind it.

Incident response team

Appropriately responding to an information security incident requires the carefully coordinated actions of a team of highly skilled individuals who have been trained on the organization's consistent process for incident response. This is simply not something that you can pull together "on the fly." Success during a security incident requires careful advance planning, including the selection and training of an incident response team.

First responder responsibilities

It's important to recognize that the first responders on the scene of an information security incident will most likely *not* be members of your trained incident response team. The first person to notice the sign of an information security incident is more likely going to be a system administrator, computer operator, or even an end user. For this reason, you should consider every member of your staff to be a member of your "extended" incident response team and provide some level of training across the organization. There are three basic elements to this training:

1. **Recognizing a security incident**   Everyone in the organization should have an understanding of what constitutes a security incident in the eyes of your firm.

2. **Activating the incident response process**   Next, first responders should have a clear, easy way to activate your formal incident response process. It should be simple for them to, in a sense, dial your "information security 911" to have trained professionals jump into action to assume control of the incident.

3. **Containing the incident**   Finally, most technical staff in your organization should know how to perform the equivalent of "information security first aid." Just as a bystander wouldn't stand by and wait for an ambulance while an accident victim bled profusely, IT staff should feel confident enough to take immediate action to stem the effect of a security incident. Actions as simple as disconnecting the network cable from a system that appears to be transmitting unencrypted credit card data to an offsite location can mean the difference between a minor and major security incident. Seconds matter when it comes to the early stages of incident response.

> *NOTE* **DON'T SHOOT THE MESSENGER**
>
> When you train large portions of your staff on first responder tactics, understand that they will make mistakes. Staff members will jump the gun and activate the incident response process in cases where there simply is no security incident. The way your organization reacts to these mistakes is just as important as your response to a true security incident. If the person who activated the process feels belittled or punished in any way, he will hesitate to ever again activate the incident response process. Even worse, others in the organization will hear the story, and it will give them pause as well. No matter what, you should always thank first responders for bringing a potential incident to your attention and make sure they understand that they made the right decision calling in the incident response team.

Of course, the level of detail that you provide should vary depending upon the role of the individuals within your organization. Staff members with no technical responsibilities whatsoever might simply get an awareness message letting them know that they should report any suspicious computer activity to a centralized security operations center or network team. System and network administrators might receive a full day of training that helps them understand how to recognize the early warning signs of a security incident and the basic steps that should be followed during incident containment.

Staffing the incident response team

Responding to an information security incident requires an interdisciplinary approach that will call upon the expertise of many different professionals from throughout your organization. Remember, responding to security incidents is not just an "infosec thing," nor is it purely a technical matter. Although information security professionals and other technical staff play an important role in incident response, it is equally important to have a well-rounded team that can handle all aspects of incident response.

There are eight categories of staff that you should consider representing on your incident response team. This does not necessarily mean that you will only have eight slots on the team, for two reasons. First, you need to plan to have a redundant team. If the attorney on your team is vacationing in Barbados when an incident occurs, you need to know that there is someone else available who can represent the legal issues. Second, some areas are broad enough that no one person can represent the entire field. For example, a network engineer would not likely be able to address database administration issues, nor would a database administrator be able to cover network issues. The categories of staff you should consider when developing your team are:

- **Management**   Quite simply, somebody needs to be in charge. Incident response without one officially designated leader can quickly devolve into many uncoordinated efforts, as everyone begins to pursue their own hunches and preferred courses of action. You need one strong leader to rein in these natural tendencies and direct the response. Additionally, difficult decisions will be made during the response to an information security incident, and you need to be sure that the team has a manager on hand with sufficient authority to make those calls without having to call in senior managers for consultation.

- **Information security**   Information security staff will play an essential role in all stages of incident response. They bring subject matter expertise to the table that can be especially helpful when attempting to identify the root cause of an incident or to quickly develop *ad hoc* controls to contain the damage caused by a security incident. Security staff also have access to unique resources, such as firewalls, intrusion detection/prevention systems, and security incident and event management (SIEM) systems that might contain data relevant to the security incident.

- **Technical staff**   In addition to information security professionals, you should have a representative from every major technical discipline in your organization on the incident response team. You certainly might not need all of these staff to respond to every incident, but you need to be prepared to react to a security incident that touches any part of your computing environment. System administrators, network engineers, database administrators, and application developers all might play critical roles in responding to an incident that either centers on or touches upon their operational domains.

- **Legal**   Many security incidents turn into legal matters, either because criminal prosecution is involved or because the firm becomes engaged in civil litigation as a consequence of the security incident. In addition, there are specific legal provisions that might dictate elements of your incident response process. For example, most states now have data breach notification laws that require the timely notification of individuals if their data is known or reasonably believed to have been compromised during an information security incident.

- **Communications and public relations**   You might need to issue some type of public statement, and you will need to react if the media gets wind of the fact that a security incident is unfolding at your organization. Communications staff should become involved early both to handle these situations and provide advice on the best time to inform outsiders that an incident is taking place.

- **Human resources**   In any incident where insider involvement is suspected, you should include representatives from your human resources department. You should definitely consult HR before interviewing any suspects who are employees of the organization. HR should also lead any disciplinary process that might take place against employees who are believed to have been involved in the incident, because such investigations are personnel matters that are within their realm of expertise.

- **Risk management**   Your organization's risk management staff will play an important role in security incidents of extended duration or impact. Individuals from this group will likely be the experts on your firm's business continuity and disaster recovery strategies and can help implement those contingency plans if it becomes necessary. Additionally, staff from the risk management area will be able to best inform the team on the provisions of any insurance policies that might cover portions of the incident response measures.

> ***MORE INFO***   **BUSINESS CONTINUITY AND DISASTER RECOVERY**
>
> Business Continuity Planning (BCP) and Disaster Recovery Planning (DRP) are discussed in detail in Chapter 4. They are both important subjects on the CompTIA Security+ examination.

- **Facilities**   If physical security is involved in a security incident, your facilities group can provide important expertise regarding your buildings and other physical infrastructure.

Developing a well-rounded incident response team is an important component of any strong incident response program. You should identify individuals to fill each of these roles and ensure that they understand the scope of their incident response functions.

Training the incident response team

The training you provide to your incident response team should cover a wide variety of topics
that prepare the team members to handle different types of information security incidents.
This training should include a core set of modules that all team members receive, covering
the following topics:

- Overview of the organization's incident response process
- Roles and responsibilities of each team member
- Activation procedures in the event of an incident
- Detection and analysis of security incidents
- Containment procedures
- Eradication procedures
- Recovery procedures
- Post-incident procedures

In addition, each team member should receive specialized training on the incident response
tools and techniques specific to her area of expertise. For example, database and system administrators should be familiar with their roles in a forensic analysis, including proper collection
procedures and the chain of custody. Attorneys should have specialized continuing legal
education on the laws and regulations that pertain to information security incidents.

All of these training modules should be conducted on both an initial and recurring basis. If
you are developing a new incident response capability, you could have large group sessions
to bring the entire team up to speed at once. If you are maintaining an existing program,
you will need to conduct initial training sessions for those staff members who are new to the
incident response team. Additionally, you will need to conduct periodic refresher training

for veteran team members to ensure both that they don't get "rusty" and that they become familiar with any changes in the incident response plan.

Finally, a critical component of any training program is giving responders hands-on experience. This is especially important in organizations that do not often activate their incident response teams. Conducting a series of drills can help familiarize staff with their roles in an actual incident. These drills can range from checklist reviews to tabletop exercises or even full-blown incident simulations.

> **MORE INFO** **CONDUCTING INCIDENT RESPONSE DRILLS**
>
> Incident response drills are actually quite similar to the tests used for business continuity and disaster recovery plans that will be discussed in Chapter 4. You might want to integrate these two programs and conduct combined drills. For example, you might conduct a drill that simulates an attacker conducting a denial of service attack against your website. The drill might begin as an incident response scenario and then evolve into a disaster recovery effort when the website becomes completely inaccessible.

Incident response life cycle

Every incident response process follows a life cycle approach, whether it is formally defined or not. The National Institute of Standards and Technology (NIST) defines one such life cycle approach, using the four-phase process shown in Figure 1-4. This includes four distinct phases:

1. Preparation
2. Detection and analysis
3. Containment, eradication, and recovery
4. Post-incident activity

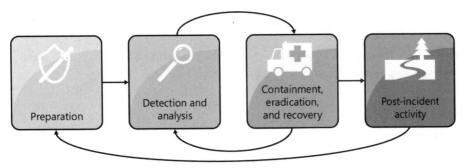

FIGURE 1-4 The incident response life cycle contains four steps (NIST).

Each of these stages has goals and objectives that will be discussed in the next several sections of this chapter. Also, be sure to take note of the multiple arrows and their directions in Figure 1-4. The incident response life cycle is not a sequential march through four phases. Rather, it is an iterative process that might loop through some steps multiple times as an incident evolves. Most notably, the steps taken during the containment, eradication, and recovery phase might identify additional information that requires analysis, causing a loop back to the detection and analysis phase.

Additionally, the entire process should be viewed as a repeating cycle. At the conclusion of each incident, you engage in post-incident activity that includes a lessons-learned session assessing the functioning of the incident response process. This information then feeds back into the preparation phase, providing valuable input regarding potential improvements to your organization's incident response process.

Preparation

The preparation phase of incident response includes establishing an incident response process, selecting a team, and training them on the plan. These steps were described earlier in this chapter.

In addition to those preparation steps, the incident response team members should ensure that they have the tools and resources needed to respond to any eventuality. Many teams choose to create a "go bag" that contains all of the tools needed to get an incident response underway quickly. At a minimum, the "go bag" should contain a forensic laptop, a variety of cables and connectors, several types of blank media for imaging systems, and other essential gear required by members of the response team. The "go bag" should be considered sacrosanct and should be inventoried periodically to ensure that nobody has "borrowed" equipment from the kit. You don't want to activate the team and get on site only to discover that essential equipment was purloined temporarily for a project and is not actually in the kit.

In addition to the incident response life cycle, NIST offers a suggested list of tools and resources that should be maintained by incident response teams. They suggest that every team have access to the following:

- **Communications and facilities resources**
    - Contact information for team members, other internal resources, law enforcement contacts, and contractors
    - On-call information for other teams within the organization that might play a role in incident response
    - Incident reporting mechanisms
    - Issue tracking system
    - Smartphones
    - Encryption software for intra-team communication and collaboration with outside parties

- A permanent or temporary war room to act as a central coordination point during incident response
- A secure storage facility for evidence gathered during an incident response effort
- **Incident analysis hardware and software**
  - Digital forensic workstations and/or backup devices to create disk images and preserve other types of digital evidence
  - Laptops for team member use that are separate from the forensic workstations
  - Spare equipment for use during the response, including workstations, servers, and network gear
  - Blank removable media (lots of it!)
  - Removable media loaded with forensic tools (potentially including bootable images)
  - A printer
  - Packet-sniffing and network protocol analysis hardware and software
  - Forensic software
  - Notebooks, cameras, recorders, and other equipment to gather evidence and notes
- **Incident analysis resources**
  - Network diagrams
  - Lists of critical information assets
  - Architectural diagrams, especially of critical/sensitive services
  - Baselines of "normal" system, network, and application activity
  - A detailed listing of firewall rules and ports

Many teams have a full-time incident response coordinator (often a member of the information security team) who is responsible for gathering resources and ensuring that everything is ready to go in the event of an actual incident. This coordinator might also facilitate the incident response planning, training, and simulation processes for the organization. Smaller organizations might choose to make this a part-time responsibility for a team member with other information security duties.

Detection and analysis

The detection and analysis phase has two distinct components. First, during periods of normal activity, trained security analysts monitor systems for signs of a security incident. This may include monitoring:

- Intrusion detection and prevention systems.
- Security incident and event management (SIEM) systems.

- Firewalls.

- Centralized antivirus monitoring software.

- Logs from critical systems, applications, and devices.

- File/system integrity monitoring software.

- Vulnerability scanners.

- External reports of malicious activity (for example, attacks emanating from your network).

- Reports from staff and customers.

Analysts monitoring these sources for signs of an information security incident will activate the formal incident response process in the event that they detect an incident.

When an incident is detected, analysts are responsible for gathering enough information to guide the response effort. This can involve coordinating information from the same sources used to detect the incident as well as activating additional information collection mechanisms. For example, analysts might begin capturing network traffic in real-time by using packet sniffers to preserve evidence of a network-related incident.

Another important part of the analysis phase is assessing the impact of the incident. This can be done by classifying the event into one of three categories:

- **Low impact**   Incidents that have minimal or no potential to affect the confidentiality, integrity, or availability of the organization's operations and/or information assets. It is unlikely that a low-impact event would warrant a major after-hours response or the activation of the full incident response team.

- **Moderate impact**   Incidents that have the potential to have a significant impact on the confidentiality, integrity, or availability of the organization's operations and/or information assets. They might disrupt some business activities and might require the activation of the incident response team.

- **High impact**   Incidents that have the potential to critically damage the confidentiality, integrity, or availability of the organization's operations and/or information assets. They might have a very serious, potentially permanent, impact on the organization and should entail immediate activation of the full incident response team.

Every organization will need to define its own criteria for triaging security incidents and determining the incident categorization scheme appropriate for its environment. Those criteria will vary depending upon the types of information handled by the organization and the criticality of various business processes supported by information technology.

Containment, eradication, and recovery

The containment, eradication, and recovery phase of an incident response typically encompasses what most security professionals consider to be the "meat" of the process. It includes steps taken to minimize the damage caused by a security incident, remove the threat, and return to normal operations. Though incident response guides typically describe this as a single phase, it is clearly divided into two different types of complementary activities: containment activities and eradication/recovery activities.

CONTAINMENT ACTIVITIES

Containment activities are focused on damage control and preventing further loss to the organization. The steps followed will vary depending upon the type of incident taking place and the technical countermeasures available. Some examples of security incident containment strategies include:

- Provisioning additional bandwidth to cope with the impact of a network denial of service attack.
- Disconnecting a potentially compromised server from the network to prevent the exfiltration of sensitive information.
- Isolation of a network segment to prevent further spread of malware that has infected systems on that segment.
- Creating temporary firewall rules to block external access to a system that is acting suspiciously.

Security professionals must work closely with other technical staff during containment activities to design a containment strategy that appropriately balances the needs of the organization with security concerns. Your organization should maintain an incident containment plan for each of the major types of attack in your planning scheme to allow for advance planning in as many situations as possible.

NIST offers six criteria that incident response planners and teams can use when developing an appropriate containment strategy:

- Potential damage to and theft of resources
- Need for evidence preservation
- Service availability (for example, network connectivity or services provided to external parties)
- Time and resources needed to implement the strategy
- Effectiveness of the strategy (for example, partial containment or full containment)
- Duration of the solution (for example, an emergency workaround to be removed in four hours, a temporary workaround to be removed in two weeks, or a permanent solution to the problem).

Another important consideration is that containment strategies are likely to alert an attacker to the fact that security responders have detected his activity. This might cause an immediate termination of the attack. Although this is certainly good from the perspective of preventing further damage, it limits the ability of responders to gather evidence that can be used to track down and prosecute offenders. The incident response plan should contain guidelines to help teams make these determinations. Incident response team leaders should ensure that all staff participating in a response understand the incident's situation-specific rules of engagement regarding the relative priorities assigned to containment and evidence collection.

ERADICATION AND RECOVERY ACTIVITIES

Eradication and recovery activities also take place during this phase and are focused on removing any aftereffects of the incident and returning the organization to normal technology operations as quickly as possible. The extent of the activities performed during this phase vary depending upon the type of incident. In some cases, there might be very little work to do. However, in cases where systems were compromised, eradication efforts might involve completely wiping affected systems to ensure that there are no lingering effects from the compromise.

Recovery includes not only restoring normal activity but also ensuring that any vulnerability that might have been exploited by attackers is remediated. If attackers found your vulnerability once, it is extremely likely that they will be able to do so a second time. You should not consider your operations fully recovered until they are functioning again and the vulnerabilities exploited by attackers are resolved so that they do not continue to pose a risk of compromise.

Post-incident activity

The final phase of the incident response process, post-incident activity, consists primarily of a lessons-learned analysis that does a postmortem look at the incident response process. It provides an opportunity for everyone who participated to reflect upon the response and any changes that might benefit future responses. In Special Publication 800-61, NIST suggests a series of questions that can be addressed during a lessons-learned session:

- Exactly what happened and at what times?
- How well did staff and management perform in dealing with the incident? Were the documented procedures followed? Were they adequate?
- What information was needed sooner?
- Were any steps or actions taken that might have inhibited the recovery?
- What would the staff and management do differently the next time a similar incident occurs?
- How could information sharing with other organizations have been improved?
- What corrective actions can prevent similar incidents in the future?
- What additional tools or resources are needed to detect, analyze, and mitigate future incidents?

The session conducted to answer these questions should have a designated facilitator who moderates the conversation. This person should have enough incident response experience to ask the appropriate follow-up questions and guide the exploration, but should not have been involved in the actual response, to preserve a sense of objectivity. It can also be helpful to have a dedicated note-taker to ensure that everyone's input is accurately captured. At the conclusion of the meeting, the facilitator should prepare a lessons-learned report that highlights the major findings of the session and key lessons learned that might benefit responders to future incidents. This document should be used to make revisions to the incident response process.

Incident communications

During an incident response, the team might need to communicate with a wide range of external parties, as shown in Figure 1-5. These are individuals who either need to be informed of the incident or might provide information valuable to the response effort. All external communications should be coordinated through the communications lead on the incident response team to ensure that the team is presenting consistent information to the outside world.

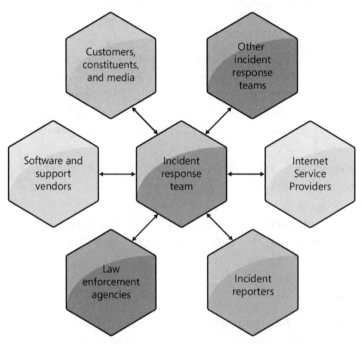

FIGURE 1-5 The incident response communications process suggested by NIST uses the incident response team as the core of all communications (NIST).

Some of the particular entities that the incident response team might communicate with include:

- **Customers, constituents, and the media**   There are many stakeholders who will be interested in learning about the potential loss of sensitive information or who are otherwise affected by the incident. These communications *must* be coordinated through your public relations group.

- **Other incident response teams**   If you are responding to an incident that affects multiple organizations, such as a widespread distributed denial of service (DDoS) attack, all responders will benefit from opening channels of communication between each organization's response team. This information sharing might help uncover important information more quickly and allows for a coordinated response.

- **Internet Service Providers (ISPs)**   In a network-based incident, your ISP might be able to provide important information or implement strategies to help you contain the incident. For example, the ISP might be able to implement filtering that prevents traffic related to a DDoS attack from reaching your network in the first place.

- **Incident reporters**   You might decide to report the incident to a state, national, or industry-specific incident response team. US federal government agencies are required to report security incidents to the United States Computer Emergency Readiness Team (US-CERT).

- **Law enforcement agencies**   Depending upon the nature of the incident, you might be required to involve law enforcement or you might choose to voluntarily do so. For example, the Payment Card Industry Data Security Standard (PCI DSS) requires that merchants suspecting a security incident that involves credit card information must immediately alert both their merchant bank's fraud unit and the United States Secret Service.

- **Software and support vendors**   You might need support from your vendors to diagnose and/or remediate the effects of a security incident.

Your incident response plan should include the procedures to be followed when involving each of the types of organizations listed here. It should describe who has the authority to initiate each contact during a security incident and should also contain contact information for each entity.

Collecting evidence

Every incident response effort involves some form of evidence collection. In some cases, the evidence gathered is used solely by the incident response team. In other incidents, evidence might be turned over to the organization's legal team for use in civil litigation, or to law enforcement for use in a criminal prosecution. In cases where evidence is used outside of the incident response team, it is absolutely critical that it be collected by following established evidence handling procedures. Evidence that is mishandled might be inadmissible in court.

Preserving the chain of custody

One of the most important aspects of evidence collection is preserving the evidence *chain of custody*. This means that you must create a paper trail that documents the history of the evidence from the time of collection until the moment it is used in court. This is done by using an evidence log that contains the following data elements:

- Identifying information that describes the nature of the evidence. This might include model numbers, serial numbers, IP/MAC addresses, user names, or other similar information.

- A description of the collection process used to gather the evidence, including contact information for the technician who collected it.

- Entries for every time the evidence was handled after collection. Each entry must include the name and contact information of the individual handling the information, the purpose for handling the evidence, and the location where it was stored after it was handled.

Quite simply, the chain of custody should tell a complete story of the life of the evidence. The evidence log should explain every single thing that happened to the evidence during and after collection, and it should document both the physical location of the evidence at all times and the names of any individuals who came into direct contact with it. The purpose of the chain of custody is to ensure that officials can provide definitive documentation of their evidence and ensure that it was not tampered with between the time of collection and the time of use.

Interviewing witnesses

In many incidents, it might become necessary to interview witnesses to gather evidence. Interviews are conducted on a voluntary basis and should have a cooperative tone to them. Individuals conducting interviews should not be hostile toward witnesses or attempt to browbeat them into providing information. If either the interviewer or interviewee is uncomfortable with the proceedings, the interview should immediately be terminated. Don't let interviewers take lessons from police dramas!

Any interview that takes place should be thoroughly documented in a manner that is known to all participants. If the interview subject consents, you might use audio or video recording to document the interview. Otherwise, the interviewer might take paper notes to record the conversation.

Remember, an interview that turns hostile is no longer an interview, but an interrogation. At no time should anyone other than trained law enforcement personnel engage in the interrogation of a witness. In the best case, interrogation by untrained individuals might result in evidence that is not usable in court. In the worst case, the interrogator may find himself guilty of a crime.

Tracking time and expense

Incident response teams should track the time and expenses associated with both evidence collection and other incident response efforts. Though these expenses might not be directly billable to any organization, they provide management with a method of identifying the resources that went into an incident response effort. At the very least, this information can be used to plan for future incident responses. In some cases, management might be able to seek reimbursement through litigation or from an information security incident insurance policy purchased by the organization.

Computer forensics

In many cases, investigators responding to an information security incident will need to collect information from computer systems believed to have played a role in the incident. This process, known as *computer forensics*, includes tools and techniques that ensure that evidence is collected in a manner that does not alter the evidence itself and preserves the chain of custody.

> *NOTE* **COMPUTER FORENSIC PROFESSIONALS**
>
> Computer forensics is a complex subfield of information security. Conducting forensic examinations of computers requires specialized training and should not be attempted by individuals unfamiliar with proper evidence collection procedures. Most law enforcement agencies have officers dedicated to the proper collection of evidence who have undergone years of training in proper tools and techniques. The moral of this story? Don't try this at home! If you need to engage in the forensic investigation of a computer system, you should seek specialized assistance.

Order of volatility

Unlike many kinds of physical evidence, computer-based evidence is often volatile. This means that it breaks down over time and, if not promptly and properly collected, it will disappear and be impossible to recover. Forensic investigators should consider the *order of volatility* when collecting evidence. Here's a summary of major computer evidence types, ordered from highest volatility (shortest life) to lowest volatility (longest life):

- RAM
- Network details
- Running process information
- System disk contents
- Removable flash media
- Removable magnetic media
- Removable optical media

Evidence from the first three elements on this list (memory contents, network details, and running process information) is only available as long as the system containing the evidence has power. For this reason, most organizations have policies specifying that first responders should never unplug a computer believed to be involved in a security incident. Doing so could destroy critical evidence before it is forensically collected. Responders seeking to contain the damage caused by a security incident should instead disconnect the system from the network, leaving it powered on. Though this may destroy some network-based evidence, it leaves important memory and process information intact while containing damage.

As forensic analysts develop an evidence collection plan for a security incident, they should begin with the most volatile evidence from categories at the top of this list and work their way downward, collecting the least volatile evidence last. This approach maximizes the amount of data that can be collected before it expires.

Hashing

Investigators make use of cryptographic *hash* values to demonstrate that one file is a true copy of another file. Hashes are values generated by a mathematical function that provide a summary of the contents of one or more blocks of data. Hash functions must be designed in such a way that they are efficient to compute. Additionally, the hash value must be collision resistant, meaning that it should not be mathematically feasible to find two different files that generate the same hash value.

If a hash value is created by using a proper hash function, it can be used to quickly and reliably compare the contents of two files. If the files are identical, they will generate identical hash values. If the hash values generated by two files do not match, then the files themselves differ in some way. It is important to note that hashing does not give you a sense of "how close" the files might be. If a single character in the files is different, the hash values might be completely different. You simply can't tell by comparing hash values whether a modification to a file was just a single letter or whether the files are completely different.

There are many software products capable of generating hash values for use in forensic examinations. Figure 1-6 shows one of these programs creating a hash value for a system file by using the well-known Message Digest 5 (MD5) hash algorithm.

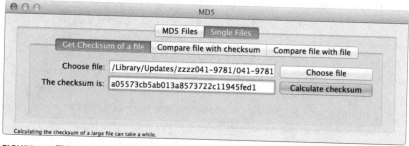

FIGURE 1-6 This screen shot demonstrates the creation of an MD5 hash.

Imaging systems

One of the most important forms of evidence captured during forensic investigations is system images. These images, gathered by using specialized forensic imaging equipment, are bit-by-bit copies of hard drives from systems involved in a security incident. System images are collected in a manner that ensures that the act of creating the image does not alter the data stored on the hard drive. Forensic investigators typically ensure that this is the case by using specialized forensic devices known as write-blockers. These are hardware connectors that sit between the drive being imaged and the hardware performing the imaging and ensure that no data can be written onto the drive, while permitting data to be read from the drive during the imaging process.

One of the major benefits of capturing a bit-by-bit image, rather than copying individual files from the disk, is that you receive a copy of the unused space on the disk. This space might contain portions of deleted files or other information that can prove very significant during the investigation.

Investigators performing forensic analysis *never* work with original media. After creating the image, investigators seal the original media in an evidence bag and securely store it in an evidence locker, being careful to preserve the chain of custody. This is because the original drive is direct evidence that might be used in court. Furthermore, investigators usually don't even work with the original image. They maintain it as a master image and make copies of that image for investigative purposes.

Network traffic and logs

Network traffic is another important source of information for forensic investigators. In some cases, you might be able to capture the full contents of the data traveling on a network. This technique, known as packet sniffing, monitors a network segment, recording every bit that passes by on the wire, and then reassembles it to provide machine-readable and human-readable forms of the data transmitted on the network.

Analysts can use tools such as the free Wireshark tool shown in Figure 1-7 to capture the full contents of network traffic. It is important to note that capturing live network traffic can quickly consume massive amounts of storage. For this reason, it is extremely unusual to capture network traffic in real time unless there is a known incident taking place. It would simply be cost prohibitive to retain network traffic for any extended period of time.

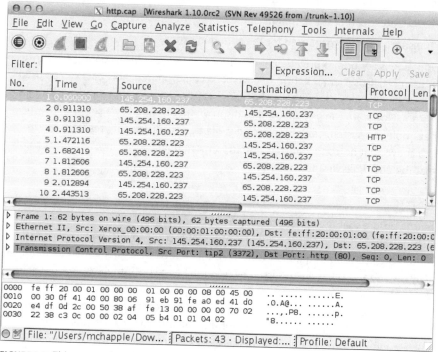

FIGURE 1-7 This screen shot demonstrates the use of Wireshark to capture network traffic.

Although analysts can't count on capturing network traffic 24 hours a day, seven days a week for use in a future investigation, there are sources of network data that might be retained for extended periods of time. First, many network devices create logs of activity that might contain information useful to a security investigation. For example, the logs on a router might show unsuccessful attempts to create administrative connections to the router that are indicative of an attack in progress. Firewalls might retain logs of permitted and blocked traffic that are useful to security investigators.

The second source of network information that is quite useful to forensic investigators is network flow data. These records, generated by network devices, track summary information about every connection that takes place on a network. They do not capture the full contents of the packet, to avoid the storage space dilemma discussed previously, but they do capture useful summary information, including:

- The source system IP address.
- The destination system IP address.
- The timestamp of the beginning of the connection.
- The timestamp of the end of the connection.
- The amount of data sent from the source system to the destination system.
- The source port for the communication.
- The destination port for the communication.
- The transport layer protocol used for the communication.

This information is enough to provide important details to those investigating a security incident. For example, if a system is known to have been compromised, flow data can be used to identify all of the remote systems that either connected to or were contacted by the compromised system. Flow data can also be used to disprove theories during a security investigation. For example, if a system contains a sensitive file that is 100 megabytes (MB) in size and flow data shows that no connections transmitted more than 25 MB, investigators can be confident that the entire file was not stolen.

Time offsets

It is important to ensure that the system clocks on all computers and devices in an organization are synchronized. This facilitates the analysis phase of security investigations. If clocks are not synchronized, it becomes quite difficult to compare log entries generated by multiple systems. Many organizations handle this issue by using the Network Time Protocol (NTP) to ensure that all system clocks are synchronized to one of the atomic clocks maintained by the United States government, or another authoritative source. Access to these clocks is freely available, and the NTP protocol is able to adjust for the network latency between your site and the clock. For more information on the atomic clocks maintained by the US Department of Commerce and the US Naval Observatory, visit *www.time.gov*.

If an investigation must take place using information from systems without synchronized clocks, investigators must make use of time offsets. The investigators determine the difference between the clock on each system and the actual time, and then use this as an offset value to adjust the times retrieved from log entries and other timestamps generated by that system. For example, if a system clock is found to be running two minutes fast, analysts must then subtract two minutes from each time value generated by that system to adjust it back to the correct time. This technique can also be used to compare data generated by systems located in different time zones.

Screen shots

If an investigator encounters a computer that is currently involved in a security incident, that investigator can also use screen shots as a valuable source of evidence. Though it is possible to gather screen shots by using the built-in operating system functionality of the target computer, this is not an advisable technique for a forensic investigator, because the keyboard interaction might be viewed as tampering with the computer itself. One simple solution to this is to simply take a photo of the screen by using a digital camera dedicated to forensic investigations. Remember to timestamp your pictures and subject the clock on the camera to the same time offset procedure used for other systems. Finally, the memory card from the camera must then be treated in the same manner as any other form of digital evidence, with secure storage and a documented chain of custody.

Video capture

Security investigators should also remember to turn to old-fashioned physical security tools when possible. For example, though it might not be possible to digitally determine who is logged onto a computer by using a stolen account, the room containing the computer might contain a surveillance camera that captures a picture of the perpetrator. If the room itself does not contain a camera, look for cameras in the hallway, at entrance points, or in other nearby areas that might have captured images of involved individuals.

 Quick check

1. What are the four phases of the incident response life cycle?

2. True or false: The incident response life cycle describes a sequential set of activities that should be followed when responding to an information security incident.

Quick check answers

1. Preparation; detection and analysis; containment, eradication, and recovery; and post-incident activity

2. False. The incident response life cycle is an iterative, cyclical process that includes the potential to repeat steps. It is not a sequential, lockstep approach to incident response.

Chapter summary

- The goals of information security professionals are to protect the confidentiality, integrity, and availability of an organization's information assets. Adversaries have the corresponding goals of disclosure, alteration, and denial.

- Vulnerabilities are weaknesses in an organization's security controls. Threats are external forces that seek to exploit vulnerabilities. Risks occur when there is an intersection between a vulnerability and a threat that can exploit that vulnerability.

- Qualitative risk assessment uses a subjective process to evaluate the likelihood and impact of a risk upon an organization. Qualitative assessments commonly use the categories of "low," "moderate," and "high" to express these attributes.

- Quantitative risk assessment calculates the financial risk that would occur if a risk materialized. It uses the concept of annualized rate of occurrence (ARO) to express likelihood and single loss expectancy (SLE) to express impact. Risks are calculated by using the annualized loss expectancy (ALE).

- Organizations have five strategy options at their disposal when determining how to manage a risk: risk acceptance, risk avoidance, risk mitigation, risk transference, and risk deterrence. They can use one or more of these strategies in response to each risk they face.

- Security professionals use controls to mitigate risk. These controls can reduce the likelihood and/or impact of a risk and are grouped into three categories: management controls, operational controls, and technical controls.

- Every organization should have a trained incident response team prepared to react in the event of an information security incident. This team should include technical, legal, communications, and management representatives that will join forces to coordinate a response.

- The incident response life cycle has four phases: preparation to get the team ready for future incidents, detection and analysis of an incident; containment, eradication, and recovery; and post-incident activity.

Chapter review

Test your knowledge of the information in Chapter 1 by answering these questions. The answers to these questions, and the explanations of why each answer choice is correct or incorrect, are located in the "Answers" section at the end of this chapter.

1. You are using encryption technology in an attempt to protect a file containing customer credit card numbers from unauthorized access. What information security goal are you pursuing?

   A. Confidentiality

   B. Integrity

   C. Disclosure

   D. Availability

2. You are performing a risk assessment of an organization and decide that the likelihood of a particular risk materializing is "low." What type of risk assessment are you performing?

   A. Operational

   B. Quantitative

   C. Technical

   D. Qualitative

3. You are conducting a quantitative risk assessment for an organization to identify the risk of a fire in a data center. The data center is valued at $10 million and you expect a fire to occur once every 50 years that will damage three-quarters of the data center (including equipment). What is your exposure factor?

   A. 75 percent

   B. 10 percent

   C. 50 percent

   D. 25 percent

4. You are conducting a quantitative risk assessment for an organization to identify the risk of a fire in a data center. The data center is valued at $10 million and you expect a fire to occur once every 50 years that will damage three-quarters of the data center (including equipment). What is your annualized loss expectancy?

   A. 75 percent

   B. $7.5 million

   C. 0.02

   D. $150,000

5. You are evaluating methods to manage the risk posed to your organization by hackers and decide that you will pursue a strategy of aggressively prosecuting anyone who attempts to break into your systems. What risk management strategy are you implementing?

   A. Risk mitigation

   B. Risk transference

   C. Risk deterrence

   D. Risk acceptance

6. You are conducting a lessons-learned session to identify gaps in your response to an information security incident. What phase in the incident response life cycle are you participating in?

   A. Preparation

   B. Detection and analysis

   C. Containment, eradication, and recovery

   D. Post-incident activity

Answers

This section contains the answers to the questions for the "Chapter review" section in this chapter.

1. **Correct Answer: A**

    A.   Correct: Confidentiality controls protect information against unauthorized access. Preventing intruders from accessing the credit card file is an example of a confidentiality control.

    B.   Incorrect: Integrity controls protect information against unauthorized modification. This is not the goal stated in the scenario.

    C.   Incorrect: Disclosure is the goal of an attacker, rather than that of an information security professional.

    D.   Incorrect: Availability controls ensure that information is available to authorized users. This is not the goal stated in the scenario.

2. **Correct Answer: D**

    A.   Incorrect: The two types of risk assessment are quantitative and qualitative. Operational is not a type of risk assessment.

    B.   Incorrect: Quantitative risk assessments use objective numeric data rather than subjective categories such as "low."

    C.   Incorrect: The two types of risk assessment are quantitative and qualitative. Technical is not a type of risk assessment.

    D.   Correct: Qualitative risk assessments use subjective categories, such as "low," "moderate," and "high," to describe the likelihood and impact of risks.

3. **Correct Answer: A**

    A.   Correct: The exposure factor is the proportion of the asset that will be damaged in the event of a fire. In this case, that is 75 percent.

    B.   Incorrect: The exposure factor is the proportion of the asset that will be damaged in the event of a fire. 10 percent is not the correct value.

    C.   Incorrect: The exposure factor is the proportion of the asset that will be damaged in the event of a fire. 50 percent is not the correct value.

    D.   Incorrect: The exposure factor is the proportion of the asset that will be damaged in the event of a fire. 25 percent is not the correct value.

4. **Correct Answer: D**

   A. **Incorrect:** 75 percent is the exposure factor.

   B. **Incorrect:** $7.5 million is the single loss expectancy.

   C. **Incorrect:** 0.02 is the annualized rate of occurrence.

   D. **Correct:** The annualized loss expectancy is calculated as the product of the single loss expectancy and the annualized rate of occurrence. The SLE is the asset value ($10 million) multiplied by the exposure factor (75 percent), or $7.5 million. The ARO is once every 50 years, or 0.02. The ALE is, therefore, $7,500,000 × 0.02 or $150,000.

5. **Correct Answer: C**

   A. **Incorrect:** Risk mitigation reduces the likelihood that a risk will be successful or the impact that the risk will have on an organization. Prosecution reduces the likelihood that an attacker will attempt to exploit your vulnerabilities.

   B. **Incorrect:** Risk transference moves the risk from one entity to another, such as through the purchase of an insurance policy.

   C. **Correct:** Prosecuting attackers reduces the likelihood that others will try to attack you and is an example of risk deterrence.

   D. **Incorrect:** Risk acceptance involves taking no other action to manage a risk. Prosecuting attackers is an active risk management approach and is a form of risk deterrence.

6. **Correct Answer: D**

   A. **Incorrect:** The preparation phase includes activities designed to prepare the team for the next incident. Though this phase might include incorporating lessons from prior incidents, it does not include the actual lessons-learned session, which is part of the post-incident activity phase.

   B. **Incorrect:** The detection and analysis phase includes activities designed to allow the team to notice that a security incident is underway and gather sufficient information to guide the response. It does not include a lessons-learned session.

   C. **Incorrect:** The containment, eradication, and recovery phase involves protecting the organization against additional loss, removing the effects of a security incident, and restoring operations to normal order. This is usually followed by a lessons-learned session, which is part of the post-incident activity phase.

   D. **Correct:** Conducting a lessons-learned session to identify potential improvements in the incident response process is an important part of the post-incident activity phase.

## CHAPTER 2

Network security technologies

Security in modern organizations is provided by a broad range of devices, from firewalls to intrusion prevention systems, as well as the underlying network switches and routers themselves. This chapter explores a typical organization's network design by using a design for Humongous Insurance, an imaginary company that uses each of the types of devices that will be discussed. As you explore their network, you will examine the security devices and technologies that they have deployed, the design decisions that guided each choice, and how Humongous uses each type of device or tool. Throughout this chapter, we will discuss common network security devices and explain their role in a modern network.

Exam objectives in this chapter:

Objective 1.1: Explain the security function and purpose of network security devices and technologies

- Firewalls
- Routers
- Switches
- Load balancers
- Proxies
- Web security gateways
- VPN concentrators
- NIDS and NIPS (Behavior based, signature based, anomaly based, heuristic)
- Protocol analyzers
- Sniffers
- Spam filter, all-in-one security appliances
- Web application firewall vs. network firewall
- URL filtering, content inspection, malware inspection

Objective 1.2: Apply and implement secure network administration principles

- Implicit deny

Network security

Any organization that connects its network to another network, whether that network is the Internet or simply another company's network, needs a way to protect its own systems and infrastructure from attack. In order to provide that protection, it needs to be able to see what is occurring on its own network, to properly handle and route traffic, and to have the ability to allow or disallow what passes through the systems and network. The key to doing of all of this is a well-designed network with network security tools and systems in place.

 Network security provides the first line of defense for most networks. In fact, almost all modern networks use a layered defense, known as *defense in depth*. Defense in depth relies on a series of protective devices, systems, policies, and procedures that combine to form layers of protection for critical systems and data. The CompTIA Security+ exam covers common elements of a secure network, so we will look at the layers that you are likely to encounter.

The first layer of defense for many companies is a firewall. Firewalls are one of the most common elements of a protected network because they allow the organization to set rules about what traffic flows through them.

Real world

Firewalls as network shields

Simple rules implemented at an organization's network border by using a firewall can dramatically decrease the total traffic that enters the organization's network. One organization that we worked with implemented a simple firewall for most of the organization and saw a 70 percent decrease in the amount of traffic simply by blocking attacks and traffic that wasn't properly formatted. That was a huge decrease in the work that the rest of the network had to do!

Behind an organization's firewall you will typically find routers and switches, network devices that control the flow of traffic through the network and connect systems together. Further into the network, in organizational data centers, you will find load balancers, which help spread traffic to multiple systems; security gateways; and proxies that filter traffic to prevent attacks or to stop users from browsing known bad sites.

Many organizations also use an intrusion detection system (IDS) or intrusion prevention system (IPS) to monitor and either warn of or stop attacks. In this chapter, we will look at how IDS and IPS work, why and where you might want to deploy them, and what their strengths and weaknesses are. We will also look at other tools for analyzing network traffic and ways to inspect it for malware and spam.

Finally, we will take a brief look at where many companies are headed with their network security tools: all-in-one appliances, which combine many of these technologies into a single system with a host of capabilities, all accessible in one place.

Humongous Insurance: a modern secure network

Throughout this chapter, we will refer to an imaginary company called Humongous Insurance, and we'll be looking at its network in detail. You can find a high-level network overview in Figure 2-1. Each section of this chapter will dig deeper into specific parts of the Humongous network as we uncover the layers of defense that it has in place.

Humongous is a large company with a large central headquarters network. Conveniently, Humongous Insurance uses most of the common network security devices we will discuss, so you'll explore the reasons and logic behind their placement and usage as you learn about the devices themselves. As you read the chapter, keep this diagram in mind, because it will help you place the devices in their proper context in an enterprise network.

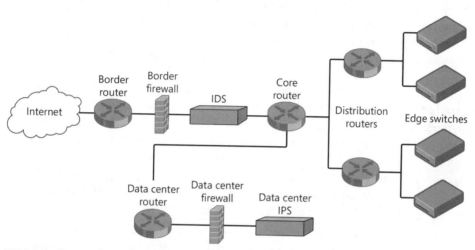

FIGURE 2-1 Humongous Insurance's overview network diagram shows a top-level view of its network.

Firewalls

Firewalls are often the first layer of defense in a network. They provide security by applying allow and deny *rules* to traffic that passes through them. Firewalls are typically deployed as either network firewalls or software-based host firewalls. Network firewalls use either a dedicated hardware device or software on commonly available hardware between two or more networks. Software-based host firewalls are installed directly on a workstation or server.

When traffic passes through a firewall, it is compared to the rules, which are part of what is called a *ruleset*, and it is either allowed through or blocked based on the results of that comparison. A well-constructed firewall ruleset always ends in a deny rule that catches anything that isn't explicitly allowed; this is known as an *implicit deny rule*. In many firewalls, this isn't actually a rule seen in the ruleset; instead, the firewall just drops anything that doesn't match the rules it does have.

There are three common types of firewalls: packet filters, stateful packet inspection firewalls, and application-layer firewalls. Let's take a look at what they do, and what their differences are.

Packet filter firewalls are the most basic form of firewall. This type of firewall works by inspecting packets based on rules. Packets that match the rules, such as "only packets from IP address 10.10.10.10 can be sent to firewall-protected system 10.11.0.5," are allowed through. Packets that don't match the allow rule are dropped. Packet filters have no concept of a conversation between machines, so every packet is checked, and rules have to be created for traffic headed both in and out of the firewall-protected network.

EXAM TIP

Chapter 3, "Secure network design and management," includes a list of common ports and protocols, along with the applications that use them. That list of ports and protocols is a key tool when you are building firewall rules, because they include some of the most frequently used services that you need to allow in and out of your network.

Stateful packet inspection firewalls use a broader view of the traffic and base their filtering on the state of communications between hosts. This technique, called *stateful packet inspection*, determines whether communications are new, whether they are part of an ongoing connection the firewall already allowed, or whether the traffic doesn't match any allow rule. If packets sent in are new and not part of an existing conversation, they are checked against the firewall's rules and, if they are allowed, a new entry is made in the firewall's state table. If the conversation already exists in the state table, then the firewall simply allows it to continue, and of course, if the traffic is on the deny list, it is blocked.

Stateful firewalls are typically preferable to packet filters because they decrease load and increase throughput by only inspecting new conversations. Fortunately, dedicated firewalls on the market today almost universally support stateful packet inspection. This means that they can apply additional intelligence to their filtering by allowing responses to traffic sent by protected systems, rather than inspecting every packet sent in or out. What stateful firewalls don't deal with is what the conversations contain, or how they should be carried on; for that, you need an application-layer firewall.

Application-layer firewalls, sometimes called third-generation firewalls, go even further into the packets they filter and examine the content of the packet itself, instead of merely looking at what IP address, port, and protocol the packet uses. This inspection capability allows application-layer firewalls to analyze data by using protocols like HTTP and applications like BitTorrent (a common peer-to-peer file-sharing application) to check if they're being used in ways that don't match the rules created by the firewall administrator.

MORE INFO   APPLICATION PROTOCOLS

We discuss application protocols like HTTP, FTP, and others in Chapter 3.

Because application-layer firewalls rely on the matching protocols and applications, they are the most likely of the three types of firewalls to unintentionally block desired traffic due to software or operating-system changes. In addition to this potential problem, there are tradeoffs when using an application-layer firewall, as you might expect when looking that deeply into packets. These tradeoffs can include application-layer firewalls often requiring more hardware horsepower to analyze packets, as well as potentially stopping traffic unintentionally when systems send traffic that doesn't match the protocol or application behaviors they expect.

Real world

Protocol inspection

Unexpected blocks in the real world aren't unheard of, particularly when a new version of software is released. We found out that a vendor's implementation of their host-to-host communication protocol added some features between versions, and these did not match the definition that their firewall used. Shortly after the update that introduced these changes was put in place, we received a panicked call from the system administrators stating that their application no longer worked!

Fortunately, this was fixed by switching the application-layer filtering to stateful filtering, but we no longer had insight into what was sent between hosts. Choices like these often involve tradeoffs between increased security and the likelihood of issues with stricter controls.

Most modern firewalls provide at least packet filter and stateful packet inspection filtering, and many next-generation firewalls add even more capabilities, like intrusion prevention or malware detection and filtering, as part of their application-layer filtering capabilities.

Network firewalls aren't the only type of firewall on the market. Most modern operating systems also provide a built-in firewall, often called a host- based or software-based firewall. Software firewalls can have the same capabilities as other firewalls, and thus typically provide stateful packet inspection or application-layer filtering capabilities. Some older host-based firewall packages can only do packet filtering, but they're relatively rare.

Host-based firewalls are part of an effective defense in depth strategy when paired with network-based firewalls. Network firewalls defend networks, or segments of networks, but typically aren't deployed to protect a single system. A software firewall can allow each system on a network to defend itself against internal threats from other systems on its local network.

EXAM TIP

Make sure you're familiar with the types of firewalls, as well as the concept of implicit deny. Can you answer questions about the differences between a stateful firewall and a packet filter?

Web application firewalls

A more specialized form of firewall that has become increasingly popular is the *web application firewall*, or WAF. Web application firewalls are specifically designed to filter HTTP and HTTPS (unencrypted and encrypted) website traffic and are intended to prevent attacks on web applications and servers. WAFs typically require specific knowledge of how an organization's applications are designed and work to be fully effective, but when properly deployed they can help prevent SQL injection, cross-site scripting (XSS), and other web attacks.

> **MORE INFO ATTACKS**
>
> We spend time looking into all of these attacks in Chapter 5, "Threats and attacks."

Web application firewalls also often add a number of features that help make website hosting easier. Current WAFs include a wide range of extra abilities:

- The ability to speed up secure web traffic (HTTPS), known as SSL acceleration
- Lookup systems to determine where users are coming from
- Reputation systems that rely on third-party data about what systems have attacked other sites
- Whitelists and blacklists to determine who should have access and which systems should be blocked due to attacks or misuse
- Authentication mechanisms to allow users to sign in to send certain types of traffic through the device
- In-depth reporting and analysis tools
- "Virtual patching," a capability that filters attack traffic to prevent exploits against known vulnerabilities, thus creating a virtual patch until the application can actually be patched

In addition, many web application firewalls have a learning mode that can analyze normal network traffic to your web servers and monitor for events and issues that go beyond what is commonly seen. This analysis can help identify problems as they occur, rather than after the fact.

In some deployments, a WAF is used to help make up for weak security in an application, whereas in others it is intended as a preventative measure for unknown issues. WAFs are available as security devices, as add-ons to traditional network firewalls, and as applications that run on web servers.

At Humongous Insurance, the example company, they use a stateful packet-filtering firewall at their border to handle the high-speed link with a minimum of slowdown (see Figure 2-2). Here, the ability to filter quickly is more important than deep inspection, because they have an intrusion prevention system in place behind it, which we'll discuss later in this chapter. The stateful firewall that Humongous uses has a rule that blocks any network traffic that is inbound to systems on their network that doesn't have a specific firewall rule allowing it, and it allows almost all types of network traffic out.

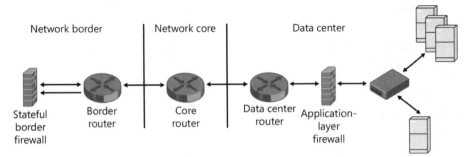

FIGURE 2-2 Stateful and application firewalls are designed to protect applications and servers.

Deeper in their network, Humongous uses application-layer firewalls to control traffic inside their data center. Here, traffic is well understood, and the ability to ensure that traffic is exactly what they expect it to be is more important than throughput

A network without a firewall

Can you responsibly run without a firewall between your organization and the Internet? It's open for debate, but if you ask Abe Singer from the San Diego Supercomputer Center in California, he'll tell you that you can have effective security without relying on a firewall because firewalls are only as effective as the rules that they use. He's right—firewall rules can be difficult to get right, especially if you don't have the right information or a skilled firewall administrator. And when he says that you can have effective security without a firewall, he's also right, but it takes a lot of work and provides more points of failure.

Thus, despite the fact that most organizations wouldn't be caught dead without a firewall in place, some have gone counter to conventional wisdom and have made the decision to not use a firewall to protect their network. That's a scary decision in the minds of most security practitioners, but the organizations that have consciously made the choice have well-thought-out reasons for their choices.

In general, the organizations that don't use a firewall value the flexibility and openness that the lack of a firewall that filters all of their organizational traffic provides. It doesn't mean that they don't use firewalls at all—rather, it means that they deploy them in specific places to protect vulnerable or sensitive systems.

System and network administrators in environments like this don't have that extra layer of protection saving them from mistakes that they make. This means that the protection in place for individual systems and network segments is even more critical than it might be in an environment where there's another layer of protection.

> **✓ Quick check**
>
> **1.** What type of firewall can make sure an application protocol like HTTP is being followed properly?
>
> **2.** What rule does traffic that doesn't match any allow rules in a firewall ruleset get handled by?
>
> **Quick check answers**
>
> **1.** An application-layer firewall
>
> **2.** The implicit deny rule

Routers

Routers interconnect networks and send packets between them. Routers maintain information about what networks they are connected to and can translate between different types of networks. Traffic that is destined for a network that your router doesn't sit in front of is sent to the next hop upstream. From there, traffic destined for remote networks passes from router to router along its path until it reaches its destination. This is the basic concept that makes the entire Internet work!

Large enterprises often have layers of routers inside their networks, with distribution routers handling traffic between geographically connected network segments, core routers handling traffic from distribution routers, and border routers sending traffic offsite to other parts of the corporate network and the Internet.

Humongous Insurance has implemented a multilayer routing approach, with a border router connected to the Internet, a pair of core routers that provide connections for the majority of their network, and distribution routers placed in each of their major buildings at their corporate headquarters (see Figure 2-3). Redundancy at the border and core allows for failures, whereas pushing routing closer to buildings allows them to operate during network outages and to apply rules to traffic closer to the endpoints in each building.

> **NOTE   ROUTER NAMING CONVENTIONS**
> Though we refer to routers with different names, like "a border router" or "a distribution router" based on their location, the main differentiators between types of routers are usually their capacity and capabilities.

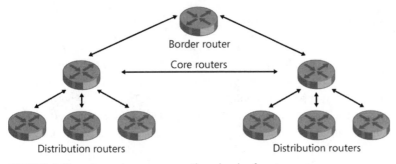

Border router

Core routers

Distribution routers   Distribution routers

FIGURE 2-3 Humongous Insurance uses three levels of routers.

In addition to their traffic routing capabilities, routers can provide a number of security-related functions, including the following:

- **Access control lists (ACLs)**   Rules that provide basic packet filter capabilities.
- **Quality of service (QoS)**   Prioritization of queues of packets and traffic, allowing higher-priority traffic to be handled first for protocols like Voice over IP (VoIP), where real-time responses are important.
- **Denial of service (DoS) attack prevention**   Some routers have protections built in to help avoid or prevent denial of service attacks on the networks they protect.

There are routers of all sizes available on the market, from simple home routers that your Internet service provider provides or that you purchase, to giant enterprise-class routers that cost hundreds of thousands of dollars. As you would expect with that wide of a range of price and usage model, routers also have a broad range of capabilities. Enterprise routers often have the ability to add redundant capabilities like extra power supplies, backup control modules, and even entire firewalls and other major devices in a single box.

Switches

Switches make up the majority of the fabric of organizational networks. Switches are used to connect network devices, or segments of networks, and use an internal table known as a CAM (content-addressable memory) table, which contains the hardware addresses (media access control addresses, typically called MAC addresses) of the systems that are communicating, to determine what traffic should go to each port. This means that two devices on the same switch can communicate with each other without their traffic having to travel beyond the switch.

EXAM TIP

It is important to know how routers and switches differ, and what their basic capabilities are. Remember that routers route traffic between networks, and that switches switch traffic between systems on a network.

Switches can be divided into two major groups: managed switches and unmanaged switches. Managed switches have a back-end management capability allowing you to change settings, monitor, and control the switch. Managed switches typically allow both a local connection to the switch via a direct cable and a network-enabled management capability that allows remote login to the switch. Unmanaged switches (sometimes called "dumb switches") simply allow you to plug network cables into them and send traffic between ports.

Switch manufacturers continue to add features to their products, and some enterprise switches have with routing features have begun to appear. These switches, known as routing switches, can help companies by allowing them to deploy routing capabilities further down in their network at a lower cost than deploying a router alone would entail.

Before switches became common, _hubs_ (also known as _concentrators_ or _repeaters_) were used. Like switches, hubs allowed many systems to be connected to a single device, but unlike switches, hubs replicated traffic from each port to every other port. Not only was this noisy, but it was also insecure, because traffic meant to be received by one system that was sent by another system was visible to every other device that was plugged into the hub.

Not that many years ago, you would find hubs still deployed in many small businesses, where they were often purchased and simply plugged into the network without regard for how their behavior could harm the network or slow down traffic. Fortunately, finding a hub is a rare event now!

Capturing data with hubs and switches

Security professionals used to keep a spare hub handy in case they had a system they wanted to monitor. After plugging the system into the hub, the security professional would connect the hub to the switch port to which the system was previously connected, and then connect a laptop. Because the hub broadcast the traffic to every port, the security professional could then use tools like the sniffers we'll talk about later in this chapter to look at the traffic the system was sending. Fortunately, we've moved past that requirement, and most modern enterprise-grade switches can provide a port, called a *span port*, that copies all of that traffic for inspection.

Span ports are a feature that most managed switches offer via their management interface. A span port can copy traffic from any or all ports, copying it to a single port. Unfortunately, most switches can only create a limited number of span ports, which means that you have to make careful decisions about which ports you copy. If you are capturing traffic for security reasons and then need to do some trouble-shooting, and your switch only supports a single span port at a time and it is in use, you'll have to choose what task is more important!

Span ports aren't a network administrator's only option. Hardware devices known as *taps* are another common choice for security professionals and network designers who need to see traffic live on the wire. Taps make a copy of the traffic that flows through them, either electronically or by splitting the light sent through a fiber optic cable. At times, taps are more desirable than span ports because they can be added without using scarce switch CPU and memory resources.

Since span ports and taps are so useful to both security professionals and network administrators, it is useful to make plans in advance for how you will use them. You will also want to make sure your network is designed to provide access to traffic via span ports or taps in the places that traffic you're interested in will pass through.

Load balancers

Load balancers allow administrators to divide the load on systems among a group of systems based on a set of rules about the traffic. Those rules can be as simple as a *round robin*, in which each request is distributed to the next member of the service pool in order, or they can be quite complex, with traffic matched to specific server capabilities or responsiveness.

There are two methods commonly used in addition to simple round-robin distribution:

- **Weighted round robin**   Each server is assigned a weight based on its capability compared to other servers. It then receives connections appropriate to its weight, after which the load balancer moves on to the next server. As its name suggests, this mode doesn't account for how heavily utilized a server is, and instead depends on moving through the group of servers.

- **Weighted least connection**   Each server is assigned a weight based on its capability to handle connections. New connections are assigned to the server with the number of connections farthest below its capacity. In this model, new connections will be handled by the server with the lowest load.

Load balancers frequently come with a broad range of other capabilities, including terminating SSL (Secure Sockets Layer) connections for secure websites, doing basic firewalling and denial of service prevention, performing health checks, compression, and caching.

Humongous Insurance uses load balancers in its data center environment to distribute load amongst its primary web servers (see Figure 2-4). Because Humongous has deployed two types of web servers, it uses weighted round robin to make sure traffic matches the capabilities of the servers. Note that the newer, more powerful web server is getting twice as many requests as the older, slower web servers.

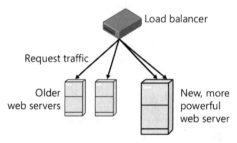

FIGURE 2-4 This load balancer distributes requests to two different types of servers.

 Quick check

1. A router is placed at what location in a network?
2. A weighted round robin load balancer chooses which server receives traffic based on what criteria?

Quick check answers

1. Routers are placed between networks to interconnect them.
2. Weighted round robin load balancers choose which server gets connections based on their relative capabilities based on a weight assigned to the server.

Proxies

A *proxy* server is an appliance, server, or application that accepts requests for access to resources on other servers and then applies filters, caches data, or translates the data that is returned. Modern proxies are most often web proxies and are used for the filtering of data to prevent access to certain types of information or websites, or to allow users to access data that is restricted to specific allowed users, networks, or systems. Proxies are typically deployed as either *explicit proxies*, which require users to have their systems configured to use the proxy, or as *transparent proxies*, which are invisible to the users.

There are three common types of proxy implementations:

- **Gateways, or tunneling proxies**   Proxies used to pass requests in an unmodified form, such as those used to access library data at universities. These merely act to centralize traffic—in the case of universities, this allows the vendor from whom the university licenses data access to have all traffic come from one system, which they permit through their own firewalls.

- **Forward proxies**   Internet-facing proxies used to retrieve data from a range of sources. These are often used to provide anonymity, to cache data to speed up data access, or to filter access to prevent access to restricted resources. Open anonymous proxies are a popular form of forward proxy used by those who want to have some anonymity while browsing the web, but they are also used by attackers in an attempt to shield themselves from identification.

- **Reverse proxies**   Proxies that allow access from the Internet to a protected resource on a local network. Load balancers are often used as reverse proxies to provide load balancing and decryption.

Network administrators and security professionals also use proxies to log and monitor traffic. Proxies are in use in many places, from libraries to companies to individual homes, where modern child safety software filters what sites children are allowed to visit and what content can be displayed to them.

> *NOTE* **PROXIES FOR SECURITY TESTING**
>
> Proxies can also be deployed on individual workstations, where they can provide the ability to inspect traffic before it is sent. Several useful security tools redirect the traffic sent by your web browser through a proxy that allows inspection as well as editing and modification of what your browser sends and receives. This is particularly useful when you are testing the security of websites, because you can send back responses that don't match what the software that runs the website expects, allowing various attack methods to be tested.

VPN concentrators

Secure remote access to networks is typically handled by *virtual private network (VPN) concentrators*. VPN concentrators allow remote users to securely connect to them, and then provide secure encrypted communications between the remote machine and the organization's network by building a secure tunnel across the Internet or other network. In addition to providing remote access for individuals, VPN concentrators are often used to build secure networks between organizational networks across public Internet connections.

As shown in Figure 2-5, Humongous Insurance has deployed an SSL VPN concentrator into its protected DMZ. Users connect to the VPN concentrators, and from there their traffic is filtered by the enterprise's firewalls before being allowed into the rest of the network. Humongous also uses an IPSec VPN to connect to its remote site in England, providing that branch office with a connection that makes its network appear to be part of the main Humongous network.

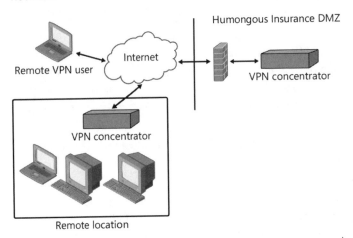

FIGURE 2-5 VPN concentrators handle secure remote access to networks.

Current VPN concentrators typically use one of two major technologies for their VPN sessions: Internet Protocol Security (IPSec) or SSL. Both have advantages and disadvantages, so we will take a quick look at the options.

IPSec VPNs have been the traditional answer to VPN needs. For IPSec VPNs to work, the client needs to have an IPSec VPN client installed and configured to work with the VPN concentrator, which can be expensive in time and effort if you have a large number of VPN users. IPSec VPNs operate at the network layer of the OSI (Open Systems Interconnection) model, meaning that the workstation that connects appears to be a part of the network where the

VPN concentrator resides—in essence, the remote machine looks like it is on the local enterprise network. This is a benefit when applications depend on being on the local network, but it also means that remote systems can appear inside your protected network!

SSL VPNs use the client's web browser to connect, meaning that there's no additional overhead for installation and maintenance of a client. This means that they're usually easier to support and deploy, and that web-based applications are easily used via the VPN. The disadvantage to this is that only web-based applications will work via an SSL VPN, meaning that client-based applications won't work out of the box without additional work to make them pass through the SSL VPN. If your organization is reliant on client-based thick client applications, printing, or storage, SSL VPN might not be the right solution.

Real world

Unexpected outsourcing

In 2012, Verizon's security team was engaged to look at a company's VPN logs due to activities that appeared to be out of the ordinary. As investigators dug into the VPN logs, they found that one of the company's developers was connecting from an address in China every day during work hours, and that this had been going on for months. This connection was a particular concern because the company used a key-fob token-based security system to access the VPN, meaning that the user's high-security token was in the possession of someone in China!

The investigators were quickly told that that user was actually at work, just around the corner from where they were conducting the investigation. After reviewing the developer's workstation, they found out that the developer's daily work consisted of browsing the Internet, spending time on eBay and Facebook and other non-work activities, and that every day ended with a summary email message to management documenting his work for the day, which had somehow been accomplished.

Further investigation and discussion with the developer showed that he had outsourced his job to China and had sent his security fob and credentials to the outsourced worker. As the investigators dug deeper, it was revealed that the same developer was actually employed at other companies in the area at the same time, and that he told those companies he was working from home. In reality, he had outsourced those jobs, too!

The lesson we can learn from this is that VPN can provide a way past your security systems for more than just your users, particularly if those users aren't careful with their credentials.

Network intrusion detection systems (NIDS) and network intrusion prevention systems (NIPS)

A *network intrusion detection system*, or *NIDS* (often shortened to IDS), is a network device or software that is designed to detect attacks as they traverse your network. IDSs are installed on the network in a location that allows them to receive a copy of network traffic for the part of the network that the organization wants to monitor. When an IDS detects an attack, it can log or send an alarm based on its configuration, allowing network and security administrators to take appropriate action.

A *network intrusion prevention system*, or *NIPS* (often shortened to IPS), takes detection a step further and resides inline with the network traffic, allowing the IPS to take action based on its rules, either logging, sending an alarm, or taking proactive action by stripping attack traffic out. An IPS can even stop all traffic from the attacker, thus preventing the attack.

IDSs and IPSs have two major methods of detection: signature-based and behavior-based. The most basic form is signature-based detection, sometimes also called pattern-based detection. Signature-based detection uses predefined fingerprints known as *signatures* to determine what attacks and malware look like. Much like the familiar methods used by antivirus software, this matches known issues well, but it doesn't effectively handle zero-day attacks that don't have a signature released yet, or attacks that change how they appear on the network.

Signature-based detection has a very low rate of false positive identification, and because the signatures are for known attacks, the response to them is easier to predetermine. The downside of signature-based detection is that it requires constant updates and a good understanding of your environment to know what to block. In addition, modern malware is intentionally designed to not be a static, easily identifiable target, making signature-based detection less effective.

Behavior-based detection, also known as *heuristic* or *anomaly-based detection*, is focused on detecting behaviors that are likely to be attacks or unwanted behaviors on the network. It focuses on detecting differences from normal behavior of users or systems on the network. To do this, behavior-based IDS and IPS systems need to build a profile of what normal traffic and behavior on your network is. Though behavior-based detection can detect new attacks that might be missed by signature-based detection, it can also be prone to false positives because behavior that is different is not always an attack.

Host-based intrusion detection and prevention

Intrusion detection and prevention software can also be installed on individual systems, in which case it is called *HIPS* or *HIDS*. Host-based intrusion detection and prevention software is often packaged with antivirus or other system security software and provides the same advantages and disadvantages as an IDS or IPS system does, but only for the host it is installed on. Thus, HIPS software can provide a useful line of defense that is far more reactive than a simple firewall ruleset. This can better protect systems from attacks that are more subtle than an easily blocked attempt to access a protected service. As you would expect, much like with an IPS system, with host-based detection a misconfiguration or a poorly designed rule can block critical traffic, taking a system offline.

False positives

IDSs and IPSs both suffer from *false positives,* when a signature-based, behavior-based, or heuristic-based detection is incorrect. With an IDS, this simply results in an alarm that must be investigated or dismissed, but with an IPS this can be more serious. IPS systems will typically be set to block attacks, resulting in legitimate traffic being blocked if a false positive occurs. In a production network, this can result in service outages or even large-scale downtime if the false positive is significant.

Real world

IPS signatures

We have worked with many popular commercial and open-source IDS and IPS technologies. One of the common issues with them is the quality of signatures that are used, because many individuals and organizations create signatures. In one recent case, a signature was released for a major new malware outbreak that attacked a newly updated version of Java, but it was designed based on a single version of the attack. Other versions were released, and malware infected systems on a protected network while the IDS sat by and didn't detect anything.

In this case, knowing how the signature was designed would have helped because we might have been able to see that it was overly narrow. Often, the opposite is true, and we deploy an IDS rule that detects traffic we want to allow on our network. Thus, we're careful to test signatures before deploying them whenever it's possible to do so. With that said, in an emergency, it's not unheard of for an organization like ours to deploy a rule knowing that the risk of blocking legitimate traffic exists.

Managing an IDS or IPS requires balancing the need to detect attacks against the possibility of false positives and inadvertent detections. Careful thought must be put into the rules used for detection, and if the rules that you use are created by a third party, or if you're not certain that they're correct, it's always safer to detect the issue and report on it than it is to block traffic outright.

EXAM TIP

The critical difference between an IDS and an IPS is the ability of the IPS to stop traffic. Because of this, IPS systems need to be installed between systems and the network where threats are likely to come from.

Remember that IDSs are installed with a view of network traffic but are not usually placed inline. This is both a benefit when preventing attacks and a downfall when a false positive occurs, stopping desired traffic. IPS network placement can also be an issue if the IPS itself crashes or fails, preventing network traffic from flowing through it.

The IDS and IPS systems used at Humongous (see Figure 2-6) are deployed based on the risks the company faces. Humongous uses an IPS behind its border firewall to protect the company against attacks from the outside world. Here, the risk of attack from the outside world outweighs the dangers of an IPS stopping traffic inadvertently. In its data center, Humongous uses an IDS to detect potential attacks. Humongous chose an IDS because it doesn't want to risk stopping its internal server traffic due to a false positive or misconfiguration.

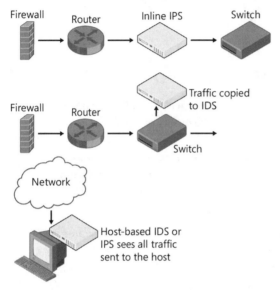

FIGURE 2-6 Humongous Insurance has deployed IPS and IDS systems on its network.

✔ **Quick check**

1. What is the danger of placing an IPS inline between your servers and workstations and your outbound connection?

2. What happens when an IDS suffers from a false positive identification of an attack?

Quick check answers

1. An IPS can block traffic between systems when it suffers from a false positive, and a failed IPS can block network traffic entirely.

2. An IDS that has a false positive will alert, log, or send an alarm due to the false positive but, unlike an IPS, will not block traffic due to the false positive.

Protocol analyzers

A *protocol analyzer*, also sometimes known as a *packet analyzer* or *packet sniffer*, is a software package or hardware device that can capture and log details about traffic as it passes through the network. It then decodes the packets, providing a view of the data each packet contains. After the packets are decoded, the protocol analyzer can provide detail on whether the packet is properly formed, if it contains errors, and what the decoded data contained in the packet is.

The most common form of protocol analyzer in today's network is the sniffer, a software tool used for packet capture and analysis. Sniffers have a broad range of uses for security professionals and for attackers. Common uses include:

- Traffic analysis to determine if packets are becoming corrupted or have the wrong source or destination address, or otherwise provide information about network issues.

- Packet content inspection to determine if the packet's payload is correct, or if it contains malware, secure data, or other information that it shouldn't.

- Capturing unencrypted passwords, sessions tokens, or other credentials as they are sent across the network and captured by attackers and penetration testers.

Sniffers are typically deployed in one of three modes, as shown in Figure 2-7 and described here:

- Inline, where traffic flows directly through them. In the figure, traffic flows from the router (a) through the sniffer (b) to the network (c).

- Tap or span, either by using a specially designed tap (a network device designed to make a copy of each packet as it goes through a network device to send to the sniffer) or a span (which configures a switch or router to copy all data from certain ports to another port where the sniffer resides). In the figure, traffic flows through a switch (a), which makes a copy and sends copies to both the sniffer (b) and the network (c).

- Host-based, which can capture traffic visible to, or sent to or from, the host on which the sniffer resides. In this design, traffic from the network (a) flows through the sniffer as it goes through the host (b).

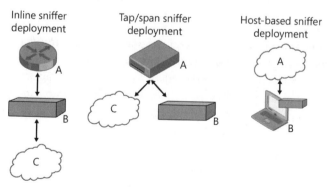

FIGURE 2-7 There are three different methods of deploying sniffers.

The diagnostic information a sniffer provides can be invaluable—system administrators often deploy sniffers to provide information about whether a new software package is connecting as it should. Networking staff use sniffers to determine whether packets are flowing properly, and whether there are issues with how the packets are being built and sent. Security professionals take advantage of sniffers to view attack traffic as it shows up, allowing them to analyze it manually if necessary.

Listening in on VoIP

Systems that use voice over IP (or VoIP, a type of network-based communication technology) often send calls between phones in an unencrypted form across the network. This means that a clever attacker can use a sniffer to capture phone calls on the network—performing a network-based wiretap. Because networks can be configured to send a copy of traffic to other places, an attacker could make copies of phone calls between users who aren't anywhere near them. Worse, tools exist that allow VoIP conversations to be modified instead of just being listened to. Imagine what you could do if you could change what the other person on the line is saying!

Attackers sometimes deploy sniffers if they are targeting specific data and they believe or know that the data will be traveling across the network unencrypted. Encrypted traffic can also sometimes be of interest, if the attacker knows how to decrypt it or can capture it before it is encrypted. This is particularly dangerous in trusted parts of a network!

Inspection

Traffic inspection takes the next step beyond packet capture and analysis and checks the traffic for attacks ranging from spam to malware to bad URLs. We'll take a deeper look at each of these.

Spam filters

Spam filters have become increasingly complex and capable as spam techniques have advanced. Modern spam filtering looks at the content of messages, the sender's IP address and its reputation, the formatting of the message, and a host of other factors to score the message. Whitelists and blacklists of trusted and untrusted sites and senders, as well as manual adjustments of the rules and scores given to messages, allow security and email administrators to have in-depth control over the messages marked as spam. As with other detection systems, there is a delicate balance between messages allowed through and messages marked as spam, and false positives are a concern.

Malware inspection

Malware inspection builds on packet capture and inspection capabilities to analyze traffic for malware. Typically, malware inspection is signature based and uses traditional antivirus detection capabilities to check for malware. An example of this type of integration can be found in Microsoft Exchange, where the Edge Transport Server processes messages by checking for malware by using a content filtering agent prior to delivery to the user, helping ensure that malware is detected and quarantined before it shows up in the user's inbox. We'll talk more about malware itself in Chapter 6.

> ***MORE INFO*** **SPAM AND MALWARE**
>
> We talk about spam and malware as threats in Chapter 5, and as part of host security in Chapter 9, "Establishing host security."

URL filtering

URL filtering typically uses a combination of content filtering, blacklisting, and heuristic detection capabilities to control web access. URL filtering is typically backed by a comprehensive logging system, allowing security administrators to monitor which users are visiting prohibited or dangerous sites on a regular basis.

Each of these three types of inspection relies on the ability to identify the targeted attacks or issues that they are intended to prevent. Much like IDSs and IPSs, they often combine heuristic capabilities that identify common behaviors or features of the attacks, or a rule-based system that looks for common elements to focus on with a signature-based or fingerprint-based detection system. Signatures are usually provided as an ongoing feed, either from the manufacturer of the device or from a third party that specializes in providing that type of feed.

In addition to these detection capabilities, spam and URL filters often use lists called Real-time Blackhole Lists, or RBLs. These are quickly updated lists that the spam or URL filter can use to check email or URL requests against to see if they are on the list. RBLs are an excellent tool, because they typically combine feedback from their customers and others with analysis of submitted spam or URLs. This combination, and the ability to check the list in real time as the traffic is analyzed, means that the filters can block developing threats more quickly than a traditional fingerprint-based detection system can.

DNS blackholing

While we're talking about inspection, it's worth mentioning another technique that has been very popular in network defense: DNS blacklisting or blackholing. The Domain Name System, or DNS, provides the ability to look up network addresses, converting from a domain name like *www.humongousinsurance.com* to an IP address, or vice versa.

DNS blackholing uses an organization's DNS and a blacklist of sites that are dangerous or prohibited. When a system on the network tries to look up a DNS entry, the organization's DNS server returns a different answer than the real answer: either nothing, leaving the user with no address to connect to, or a redirection to a website that informs the user that he was trying to visit a blocked site.

This technique only works for systems inside a network where DNS blacklisting is enabled, but it's a clever way to neutralize threats that try to direct your users or systems to external sites and systems. It has gained popularity in higher education, with home users who want to protect their children, and with organizations that want to remain open and don't want to filter by using a proxy, but that do want to have some form of protection against known bad sites.

DNS will be covered in more detail in Chapter 3, when we discuss the protocol itself, and in Chapter 5, when we focus on DNS attacks.

 Quick check

1. If your organization needs you to review traffic to determine whether systems are properly connecting to each other, what tools would you use?

2. What type of filtering would be most effective to prevent users from visiting links included in spam email messages?

Quick check answers

1. A sniffer or protocol analyzer

2. URL filtering

Web security gateways

Websites are a major part of today's threat environment. Employees expect to be able to browse the web at work in most organizations, and when they do, they don't always make good choices about where they browse. Even if your employees always click on the right links, and don't end up in the seedier portions of the Internet, hackers will bring the threats to your door by sending tempting phishing links via email (which we will discuss in Chapter 4, "Operational and environmental security," and Chapter 5). Some attacks even take advantage of ad networks to push attacks to users of popular websites via paid ads that later become attacks aimed at vulnerable web browsers and plug-ins.

This has led to the development of an entirely new class of devices focused on protecting browsers from the wide variety of attacks that are aimed at them. Browsers are particularly attractive because they are widely used, they are often not updated because a specific version is required for compatibility or because the users didn't remember to install the updates, and because of the wide variety of plug-ins that most users have installed.

We used to deploy only anti-spam and anti-malware tools, but now we find that we need to deploy centralized systems to protect the most common way that our users access data— their web browsers. Thus we deploy *web security gateways*.

Web security gateways are combination devices that fuse URL filtering, malware inspection, and additional controls for web applications and other tools into a single device to protect users from attacks and malware while browsing the web. Much like an IDS or an IPS, they often have:

- Heuristic detection capabilities to catch behaviors that are common to attacks.
- Whitelists and blacklists for allowed and prohibited traffic types and websites.
- An antimalware scanning capability.
- The ability to set rules about behaviors.

In addition, they often offer reputation-based filtering by using services that identify systems or networks based on what they have done that was seen by similar devices or a company that specializes in providing attack data.

Unlike web application firewalls, which protect your web applications against attacks, web security gateways protect users against attacks like malicious websites, browser attacks, and compromise of browser plug-ins.

At this point, you may be wondering why you would choose to deploy a web security gateway if you're already doing URL filtering. But URL filtering focuses on blocking known bad URLs. This means that new sites that are infected or filled with malware won't be caught until they are reported and added to the list of known bad sites. Worse, URL filters can't catch attacks aimed at browser plug-ins, because they only look at where your users are browsing to, not what the content of the traffic is!

Web security gateways are often configured as transparent proxies, meaning that user network traffic passes through them without users being aware of them. They are effectively invisible on the network but provide protection to users by inspecting traffic; checking the traffic against blacklists, fingerprints, and other filtering tools; and then passing legitimate traffic through.

All-in-one security appliances

Many network security vendors have integrated the capabilities we've discussed thus far into a single device that can provide a broad range of network security services. These *all-in-one appliances* are often called Unified threat management or UTM devices. These all-in-one security appliances typically provide routing; switching; firewalling; IDS and IPS capabilities; content inspection with malware, spam, and URL filtering; and a variety of other services like bandwidth shaping, logging, and reporting. Though expensive, these devices can help simplify secure network design by replacing a multitude of devices with a single device, but this can also introduce some new dangers into your network. These dangers can include risks created by relying on a single vendor to provide multiple layers of protection, as well as the potential issues that a single point of failure can create in a network. As all-in-one appliances have matured, they have become better solutions for small to mid-size networks, but they are still relatively uncommon in large enterprises.

Chapter summary

- There are three common types of network firewalls: packet filters, which inspect every packet for source, destination, port, and protocol; stateful packet inspection firewalls, which can maintain information about the state of traffic, decreasing the effort required to permit traffic; and application firewalls, which apply deeper inspection to application-layer traffic, checking protocols and other details. There are also web application firewalls, which specifically protect websites and servers from attacks.

- The concept of implicit deny, a critical part of firewall design, is applied in firewalls by stopping any traffic that is not specifically allowed to pass through them.

- Routers are devices that direct traffic between networks and switches, which carry network traffic between systems and other switches and routers. Together, they are the underlying fabric of networks.

- Load balancers are network devices that direct traffic to multiple systems to spread the load on their services. This chapter looked at the three most common load balancing schemes, from simple round robin to more complex schemes that pay attention to server capability and current load.

- There are three types of proxies: gateways, which aggregate traffic through a single point; forward proxies, which filter Internet access; and reverse proxies, which funnel outside traffic back into a network.

- Virtual Private Network concentrators allow remote users to tunnel back in to your private network, providing either direct access to the internal network or a tunnel to provide access to applications via SSL.

- Network intrusion detection and intrusion prevention systems use their view of a network to apply heuristic-based or behavior-based analysis as well as pattern- based or fingerprint-based analysis to detect attacks. An IDS detects, whereas an IPS is placed inline with the traffic, allowing it to block attacks. An IPS can be a danger, because it can block legitimate traffic, but an IDS has no chance to stop an attack.

- Protocol analyzers and sniffers are the tools that security professionals, as well as server and network administrators, use to inspect and analyze traffic on the network. Sniffers are useful for many things, from checking to make sure packets are arriving to diving deep into the packets to find attacks.

- Content inspection, including spam filtering, malware inspection, and URL filtering, is a way for security professionals to protect networks by using network filtering. Web security gateways are an additional useful layer of protection for users doing web browsing.

- All-in-one security devices combine many of the technologies covered in this chapter into a single device with a broad array of capabilities.

Chapter review

Test your knowledge of the information in Chapter 2 by answering these questions. The answers to these questions, and the explanations of why each answer choice is correct or incorrect, are located in the "Answers" section at the end of this chapter.

1. If your organization wants to monitor for attacks but is worried about possible outages if your network traffic is accidentally blocked, what technology should you deploy?

    A. A sniffer

    B. An IPS

    C. An IDS

    D. A firewall

2. A firewall that can block traffic based only on the IP address, protocol, or port that traffic is sent to is what type of firewall?

    A. A stateful firewall

    B. A host firewall

    C. A network firewall

    D. A packet filter

3. Which of the following network devices connects two networks and sends traffic to the appropriate network based on its destination?

   A. A switch

   B. A firewall

   C. An IPS

   D. A router

4. If you wanted to use a proxy to send traffic directly in an unmodified form to its destination, what type of proxy would you use?

   A. A gateway

   B. A reverse tunneling proxy

   C. A reverse proxy

   D. A side-to-side proxy

5. An attack on a device that fills the device's CAM table, making it send traffic to every port, is an attack against what type of device?

   A. A firewall

   B. A router

   C. A packet filter

   D. A switch

6. What type of network security tool would you use to manually inspect traffic?

   A. An IDS

   B. An IPS

   C. A sniffer

   D. A firewall

Answers

This section contains the answers to the questions for the "Chapter review" section in this chapter.

1. **Correct Answer: C**

   A. **Incorrect:** A sniffer is used to view traffic but does not monitor for attacks.

   B. **Incorrect:** An IPS, or intrusion prevention system can detect attacks, but it is designed to block them, thus creating the risk of causing an outage.

   C. **Correct:** An IDS is designed and deployed in a way that allows it to monitor attacks without blocking them.

   D. **Incorrect:** A firewall uses rules to allow or deny traffic, but does not detect attacks.

2. **Correct Answer: D**

   A. **Incorrect:** A stateful firewall could filter only based on an IP address or port, but it also has the ability to understand when a conversation is permitted between hosts.

   B. **Incorrect:** A host firewall is a firewall that is installed on a single system and could be an application firewall, a stateful firewall, or a packet filter. "Host firewall" alone does not tell us enough to know what type of firewall it is.

   C. **Incorrect:** A network firewall is a firewall that is installed on a network. It could be a packet filter, a stateful packet inspecting firewall, or an application firewall.

   D. **Correct:** A packet filter has a limited understanding of traffic and only filters on the IP address, port, or protocol of the traffic.

3. **Correct Answer: D**

   A. **Incorrect:** A switch interconnects systems on a network and sends traffic to ports based on the address of the destination system, but it does not make decisions about appropriate networks to send traffic to.

   B. **Incorrect:** A firewall applies a set of rules to inbound or outbound traffic.

   C. **Incorrect:** An IPS (intrusion prevention system) monitors traffic for attacks and can stop those attacks by dropping the related traffic.

   D. **Correct:** Routers sit between networks and, as their name implies, route traffic to destination networks.

4. **Correct Answer: A**

   A. Correct:. A gateway is used to centralize traffic. Gateways are often used for database searches conducted from university campuses to allow authorized users access to library databases from a single, trusted system

   B. Incorrect: Gateways are tunneling proxies, but reverse tunneling proxies that reach out of the network to allow traffic in via a secure tunnel are usually used by malware to stealthily get traffic out of a network.

   C. Incorrect: Reverse proxies allow access from the Internet to a protected resource.

   D. Incorrect: This is a made-up answer—side-to-side proxies don't exist!

5. **Correct Answer: D**

   A. Incorrect: A firewall uses rules to block or allow traffic, but it does not use a CAM table to send traffic to ports.

   B. Incorrect: Routers route traffic between networks and typically have far more memory that a switch, preventing attacks like this.

   C. Incorrect: A packet filter is a type of firewall.

   D. Correct: Switches use CAM tables to look up what hardware-address-to-IP-address pairing is associated with each port. An attack that fills the CAM table prevents the switch from looking up the data, resulting in the switch defaulting to sending traffic to all ports.

6. **Correct Answer: C**

   A. Incorrect: An IDS is used for automated inspection and detection of attacks.

   B. Incorrect: An IPS is used for automated inspection and prevention of attacks.

   C. Correct: A sniffer is a tool used to capture and analyze network traffic. It is sometimes known as a protocol analyzer.

   D. Incorrect: Firewalls are used to block and allow traffic based on a ruleset.

Secure network design and management

Network design and management is an important part of securing organizations. Knowing the major elements that make up a network, and what the underlying technologies, protocols, and applications are, will help you better understand the choices you will face when designing and securing networks. In this chapter we will examine what makes networks work, including the underlying building blocks of local networks and the Internet. From there, we will move on to application protocols and the ports that are commonly used for those applications, and how networks are designed and segmented. Along the way, we will dig into virtualization, remote access, and telephony.

Finally, we will look at how to securely manage a network and how to design and implement wireless network security.

As you read this chapter, bear in mind the Humongous Insurance network we looked at in Chapter 2, "Network security technologies." By the time you are done, you will have a better understanding of how all of these elements work together in a network.

Exam objectives in this chapter:

Objective 1.2: Apply and implement secure network administration principles

- Rule-based management
- Firewall rules
- VLAN management
- Secure router configuration
- Access control lists
- Port Security
- 802.1x
- Flood guards
- Loop protection
- Implicit deny

- Prevent network bridging by network separation
- Log analysis

Objective 1.3: Distinguish and differentiate network design elements and compounds

- DMZ
- Subnetting
- VLAN
- NAT
- Remote Access
- Telephony
- NAC
- Virtualization
- Cloud Computing
  - Platform as a Service
  - Software as a Service
  - Infrastructure as a Service

Objective 1.4: Implement and use common protocols

- IPSec
- SNMP
- SSH
- DNS
- TLS
- SSL
- TCP/IP
- FTPS
- HTTPS
- SFTP
- SCP
- ICMP
- IPv4 vs. IPv6

Objective 1.5: Identify commonly used default network ports

- FTP
- SFTP
- TFTP

- Telnet
- HTTP
- HTTPS
- SCP
- SSH
- NetBIOS

Objective 1.6: Implement wireless network in a secure manner

- WPA
- WPA2
- WEP
- EAP
- PEAP
- LEAP
- MAC filter
- SSID broadcast
- TKIP
- CCMP
- Antenna Placement
- Power level controls

Network design and implementation

The ability to successfully secure a network is rooted in an understanding of network design and concepts. In this chapter, we will explore the underlying protocols that are commonly used in networks, applications that use them, common ports associated with these protocols, and security concepts and techniques that are available to network administrators and security professionals. We will also look at wireless networks, telephony and network telephony, and virtualization, which are newer topics of concern for security professionals.

IP: the Internet Protocol

 Most modern networks, including the Internet, use a set of core protocols known as the *Internet Protocol (IP)* suite. This is the *IP* in *TCP/IP*, and it has played a critical role in the development of modern networks and the Internet as we know it. IP provides routing of network packets between local and remote networks, and thus is the glue that holds together the Internet.

IPv4

IPv4 is the most widely deployed version of the IP protocol today. It uses 32-bit addresses composed of four 8-bit bytes, resulting in 4,294,967,296 possible addresses for systems. Those four 8-bit addresses are commonly represented in what is known as dotted quad notation, typically written in the form 1.2.3.4, with each number ranging from 0–255.

> **NOTE BINARY BASICS**
>
> A basic understanding of binary numbers is useful here to understand how these addresses are built. Remember that computers operate by using the binary system, which represents data as a series of 1s and 0s (or bits)—this allows computers to use electrical charges representing on or off to do their processing. A byte, the basic building block that bits are assembled into, is composed of 8 bits. In IPv4 addresses, each number in the address is composed of 8 bits (one byte), with the order and value of each bit indicating a power of 2. Thus, you can add each value together to get numbers from 0 to 255, as shown in Figure 3-1.

128	64	32	16	8	4	2	1
1	0	1	1	0	0	0	1

FIGURE 3-1 This table shows the binary address representation of the number 177.

IP addresses originally had only two parts, the network identifier at the beginning of the address, and the host identifier, found at the end of the address, which was specific to that system. As use of IPv4 networks grew, this was found to be insufficient, and more networks were needed, along with ways to identify them. Thus, the concept of classes was developed. Five network classes were created and called A,B,C,D, and E (see Figure 3-2 for a partial representation). Each network class described a set bit length for network identification and left the rest for host identification. Over time, this too was found to not be flexible enough, and a new scheme called Classless Inter-Domain Routing (CIDR) was developed, although references to network classes such as "MIT has an entire class A network allocated to them!" are still common.

Class	Addresses per network	Number of networks
Class A	16,777,216	128
Class B	65,536	16,384
Class C	256	2,097,152

FIGURE 3-2 This table shows the statistics for network classes A, B, and C.

IP addresses

By now you're probably wondering who is responsible for handing out IP addresses and making sure that there aren't duplicates. That task is handled by the Internet Assigned Numbers Authority (IANA), which maintains and allocates IP address space. IANA is assisted by regional Internet registries (RIRs) such as the American Registry of Internet Numbers (ARIN), the Asia-Pacific Network Information Centre (APNIC), the African NIC (AfriNIC) and others. Internet service providers and other organizations purchase address space from the RIRs and allocate that space to their users.

IPv4 address space exhaustion

The issue of address exhaustion has been a fear for several years due to the limited number of IPv4 addresses, resulting in the development of IPv6 to allow for more address space. In the intervening time, technologies such as network address translation (NAT) and CIDR have helped make the limited number of addresses work for the growing number of systems on the Internet. Will we run out of IPv4 addresses? The last unassigned address blocks were assigned in February 2011, meaning that there are no new blocks for Internet service providers to acquire. Now organizations are starting to look at IPv6, and how to most efficiently use their IPv4 space.

IANA maintains a list of all of the space that exists in the IPv4 address range and which RIR is assigned to manage it. Each of the RIRs then provides lookup capabilities for the IP address ranges it controls, allowing you to look up both customers and IP addresses. This is particularly handy when you are attempting to find a contact for a system that is compromised or that has attacked your network.

Subnets and CIDR

IPv4 networks are partitioned into blocks of addresses by using *Classless Inter-Domain Routing (CIDR)*. CIDR allows address blocks like the class A, B, and C networks discussed earlier to be partitioned into larger networks called *supernets* or smaller network blocks called *subnets* as they are allocated to organizations and users (see Figure 3-3). CIDR notation uses a / (slash) and a number, as well as a subnet mask, to designate how much of the address is the network address and how much is the host address. This approach allows for more flexibility than the A, B, and C network classes alone offered. For example, if your address is 192.168.10.1/25 and your subnet mask is 255.255.255.128, your network consists of all systems in the lower half of the 192.168.10 network: 192.168.10 through 192.168.10.128. The / notation also provides information about the mask that you can apply to the address to determine what the local network is. Because masks are binary, an increase from /24 to /25 means that a /25 network is half the size of a /24 network. Similarly, a /23 network is twice as big as a /24 network.

IMPORTANT VIEW YOUR CURRENT IP ADDRESS

You can try a hands-on example of this by checking your PC's IP address. On Windows-based PCs, open a command prompt from the Start menu and enter *ipconfig*. On Mac and Linux PCs, open a console window and enter *ifconfig*. You'll see a listing of your system's IP address and subnet mask. If you're behind a home router, the mask will probably be 255.255.255.0, meaning that your local network has 256 addresses available to it.

CIDR notation	Mask	Number of hosts	Size
x.x.x.x/25	255.255.255.128	128	Half of a class C subnet
x.x.x.x/24	255.255.255	256	Class C subnet
x.x.x.x/23	255.255.254	512	Two class C subnets

FIGURE 3-3 This table shows examples of CIDR, subnets, and supernets.

IPv6

IPv6 is the replacement for IPv4. It uses a 128-bit address space, hugely increasing the number of IP addresses to approximately 3.4x10^38, or exactly 340,282,366,920,938,463,463,374,607, 431,768,211,456 addresses, versus the 4.3 billion addresses IPv4 provides. If you're trying to talk about that many addresses, you can say that there are 340 trillion trillion trillion addresses, or 340 undecillion addresses in total—it's a mouthful! Because of the huge number of addresses, IPv6 needs eight groups of four hexadecimal digits separated by colons to represent addresses instead of IPv4's simple four numbers.

Figure 3-4 shows a typical Windows 7 machine's IPv4 and IPv6 addresses. Note the IPv6 address, fe80:3087:1eea:6937:75f6, and the IPv4 address, 192.168.2.113. IPv6 addresses are composed of eight groups of hexadecimal numbers with values 0-9 and A-F, providing a total of 16 possible values for each digit, adding up to a 128-bit address. In contrast, IPv4's 32-bit address space is recorded as numbers between 0 and 255 for each of four bits. Sharp-eyed readers will note that the Windows-based system's local IPv6 address is missing three groups of four digits—something is wrong here! Windows trims the zone index from IPv6 addresses, thus resulting in the shortened display.

```
Ethernet adapter Local Area Connection:

   Connection-specific DNS Suffix  . : wan
   Description . . . . . . . . . . . : Realtek PCIe GBE Family Controller
   Physical Address. . . . . . . . . : 00-1F-BC-08-44-06
   DHCP Enabled. . . . . . . . . . . : Yes
   Autoconfiguration Enabled . . . . : Yes
   Link-local IPv6 Address . . . . . : fe80::e087:1eea:6937:75f6%9(Preferred)
   IPv4 Address. . . . . . . . . . . : 192.168.2.113(Preferred)
   Subnet Mask . . . . . . . . . . . : 255.255.255.0
   Lease Obtained. . . . . . . . . . : Thursday, July 11, 2013 8:07:15 PM
   Lease Expires . . . . . . . . . . : Friday, July 12, 2013 12:48:35 AM
   Default Gateway . . . . . . . . . : 192.168.2.1
   DHCP Server . . . . . . . . . . . : 192.168.2.1
   DHCPv6 IAID . . . . . . . . . . . : 234889148
   DHCPv6 Client DUID. . . . . . . . : 00-01-00-01-13-F8-CD-17-00-1F-BC-08-44-06

   DNS Servers . . . . . . . . . . . : 192.168.2.1
   Primary WINS Server . . . . . . . : 192.168.2.1
   NetBIOS over Tcpip. . . . . . . . : Enabled
```

FIGURE 3-4 This screen shot shows typical IPv4 and IPv6 addresses for a Windows 7–based system.

IPv6 also adds additional security capabilities, including Internet Protocol Security (IPsec) support (which is discussed when we look at network and application protocols later in this chapter) and additional multicast capabilities for sending to multiple machines at the same time. It also focuses on automatic configuration of devices on the network, which is intended to decrease the effort required to maintain an IPv6 network. Unfortunately, IPv6 and IPv4 are not interoperable, meaning that dedicated IPv6 gateways are the only way for IPv4 networks to send traffic into IPv6 networks, and vice versa.

Information security staff often encounter IPv6 because it is enabled by default in many new operating systems, and some traffic might be sent via IPv6-connected systems that have automatically configured themselves on a supported network. If you tried the *ipconfig* or *ifconfig* command a earlier in this chapter, you might have seen two IP addresses configured on your system: an IPv4 address, and a long IPv6 address.

Security devices such as firewalls, intrusion detection systems, and packet sniffers are starting to provide IPv6 support out of the box, but it isn't always on, and in many cases it isn't as fully featured as the IPv4 support. Attackers have noticed this and in some cases have used IPv6 tunnels or even local IPv6 networks to avoid security systems designed to block IPv4 traffic on the network.

IPv6 and firewalls

IPv6 creates new challenges for traditional firewalls, which have used IP addresses and IP address ranges to control network traffic flow. A typical firewall rule to allow local users access to a web server via an IPv4 firewall might read "allow 10.10.11.0/24 to 10.10.12.6 via TCP port 80." In an IPv6 network that relies on automatic configuration, this can be much more difficult to do.

As organizations move to IPv6, they will have to carefully examine their choice of network configuration and security design to make sure that they retain the control they require.

The Internet Protocol suite

The three protocols that security professionals typically focus on are TCP, UDP, and ICMP, each of which is commonly used to send traffic on networks every day.

The most commonly used of these is *TCP*, or *Transmission Control Protocol*. TCP is a stateful protocol, which means that both sides of the communication track the status of the transaction, and it is both reliable and connection-oriented. With TCP, this means that communications start with a three-way handshake between the systems. As shown in Figure 3-5, in a three-way handshake the client that initiates the connection sends a SYN , (meaning *synchronize*) to the server or other system it wants to connect to. That system responds with a SYN-ACK, to acknowledge the SYN. The first system then responds with an ACK to acknowledge that communication has been accepted, and communication of data starts.

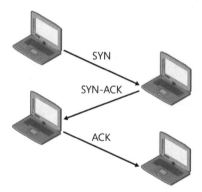

FIGURE 3-5 The TCP three-way handshake is shown in this diagram.

As communications continue, systems check the sequence number of packets that are sent, verifying that all packets are received and that the packets are intact. Data integrity checking, the three-way handshake, the ability to reset connections, and a process to cleanly end communications all help make TCP able to handle errors and to ensure that communications are properly received. As shown in Figure 3-6, when communication is done, the client sends a FIN, meaning "no more data," which the server acknowledges with an ACK and a FIN, which the client then acknowledges with an ACK, ending the session.

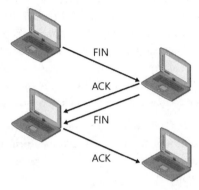

FIN

ACK

FIN

ACK

FIGURE 3-6 TCP session termination is shown in this diagram.

 The *User Datagram Protocol (UDP)* is not connection-oriented like TCP is—in fact, it is a common joke that the *U* stands for *unreliable*. Instead of the handshaking process that TCP uses, UDP sends packets without any means of verifying that they have arrived. This saves network bandwidth and packet overhead because packets don't need to check that they're being received, and can allow for faster transmission. UDP is commonly used for traffic that doesn't need to be guaranteed to be received, or where traffic is unidirectional, rather than an ongoing conversation between two systems. This makes it a common choice for multicasting traffic to many systems, for bootstrapping systems when they need information to boot (which is commonly done via the Trivial FTP protocol or TFTP on port 69), or for applications in which transmission delays are a problem, such as real-time audio. Much like in TCP, UDP packets are sent to a port on a system with an IP address.

TCP and UDP differences

TCP's connection-oriented design means that TCP sessions that end properly communicate the end of their traffic by sending a FIN. Unlike TCP, UDP doesn't require the systems that are communicating to specify that they're done.

This is important in secure networks because proxies and firewalls that inspect application traffic have timeouts for the sockets they create between systems. For TCP, this is often longer because most TCP sessions will send a FIN—in essence, saying "goodbye" and hanging up the connection. UDP doesn't do this, and if you inadvertently use a timeout that is suitable for a TCP session for a UDP session, you can quickly run out of sockets as more and more UDP sessions wait to end. This means that UDP needs to time out relatively quickly, whereas TCP can be allowed a longer time before the receiver decides that the conversation is done.

If you run out of sockets on a firewall or on a server, no new connections can be created. It might take some time for this to be visible, particularly if your network or the service you're trying to connect to isn't busy, but it can create a major outage if it occurs on a busy network.

 The *Internet Control Message Protocol (ICMP)* provides diagnostic, control, and error messaging for networked devices. The most common ICMP traffic you are likely to encounter is ping, which sends an ICMP echo request and ICMP echo reply. Beyond simple pings, ICMP is used to trace network traffic routes and to respond to hosts when a system is down or unreachable.

Because ICMP provides information about systems and how long it took to reach them, it can be used to map the layout of a network behind a security device such as a firewall. You can think of this as similar to a bat using echoes to locate objects around it. Attackers send ICMP traffic such as pings, or performs traceroutes to each system behind a firewall, and then plot the responses they receive. This tells them how many hops away the system is and can even help point out hidden intrusion prevention systems or firewalls in some cases.

 EXAM TIP

Remember the key differences between protocols when you are studying: TCP is connection oriented and emphasizes reliability; UDP simply sends data, allowing for greater speed and less overhead in the protocol. ICMP is used for diagnostics and control.

Fortunately, there is a defense: most firewalls have default settings that can prevent ICMP packets from going through the firewall, and many firewall administrators choose to prevent

ICMP traffic from passing into their secure networks. This can help prevent attackers from using ICMP to map the inside of your network by pinging or getting traceroute information about what lies behind your firewall. As you might imagine, blocking ICMP entirely can prevent useful diagnostic and status information from being sent, which means that many network administrators choose to block some types of ICMP, and control the amount of others, (known as rate limiting) to balance security and usability of the network.

> **MORE INFO ICMP ATTACKS**
>
> ICMP-based attacks are discussed further in Chapter 5, "Threats and attacks," where attacks such as ping floods and the ping of death are covered.

 Quick check

1. The 10.11.0.0/16 network contains how many available host addresses?
2. What is the major difference between IPv4 and IPv6?

Quick check answers

1. You know that there are 32 bits in an IPv4 address, and that /16 means that you have the other 16 bits available as host addresses. This means there are 2^16 addresses, or 65,536 total addresses available.

2. IPv6 has a much, much larger address space than IPv4 does. IPv4 has 4.3 billion addresses, whereas IPv6 has 340 trillion trillion trillion addresses.

Network and application protocols

A broad variety of network and application protocols are used to connect machines and applications on the Internet and on local networks. These protocols define the rules and methods that network devices and services use to communicate with each other. This section takes a look at some of the most common protocols.

 The Internet Protocol Security suite (IPsec) is an open standard for a set of protocols designed to provide security for IP-based communication. This means that IPsec can be used to secure TCP or UDP traffic—anything that you can send via IP can be protected in an IPsec protocol.

IPsec provides both encryption and authentication capabilities, ensuring that traffic sent is secure from snooping, and that traffic is from the system you expect it to be from. Thus, IPsec can be used to provide assurance of both integrity and confidentiality. Unlike protocols such as SSL and TLS, which are discussed later in this chapter, IPsec encapsulates IP traffic, meaning that applications that aren't natively designed to be secure can be protected.

IPsec has three main elements:

- **Authentication header** This ensures that the origin of a packet is authenticated and that the packet itself has not been modified.
- **Encapsulation security payload (ESP)** This can provide confidentiality, integrity, and verification of the origin of packets.
- **Security association** This is a capability that allows security to be added to IP communications by using, the Internet Security Association and Key Management Protocol (ISAKMP).

To support this, IPsec provides protocols that allow systems to authenticate each other (known as mutual authentication) and to negotiate encryption key use. The protocols can be used in either transport mode, in which only the data payload of the IP packet is encrypted, or in tunnel mode, in which the entire IP packet is encrypted, allowing you to choose how the data is protected based on what type of security your organization requires.

IPsec is commonly used to provide VPN tunnels for remote access, and implementations exist for every current major operating system, resulting in widespread use.

> **MORE INFO   IPSEC**
>
> Chapter 12, "Cryptography," discusses IPsec in greater detail as part of Objectives 6.1 and 6.2.

 Telnet was created to provide a command-line console on a remote machine. As you can imagine, this is very useful for remote access, particularly before graphical user interfaces became common. Telnet was used for decades to provide access to network devices, servers, and almost every other device one could find on a network, but it has been largely replaced by the Secure Shell protocol (SSH) in common use for one simple reason: Telnet isn't secure; it sends all of its data in unencrypted form across the wire, making it vulnerable to attackers who can view network traffic and capture commands, logon information, and passwords. Telnet is typically associated with port 23 and is a TCP protocol.

 SSH provides a secure, encrypted connection between two systems running an SSH client and an SSH server. SSH can use public-key cryptography to secure its credentials (you can read more about public-key cryptography in Chapter 12). This allows users to have a secure connection without having to store a password on the remote server—instead, the server simply stores a public key, while the user keeps the secure private half of the key, which allows authentication. In addition to its command-line capabilities, SSH also supports file transfer via SFTP (SSH File Transfer Protocol) or SCP (Secure Copy Protocol). SSH uses TCP port 22 as its default port.

The problem with SSHv1

In 1998, significant vulnerabilities were found in the first version of SSH, called SSHv1, which allowed attackers to insert data into SSH communication. Various patches were released, but many of them made the issue worse, and allowed attackers to run code as the user running the SSH server itself. This often resulted in the code running as root, the local administrator of the system. Other vulnerabilities continued to be discovered, and SSHv1 is no longer considered a usable or secure protocol. If you perform a security review of a system, look for SSHv2 instead of SSHv1 for secure console access.

The *Domain Name System (DNS)* provides a system that translates IP addresses into human-readable names for devices connected to the Internet or other networks. As such, it is one of the underlying protocols for almost everything that happens on the Internet. It is used to associate a name and other data about the domain or host such as the name of the registrant, his or her contact information, and details about that registrant's organization to the IP address that the registrant is assigned. In common use, the DNS protocol uses UDP via port 53 to query a hierarchy of servers. In practice, this means that when a client sends a DNS request, if the server it requests the response from does not know the answer to the request, the request is then passed along upward until it finds a server that can respond. Note that DNS can use TCP (still on port 53) but typically only uses it for very large queries or for zone transfers, which are used to copy entire DNS databases between servers.

As shown in Figure 3-7, DNS servers operate as part of a hierarchical system, with each major top-level domain such as .com, .net, or .org having its own domain servers. Second-level domains such as *humongousinsurance.com* or *treyresearch.net* again have their own domain server or servers, with this continuing down the chain to individual hosts that query upward.

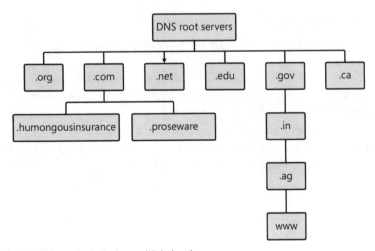

FIGURE 3-7 The DNS hierarchy includes multiple levels.

Targeting DNS

There are 13 root nameserver clusters at the top of the DNS system hierarchy that provide the foundation for the Internet as we know it, making them an attractive target for attacks because attacks against them could theoretically cause the entire DNS system to fail. Fortunately, the hierarchical design of DNS, as well as the caching of responses that occurs at each level in the DNS hierarchy, means that it is difficult to attack. In fact, it would probably be days before an attack would begin to have any major effect, which would provide time to either extend the lifespan of cache entries or bring up alternate DNS infrastructure.

Two major attacks have been conducted on the root DNS nameserver clusters. The first occurred in 2002 and caused a failure for about an hour. The second major attack in 2007 lasted for a full day and caused outages and slowdowns for four of the 13 nameservers. In response, the United States' Department of Defense noted that it would consider bombing the source of an attack (*http://www.networkworld.com/ news/2007/020807-rsa-cyber-attacks.html*).

 Secure Sockets Layer (SSL) was originally designed to provide security for web traffic. Early versions of SSL had several flaws that led to the creation of SSL 3.0, and then to the creation of *Transport Layer Security (TLS)* 1.0, which is broadly used today. TLS is an encryption protocol used to provide secure communication over networks to protect web traffic, email, VoIP, and other protocols. Today, SSL and TLS are often used as interchangeable terms, although TLS is most often the correct term. Many services are provided with both a TLS-protected version and a non-TLS version of the service, such as secure web traffic on port 443 as HTTPS, and unencrypted web traffic on port 80 for normal HTTP. TLS has a broad range of uses, from protecting services to providing the underlying security layer in SSL virtual private networks.

> *MORE INFO* **SSL AND TLS**
>
> Chapter 12 discusses SSL and TLS in greater detail as part of Objectives 6.1 and 6.2.

 The *File Transfer Protocol (FTP)* was one of the first protocols used on Internet-connected systems. As its name suggests, FTP is designed to transfer files between two systems. In its original design, FTP does not make use of encryption, which results in the user name, password, and all sent data traversing the network in the clear. Alternatives such as SCP and SFTP, discussed earlier in the chapter, as well as FTPS, discussed next, are preferable for organizations that want to secure their data transfers or credentials.

FTPS is a secure, encrypted implementation of FTP that adds support for TLS and SSL encryption. Unlike SFTP, which leverages SSH as its underlying secure transfer method, FTPS actually wraps FTP, allowing it to support a legacy compatibility mode when it has to connect to an FTP server that does not support encryption.

Real world

FTPS and firewalls

FTP uses a secondary port that it sets dynamically as it transfers data. This works well in non-firewalled environments because there isn't anything to stop the FTP client and server from opening ports as needed. Firewalled networks, however, require more care, because firewalls need to know what ports to allow.

Most firewalls implement a special listener or handler that watches FTP connections and recognizes when the secondary port is selected. They then add a short-term allow rule that permits traffic to flow to that port for the duration of that connection. This inspection fails for FTPS connections because the firewall cannot see through the encryption provided by the TLS or SSL connection! If you encounter this issue, you'll be glad to find that most FTPS clients can be limited to a small range of dynamic ports that you can allow through via a firewall rule to your FTPS-enabled server.

There is good news if your client's network or system firewall doesn't implement a listener or handler for active FTP sessions that set ports dynamically. FTP's passive mode allows the client to initiate both connections to the server, based on a port that the server sends in response to the client's first query. This allows you to work around firewalls that won't let the server connect directly to clients, because most firewalls allow clients to reach out.

The *Hypertext Transfer Protocol (HTTP)* is the application protocol that makes the World Wide Web work. Hypertext, the underlying concept behind HTTP, relies on links to connect concepts and other data. HTTP relies on a client-server model, with the user's web browser (or various other tools) acting as the client and a server providing the webpages it requests.

HTTPS is the most widely used way to secure HTTP traffic. Unlike HTTP, HTTPS is not an application protocol itself. Instead, HTTPS wraps HTTP traffic in a TLS or SSL wrapper, providing a secure session. One of the key advantages HTTPS provides over HTTP is site authentication that uses certificates, thus proving the identity of the site. The other advantage of HTTPS is the confidentiality that encrypted traffic provides. Websites that send all traffic via HTTPS ensure that nobody between the sender and the receiver can read the contents of their packets.

Certificates and certificate authorities

When a web browser opens an HTTPS connection, it checks for the server's certificate, and then checks that certificate against its certificate store. That store contains a list of the valid, trusted certificate authorities. (Certificates are part of the x.509 public key infrastructure that is discussed in Chapter 12 in more depth).

Certificate authorities (CAs) play an important role in the security of the Internet. They own the root certificates that are used to sign certificates sold to websites, developers, and individuals. As part of their responsibility when signing certificates, they are expected to provide a review process to ensure that their clients are who they claim to be. Every web browser includes a list of known, trusted certificate authorities, allowing them to identify when a certificate has been issued by a trusted CA.

In 2011, DigiNotar, a Dutch certificate authority, experienced a security breach resulting in fraudulent certificates being issued, including a wildcard certificate for Google, allowing the attackers to represent themselves as any Google site with a certificate that would appear valid. The certificate was used to conduct attacks on Internet traffic in Iran.

In response to this compromise, Microsoft removed DigiNotar as a valid CA, as did Mozilla, Apple, and Google. DigiNotar's ability to be a usable certificate authority ended when it was removed as a trusted CA, and it ended up declaring bankruptcy before the end of 2011.

 The *Simple Mail Transfer Protocol (SMTP)* is one of the oldest protocols used on the Internet and is still broadly used today. It defines how mail servers send and receive email, and mail clients typically use it to send email messages for relay via those servers. Mail clients tend to use the Post Office Protocol (POP), the Internet Message Access Protocol (IMAP), or the Messaging Application Programming Interface (MAPI) used by Microsoft Exchange to access email.

 NetBIOS provides network name service, as well as the ability to connect to other PCs on a local area network. NetBIOS is typically associated with Windows-based PCs, which use it over TCP/IP in modern networks where it uses TCP and UDP ports 137, 138, 139, and 445. NetBIOS provides its own 16-character naming scheme, which can be separate from DNS. NetBIOS is often targeted by attackers in Windows-based networks because of common vulnerabilities and insecure default configurations that can reveal information about systems, shared resources, and users on a network. In modern networks, NetBIOS is largely outmoded, but it is still found in smaller networks or in older environments. NetBIOS isn't alone; other older network protocols such as IPX/SPX, AppleTalk, and DECnet were popular before TCP/IP came to dominate networks and might still be encountered occasionally.

Targeting NetBIOS

A Windows-based system with NetBIOS turned on for file and print sharing was a classic target for hackers. In older versions of Windows, NetBIOS provided a wide range of information about the system, its users, and what folders and devices it was sharing. Given this information, an attacker could attempt to guess passwords, or in some cases, could simply connect to a system that didn't require a password to access the directories it was sharing. Some users even shared their entire hard drive, making compromise even easier! With capabilities like these, NetBIOS and the Linux package called Samba, which replicates its functionality, have both been popular targets for exploit.

Ports and protocols

TCP and UDP each provide a range of 65,535 ports for services to operate on. Some services are commonly associated with specific ports, and the first 1,024 ports are known as the "well-known ports." Figure 3-8 shows some of the most critical ports to know for common applications. Bear in mind that these are not the only ports the applications can run on. Rather, they are the ports that the server or service typically defaults to. You can easily find lists of these ports on the Internet by searching for *well-known ports*, and you'll see them frequently as a security professional.

Port	Protocol	Application
21	TCP	FTP
22	TCP	SSH
22	TCP	SFTP
22	TCP	SCP
23	TCP	Telnet
25	TCP	SMTP
53	UDP/TCP	DNS
69	UDP/TCP	TFTP
80	TCP	HTTP
110	UDP/TCP	POP3
123	UDP/TCP	NTP
443	TCP	HTTPS
137–139, 445	UDP/TCP	NetBIOS
990, 989	TCP	FTPS

FIGURE 3-8 This table lists common ports and protocols.

Quick check

1. What port does SSH use?

2. What port does unencrypted WWW traffic commonly use?

3. What port does encrypted WWW traffic commonly use?

Quick check answers

1. 22

2. 80

3. 443

Network design and segmentation

Now that you've learned how to get traffic to and from machines, you can dig into how to keep traffic from flowing between them when you don't want it to. This is accomplished by using a concept called *network segmentation*. Network segmentation is a key part of network security design, because it allows you to choose who and what gets to systems and networks you control.

As you learned in the first half of this chapter, systems connect by using various protocols to services hosted on servers, which are pointed to via ports. Chapter 2 discussed firewalls and other network devices that can help divide a network into segments or networks, so now we will take a look at what those divisions look like. Three of the key elements of most segmented designs are the demilitarized zone (DMZ), virtual LANs, (VLANs), and Network Address Translation (NAT).

 The *DMZ* is a networking reference stolen from the real world, where a DMZ separates two warring countries. In a network, a DMZ is the part of the network that is exposed to the outside world where it is likely to be attacked. Thus, inside users can access the DMZ, and the outside world can access the DMZ, but typically traffic is not allowed directly into the protected zone. As you can see in Figure 3-9, a DMZ often contains web servers or other services that an organization wants to make available. Most DMZ networks are separated from the outside world by using a firewall. That single firewall often has a connection to the non-DMZ internal network as well, in which case it is called a three-legged DMZ. More complex DMZ network designs use two firewalls, one to protect the DMZ and organization from the outside world, and one placed deeper inside the network to prevent DMZ systems from accessing the internal network.

In Figure 3-9, notice that the single firewall has two internal trusted interfaces, with one for the DMZ and one for the rest of the organization's network behind it. It also has a connection to the outside world (the Internet) on its untrusted interface. A two-firewall design would place a firewall in front of the DMZ and second firewall behind that to protect the rest of the network from the DMZ.

It is worth noting that the fact that we show the firewalls as separate devices doesn't mean that they always have to be. Some firewalls can be logically separated internally, allowing a single firewall to provide multiple virtual firewalls for your organization.

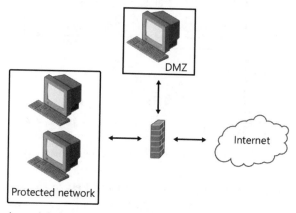

FIGURE 3-9 This three-legged design includes a DMZ, the Internet, and a protected network.

 VLANs create segregated networks. Packets that travel between these networks must be routed by a router, rather than passing between the systems as they would on a flat network composed only of switches. In practice, this results in a switch supporting multiple separate networks without requiring separate physical switches to provide separation. This can help provide a layer of separation for systems, which can improve security, help with scalability by limiting the number of systems that are in a single broadcast domain, and help with management of the network by providing smaller slices to deal with. VLANs are heavily used in modern networks, but switches must be secured to prevent attackers from hopping VLANs on the switch.

In Figure 3-10, ports 1, 2, 4, 6, 7, 9, 10, 11, 13, and 14 are part of VLAN 5; ports 3, 5, and 12 are part of VLAN 10; and ports 8, 15, and 16 are part of VLAN 81. These VLANs cannot contact each other without the help of a router, providing logical separation between the networks, despite the fact that they are on the same switch.

VLAN hopping is an exploit in which attackers seek to gain access to other VLANs that are normally inaccessible to them. To do this, they either exploit protocols intended to combine or trunk VLANs to view traffic on other VLANs, or they send two sets of VLAN tags, which are removed as traffic goes from switch to switch. In a double-tagging attack, the first switch the traffic encounters removes the tags for the traffic's native VLAN, and the second switch it encounters sees the fake VLAN tag, which the host interprets to mean that the traffic is bound for a system on a different VLAN. This only works in one direction, because there is no way to force the receiver to spoof tags back!

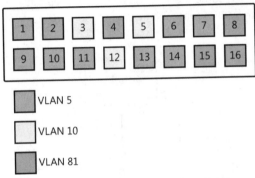

VLAN 5

VLAN 10

VLAN 81

FIGURE 3-10 This simplified view shows a switch that supports three VLANs.

NAT is a tool frequently used to convert an external address to an internal address. This offers two major benefits: First, it means that internal addresses cannot easily be determined by outside attackers or users, which can help protect your internal network. Second, it can allow a single external address to be used for multiple hosts. NAT can also be used to change port numbers or to modify IP ID fields and other information.

There are two common types of NAT:

- **Static NAT** Translates an internal address into an external address, permitting private networks to be reached from the outside world.

- **One-to-many NAT** Maps many addresses on one side to a single address on the other by using a table of ports to track which traffic goes back to which host.

Some applications don't handle NAT well and break when they pass through a NAT device. This is often because the application transmits the IP address of the system sending the traffic as part of its data, and the client then attempts to use that address to reach the server. Because the server is behind a NAT device, unless the NAT device reaches into the traffic to change this, the remote system will never find its IP address. Figure 3-11 shows NAT in action.

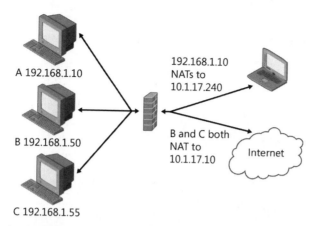

A 192.168.1.10

192.168.1.10
NATs to
10.1.17.240

B 192.168.1.50

B and C both
NAT to
10.1.17.10

Internet

C 192.168.1.55

FIGURE 3-11 Network Address Translation can allow multiple systems to share a single outside IP address. Note that system A uses static NAT to allow outside systems to access it, whereas B and C both share the same outside IP address to access the Internet.

Remote access

After a network has been partitioned and armored against attack, you're faced with a problem: how do you get back into it from outside?

The ability to remotely access a network or system is a key component of almost any network design. Historically, most remote access was done by using dial-up modem access via phone lines. Individual users would typically use a protocol called PPP, the Point-to-Point Protocol. PPP is still in use for some connections to Internet service providers, but most users no longer use modems to access networks.

In most current networks, that role is fulfilled by a virtual private network (VPN), but there are a wide range of technologies that exist to allow remote access. We'll take a look at some of the most common remote access technologies and the underlying systems that make them work.

Virtual private networks

A *virtual private network (VPN)* uses either encryption or a tunneling protocol (or both) to create a virtual network connection through other networks. In practice, this is usually either a user connecting from a remote location to an organization's network or the organization itself connecting two remote sites across the Internet.

In order to create this private connection, you need a way to authenticate the connection, and then you need a tunnel to be established between the endpoints. In Figure 3-12, the top of the illustration, shows tunnels established between a remote user and the main office, allowing that user to access internal network resources. In the bottom configuration a tunnel is established between two remote offices, allowing the remote offices to act like they are on the same network.

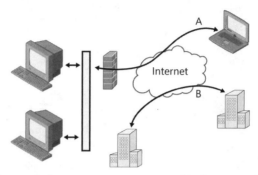

FIGURE 3-12 VPN tunnels can exist between systems at geographically separated sites.

Virtual private networks offer three things that security professionals look for: the ability to provide confidentiality by encrypting data, the ability to provide integrity by ensuring that messages remain intact, and the ability to verify the sender by authenticating the VPN connection.

VPNs can also provide the ability to connect networks by using a different or additional protocol. The IPv6 networks discussed earlier in this chapter can use a VPN to connect across an IPv4 network because the IPv4 network never sees the private IPv6 traffic.

Common VPN technologies include the Point-to-Point Tunneling Protocol (PPTP), which was used for many older VPN systems; IPsec, which uses the IPsec security capabilities discussed earlier in the chapter; SSL/TLS, which uses the same SSL/TLS wrappers as other secure traffic; and the Layer 2 Tunneling Protocol (L2TP).

The problem with PPTP

The PPTP protocol was used for VPN traffic for years and was very popular because it was integrated in common operating systems, making it easy to set up and use. Unfortunately, PPTP has a variety of vulnerabilities, including issues that can allow the encryption used on data sent via PPTP to be cracked with relative ease. This potential exposure means that PPTP isn't a safe VPN technology.

Perhaps worse, in the view of some organizations, common PPTP implementations had vulnerabilities that allowed them to be attacked by using a denial of service attack. When the PPTP VPN server was attacked, the server would crash or stop providing service, taking down VPN access for all users who relied on it.

The vulnerabilities in PPTP resulted in a move to IPsec VPN technology for many organizations, and provides an important lesson: remember to check that technologies you're implementing for security purposes aren't themselves vulnerable!

The two most common modern VPN types are IPsec VPNs and SSL/TLS VPNs, which are often simply called SSL VPNs. IPsec VPNs offer the advantage of tunneling all data, which can make the client system appear to be entirely on the remote organization's network. Their downfall is the requirement for client configuration, and some IPsec VPNs require client software to be installed. SSL VPNs come in two flavors: SSL Portal VPNs and SSL Tunnel VPNs.

> **MORE INFO   SSL VPNS**
>
> You can find the National Institute of Standards and Technology (NIST) guide to SSL VPNs at *http://csrc.nist.gov/publications/nistpubs/800-113/SP800-113.pdf*. It provides information about SSL VPNs including their functions, features, and details of their capabilities as well as recommendations on how to select and implement them.

SSL Portal VPNs provide a secure SSL connection to a website, allowing the remote user to access network services. They are increasingly popular as applications move to the web, and they don't require a special client or configuration. Instead, they only need a current web browser. SSL Tunnel VPNs use a web browser to create a tunnel. This can provide access to a variety of other network services beyond those simply accessible via a web browser. SSL Tunnel VPNs require browsers to support plug-ins such as Java or ActiveX to handle the tunneling capabilities they provide.

> **MORE INFO   VPN AUTHENTICATION**
>
> Authentication for VPNs and other remote access technologies uses a variety of mechanisms. You can read more about them in Chapter 11, "Identity and access control."

Remote access services

Dial-up remote access is still used by some organizations that have a specific need that is met by using modems. In some cases, this is due to users who only have access to phone lines instead of high-speed Internet connections. Other organizations retain their remote access capabilities for emergencies in case their Internet connection is down.

The systems that provide this access via any of several methods, including dial-up, are referred to as *Remote Access Services*.

Telephony and VoIP

Telephony in organizations used to be limited to what is frequently called *POTS lines*, or *plain old telephone service lines*. A company would deploy its own business telephone system, often with a private branch exchange (PBX). PBX systems allowed companies to handle internal phone calls completely inside the organization, routing calls between buildings from a central location. Over time, PBX systems started to become more tightly integrated into computer systems, allowing them to interoperate with networks.

Now network-based telephony is a big part of many corporate networks. Traditional PBX systems that ran phones throughout an organization brought a lot of cost with them, including a separate wiring plant, administration, and the costs of upgrading a phone system as the company expanded or needed more lines. Perhaps most important, traditional phone lines brought significant expense when the cost of long-distance and local phone trunks were considered.

Many organizations have transitioned to *Voice over IP* (VoIP). VoIP moves telephone calls to the data network, allowing the same network to carry both voice data and other network data. As you might imagine, this does create its own list of concerns. A few of these include:

- **Security for the phone network** When phones become network devices, they can also be attacked like other network devices.

- **Security for VoIP servers** As with VoIP phones, an attack on the central VoIP servers can be conducted via the network, possibly taking down some or all of the VoIP calling capability.

- **Separation and segmentation for VoIP calls** Unless VoIP traffic is encrypted, placing VoIP traffic on the same networks as workstations can make capturing and decoding phone calls relatively easy. Separating VoIP onto its own VLANs is useful; however, this can be a challenge because many organizations want to use software-based phones to allow desktop and laptop machines to make phone calls, which requires them to be able to be on the phone network.

- **Power and reliability for the phone network** Older telephone systems provided their own power via the phone lines, which meant that in many outages the phone system would stay up. When phones move to local switches, providing power to the phones is important.

VoIP is also used in the homes of individual consumers and is provided by both dedicated VoIP phone services and Internet service providers who bundle it as part of their Internet and TV services.

Virtualization

Virtualization has changed the way networks and data centers are built and designed. In a system that uses a virtual environment, switches, firewalls, routers, and the rest of the data center can operate as virtual devices, all operating on the same underlying hardware.

The basic concept behind virtualization is that hardware can be presented to software in a virtualized mode. In other words, the real hardware is not accessible to the operating system or software; instead, the underlying virtualization layer provides an abstracted version of that hardware or resource. This allows a single system to run multiple servers or other platforms, sharing resources that would have otherwise been reserved for a single system.

The underlying software that runs virtual machines is called a hypervisor. The hypervisor provides all of the virtual resources to the virtual machines (VMs) that it runs and can control what resources, access, and capabilities those virtual machines have. Some hypervisors are an entire operating system by themselves, whereas others run as an application on a traditional operating system.

Hypervisor classifications

Hypervisors are typically separated into two major types. Type 1, or "bare metal" hypervisors, run directly on the underlying hardware to control the hardware and to provide resources to guest operating systems. This is the classic hypervisor model and is used for common hypervisors such as VMWare ESX/ESXi and Microsoft's Hyper-V hypervisor. Type 2, or "hosted" hypervisors, run inside of a typical operating system as a software layer, with guests running as a third layer above the system's hardware. VirtualBox and VMWare Workstation and Player are all examples of Type 2 hypervisors.

The level of control that hypervisors provide makes it easier to provision the capabilities needed for the purpose of the server. In many organizations, servers run by using a tiny fraction of the CPU, memory, and network bandwidth that the physical servers they are installed on have. In a virtualized environment, you can optimize your use of hardware by placing multiple machines on the same underlying hardware. If you need more speed, memory, or network bandwidth, your hypervisor can allow the machine to scale upward, or in more complex environments, it can send that virtual machine to another system to run with more resources. Virtualized systems run on one or more underlying servers, allowing multiple machines to share the same resources. A virtual cluster as shown in Figure 3-13 can host dozens of servers by using only a few machines.

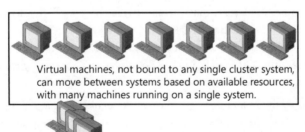

Virtual machines, not bound to any single cluster system, can move between systems based on available resources, with many machines running on a single system.

Hypervisor cluster

FIGURE 3-13 Virtualization servers act as a platform for many virtual servers.

Virtualization makes it easier to migrate machines between different underlying hardware, because virtualized hardware can appear identical. This makes concerns about hardware drivers, networks, and even CPU models no longer an issue, and means that virtualizing systems even on their own hardware is attractive for disaster recovery and flexibility reasons. When every hardware platform that you own appears the same, you can quickly and easily move between them instead of having to make sure that you keep exactly matching hardware.

In a virtual environment, systems can be paused and copied, and backups can be made easily and quickly by simply copying the live machine. If you need to move a live environment to another location, tools exist that allow you to simply migrate the system to that site. If you have virtualized the network that the system connects to, the entire infrastructure for the system can move at the same time!

Virtualization is being extensively used to increase efficiency of hardware use, to help with disaster recovery, and to allow for more flexibility with deployment, patching, and scaling.

Real world

Virtualization attacks

Attackers know that virtualization means that multiple machines might exist on the same underlying hardware. That means that if they could somehow escape the virtual machine and attack the hypervisor underneath, they could potentially control all of the virtual machines that run on the physical system.

There are two ways to go about doing this. First, the attacker could look for a vulnerable system that is running virtualization software. Attackers would look for vulnerable management utilities or an unpatched version of an operating system that is running the hypervisor. The second way to attack is to attack via one of the virtual machines. The first step in doing this is to identify whether the machine that has been compromised is a virtual machine. Researchers have identified a number of ways to check whether the machine that is running is a VM. When an attacker has done that, he or she needs a tool that can break out of the virtual machine and take over the hypervisor. Fortunately, tools to do this haven't appeared yet except those created for proof-of-concept research.

Most organizations with more mature virtualization deployments are balancing the flexibility that full virtualization can provide with the need to keep sensitive data secure. In a traditional data center, this was done by separating machines into a DMZ and more protected areas. In a fully virtualized environment, this can create extra costs, because physical separation means that you can't fully optimize your use of VMs.

Designing secure virtual data centers

Virtual data center design is an emerging field, and there are many ideas about how to design a secure, flexible environment. Currently, there are two main design philosophies, with organizations frequently choosing to implement parts of each to meet their own needs, as shown in Figure 3-14. In design A in the figure, all segmentation is handled inside of the virtual environment, creating red and green zones that the hypervisor separates. This provides maximum flexibility and allows the hypervisors to allocate resources by using all of the virtualization hardware as necessary. In design B, physical separation of virtual environments is enforced by having both red and green virtualization clusters, limiting the hypervisors to using resources in the same security zone, but limiting the effect of a hypervisor escape or compromise. Note that in A, all four servers are available to share the load, whereas B only has two servers for each zone, limiting resource flexibility.

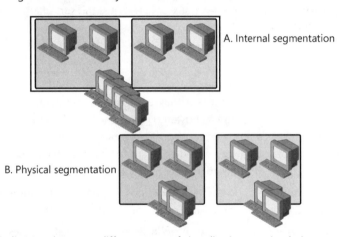

FIGURE 3-14 This diagram shows two different types of virtualization security design.

One design focuses on the capabilities of virtualization and relies on the built-in security tools to build an entirely virtualized environment. This is becoming a more and more attractive option, because hypervisors are adding additional security capabilities on a frequent basis, and they are getting closer and closer to having the same capabilities that a traditional data center network can support.

The competing train of thought chooses to build virtualization into a traditional data center design. In this design model, a virtualization cluster might be placed in a traditional DMZ, rather than attempting to partition DMZ machines inside the hypervisors themselves by using virtual firewalls and networks. This design is more common in organizations with strong confidentiality requirements, or those that don't put as strong of an emphasis on maximum efficiency over potential security concerns if escape from the virtual machine to the underlying hypervisor occurred.

Virtualization attacks

One of the most interesting threats that exists in virtual environments is the possibility of a vulnerability allowing an attacker to escape from within a compromised virtual machine. If this occurred, and the attacker could gain access to the underlying hypervisor, that attacker could end up with control over all of the virtual machines the hypervisor controls. Obviously, this would be a major security issue, particularly in organizations that use large virtual platforms to control hundreds or thousands of machines. Segmentation, either physical or logical, remains an attractive control, although no VM escape vulnerability has been widely exploited in the wild. Vulnerabilities that could allow just such an attack do exist, as demonstrated by the US Computer Emergency Response Team (US-CERT)'s advisory in 2012 about the Xen virtualization platform being susceptible to just this sort of attack on Intel CPU–based hardware.

Cloud computing

Organizations of all types are finding that virtualization means that they can now move their internal infrastructure into environments hosted by third parties in large-scale data centers with support and capabilities that they can't afford to recreate themselves. Computing in the cloud—outsourcing systems, platforms, and software to others who can run them more efficiently, more cheaply, or more reliably—is a quickly growing option.

There are several common cloud computing designs that have been adopted by vendors and organizations as they build public and private clouds. The most common are:

- *Infrastructure as a service (IaaS)*   A cloud service model that provides underlying resources such as servers, storage, and networking. This form of utility computing focuses on capabilities such as dynamic scaling and highly reliable services. Organizations are increasingly using IaaS as a means of providing remote data center capabilities with greater bandwidth and reliability than their own data centers have.

- *Platform as a service (PaaS)*   A cloud service model in which customers use vendor-provided tools to create their service. Vendors provide a complete infrastructure to support the tools, allowing customers to develop, test, deploy, and maintain their applications without having to support the underlying hardware and network.

- *Software as a service (SaaS)*   These cloud environments provide software and data storage via a cloud service. SaaS is a common model for complex software packages such as customer relationship management and content management, as well as services such as vulnerability management or even photo editing.

Other less common cloud service models include backend as a service (BaaS), where back-end technologies such as databases are provided via the cloud, and desktop as a service (DaaS), which provides a virtualized, cloud-hosted desktop.

✔ Quick check

1. What is network-based telephony called?
2. What does a hypervisor do?

Quick check answers

1. VoIP
2. A hypervisor provides the environment for virtual machines to run in.

Network administration and management

A well-designed network is never secure without good administration, and several key concepts are critical to that. This section digs into the basics of rules and access control lists, as well as the configuration options and device capabilities that are important to understand to implement a secure network.

 The first major concept that most networks rely on is *rule-based management*. Networks implement multiple types of rules, including access control lists, firewall rules, and, of course, the procedural rules set as part of the organization's administration. In this section we will look at the technical rules applied to network devices: access control lists and firewall rules.

Access control lists (ACLs)

 Access control lists (ACLs) are typically deployed on network routers. These are lists of systems, networks, or ports that are allowed or blocked. ACLs provide a basic type of firewalling similar to that of a packet filter and are often used to provide very coarse filtering of traffic when a firewall isn't available, or when the router is well-placed to provide control of the traffic.

Firewall rules

Firewall rules allow or deny traffic based on attributes such as the IP address source or destination, the port or protocol the traffic uses, its compliance with the application protocol, the time of day, or even whether the user sending the traffic has authenticated to the firewall. Rules can be as broad or as narrow as necessary to accomplish their task, but the best practice for firewall rules is to limit access to only that which is required. Most firewalls process firewall rules in a set order, usually from the top down, or "first match."

A group of firewall rules is often referred to as a ruleset. Ruleset management is a major part of network security. If your firewall is well designed and has a deny-by-default rule in place, rules have to be added to allow new traffic through as applications, servers, and devices are added to the network. The rules also have to be trimmed and cleaned up when old systems and services are removed from the network.

> **MORE INFO   FIREWALL RULES**
>
> Firewall rules were discussed in Chapter 2 in relation to the topic of implicit deny and other details of firewall ruleset best practices.

Logging

Even if you have designed and built a well-managed network, things do occasionally go wrong. When this occurs, or when you have to investigate an event in progress, the ability to review logs to see what happened is critical. Network devices such as switches, routers, firewalls, VPN concentrators, and almost any other sort of system that can connect to a network have the ability to provide logs. Logs for network devices have the same pitfalls that logs for any system have: if you don't log the right things, you will miss out on important messages and information, but if you log too much, you'll never be able to keep up.

In general, logging should be set to the minimum level required to meet the information needs your organization has. Often, that level is one that sends critical errors, rather than everything that the network device does. For a VPN concentrator, for example, you might choose to log every user who authenticates, and every connection that receives an incorrect password.

After you have chosen your logging level, you will want to determine where to store your logs. Most devices have the ability to store some logs locally, but if the device crashes, has an error, or is hacked, you'll want to have a copy of the log elsewhere. Log servers set up to accept logs from many devices perform a crucial service by providing a secure location where logs can be centralized and reviewed.

Most devices that support logging provide support for the Unix syslog log format. This format is designed to be sent via the network, either via UDP or TCP. As you would expect, TCP syslog has more overhead but is guaranteed to be delivered, whereas UDP syslog is simply sent to the receiving system.

Log analysis

Log analysis is a critical part of securing a network. Almost every device on your network and in your organization can generate logs of some type, and what you choose to log, and how you choose to consolidate, review, and analyze those logs can make the difference between discovering issues and continuing to have a compromised network.

In its most basic form, log analysis is simply a review of the logs provided by a device or system. Most logs will show errors, and you can typically change logging settings to greater levels of sensitivity, resulting in logs that can display a range of events from a log of everything that happened on the device to a log that only shows absolutely critical information.

When you are considering log analysis and review, you need to first determine whether you intend to look at logs on the system that generates them or on a central system. In general, it is preferable to have devices send their logs to a central secure location for two reasons: first, because log analysis is simpler when all of the data is in one place, and second, because attackers often wipe logs after they compromise a system. A central, secure system that stores logs can help with both cases.

After you have figured out where you want to store logs, it is important to consider what information your organization requires from the logs. Setting an appropriate log level for your systems can make a huge difference in the amount of data you store and have to sort through to find the information you are looking for.

The sheer volume of log information available has led to the development of a variety of log analysis tools including security information management (SIM) devices, which provide log management and alerting; security event management (SEM) devices and software, which provide event management and correlation; and combined SIEM tools, which apply additional intelligence via software to log analysis, allowing automation of detection and even automated response capabilities.

Secure switch and router configuration

A well-managed network also requires the switches and routers that connect systems and networks together to be configured to provide security. Several common security settings and capabilities help with this. Now that you've learned how management works, we will look at some of the security practices that are commonly used to ensure network and device security. These include VLANs, port security, 802.1x authentication, flood guards, and loop protection.

VLAN management

As discussed earlier, VLANs allow you to separate switch ports into segmented groups. By creating a VLAN, you can create a virtual network that can be accessed across multiple switches throughout your organization. Rather than buying multiple switches to create separate physical networks, you can use VLANs to provide that separation. It is worth keeping in mind that systems on different VLANs can't communicate with each other without a router, although some switches have basic routing functionality and can bridge that gap.

When VLANs are used to separate parts of a network, the obvious target for an attacker is a more sensitive VLAN than the one that the attacker is currently in. VLAN attacks typically focus on attempting to hop VLANs, resulting in traffic being sent to the secure VLAN. VLAN hopping attacks can be easily prevented by configuring switch ports with the proper security settings.

Port security

 Switches provide a capability called *port security*, which can allow you to control what and how many systems are allowed to connect to each port on the switch. When port security is enabled on a port, the port limits what network hardware addresses (MAC addresses) are allowed to send traffic through that port. If the MAC address is not allowed to access that port, then no traffic from it is sent onward from the port.

Port security has three modes that it typically supports:

- **Static learning** Requires you to configure each port to allow specific MAC addresses to work on that port. This is useful when you want only one system to ever access that port, such as a dedicated hardware device or a trusted PC.

- **Dynamic learning** Allows the port to learn MAC addresses when they connect. Typically this mode is configured with a limit on the number of MAC addresses that can connect to a port, allowing you to decide that only a few machines can connect to the port.

- **Sticky learning** Stores addresses so that they remain in memory through reboots. Like dynamic learning, this can be used to limit how many systems can connect to a port, but it also makes sure that attackers can't cause a power outage or switch reboot to allow them access.

802.1x authentication

In addition to using port security, networks can authenticate systems that attempt to connect to them. The IEEE *802.1x* authentication standard is a standard for port-based network access control (NAC). The 802.1x standard uses three things to authenticate systems: a supplicant, which the client runs to request access; an authentication server, which checks the user's credentials; and the device that provides access, known as the authenticator. The authenticator is often a wireless access point or switch, and when the authentication server approves access, the authenticator then allows the supplicant system access.

The 802.1x standard usually relies on VLANs to create separation between various groups of users. Unauthenticated users, users with different roles, and network devices might each be placed into different VLANs. Because 802.1x doesn't require switches or access points themselves to know how to authenticate users, relying instead on the authentication server, it is relatively lightweight and can be deployed without great expense for powerful, capable endpoints.

Real world

Taking NAC further

A few years ago, network access control systems that used proprietary software clients were common. These systems added enhanced capabilities such as anti-virus scanning, configuration verification, and other checks that ensured that systems that connected to the network were in compliance with network security policies. As 802.1x has become more broadly integrated into operating systems and network devices, this technology has largely been retained only by companies with strict security requirements. Though it is an attractive idea to test every system that connects to the network for security, dropping a system from the network can cause issues that might not be worth the security advantages.

Flood guards

There are two types of flood protection commonly found on a secure network: IDS/IPS-based protection, and switch-based protection. Both have a role to play in network security and usability.

Intrusion detection systems (IDSs) and intrusion prevention systems (IPSs), which were discussed in Chapter 2, target port scans and denial of service attacks such as ping floods, SYN floods, and other types of floods that focus on excessive amounts of traffic. IDS systems can be configured to detect and alarm if this type of flood is seen, but they can't stop it. IPS systems, as you learned in Chapter 2, can take active steps to prevent attacks and could stop a flood.

Switch-based flood protection, sometimes called *storm control*, helps prevent network traffic floods (or storms) that occur when packets flood the network, resulting in heavy traffic and poor network performance. Broadcast storms, which are sent to all hosts on a network; multicast storms, which are sent to multiple targeted systems simultaneously; or unicast storms, which are sent to a single host; can all cause this issue.

Flood guard tools monitor one of two things:

- The bandwidth as a percentage of the total available bandwidth of a port that is used for broadcast, multicast, or unicast traffic.

- The traffic rate of broadcast, multicast, or unicast packets in packets per second.

When a value set in the switch configuration is reached, the storm control capability blocks traffic and continues blocking traffic until the traffic falls below the threshold.

Loop protection

Loop protection is very important in a network because it is very easy to accidentally create a loop in a network. If you simply plug a switch into another switch in a way that makes traffic loop through the two switches, you can cause huge amounts of network traffic congestion as your network repeats traffic sent through it. Fortunately, the IEEE 802.1D standard defines the *spanning tree protocol* (STP), which provides loop protection by detecting loops and shutting them down. A network with STP determines where the potential for a loop exists and then blocks the port where that loop might happen. If the network is later reconfigured, or if the ports that would have created the loop will no longer create a loop, STP is smart enough to update its configuration to allow traffic to flow properly.

Preventing network bridging

In addition to protecting from floods and loops, switches can prevent network bridging when they detect it. Network bridging occurs when two networks are connected together, creating a bridge between the networks. In most cases, this is due to a single machine with multiple network cards that can be connected to two distinct networks at the same time, allowing traffic to flow through it to both.

This is a particular concern when two separate networks are maintained for security, either via physical separation, VLANs, or virtualization. In those cases, network devices should be configured to detect and disable the bridged network port.

Wireless protocols: encryption and authentication

Wireless networking uses several protocols for encryption and authentication. As vulnerabilities and other issues are found in a current-generation protocol or standard, newer versions are usually released. Unfortunately, from the perspective of security professionals, the older technologies are often broadly used, and organizations and individuals frequently don't upgrade quickly, leaving their networks and data vulnerable.

When examining wireless security, the first layer that most users encounter is the type of encryption used. Encryption protocols have been an important part of wireless networks since the late 1990s, because designers were aware that data travelling wirelessly is susceptible to capture, and unlike with a wired network, attackers could now simply aim an antenna at a wireless network and see what was sent. Thus, the first broadly accepted and used wireless security protocol, *Wired Equivalent Privacy (WEP)* was designed. WEP was originally introduced in 1999 and was intended to provide confidentiality equivalent to that of a wired network, as its name suggests. WEP was widely adopted and used, but it suffered from several critical security issues, allowing it to be cracked with relative ease.

The most common form of WEP security, 64-bit WEP, uses a 40-bit key and a 24-bit initialization vector (IV) to build an RC4 encryption key by simply concatenating the key and the IV; in other words, it simply glues the two values together. Unfortunately, the use of such a small initialization vector meant that the keys used in WEP's RC4 stream cipher repeated during longer communications, because there are only 2^{24}, or 16,777,216, possible initialization vectors. As repetitions occurred, it becomes easier and easier to crack the key, making WEP vulnerable to any attacker who could capture traffic on the network over time. On busy networks, and as attacks improved, this meant that the WEP key for the network could be retrieved in almost all cases in less than a minute.

WEP and data breaches

In 2006, a major breach of TJX, the parent company of the TJ Maxx and Marshalls chain of stores, was revealed. The hackers had attacked the WEP encryption used to protect the company's wireless networks, which carried credit card and other customer data. The hackers had gained access with relative ease, and even targeted the TJX network during peak times to steal the most data possible.

TJX was eventually revealed to have lost as many as 96 million consumers' personal information, and costs to the company totaled over $168 million. Shockingly, many other stores and companies continued to use WEP for years.

As WEP became outmoded, *Wi-Fi Protected Access (WPA)* was adopted. WPA implemented most of the IEEE 802.11i standards, including the *Temporal Key Integrity Protocol (TKIP)*, which was designed to prevent the issues with keys that WEP suffered from. TKIP uses three techniques to prevent those attacks:

- It implements key mixing to combine a secret key with the initialization vector, thus preventing most of the attacks that the simple initialization vector usage in WEP created.

- It uses message integrity checking to ensure that messages have not been modified.

- It uses a sequence counter to ensure that packets aren't being received out of order, preventing attacks previously seen in WEP networks that took advantage of out-of-order packets.

TKIP also uses a rekeying mechanism, preventing the key reuse found in WEP, which means that attackers can't rely on capturing traffic encrypted with the same key repeatedly to make their attacks easier.

Finally, *WPA2* was delivered as a replacement for WPA and introduced CCMP (Counter Cipher Mode Protocol), an encryption mode based on the Advanced Encryption Standard (AES). WPA2 fixes issues found in WPA that allowed shorter packets to be used to reinject data or to spoof packets.

> ### MORE INFO   AES ENCRYPTION
>
> You can learn more about AES in Chapter 12.

Authentication is the other half of wireless network security, because it keeps unauthenticated users off of your network. Authenticating to wireless networks is commonly done by using the *Extensible Authentication Protocol (EAP)*, *Lightweight EAP (LEAP)*, or *Protected EAP (PEAP)*, although there are a multitude of protocols supported by various vendors.

EAP provides a framework for authentication. It supports a broad variety of methods, each defined by a vendor or an RFC, and each of which allows keys and parameters to be sent and used. EAP is used in both WPA and WPA2, using five different EAP types as authentication mechanisms, with EAP versions including EAP-TLS, EAP-TTLS, EAP-FAST, EAP-SIM, and EAP-AKA all supported, allowing for interoperability between different vendors' implementations of WPA and WPA2 devices.

> **MORE INFO** **REQUESTS FOR COMMENT**
>
> RFCs (Requests for Comment) are memorandums describing methods, behaviors, protocols, and other information that are collected by the Internet Engineering Task Force (IETF) and the Internet Society. Computer scientists and engineers submit RFCs, some of which the IETF adopts as standards for the Internet.

EAP's design presumed that its communications channels would be protected, which isn't always the case in wireless networks. Fortunately, *PEAP* wraps EAP in an encrypted tunnel by using TLS, providing enhanced security for the authentication that EAP handles.

The last of the common protocols is Cisco's proprietary authentication protocol, LEAP. LEAP is considered to be outmoded due to security issues that left user credentials vulnerable; however, it is still found in some Cisco networks. The security issues found in LEAP were used in various attack tools, allowing LEAP networks to be easily compromised. Cisco has since updated their protocol to a newer version called LEAP-FAST, which doesn't have the vulnerabilities that affected LEAP.

Designing and implementing secure wireless networks

The design of wireless networks is also a critical part of their security. Important decisions must be made about the visibility of the network, how it is laid out, and whether the network should filter for specific hardware addresses before allowing them to connect.

In many larger organizations, 802.1x is used in conjunction with WPA2 in enterprise mode to allow systems to authenticate to the network and to then communicate in a secure mode. In smaller networks, however, the settings on individual access points become more important. A few of the settings most commonly used are:

- **SSID broadcast**   The service set identifier (SSID) is the name of the wireless network. If an organization doesn't want casual users to try to connect to its network, it can disable SSID broadcast to help protect the network. Though this can help provide some obscurity, the network still uses its SSID, and attackers who are in range of an unencrypted wireless network can still determine its SSID.

- **Power level controls**   Most enterprise access points and some small office/home office access points have the ability to control the power levels they use to broadcast a Wi-Fi signal. By carefully tuning the power levels used by your access points, you can limit the range and area they cover. Enterprise wireless controllers often have automated signal strength tools built in, allowing the network to self-adjust to provide the best coverage without signal issues.

- **MAC filtering** Often used for small offices and home use, MAC filtering uses a list of known hardware addresses for wireless network cards. This requires manually updating the list to allow new devices to connect, but it also ensures that only trusted systems can use your network—unless attackers figure out the MAC address of a trusted system, which is trivial without encryption!

In addition to these, your organization can choose to take advantage of the variety of designs of the antennas used on the access points themselves. The most common antennas are omnidirectional, allowing the access point to broadcast in all directions, resulting in 360-degree coverage. This obviously isn't ideal when putting access points into locations where control over signal coverage is important. In those cases, wireless network designers will use a directional antenna or will change the power level as previously discussed.

 Quick check

1. What major issues with WEP led to its replacement with WPA?

2. If you are trying to prevent wireless signal bleed over into areas you don't want Wi-Fi to be accessible in, what strategies might you use?

Quick check answers

1. WEP has a limited number of initialization vectors, resulting in repeated use and easy cracking of its encryption.

2. Power level controls and antenna choice and placement are both common methods of controlling signal levels.

Chapter summary

- IP is the underlying protocol of the Internet. IPv4 is currently the most broadly deployed version, but IPv6 is slowly gaining ground as address exhaustion drives adoption.

- TCP, UDP, and ICMP are IP protocols used to send traffic via most modern networks. TCP is a connection-oriented protocol, whereas UDP is not. ICMP is used to send information about network and host status information.

- IPsec, the Internet Protocol Security protocol suite, provides a way to secure IP-based communication. IPsec relies on authentication headers, encapsulation security payload, and security association to provide security.

- Many frequently used services have ports that are commonly used to access them. Common ports/service pairs include: SSH/TCP 22, HTTP/TCP 80, HTTPS/TCP 443, and NetBIOS, which uses TCP and UDP 137-139 and 445.

- Network segmentation is used to separate parts of a network. Segmentation often takes advantage of DMZs, VLANs, and NAT.

- Remote access was historically provided via dial-up servers and remote access systems. Most networks now use virtual private networks (VPNs) to allow remote users in.

- Telephone service has moved to a data network–based technology called Voice over IP (VoIP). VoIP provides significant advantages by using existing networks, but it requires special care to ensure that telephone service is secure and usable in emergencies.

- Virtualization allows systems to exist in a virtual environment where hardware is abstracted. This allows multiple operating systems and servers to coexist on the same underlying hardware or virtual network, providing scaling, disaster recovery, and a host of other benefits.

- Cloud services provide infrastructure, software, and platforms as a service, allowing organizations to outsource to remote providers, often at a lower cost, by using economies of scale.

- Network administration relies on rules-based management to ensure proper function. Routers use access control lists (ACLs), whereas firewalls use their own rules. Ongoing logging of events and issues is important when problems are detected.

- Switches and routers provide a variety of tools to help them remain secure, including VLAN management, port security, 802.1x authentication, flood guards, and loop protection.

- Wireless networks can be designed to be more secure by using encryption, as well as through configuration choices such as SSID broadcast limitations, antenna design, and broadcast power limitations.

Chapter review

Test your knowledge of the information in Chapter 3 by answering these questions. The answers to these questions, and the explanations of why each answer choice is correct or incorrect, are located in the "Answers" section at the end of this chapter.

1. What major issue led to the creation of IPv6?

   A. IPv4 was vulnerable to attacks.

   B. IPv4 address space was limited to 4.3 billion addresses.

   C. IPv5 was updated.

   D. Major vendors released the new version to add additional networking features.

2. Which protocol uses a three-way handshake to establish sessions?

   A. ICMP

   B. IPsec

   C. TCP

   D. UDP

3. What advantage does an IPsec VPN have over an SSL or TLS VPN?

   A. IPsec VPNs work with IPv6.

   B. IPsec VPN devices are less expensive.

   C. An IPsec VPN can be established by using a web browser.

   D. IPsec VPNs can tunnel all traffic from a system.

4. What ports do SSH, HTTP, and NetBIOS use?

   A. 22, 80, 137–139, and 445

   B. 21, 88, and 443

   C. 22, 8080, 123, and 443

   D. 1024, 4000, and 8888

5. What technology is frequently used for secure remote access to networks?

   A. VPN

   B. Routers

   C. 802.1x

   D. IPv6

6. If you want to outsource an entire Linux server without having to install the operating system itself to the cloud, what type of cloud service would you look for?

   A. IaaS

   B. SaaS

   C. PaaS

   D. BaaS

7. What are the rules routers use to restrict the flow of traffic through them?

   A. Port security

   B. VLANs

   C. PEAP

   D. ACLs

8. What switch security tool can help you limit the systems that can connect to a specified port based on the hardware MAC address of the system?

   A. VLANs

   B. Port security

   C. Flood guards

   D. 802.1x

Answers

This section contains the answers to the questions for the "Chapter review" section in this chapter.

1. **Correct Answer: B**

    A. **Incorrect:** IPv4 does not have specific vulnerabilities that separate it from IPv6.

    B. **Correct:** IPv4 address space was limited to 4.3 billion addresses, resulting in address space exhaustion. IPv6 provides 3.4 trillion, trillion, trillion addresses.

    C. **Incorrect:** IPv5 was not the issue that led to IPv6.

    D. **Incorrect:** Major vendors did not release a new version of IPv4 to add additional networking features.

2. **Correct Answer: C**

    A. **Incorrect:** ICMP is used for network status monitoring and does not perform a three-way handshake.

    B. **Incorrect:** IPsec is a security protocol and uses a distinct connection protocol.

    C. **Correct:** TCP uses a three-way handshake to establish sessions. The initiator sends a SYN, the recipient sends a SYN-ACK, and the initiator responds with a final ACK.

    D. **Incorrect:** UDP is a stateless protocol and does not perform a handshake.

3. **Correct Answer: D**

    A. **Incorrect:** IPsec and SSL VPNs can both work with IPv6 if they are implemented to do so.

    B. **Incorrect:** IPsec and SSL VPN devices are available at a range of price points. This is not a point of distinction between the two.

    C. **Incorrect:** An IPsec VPN cannot be established by using a web browser.

    D. **Correct:** IPsec VPNs can tunnel all traffic from a system. As far as applications are concerned, the system appears to be on the remote network. SSL (TLS) VPNs cannot do this.

4. **Correct Answer: A**

    A. **Correct:** SSH uses 22, HTTP uses 80, and NetBIOS uses 137–139 and 445.

    B. **Incorrect:** 21 is the common port for FTP, 88 is a port used for Kerberos, and 443 is used for secure HTTP via TLS or SSL.

    C. **Incorrect:** 22 is used for SSH, but 8080 is a common alternate HTTP port, 123 is used for the Network Time Protocol, and 443 is used for secure HTTP via TLS or SSL.

    D. **Incorrect:** 1024, 4000, and 8888 are all over port 1023, meaning they are not in the list of well-known ports.

5. **Correct Answer: A**

   A. **Correct:** VPN (virtual private network) technology is frequently used to provide remote secure access to networks, or to securely connect two networks together over a public network.

   B. **Incorrect:** Routers provide traffic control and send traffic destined for other networks to their external interface, but are not a tool for secure remote connections.

   C. **Incorrect:** 802.1x can allow port-based authentication for networks but is not a tool for secure remote connections.

   D. **Incorrect:** IPv6 is an updated version of IP, but it is not itself a secure remote access method.

6. **Correct Answer: C**

   A. **Incorrect:** IaaS, or infrastructure as a service, provides an entire virtual data center as services.

   B. **Incorrect:** SaaS, or software as a service, provides virtual software such as enterprise resource management or customer relationship management software as a service.

   C. **Correct:** PaaS, or platform as a service, provides an entire operating system platform in the cloud.

   D. **Incorrect:** BaaS, or backend as a service, focuses on providing back-end technologies such as databases as a cloud service.

7. **Correct Answer: D**

   A. **Incorrect:** Port security uses a list of MAC addresses to filter which hosts can connect to a switch.

   B. **Incorrect:** VLANs provide network separation on the same hardware, allowing you to separate networks as you would using separate physical switches.

   C. **Incorrect:** PEAP is a wireless authentication protocol.

   D. **Correct:** Routers use access control lists (ACLs) to provide basic limitations on what systems can send traffic through them. ACLs typically rely on IP addresses or ranges, as well as ports and protocols, to limit what traffic is allowed.

8. **Correct Answer: B**

   A. **Incorrect:** VLANs provide network separation on the same hardware, allowing you to separate networks as you would by using separate physical switches.

   B. **Correct:** Port security provides the ability to limit what systems connect to a port based on their MAC addresses, the number of unique MAC addresses that can connect, or to a single host.

   C. **Incorrect:** Flood guards prevent floods of traffic by shutting down or restricting ports when traffic floods are detected.

   D. **Incorrect:** 802.1x provides port-based authentication, rather than MAC address–based connection restriction.

CHAPTER 4

Operational and environmental security

Although information security professionals spend a large amount of time concerned with technical issues, the nontechnical components of information security are equally important to preserving the confidentiality, integrity, and availability of information. In this chapter, we look at two major elements of an information security program: operational controls, such as security policies, awareness training, and business continuity/disaster recovery; and environmental controls, such as cooling, humidity controls, and monitoring.

Exam objectives in this chapter:

Objective 2.1: Explain risk related concepts

- Importance of policies in reducing risk
    - Privacy policy
    - Acceptable use
    - Security policy
    - Mandatory vacations
    - Job rotation
    - Separation of duties
    - Least privilege

Objective 2.2: Carry out appropriate risk mitigation strategies

- Implement policies and procedures to prevent data loss or theft

Objective 2.4: Explain the importance of security related awareness and training

- Security policy training and procedures
- Personally identifiable information
- Information classification: Sensitivity of data (hard or soft)
- Data labeling, handling and disposal
- Compliance with laws, best practices and standards

- User habits
  - Password behaviors
  - Data handling
  - Clean desk policies
  - Prevent tailgating
  - Personally owned devices
- Threat awareness
  - New viruses
  - Phishing attacks
  - Zero-days exploits
- Use of social networking and P2P

Objective 2.5: Compare and contrast aspects of business continuity

- Business impact analysis
- Removing single points of failure
- Business continuity planning and testing
- Continuity of operations
- Disaster recovery
- IT contingency planning
- Succession planning

Objective 2.6: Explain the impact and proper use of environmental controls

- HVAC
- Fire suppression
- EMI shielding
- Hot and cold aisles
- Environmental monitoring
- Temperature and humidity controls
- Video monitoring

Objective 2.7 Execute disaster recovery plans and procedures

- Backup/backout contingency plans or policies
- Backups, execution and frequency
- Redundancy and fault tolerance
  - Hardware
  - RAID

- Clustering
- Load balancing
- Servers
- High availability
- Cold site, hot site, warm site
- Mean time to restore, mean time between failures, recovery time objectives and recovery point objectives

Security policies

Security policies serve as the foundation of every strong information security program. They provide everyone in an organization with clear, written expectations for behavior and are essential to achieving consistent implementation of security controls across an organization. They also serve as the basis for the authority of information security staff to take action when risks materialize to the confidentiality, integrity, or availability of the organization's information assets. Finally, they provide a mechanism for disciplinary action against staff who intentionally or accidentally violate the policy.

Though many people use the term "policy" broadly to describe any written document that outlines expectations, there are actually four separate types of document commonly used to build the foundation of a security program:

- **Policies** Formal, written statements that outline, normally in broad terms, the objectives of an organization's management. Policies typically require executive-level approval and are normally written in a manner that allows them to endure unchanged for long periods of time. Policies rarely specify technical details, allowing the policy language to survive changes in technology. It is not uncommon to see policies that are 10 or more years old still serving a useful purpose. Compliance with policies is mandatory for all individuals covered by the policy.

- **Standards** Written descriptions of the specific controls that must be used to achieve an organization's policies. Standards derive their authority from policy and are usually approved by middle management. Unlike policies, standards do describe very specific technical measures and can change on a regular basis. Compliance with standards is also mandatory.

- **Guidelines** Recommendations of controls that should be implemented as best practices within an organization. Unlike with policies and standards, compliance with guidelines is not mandatory and is left to the discretion of the individual.

- **Procedures** Specific, step-by-step directions for implementing a control. Procedures might or might not be mandatory, depending upon the requirements of the organization. Procedures can be based upon standards and/or guidelines.

For example, consider an organization that wants to ensure the confidentiality of sensitive information that is sent over the Internet. This organization might create the following set of documents to describe those requirements:

- An information security policy that requires the use of encryption to protect any sensitive information sent over an insecure network

- An encryption standard that requires the use of Advanced Encryption Standard (AES) encryption with a minimum key length of 128 bits for use when transmitting information via an Internet connection

- A guideline that recommends the use of an encryption key escrow mechanism to protect the organization against loss of the encryption key used to protect this sensitive information

- A procedure that describes the process for using the organization's encryption software to encrypt a file and attach it to an email message for transmission to the recipient

A user in this organization can then look at this set of documents and realize that, at a minimum, he or she must use AES encryption with a 128-bit key to protect sensitive information sent via email. These actions are mandatory, and failure to use 128-bit AES encryption would subject the user to the disciplinary procedures outlined in the policy. The user also has additional guidance recommending the use of key escrow and providing step-by-step instructions for a procedure that will ensure compliance with the policy. Though the user does not need to use escrow or follow the process outlined in the procedure, he or she knows that following the procedure will result in compliant encryption.

Now imagine that three years in the future, cryptographers discover a new technique for breaking AES encryption that renders the use of a 128-bit key insecure. In this scenario, they might recommend that users immediately upgrade to 256-bit AES encryption for all sensitive information. In this case, the organization does not need to change the policy document (which would require executive approval) because the policy document does not get into the specifics of encryption technology. Instead, they simply need to update the encryption standard, replacing the 128-bit requirement with a 256-bit requirement. This likely only requires the approval of the Director of Information Security or someone in a similar capacity and can be accomplished quickly.

> **NOTE USING POLICY TO PREVENT DATA LOSS OR THEFT**
>
> One of the primary objectives of information security policies is to preserve the confidentiality of sensitive information possessed by an organization. For this reason, policies and standards normally contain several specific provisions designed to protect against the loss or theft of sensitive information. This might include the specification of mandatory technical controls, such as the use of encryption techniques and data loss prevention systems. It also might include physical controls that protect against the theft of devices containing sensitive information, and administrative controls that ensure that only authorized personnel with complete background checks obtain access to sensitive information.

Security policy

One of the first policies created by an organization is known as either the security policy or the information security policy. This policy is the bedrock of the information security program and typically contains the following elements:

- A management statement that the organization is committed to preserving the confidentiality, integrity, and availability of sensitive information under its control

- Designation of a specific individual (normally the Director of Information Security, Chief Information Security Officer [CISO], or similar role) as holding primary responsibility and accountability for information security

- A statement granting the CISO authority to create standards, guidelines, and procedures that implement the security policy

- Disciplinary penalties for individuals who violate the organization's information security policy or supporting standards

- A description of the process and authority for granting exceptions to the policy, as needed

- Contact information for individuals who have questions about the policy or its proper implementation

As with most policies, it is best if the actual policy statement can be summarized in a few clear sentences. After information on roles, responsibilities, violations, exceptions and contacts has been added, the entire policy document shouldn't be longer than two or three pages. If you find yourself trying to write much more that, you should reevaluate your document. It is likely that you might be including information in the security policy that is more appropriate for a standard or other document.

Privacy policy

Many but not all organizations also adopt a privacy policy that outlines the expectations that individuals can rely on when entrusting the organization with personally identifying information (PII). This policy might apply to the personal information that the organization collects about employees, customers, or third parties.

> **MORE INFO** **PERSONALLY IDENTIFYING INFORMATION (PII)**
>
> For more about identifying and classifying PII, see the section "Information classification and labeling" later in this chapter.

Many organizations choose to adopt a privacy policy in an attempt to achieve "safe harbor" status under the United States Department of Commerce's U.S.-EU Safe Harbor program. This allows organizations to exchange private information with entities in European Union (EU) member nations that are subject to the EU Data Protection Directive (DPD). The Safe Harbor program has seven components:

- **Notice** Under the Safe Harbor program, organizations must provide individuals with the reasons they collect information, the identities of third parties who receive information from them, complaint procedures, and the organization's process for allowing individuals to limit the use and disclosure of sensitive information.

- **Choice** Individuals must be given the ability to opt out of uses of their personal information that involve third parties or purposes other than those that they specifically agreed to allow when the information was collected.

- **Onward Transfer** Organizations cannot disclose information to third parties unless they comply with the notice and choice requirements described previously. In addition, it is the responsibility of the organization sending the information to ensure that the organization receiving the information is either subject to the EU DPD or an approved Safe Harbor program (such as the U.S.-EU Safe Harbor program).

- **Access** Organizations that collect personal information must provide individuals with access to their own personal information. In addition, the organization must provide individuals with the ability to correct inaccuracies in the information held by the organization.

- **Security** Organizations must take steps to protect the confidentiality, integrity, and availability of personal information under their care.

- **Data Integrity** Organizations should only hold information that is relevant to the business purpose approved by the individual. In addition, the organization, must take steps to protect the integrity of that information.

- **Enforcement** The Safe Harbor program must include complaint mechanisms, auditing processes to ensure that companies implement the practices they describe, and sanctions that punish organizations that fail to maintain compliance with the program's requirements.

Although the United States does not have broad laws requiring the adoption of privacy policies, many organizations wind up being subject to the Safe Harbor requirements due to their business interests in European Union member states. Additionally, industry-specific regulations require the adoption of privacy policies by US organizations involved in health care, education, financial services, and other fields.

Acceptable use policy

Acceptable use policies (AUPs) outline the ways that users are allowed to behave when interacting with your organization's information systems and networks. AUPs often include provisions that outline:

- **Types of impermissible behavior**   For example, the AUP might explicitly prohibit the use of the organization's computers and networks to access obscene or illegal content.

- **Allowable personal use**   Most organizations allow some incidental personal use of the organization's computers and networks. The AUP should outline what constitutes acceptable incidental use. It should explicitly address whether the organization's systems can be used for personal business purposes.

- **Consequences for AUP violations**   The AUP should designate an individual or group to investigate suspected AUP violations and specify the disciplinary procedures that apply to individuals who violate the policy.

The AUP serves as a guiding document for the relationship between the organization and its employees or other users. A review of the AUP should be included in orientation programs that welcome new individuals to the organization.

Personnel security best practices

Personnel security practices ensure that an organization's staff are hired, monitored and dismissed in an appropriate manner. Improper decisions in any of these areas could significantly undermine an organization's security, because individuals can have significant insider access to information and systems. Organizations should consult with their human resources (HR) departments and cooperatively design a set of personnel security policies that provide added protection for individuals with access to sensitive information and/or information systems. Some of the best practices typically included in these personnel policies include mandatory vacations, job rotation, separation of duties, and least privilege.

Mandatory vacations and job rotation

Mandatory vacation policies require that individuals in sensitive positions use a minimum amount of their vacation time during a calendar year and that they have no contact with the office during that vacation time. They also normally require that at least one vacation period be two weeks long. Job rotation programs require that individuals move from their primary position to a secondary position for a determined period of time. Under both mandatory vacation and job rotation programs, employees should not have access to sensitive systems while they are away from their normal responsibilities.

Though these policies might be difficult to understand at first glance, they actually play a very important role in protecting the organization against embezzlement, fraud, and other malicious actions taken by insiders with access to systems. In many cases, individuals engaged in malfeasance must take actions on a regular basis to ensure that their untoward activity remains concealed. Forcing them to spend time away from their positions serves two purposes. First, it denies them the ability to take concealment actions during their absence. Second, it provides other individuals with access to the same systems while they are gone. The combination of these two circumstances greatly increases the likelihood that malfeasance will be detected during an individual's absence. It also serves as a deterrent to insider malfeasance if individuals know that they will have a forced absence from their normal responsibilities and privileged access.

Separation of duties

The separation of duties principle says that one individual should never have the necessary permissions to perform an entire sensitive operation without the involvement of a second person.

The classic example of separation of duties comes from the military. US Air Force officers are assigned to intercontinental ballistic missile launch facilities in pairs. The facility is configured so that a missile launch requires that both officers turn their launch keys simultaneously. The keys are positioned sufficiently far apart so that one individual cannot turn one key and then rush over to turn the second key within the allowed time period. This is an example of two-person control—the coordinated action of two individuals is required to perform a sensitive operation.

In the business world, separation of duties is often used to protect vendor payment processes. One common way that individuals embezzle from an organization is by issuing checks to a business that is actually under their control. For this reason, accounting departments normally adopt a separation of duties approach that requires that no one individual has the authority to both create a vendor in the accounting system and issue checks to that vendor. Under this circumstance, an individual seeking to embezzle from the organization might have the authority to create the fake vendor in the system, but would lack the authority to issue a check to that vendor. Similarly, the individual might have the authority to issue a check, but would lack the authority to create a new vendor. Under this arrangement, embezzlement would require the collusion of two individuals to succeed, a situation that is far less likely than a lone individual seeking to steal money from the organization.

Least privilege

The principle of least privilege dictates that individuals should have only the minimum level of access necessary for them to complete the responsibilities of their jobs. This limits the likelihood of malfeasance by restricting the types of actions that an individual can take. Least privilege is often implemented through the use of role-based access controls.

One of the barriers to least privilege is a concept known as *privilege creep*. Privilege creep occurs when an individual changes roles in an organization, perhaps multiple times. Each time an individual assumes new responsibilities, that person quickly notices that he or she does not have the permissions necessary to perform the new job, and requests those permissions from IT. Unfortunately, nobody ever thinks to ask IT to remove the old permissions that are no longer needed. After several such moves, an individual might amass a large set of inappropriate permissions that might violate not only the principle of least privilege but also the separation of duties principle.

 Quick check

1. Of the four types of security documents, which always include mandatory requirements that must be followed?
2. What is the name given to the personnel security best practice that prevents one individual from having sufficient permission to perform a critical action without colluding with another individual?

Quick check answers

1. Policies and standards are always mandatory. Guidelines are not mandatory. Procedures might be mandatory, depending upon the organization's philosophy.
2. Separation of duties

Security awareness and training

Defining security policy is not sufficient—a policy can only be effective if those affected by the policy know that it exists and are aware of the methods available to them to help them comply with the policy. For this reason, organizations develop security awareness and training programs designed to educate users about the organization's policy and their information security responsibilities.

Security policy training

The most common type of security training provides an overview of the organization's information security program and might contain specialized modules that provide specific information about the responsibilities of individuals in particular roles. For example, a security training program might contain a 30-minute overview of the organization's information security program and then contain a series of 30-minute modules covering:

- Handling of Social Security numbers (SSNs).
- Use of encrypted electronic mail.
- Combating social engineering attacks at the switchboard.
- Physical security procedures.

These modules are provided only to employees with relevant responsibilities. For example, the general security awareness module might contain a warning that employees should not use Social Security numbers outside of an approved program. This gives the general user population enough information to know that they should not see SSNs in their routine business and that they should inform management if they do encounter this highly sensitive information. The smaller population of employees who do have a business need to handle SSNs would receive detailed instructions on their proper storage, processing, and transmission during the SSN-handling module.

Security training programs should include at least three components:

- **Initial training**   This type of training should be provided to new employees and those entering new roles within the organization. It is normally the most comprehensive training program, offering a complete overview of security and compliance requirements.
- **Refresher training**   This type of training provides periodic updates to users. It might include new information but primarily serves as a reminder of security responsibilities. Common practice is to conduct refresher training on at least an annual basis.
- **Security awareness**   Not a formal training program, security awareness uses techniques such as email newsletters, posters, giveaways, and other reminders to keep security present in the minds of users in between formal training programs.

Strong security training programs will include all three of these elements, mixed in a manner to provide users with regular reminders of their security requirements.

Compliance training

In addition to training on security policies, individuals should also receive training on the laws, standards, and best practices that affect their daily work. This training ensures that users are aware of their compliance responsibilities, limiting the risk that the organization will run afoul of regulators. The contents of these training programs will vary depending upon the type of business conducted by the organization. Examples of specific compliance requirements affecting various industries include:

- **Payment Card Industry Data Security Standard (PCI DSS)**   Regulates merchants and service providers involved in the storage, processing, and transmission of credit and debit card information
- **Family Educational Rights and Privacy Act (FERPA)**   Governs the handling and disclosure of student educational records by educational institutions
- **Gramm-Leach-Bliley Act (GLBA)**   Requires that financial institutions develop and implement an information security program that is based upon a risk assessment and a formal written security plan
- **Health Insurance Portability and Accountability Act (HIPAA**)   Requires that health care providers, health plans, and health care information clearinghouses follow a set of security and privacy standards for protected health information
- **Sarbanes-Oxley Act (SOX)**   Governs the financial accounting practices of publicly traded companies and the implementation of security controls around systems that handle financially significant information
- **Children's Online Privacy Protection Act (COPPA)**   Regulates the ways that website operators can interact with children under the age of 13

> **IMPORTANT   INDUSTRY-SPECIFIC COMPLIANCE REQUIREMENTS**
>
> These are just a small sampling of the information security compliance obligations facing organizations today. The specific laws and regulations governing particular industries vary, and it is always a good idea to engage legal counsel when identifying your security compliance requirements.

User habits

When developing your security awareness and training program, it is important to remember that you must combat bad user habits that might arise from convenience or ignorance. You are responsible not only for providing users with information on proper practices, but also providing the motivation to spur them to action and inspire them to break bad habits. In this section, you will learn some of these habits and some best practices that you can include in your security awareness programming.

Passwords

Despite the widespread availability of multifactor authentication technology, passwords remain, by far, the most common authentication technique in use today. It is very common to find that a username and password make up the only security control between a potential intruder and highly sensitive information. For this reason, it is essential that users follow password management best practices, including the following:

- **Change passwords regularly** The organization should dictate the maximum age of a password. Many organizations choose to set a maximum password lifetime of 90 days.

- **Use long, complex passwords** Passwords should consist of a minimum of eight characters that are a mixture of uppercase and lowercase letters, numbers, and symbols.

- **Don't use the same password in multiple places** Users must understand the impact of a password breach at a third-party site and ensure that they use passwords for their accounts with your organization that are not used anywhere else.

- **Don't share passwords** Passwords provide a means for individual user accountability. Sharing passwords among multiple individuals prevents the organization from uniquely identifying the individual who performed a particular action.

In addition to following these best practices, organizations should also consider the adoption of multifactor authentication systems to protect their most sensitive information assets.

> *MORE INFO* **AUTHENTICATION FACTORS**
>
> For more information about passwords and multifactor authentication, see Chapter 11.

Data handling and disposal

Most likely, many users in your organization handle sensitive information on a daily basis and often produce printouts and other media that require proper handling and disposal. Your security awareness program should include specific training in the approved methods for handling and disposing of sensitive information. At a minimum, you should answer the following commonly asked questions:

- Under what circumstances must encryption be used for data at rest and data in transit?

- What encryption technologies are approved for use with sensitive information, and how do they function?

- How should users exchange sensitive information with coworkers? Does internal electronic mail provide sufficient security? How should large files containing sensitive information be exchanged and stored?

- How should users exchange sensitive information with external parties? Does the organization provide a secure messaging facility for use with suppliers and customers?

- How should paper documents containing sensitive information be discarded? If the organization offers a centralized document destruction program, how does it work?

- Can unneeded electronic media be discarded through the centralized program? If not, how should it be destroyed?

These are all issues that should be addressed up front to avoid confusion and mistaken assumptions in the minds of end users.

Clean desk policy

Clean desk policies require that employees clear off their working surfaces before they leave the office at the end of the day. Though at first glance this might seem like a strange policy that is directed more at tidiness than at information security, it is indeed a sound security practice. Clean desk policies ensure that sensitive information is locked away before the evening hours, when ancillary personnel, such as cleaning staff, might be alone in the work area. Additionally, the use of a clean desk policy limits clutter and reduces the likelihood that sensitive information will be misplaced.

> **NOTE** **"SELLING" A CLEAN DESK POLICY**
>
> Because clean desk policies might seem trivial to employees, your security training program should not only tell staff about the policy but also educate them about the security impact of maintaining a clean work area.

Tailgating prevention

Many organizations use physical door-locking mechanisms to prevent unauthorized individuals from entering a work area. These mechanisms often require that employees swipe their badges, submit to biometric screening, or provide some other authentication factor before entering.

Individuals seeking to gain unauthorized access to the work area might engage in social engineering designed to prey upon the kindness of individuals who have authorized access to an area. For example, they might show up at the front door struggling with a full armload of equipment, hoping that an individual authorized to access the area will see their plight and hold the door open for them. This practice, known as tailgating, can undermine all of your carefully designed physical security defenses.

Employees must be specifically educated about the risks associated with tailgating and trained to insist that each individual seeking to gain access to a sensitive area submit to the same authentication procedures. It's fine to help fellow employees through the entry area, but only after they are certain that the individual has successfully authenticated. This should be a key theme of your security training program, and the use of skits and roleplaying might be particularly effective.

MORE INFO PHYSICAL SECURITY

You'll learn more about physical security, including information on mantraps and other tailgating prevention techniques, in Chapter 6, "Monitoring, detection, and defense." For more information on social engineering threats and techniques, see Chapter 5, "Threats and attacks."

Personally owned devices

Over the past few years, many businesses have adopted new policies surrounding the use of personally owned devices on corporate networks and for accessing corporate information. The widespread use of smartphones and tablet computers places increased importance on this area, because many users expect to have the same access to resources and information regardless of the device they happen to be holding.

Every organization should adopt clear policies surrounding the acceptable use of personally owned devices. Though the organization's security requirements will dictate the proper approach for their own organization, security training must describe these requirements in detail for all organizations.

Real world

BYOD policy

One recent trend is the adoption of "bring your own device" (BYOD) policies in many organizations. These policies might allow (or even *require*) the use of personally owned smartphones, tablets, or computers for business purposes. BYOD policies should be carefully coordinated with the organization's security policies and training programs to ensure that they present a consistent message to end users. Several US federal government agencies have adopted BYOD approaches; a summary of those efforts appears on the White House website at *http://www.whitehouse.gov/digitalgov/bring-your-own-device*.

Social networking

It's very unlikely that there are any users in your organization who do not have at least one social networking account. Between Facebook, LinkedIn, Twitter, and Pinterest, almost everyone with Internet access participates in social media in one fashion or another. Your security awareness program should provide employees with clear guidance on what types of activity are acceptable and unacceptable when it comes to social networking activities. Clearly, social media should never be used to share sensitive information. Your policy should also outline the responsibilities of employees regarding other types of participation in social networking activities.

P2P computing

Peer-to-peer (P2P) computing software provides individuals with a means for direct interaction between their personal computers without the intervention of a centralized server. P2P technology is commonly used for file sharing, communications, and similar activities. Though it does have legitimate uses, P2P technology is widely recognized as a technique used for illegally sharing content such as copyrighted material and pornography. P2P software can also pose a risk to the organization's security posture, because it might provide an external attacker with a foothold in internal systems.

Your security awareness program should explain the risks of P2P computing and advise users on the acceptable uses of P2P technology, if any exist, within your organization. Users might not realize that the installation of P2P software can open their computers to outside users without their explicit consent.

Threat awareness

Security training programs should also be used to educate users about current and emerging information security threats. This might include sharing information on new viruses and the weaknesses they exploit in periodic information security bulletins sent to all employees.

> **NOTE** **ZERO-DAY EXPLOITS**
>
> Many new types of malicious code spread through the use of zero-day exploits. These exploits use newly identified weaknesses in operating systems and applications that attackers take advantage of before the software developer has the opportunity to provide a security update.

Threat awareness training should also educate users about the prevalence of *phishing attacks* that attempt to acquire sensitive information, such as passwords, financial account numbers, and Social Security numbers, by posing as a legitimate requestor in an email message. These requests might use the logos and branding of a legitimate organization in a false manner.

Figure 4-1 shows an example of a phishing message sent to one of the authors purporting to be from Navy Federal Credit Union. Following the link in the message would lead an individual to a phishing website designed to harvest sensitive account information for use in additional attacks. This email message was part of a widespread campaign that occurred in early 2013 and was later highlighted in media reports as a phishing scam. (See *http://threattrack.tumblr.com/post/43078643317/navy-federal-credit-union-credentials-phish* and *http://www.defense.gov/news/newsarticle.aspx?ID=59099* for more information about this attack.)

NAVY FEDERAL Credit Union

🔒 EMAIL SECURITY ZONE
Secure Member
March 27 2013

Navy Federal Online Account Secure e-Message

Unauthorized Access

Unauthorized Access Notice

We recently have determined that different computers have logged on to your Online Account and multiple password failures were present before logons.

We now need to re-confirm your account information with us.

If this is not completed by **March 27, 2013** we will be forced to suspend your account indefinitely, as it may have been used for fraudulent purposes.

We thank you for your cooperation in this matter.

Please click here immediately to verify your identity and automatically reverse the change.

E-mail Security Zone
At the top of this message, you'll see an E-mail Security Zone. Its purpose is to help you verify that the e-mail was indeed sent by Navy Federal Online. If you have questions, please call 1-888-842-6328. To learn more about fraud visit NavyFederal.org and click "Security" at the bottom of the screen

ABOUT THIS MESSAGE Please do not reply to this Customer Service e-mail. For account-specific inquiries, kindly call 1-888-842-6328 (TTY: 1-703-255-8837) or visit NavyFederal.org.

FIGURE 4-1 This phishing attack message is an attempt to entice the recipient to disclose sensitive information.

Information classification and labeling

Information classification programs ensure that organizations have consistent mechanisms for identifying, labeling, and handling sensitive information. The primary purpose of an information classification program is to assign data elements to a consistent categorization scheme describing the sensitivity of the information.

The most well-known information classification program is the one used by the U.S. government for classified national security information. This categorization scheme has four primary levels:

- **Unclassified**   Information that is approved for public disclosure
- **Confidential**   Information that, if disclosed to unauthorized individuals, would cause damage to national security
- **Secret**   Information that, if disclosed to unauthorized individuals, would cause serious damage to the national security
- **Top Secret**   Information that, if disclosed to unauthorized individuals, would cause exceptionally grave damage to national security

Government officials handling classified information are obligated to ensure that individuals receiving classified data possess both a sufficient security clearance and a valid need to know the information. If either of these factors is absent, an individual must not be granted access.

Though businesses rarely use the same names, they often adopt similar categorization schemes with more "business-friendly" names. For example, one common civilian information classification scheme uses these levels:

- **Public**   Information that can be freely disclosed to the public and would commonly be published on the organization's website, included in sales brochures and similarly promotional materials.
- **Internal**   Information that is not normally disclosed to the public, but would not cause much damage if it were accidentally or maliciously disclosed. This might include an organization's internal telephone directory, calendar of employee events, and similar information.
- **Sensitive**   Information that would damage the firm's business interests if it were disclosed to unauthorized individuals. Sensitive information might include pricing strategies, marketing plans, and staffing scenarios.
- **Highly sensitive**   Information that would cause serious damage to the firm if it were disclosed to unauthorized individuals. Highly sensitive information might include Social Security numbers of employees, customer credit card information, blueprints for proprietary products, and similar information.

Some firms choose to use a three-category scheme rather than a four-category scheme. Whatever approach your organization adopts, it is important to educate employees about the classification scheme, the types of information that fit into each category, and the controls required to safeguard information at each classification level.

In addition, organizations should adopt data-labeling standards that specify the types of sensitive information that must be labeled and the method used to label media containing this information. For example, an organization might decide that any documents containing highly sensitive information must contain the words "Highly Sensitive" in the header and footer of the document to help employees easily identify and properly protect those documents.

Personally identifying information (PII)

Organizations have a special responsibility to protect private personal information that they collect about individuals. This category of information, known as *personally identifying information (PII)*, includes information that is about an individual and is defined by the National

Institute of Standards and Technology (NIST) in their Special Publication 800-12 as falling into one of two categories:

1. Any information that can be used to distinguish or trace an individual's identity, such as name, Social Security number, date and place of birth, mother's maiden name, or biometric records.

2. Any other information that is linked or linkable to an individual, such as medical, educational, financial, and employment information.

These categories are quite broad and can be used to help you form a general idea of the types of information that should be treated as PII. Organizations might want to turn to the specific laws and regulations governing their industry and operating locations for more specific advice. For example, the California data breach notification law (SB 1386) defines personal information as an individual's first name (or first initial) and last name in combination with one or more of the following three data elements:

- Social Security number

- Driver's license number or nondriver's state identification card number

- Account number or credit or debit card number, in combination with any required security code, access code, or password that would permit access to an individual's financial account

> **NOTE COORDINATING INFORMATION CLASSIFICATION AND PII**
>
> When designing an information classification scheme for your organization, you should consider the types of PII held by your organization. Although not all PII might meet the criteria for your highest classification level, the list of PII elements is an excellent cross-check to ensure that you have accurately identified the sensitive information stored, processed, or transmitted by your information systems.

 Quick check

1. What is the recommended maximum age for a user's account password that should be required as a best practice?

2. What are the three types of security awareness training that every organization should conduct?

Quick check answers

1. 90 days

2. Initial training, refresher training, and ongoing security awareness

Environmental controls

Though security professionals are not normally directly engaged in the development of the specialized environmental controls used to maintain proper operating conditions in a data center, it is important that they are familiar with the basic concepts of environmental control. In this section, we examine heating, cooling, and humidity controls as well as fire suppression, electromagnetic shielding, and monitoring.

Heating, ventilation, and air conditioning (HVAC)

Maintaining proper temperature and humidity is critical to prolonging the life of the sensitive electronic equipment housed in a data center. For this reason, data centers normally have separate heating, ventilation, and air conditioning (HVAC) systems designed to regulate the temperature on the data center floor separately from other areas of the building. These systems are normally supported by backup power sources designed to maintain the temperature in the event of a power outage.

Data center environmental specifications are the subject of some argument within the data center management community. In 2008, the American Society of Heating, Refrigeration, and Air-Conditioning Engineers (ASHRAE) released new guidance that greatly loosened the operating parameters of a data center. The new parameters, known as the "expanded environmental envelope," allow operation within these ranges:

- Temperature can vary within a range of 64.480.6 degrees Fahrenheit (18-27 degrees Celsius).

- Humidity should be measured by using the dew point, which should be held within a range of 41.9-59.0 degrees Fahrenheit (5.5-15 degrees Celsius). The relative humidity should not exceed 60 percent.

> **NOTE HOT AND COLD AISLES**
>
> Many data centers follow a "hot aisle/cold aisle" heat management strategy that is designed to efficiently manage the cold air in a data center. Servers stored in data center racks pull cool air in through the front and exhaust hot air out the back. If racks are aligned in standard rows, the front of one rack faces the back of the rack in the row ahead of it. With this approach, the servers are pulling in warm air exhausted by the rack in front of them.
>
> In the hot/cold aisle approach, racks face each other, so that they both pull cool air in from the same aisle. This results in an alternating sequence of hot aisles and cold aisles in the data center. HVAC systems are then configured to supply cool air to the cold aisles and remove warm air from the hot aisles. Using this approach can greatly reduce data center cooling costs.

You might encounter data center managers who still follow the outdated 2004 ASHRAE recommendations that require tighter temperature and humidity controls. Loosening standards to follow the 2008 guidelines allows for more effective heat management and might reduce operating costs.

> *MORE INFO* **ASHRAE EXTENDED ENVIRONMENTAL ENVELOPE**
>
> If you encounter data center managers who doubt the reasonableness of the new standards, you might want to refer them to the ASHRAE standards at *http://tc99.ashraetcs.org/documents/ASHRAE_Extended_Environmental_Envelope_Final_Aug_1_2008.pdf.*

Fire suppression

Data centers contain large amounts of electronic equipment that generate significant quantities of heat. These conditions are ripe for fire, and normal water-based fire suppression techniques can be catastrophic in the event of an electrical fire in a data center.

You probably recognize the fire triangle shown in Figure 4-2 from your days in elementary school. The triangle describes the three elements necessary for a fire to continue to burn:

- Oxygen
- Heat
- Fuel

FIGURE 4-2 The fire triangle shows the three elements that must be present for fire to burn.

Removing any one of these elements is sufficient to extinguish a fire. In traditional fire-fighting, massive quantities of water is used to remove the heat from the fire. However, applying water to an electrical fire in a data center has the potential to completely destroy the electronic equipment in the data center and harm the personnel attempting to extinguish the fire.

Fire suppression equipment generally takes two forms: handheld fire extinguishers and full-room fire suppression systems. Fire extinguishers come in five classes:

- **Class A Extinguishers** Designed for common wood, paper, cloth, and trash fires
- **Class B Extinguishers** Used on fires consisting of flammable liquids, such as gasoline and oil

- **Class C Extinguishers**   Designed for electrical fires, such as those that may occur in a data center
- **Class D Extinguishers**   Designed to combat heavy metal fires in industrial applications
- **Class K Extinguishers**   Designed for kitchen fires with a fat or oil-based fuel source

Many fire extinguishers contain suppression technologies suitable for use on multiple types of fires and will be labeled with the classes of fires they can combat. You should always ensure that any fire extinguisher used on computer equipment has a Class C label before using it. Spraying an electrical fire with a non-Class C extinguisher might result in life-threatening injury.

Data centers also normally contain room-based fire suppression systems. These might be water-based systems or they might use advanced suppression agents that will not damage electronic equipment. When water-based systems are used, they are typically deployed in a "dry pipe" scenario that uses valves that keep water from entering the pipes until smoke is detected in the room and electrical power has been automatically or manually disconnected by using an emergency power off (EPO) mechanism. This prevents the dangerous combination of electricity and water from occurring.

EMI shielding

Electromagnetic interference (EMI) consists of the radio emanations from an electronic device. It is possible to intercept these electronic signals and reconstruct some or all of the activity on the electronic device. Some data centers that process extremely sensitive information (such as top secret national security information) use special shielding to prevent these electronic emanations from leaving the data center and being used for intelligence-gathering purposes. One type of EMI shielding is a device known as a *Faraday cage*. Faraday cages use a combination of metal shielding and electromagnetic charges to prevent EMI signals from entering or leaving the cage.

Environmental and video monitoring

Due to the sensitive nature of the equipment and information stored in data centers, data center management staff should employ monitoring mechanisms to keep watch over the environmental and physical security of the facility 24 hours a day, seven days a week. This should include automated monitoring that alerts staff when any of the following undesirable conditions occur:

- Temperatures in the data center fall outside of the approved range of 64.4-80.6 degrees Fahrenheit (18-27 degrees Celsius).

- The dew point in the data center falls outside the range of 41.9-59.0 degrees Fahrenheit (5.5-15 degrees Celsius).

- Relative humidity in the data center rises above 60 percent.

- Smoke is detected in the data center.

- Water is detected in the data center.

- Motion is detected in the data center when the facility is expected to be unoccupied.

In addition, most data centers employ constant video monitoring with a recording capability to record the physical presence of individuals in the facility and their activities while present in the data center. These recordings can be maintained for an extended period of time in the event that questions later arise about an individual's actions.

> **NOTE   PCI DSS AND VIDEO MONITORING**
>
> Data centers that store, process, or transmit payment card information must adhere to the video monitoring requirements of the Payment Card Industry Data Security Standard (PCI DSS). Section 9.1.1 of the PCI DSS specifies that data centers must "Use video cameras and/or access control mechanisms to monitor individual physical access to sensitive areas. Review collected data and correlate with other entries. Store for at least three months, unless otherwise restricted by law."

 Quick check

1. What type of fire extinguisher can be used on an electrical fire in a data center?
2. What is the acceptable dew point range for data center humidity?

Quick check answers

1. Class C
2. 41.9-59.0 degrees Fahrenheit (5.5-15 degrees Celsius)

Business continuity planning

Availability is perhaps the most overlooked of the three legs of the confidentiality, integrity, and availability triad. Though security professionals spend quite a bit of their time preserving the confidentiality and integrity of sensitive information, availability is often left as "someone else's concern." It is, however, one of the cornerstones of the profession, and *business continuity* is one of the primary mechanisms used by security professionals to ensure availability.

Business continuity is the practice of designing systems and business processes so that they can continue uninterrupted in the face of a human-made or natural disaster. Business continuity planners must perform business impact assessments to identify the risks facing their business, remove single points of failure, and then design and test business continuity plans to preserve business operations. This section examines each of these steps in further detail.

Business impact assessment (BIA)

The business continuity planning process begins by performing a *business impact assessment (BIA)*. The BIA is a risk assessment designed to identify the risks that might disrupt business operations and prioritize those risks based upon their likelihood of occurrence and potential impact. The BIA can follow either a quantitative or qualitative methodology, depending upon the needs of the business.

> **MORE INFO** RISK ASSESSMENT
>
> The tools used to perform the BIA are the same as the tools used to conduct any risk assessment. Chapter 1, "Risk management and incident response," described the process used to conduct both quantitative and qualitative risk assessments. The annualized loss expectancy (ALE) approach described in Chapter 1 is a very common quantitative approach to conducting a BIA. If you're not familiar with the details of calculating ALE, you might want to revisit that material in Chapter 1 before continuing.

The output of a BIA is a prioritized list of risks facing the business. Organizations that adopt a quantitative BIA methodology might choose to include the annualized loss expectancy (ALE) in their prioritized list. An example of BIA output appears in Figure 4-3.

Risk	Annualized loss expectancy (ALE)
Hurricane damages data center	$142,178
Data center flooding	$136,150
Fire in data center	$18,912
Theft of equipment from data center	$2,145
Prolonged power outage	$1,765

FIGURE 4-3 An example of a BIA work product shows the ALE for a variety of risks.

Notice that the risks listed in the BIA risk listing are ordered by ALE in descending order. It is fair to say that the risk listed at the top of the list, hurricane damage to the data center, is the greatest risk facing the organization. This information will play an important role in subsequent steps of business continuity planning. For example, it would not make sense to spend $5,000 annually to mitigate the risk of equipment theft, because that amount exceeds the expected loss for the year.

Removing single points of failure

The list of risks you develop during your BIA can help you identify specific issues with your business processes and technical infrastructure through a process known as single-point-of-failure analysis. A *single point of failure* is a system or process component that, if it fails, can cause an entire business function to fail in a cascading manner. Single-point-of-failure analysis involves mapping out a technology function or business process and identifying any situations where single points of failure exist. This information can then be used to resolve the single points of failure where it is cost effective to do so.

For example, consider the web server infrastructure shown in Figure 4-4. This is a very basic environment, consisting of a single web server supported by a single firewall that is connected to the Internet. A business continuity analyst performing a single-point-of-failure analysis of the web server function might immediately notice that this environment has a single point of failure located at the web server. If the web server fails, for any of a myriad of reasons, the websites run by the server will be unavailable to end users, resulting in business disruption.

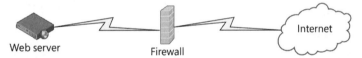

Web server   Firewall   Internet

FIGURE 4-4 The initial web server infrastructure in this scenario uses only a single web server behind a firewall.

The analyst facing this situation might recommend that the server be replaced with a clustered server farm that is capable of withstanding the disruption of a single server. If one server goes down, the other servers in the cluster are able to automatically assume responsibility for the full load. In fact, the cluster can be designed to have enough capacity to support the simultaneous failure of two or more servers, depending upon the organization's business continuity requirements. Figure 4-5 shows the clustered web server scenario.

> *MORE INFO* **CLUSTERING AND HIGH AVAILABILITY**
>
> You'll learn more about clustering and high availability technologies in the section "Disaster recovery planning," later in this chapter.

Continuing to look at this function, the analyst might note that the firewall in Figure 4-5 represents another single point of failure. If the firewall goes down, network traffic will not be able to pass between the Internet and the web servers.

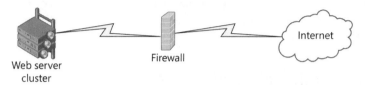

FIGURE 4-5 The first revised web infrastructure replaces the single web server with a clustered web server approach that avoids the web server becoming a single point of failure.

To address the risk of a firewall failure, the analyst might recommend the use of high-availability firewalls. In one possible high-availability environment, one firewall is designated as the primary firewall while the other is designated as the secondary firewall. The two firewalls constantly communicate with each other about their status. If the secondary firewall fails to hear from the primary firewall for a predetermined period of time, it assumes that the primary firewall has failed and immediately assumes the role of the primary firewall. When the failed firewall comes back online, it notices that the other firewall is serving as the primary firewall, and it reverts to secondary firewall mode.

The scenario shown in Figure 4-6 illustrates an environment that addresses both the firewall and web server single points of failure.

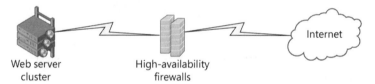

FIGURE 4-6 The second revised web infrastructure adds high availability firewalls that remove the firewall as a single point of failure.

The business continuity analyst might then note that, although the server and firewall components now have redundancy that prevents them from becoming single points of failure, the environment is still dependent upon single network connections between the firewall and the Internet and between the firewall and the web server network. A failure of one of those network segments would disrupt connectivity and knock the web server cluster offline.

Figure 4-7 shows an environment architected to remove the single point of failure on the network. This scenario adds network redundancy to the equation by adding dual communications links to both sides of the firewall. In practice, this might be implemented by purchasing a second Internet connection from an alternate provider and by connecting the firewall to the web server network via multiple network connections that do not traverse the same switches.

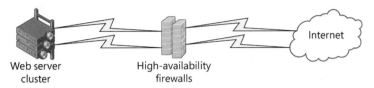

Web server   High-availability   Internet
cluster   firewalls

FIGURE 4-7 The fully redundant web server infrastructure supplements the clustered web servers and high availability firewalls with redundant communications links.

> **NOTE   FIGURING OUT WHEN TO STOP**
>
> As with any analysis, it is always possible to carry single-point-of-failure analysis to another step. For example, the next step in the scenario described in this chapter might involve looking at the physical paths used to bring network connections into the building. In many cases, networking vendors share common conduit paths from the street into a building. If you purchase network connections from vendors that share a conduit path, that conduit is now a single point of failure.
>
> Wondering how a conduit could be a single point of failure? It only takes one experience with an errant jackhammer to discover how disruptive a physical break in a fiber optic cable can be to business operations!

Designing and testing the business continuity plan

The business continuity plan is the organization's written documentation of its approach to maintaining the continuity of business operations. The written continuity plan should include the results of a business impact assessment, single-point-of-failure analysis, and the methods used to address other risks.

> **NOTE   THE BUSINESS CONTINUITY PLAN AND THE DISASTER RECOVERY PLAN**
>
> In practice, it's often efficient to combine both the business continuity plan and the disaster recovery plan into a single set of documents. This helps planners identify not only the controls put in place to prevent the disruption of the business but also the steps to be followed in the event that the continuity controls fail and the business is actually disrupted.

Many business continuity plans gain the undesirable designation of "shelfware"—a thick binder full of good intentions that managers place on their bookshelves and never reference. When disaster strikes, they pull out the plan and might discover that it is woefully out of date. Personnel, business processes, and technology all change over time, and these changes often require updates to the business continuity plan. After it has been developed, the plan should be placed on a regular review and update cycle to ensure that it remains relevant to the evolving business needs of the organization.

In addition to keeping the plan updated, the personnel involved in business continuity and disaster recovery operations should conduct periodic tests of the plans to ensure that the controls are functioning properly. There are several common types of test used to validate business continuity and disaster recovery plans:

- **Checklist reviews**   During a checklist review, which is the simplest type of test, the test coordinator distributes copies of the business continuity/disaster recovery plan to all of the personnel involved in the plan. They then review the plan at their convenience and return feedback to the coordinator. Staff members reviewing the plan should verify that they are able to perform all of the tasks assigned to them and that there are no additions, modifications, or deletions needed. Conducting regular checklist reviews is essential to both maintaining the currency of the plan and keeping individuals aware of their roles and responsibilities in the event that an actual disaster strikes.

- **Tabletop exercises**   These go a step beyond the checklist review and gather the affected staff together to walk through a simulation. This can be as simple or as elaborate as the organization wants. The goal is to move the staff into "disaster mode," where they are living the plan and gaining experience that will be useful in the event of an actual activation.

Real world

Conducting tabletop simulations

One organization that the authors work with conducts annual tabletop simulations that are quite complex and well orchestrated. The exercise gathers together very senior executive leaders, including the CEO, on an annual basis for a half-day disaster simulation. A dedicated exercise team develops an elaborate, realistic scenario in advance and uses it to guide the team through the simulation, which typically targets improvements in one or two specific areas of disaster response. The exercise planners use mock news footage and telephone "reports from the field" to lend authenticity to the exercise.

- **Parallel tests**   These test go beyond talking about business continuity and involve the actual activation of business continuity/disaster recovery plans. In a parallel test, the organization assumes that a disaster has occurred and immediately begins activating contingency plans designed to compensate for the disaster. This includes activating a disaster recovery site, if applicable, and conducting operations at that site. It is important to note, however, that the organization does not rely upon the recovery site for production operations. Instead, all of the transactions conducted at the primary site are conducted at the recovery site in parallel.

- **Full interruption tests** During a full interruption test, the primary site is taken offline and operations are shifted to the recovery site. Full interruption tests provide planners with the best assurance that their plan is complete and will function, but they also introduce a high degree of risk—if the recovery plan fails, the business will be interrupted for real during the test. For this reason, full interruption tests are rarely used in practice.

Designing a well-rounded business continuity and disaster recovery testing program is an essential component of every organization's IT contingency planning operations.

Succession planning

"People are our most important asset." "Our team makes us who we are." There's probably a poster or other corporate material with a slogan along those lines somewhere near your workspace. If this declaration is true, why is it that IT contingency planning operations often overlook the human resources needed for the business to continue to function as a viable technology operation?

Succession planning is an important human resources tool that can be used to identify employees with the potential to move into higher level roles and provide them with the career development necessary to prepare them for a new position. During a succession planning exercise, an organization's leadership team identifies individuals who, if needed, could quickly step in to fill the role of another person in the organization. It is common to perform succession planning for all management roles within an organization, and many IT groups now also conduct succession planning for critical technology roles as well.

 Quick check

1. What term is used to describe a system component that, if it fails, could cause the entire system to fail?

2. What are the common types of business continuity/disaster recovery plan tests that an organization might conduct?

Quick check answers

1. Single point of failure

2. Checklist review, tabletop exercise, parallel test, and full interruption test

Disaster recovery planning

 Disaster recovery is the practice of contingency planning for the actual disruption of business operations by a natural or human-caused disaster. The goals of disaster recovery plans are twofold:

1. The disaster recovery plan should get business operations up and running again as quickly as possible. Depending upon the nature of the disruption and the criticality of operations, this might involve activating an alternate data center facility for the duration of the disruption.

2. If an alternate site is activated, the disaster recovery plan must include measures to transition operations back to the primary site as soon as practical.

> **NOTE** **IT CONTINGENCY PLANNING**
> Organizations often use the term "IT contingency planning" to refer to the combination of the fields of business continuity and disaster recovery. The use of this term acknowledges the fact that the two types of planning are closely related. The goal of the business continuity plan is to prevent the disruption of business activity in the face of a disaster. Disaster recovery plans serve as the backstop that protects the business when the business continuity plan fails. If the business is actually disrupted, the disaster recovery plan describes the actions that the organization will take to resume normal operations as quickly as possible.

In this section, you will learn about three key disaster recovery concepts: backups, fault tolerance, and disaster recovery metrics.

Disaster recovery metrics

Disaster recovery planners use a variety of metrics to help guide disaster recovery efforts. The most common metrics include the recovery time objective (RTO), recovery point objective (RPO), mean time to restore (MTTR), and mean time between failures (MTBF).

Recovery time objective

 The *recovery time objective (RTO)* is the organization's desired recovery time for a particular service in the event of a disaster. The RTO should be calculated based upon a realistic understanding of the technical environment and staff capabilities. It is normally expressed as an amount of time, in hours and minutes.

Recovery point objective

Whereas the RTO designates a particular amount of time that can pass before service is restored, the *recovery point objective (RPO)* indicates the amount of data that is considered an acceptable loss by the organization. For example, if an organization sets an RPO value of two hours, they understand that they might lose two hours' worth of data in the event of a disaster. As you will read later in this chapter, RPO values are critical to designing a backup frequency strategy.

Mean time to restore

The *mean time to restore (MTTR),* also known as the mean time to repair, is the average amount of time required to repair a defective piece of equipment or otherwise restore it to operation. The MTTR is a critical metric for disaster recovery planning because the MTTR values for equipment might influence the organization's recovery time objectives.

Mean time between failures

The *mean time between failures (MTBF)* is the average amount of time that passes between failures for a particular piece of equipment. The MTBF rate can be used to estimate the reliability of a particular piece of equipment and often serves as a selection criterion when comparing different models or brands of equipment for use in an organization. Equipment with a higher MTBF is more reliable and, generally speaking, also more expensive than equipment with lower MTBF values.

Backups

Backups preserve information in an archival form so that it can be restored in the event of accidental or intentional loss. System and data backups play a critical role in disaster recovery plans because they allow administrators to reconstruct the environment that existed prior to the disaster. Administrators should conduct backups on a regular basis by using an automated process that minimizes the possibility of error.

Backup software copies the data stored on a disk to another type of media. Magnetic tapes continue to serve as the primary destination for most backups (disk-to-tape backups), although the use of other disks (disk-to-disk backups) is also common. It is important to remember that, for backups to be effective, a copy should always be stored at a separate location from the servers containing the source data. After all, you wouldn't want a fire or other physical disaster to wipe out both your primary system and your backup!

> *NOTE* **BACKOUT PLANS**
>
> In addition to backup plans, technology groups should also develop backout plans for critical changes to systems, applications, or data. Good configuration and change management practice dictates that you should always have a fallback plan to revert systems to the condition prior to an attempted change. These backout plans provide you with a contingency option in the event that the change fails or has unintended consequences.

Backup systems are capable of performing three different types of backup, which differ based upon the specific data that they back up:

- *Full backups*   These simply copy every file stored on the source disk to the backup media. Full backups are both time-consuming to perform and consume large amounts of disk space. However, they are the easiest to restore, because the backup software simply needs to copy all of the data from the backup media back to the source media. Performing a full backup is a prerequisite for performing a differential or incremental backup.
- *Differential backups*   These only copy files that have changed since the last full backup. Depending upon the level of activity on the system, differential backups can be quite small. Restoring a system from differential backups requires first restoring the most recent full backup and then restoring the most recent differential backup.
- *Incremental backups*   These copy any files that have changed since the most recent full or incremental backup. Restoring a system from incremental backups requires first restoring the most recent full backup and then restoring the full series of incremental backups taken since that full backup. Incremental backups are the most time-efficient and space-efficient to create, but they are also the most time-consuming to restore.

Backup administrators typically design a backup frequency schedule that takes advantage of multiple backup types. For example, all of the following strategies are valid approaches to backing up systems:

- Weekly full backups with daily differential backups
- Weekly full backups with daily incremental backups
- Weekly full backups with daily differential backups and hourly incremental backups

The selection of a specific backup schedule depends upon the criticality of the organization's data and the chosen recovery point objective (RPO).

Building fault-tolerant environments

One of the major responsibilities of disaster recovery and business continuity planners is creating high-availability environments that are capable of continued operation in the event of one or more component failures. This concept, known as fault tolerance, is a critical tool used to resolve single points of failure in a technology infrastructure. Fault tolerance exists at many levels and might rely upon hardware redundancy, server redundancy, and/or disk redundancy to support highly available environments.

Hardware redundancy

Hardware redundancy uses multiple pieces of equipment or components to provide fault tolerance in the event that one of the components fails. For example, power supply failures are one of the most frequent hardware failures that occur on server hardware. To compensate for this, most data center–grade servers contain multiple power supplies that have separate connections to the power in the data center. In the event that one power supply fails, the other power supply continues providing power to the server. In many cases, the two power supplies are connected to different power sources, providing fault tolerance against not only a power supply failure but also an electrical power outage.

Server redundancy

In addition to building hardware redundancy into server hardware, engineers might also use redundant servers to protect against a hardware or software failure in one server. This can be accomplished in two ways:

- **Standby servers** These sit dormant and monitor for a failure of the primary server they support. In the event that the primary server fails, the standby server takes over the primary role and continues to service requests. When the former primary server comes back online, it can either reassume its responsibilities or assume the standby role, depending upon the configuration.

■ **Clustered servers**   These consist of two or more servers performing the same function. In the event that one server fails, the other server or servers in the cluster simply carry the load that would normally be carried by the failed server.

> **IMPORTANT   DESIGNING SERVER CLUSTERS**
>
> It is important to design server clusters with enough capacity to withstand the failure of one or more servers. If normal operations use the full capacity of the servers in the cluster and one of those servers fails, the remaining servers in the cluster will not have enough capacity to meet the demand. This will result in, at best, degraded service and, at worst, a complete system failure.

Clustering is a form of *load balancing*, the practice of spreading requests across multiple servers with the same capabilities.

Disk redundancy

Disks are also a primary source of failures because they often contain moving parts. They are also relatively inexpensive and easily replaced. *Redundant array of independent disks (RAID)* technology takes advantage of these facts to provide fault tolerance in the event that one or more disks fail. There are many different types of RAID, each described by a numeric RAID level. The most common RAID levels are:

■ **RAID 1**   Also called disk mirroring, RAID 1 requires two disks and simply creates a copy of the data stored on one disk on the other disk and maintains that copy over time. In the event that one disk fails, the system simply uses the other disk to continue operations and restore the mirrored disk.

■ **RAID 5**   Also know as disk striping with distributed parity, this type of RAID uses parity information stored on the disks to allow the regeneration of a single disk that fails. RAID 5 requires the use of at least three disks.

■ **RAID 10**   Also known as RAID 1+0, this type of RAID combines disk striping with parity and disk mirroring.

> **IMPORANT** **RAID IS NOT A BACKUP STRATEGY!**
>
> Some system administrators mistakenly believe that, because RAID protects against a disk failure, it can be used in lieu of backups. This is a terrible idea for several reasons. First, the disks are stored in the same physical server. If one is physically destroyed, chances are that the others will also be physically destroyed. Second, RAID provides no protection against the accidental deletion of a file. If you remove it, it's gone!

Disaster recovery sites

In the unfortunate case that business operations are disrupted at the primary facility and it is not practical to restore them at that location within the designated recovery time objective, disaster response teams must activate an alternate processing site. There are three main categories of disaster recovery site: hot sites, warm sites, and cold sites. They differ based upon the type of equipment and infrastructure that they contain and whether applications and data are live at the site.

Hot sites

Hot sites are the most advanced disaster recovery sites. They contain basically everything needed to assume responsibility for the business's operations on extremely short notice. Hot sites have live servers running critical business applications and contain copies of the organization's data, current to at least the organization's recovery point objective. Hot sites operate on a 24-hour, seven-days-a-week availability basis, and many are configured to instantly assume operational responsibility in the event of a disruption at the primary site. Of course, the trade-off is that hot sites are extremely expensive to equip, staff, and operate.

Warm sites

Warm sites are equipped in a manner similar to hot sites—all of the servers and infrastructure necessary to assume business operations are present at the site. The one thing missing is the data. Although the warm site might contain copies of the organization's backup media, that data is not loaded and ready to run. The activation of the warm site requires restoring the data from backup (or, if time permits, from the primary site). This process can take several hours to complete.

Cold sites

The most inexpensive disaster recovery option is the use of cold site facilities. These sites contain the basic infrastructure—power, HVAC, and telecommunications—necessary to run the business's operations, but they do not have the applications or data installed. Resuming operations at a cold site is extremely time intensive and might take days or weeks.

> ✔ **Quick check**
>
> 1. What two related metrics are used to describe the amount of time that an organization can be without a service and the amount of time that service recovery is expected to take?
>
> 2. What technology uses two disks that each store an entire copy of the data stored on the other disk for use in the event of a disk failure?
>
> **Quick check answers**
>
> 1. MTO and RTO
>
> 2. RAID 1 or disk mirroring

Chapter summary

- Security policies are formal, written statements that outline management objectives. Standards describe the specific controls used to achieve an organization's security objectives. Compliance with policies and standards is mandatory.

- Guidelines offer recommendations for security controls that can be implemented as best practices. Procedures provide specific, step-by-step directions for completing a process. Compliance with guidelines and procedures might be optional.

- The seven elements covered by a European Union privacy Safe Harbor arrangement are notice, choice, onward transfer, access, security, data integrity, and enforcement.

- Separation of duties is a best practice stating that one individual should never have the necessary permissions to perform an entire sensitive operation. Least privilege requires that individuals only have the minimum level of access necessary to complete their job functions.

- Security training programs should include initial training for new employees or those changing roles, refresher training that offers periodic updates, and ongoing awareness components that keep security concepts fresh in the minds of staff.

- Information classification programs divide an organization's information assets into categories based upon level of sensitivity. Classified information should normally be labeled, especially at higher levels of sensitivity.

- Heating, ventilation, and air-conditioning (HVAC) systems play an important role in maintaining data center temperature and humidity at levels appropriate for sensitive electronic equipment.

- The business impact assessment (BIA) is a risk assessment designed to identify risks that might disrupt business operations and prioritize the remediation of those risks based upon their likelihood of occurrence and potential impact on the business.

- Business continuity operations often identify and remove single points of failure from a process or technology environment that could cause an unscheduled interruption to the business.

- Redundancy plays an important role in keeping systems functioning in the event of a component failure. RAID technology applies redundancy to storage to protect against disk failure.

- Backups ensure that an organization's data remains available, even if it is accidentally or intentionally destroyed in the primary data center. Backups should be stored offsite.

- Organizations use disaster recovery sites to resume operations after they are disrupted by a disaster. The organization can use a hot site, warm site, or cold site, depending upon the cost/benefit analysis.

Chapter review

Test your knowledge of the information in Chapter 4 by answering these questions. The answers to these questions, and the explanations of why each answer choice is correct or incorrect, are located in the "Answers" section at the end of this chapter.

1. Richard is the director of information security for A. Datum Corporation. He is developing a set of documents that will guide the organization's information security efforts and is working on language that will require the use of appropriate network security controls. He wants to describe the specific models of firewall that are authorized for use within the organization. He expects to add and remove models from this list every few months and needs to create a document that is mandatory but can be easily changed. What type of document would be best suited for Richard's needs?

    A. Standard

    B. Policy

    C. Guideline

    D. Procedure

2. Renee is an information security professional for a retail business that accepts credit cards at several locations around the country. She is concerned about the compliance obligations that her firm might have when handling payment card transactions. What regulation governs the storage, processing, and transmission of credit card information?

    A. COPPA

    B. PCI DSS

    C. SOX

    D. HIPAA

3. Matthew is designing a password security poster as part of his company's information security awareness program. Which one of the following is NOT a password best practice that he might include on his poster?

   A. Use different passwords for each website you visit.

   B. Use long, complex passwords.

   C. Change passwords regularly.

   D. Store shared passwords in a secure location.

4. Christopher is verifying that the temperature in his data center is within the standard acceptable range, as recommended by ASHRAE. Which one of the following temperatures is within ASHRAE's extended environmental envelope?

   A. 52 degrees Fahrenheit

   B. 62 degrees Fahrenheit

   C. 72 degrees Fahrenheit

   D. 82 degrees Fahrenheit

5. Darcy is reviewing the disaster recovery plan for an organization and would like to know the amount of time that the organization believes it will take to restore a critical technology function. What metric should Darcy review?

   A. MTO

   B. RPO

   C. MTBF

   D. RTO

6. Samantha would like to configure RAID 5, disk striping with distributed parity, to preserve information in the event of a disk failure. What is the minimum number of disks that she must use to implement RAID 5?

   A. One

   B. Two

   C. Three

   D. Five

Answers

This section contains the answers to the questions for the "Chapter review" section in this chapter.

1. **Correct Answer: A**

   A. **Correct:** Standards are mandatory requirements that are easily changed. They often contain specific details of security controls.

   B. **Incorrect:** A policy is mandatory but not easily changed. Policies should not contain specific details of security controls but rather make broad general objective statements.

   C. **Incorrect:** A guideline can be easily changed to adapt to new technologies, but it is not suitable for Richard's use in this scenario because compliance with a guideline is not mandatory.

   D. **Incorrect:** A procedure offers step-by-step instructions for performing an action. This is not Richard's objective, so a procedure is not the appropriate document. After Richard creates a firewall standard, he might follow up with model-specific procedures for firewall installation, rule changes, and similar instructions.

2. **Correct Answer: B**

   A. **Incorrect:** The Children's Online Privacy Protection Act (COPPA) governs the ways that website operators can handle information collected from children under the age of 13.

   B. **Correct:** The Payment Card Industry Data Security Standard (PCI DSS) regulates merchants and service providers involved in the storage, processing, and transmission of credit and debit card information.

   C. **Incorrect:** The Sarbanes-Oxley Act (SOX) governs the financial reporting practices of publicly traded companies.

   D. **Incorrect:** The Health Insurance Portability and Accountability Act (HIPAA) imposes privacy and security requirements on those organizations handling protected health information.

3. **Correct Answer: D**

   A. **Incorrect:** Using different passwords for each website you visit is a password security best practice, because it reduces the risk that a compromise at one site will affect the security of your account at other sites.

   B. **Incorrect:** The use of long, complex passwords is a password security best practice because it reduces the susceptibility of your passwords to brute-force password guessing attacks.

C. **Incorrect:** Periodic password changes are a password security best practice because they reduce the duration of time that an attacker might have access to a compromised account.

D. **Correct:** As a password security best practice, shared passwords should never be used. Instead, each individual should be assigned a unique account and granted shared permissions.

4. **Correct Answer: C**

A. **Incorrect:** Data center temperatures can vary between 64.4-80.6 degrees Fahrenheit (18-27 degrees Celsius). 52 degrees is below this range.

B. **Incorrect:** Data center temperatures can vary between 64.4-80.6 degrees Fahrenheit (18-27 degrees Celsius). 62 degrees is below this range.

C. **Correct:** Data center temperatures can vary between 64.4-80.6 degrees Fahrenheit (18-27 degrees Celsius).

D. **Incorrect:** Data center temperatures can vary between 64.4-80.6 degrees Fahrenheit (18-27 degrees Celsius). 82 degrees is above this range.

5. **Correct Answer: D**

A. **Incorrect:** The maximum tolerable outage (MTO) is the amount of time that the organization believes it can be without a function during an outage.

B. **Incorrect:** The recovery point objective (RPO) is the amount of data that the organization feels would be an acceptable loss during a disaster.

C. **Incorrect:** The mean time between failures (MTBF) is the average amount of time that it will take for a particular type of device to fail.

D. **Correct:** The recovery time objective (RTO) is the amount of time that the organization believes it will take to restore a service after a disaster.

6. **Correct Answer: C**

A. **Incorrect:** Disk striping with parity (distributed or dedicated) requires a minimum of three disks. One disk does not meet this minimum threshold.

B. **Incorrect:** Disk striping with parity (distributed or dedicated) requires a minimum of three disks. Two disks does not meet this minimum threshold.

C. **Correct:** Disk striping with parity (distributed or dedicated) requires a minimum of three disks.

D. **Incorrect:** Though Samantha could implement disk striping with five disks, that is not the minimum number of disks required by RAID 5. She could implement it with as few as three disks.

## CHAPTER 5

Threats and attacks

An understanding of the threats that systems and networks face is a critical part of the CompTIA Security+ body of knowledge. In this chapter, we will explore the many types of client-side attacks such as malware and attacks against applications. You will learn about web-based attacks, including cross-site scripting and SQL injection. Next we will explore attacks against both wired and wireless networks, and you will finish by learning about attacks against the vulnerabilities in human behavior, a technique known as social engineering.

Throughout this chapter you will learn not only how these attacks work, but why they are used, and what their targets typically are. In addition, you will gain insight into historical attacks and why they worked, in order to help you plan to counter unexpected threats and design defenses against new attacks.

Exam objectives in this chapter:

Objective 3.1: Analyze and differentiate among types of malware

- Adware
- Virus
- Worms
- Spyware
- Trojan
- Rootkits
- Backdoors
- Logic bomb
- Botnets

Objective 3.2: Analyze and differentiate among types of attacks

- Man-in-the-middle
- DDoS
- DoS
- Replay
- Smurf attack
- Spoofing

- Spam
- Phishing
- Spim
- Vishing
- Spear phishing
- Xmas attack
- Pharming
- Privilege escalation
- Malicious insider threat
- DNS poisoning and ARP poisoning
- Transitive access
- Client-side attacks

Objective 3.3: Analyze and differentiate among types of social engineering attacks

- Shoulder surfing
- Dumpster diving
- Tailgating
- Impersonation
- Hoaxes
- Whaling
- Vishing

Objective 3.4: Analyze and differentiate among types of wireless attacks

- Rogue access points
- Interference
- Evil twin
- War driving
- Bluejacking
- Bluesnarfing
- War chalking
- IV attack
- Packet sniffing

Objective 3.5: Analyze and differentiate among types of application attacks

- Cross-site scripting
- SQL injection

- LDAP injection

- XML injection

- Directory traversal/command injection

- Buffer overflow

- Zero day

- Cookies and attachments

- Malicious add-ons

- Session hijacking

- Header manipulation

Client-side attacks

In many organizations, the most common attacks are those made on desktop PCs, often known as clients. For most companies, that means systems that use the Windows XP, Windows 7, and Windows 8 operating systems, as well as those that use Mac OS and Linux. Most of those clients have an always-on Internet connection, a sizeable hard drive, plenty of CPU horsepower, a web browser and other common applications and plug-ins, and access to your organization's corporate data. That combination makes a workstation or a laptop an attractive target to an attacker.

In the first part of this chapter we will look at many of the ways that attackers target PCs: via malware, in its many different flavors; through application attacks and privilege escalation; and through operating system vulnerabilities.

> **MORE INFO**   **VULNERABILITY SCANNING FOR ASSESSMENT**
>
> We discuss vulnerability scanning tools and techniques that can help you assess system vulnerabilities and stay ahead of attackers in Chapter 7, "Vulnerability assessment and management."

Malware

Malware is a catch-all term for a variety of kinds of malicious software, covering everything from relatively innocuous adware that delivers ads to users who inadvertently install it to serious threats focused on stealing personal or corporate data or disrupting operations. We'll start with the lower level-threats and progress to much more dangerous tools.

Adware

The first and typically least threatening member of the malware family is adware. *Adware* is relatively innocuous malware that pushes ads to users. Some adware is actually legitimate and uses the advertising that it carries to help fund development of the software itself. In general, however, the term *adware* means malicious software that displays ads that users didn't sign up to receive. Adware ads are often pop-up ads that, although irritating, usually aren't a significant threat.

> **MORE INFO   DEFEATING MALWARE**
>
> We talk more about ways to defeat the malware we discuss in this chapter, including anti-virus, anti-spam, and anti-spyware tools, in Chapter 9, "Establishing host security."

Spyware

Unlike adware, *spyware* is a far more real threat. In fact, spyware has one purpose: to gather data. Spyware, like adware, can be somewhat innocuous, tracking users for the purposes of advertising and to better target ads. Other spyware is intended to help with digital rights management for software or media. The majority of spyware has a far more sinister intent: to steal personal data such as bank account information, passwords, and credit card numbers. Some spyware is used to help identity thieves acquire information about new victims.

Companies even sell spyware to help individuals spy on others! Couples going through a divorce or people who are worried that their partners might not be faithful can purchase spyware that tracks their online activities, logs their chats, and monitors their email.

> **Real world**
>
> **Layering malware protection**
>
> Removing adware and spyware can sometimes require a lot of effort. A good practice is to have a second anti-malware product in your toolbox to help get rid of particularly difficult-to-remove bugs.

Viruses

Computer *viruses* are programs that make copies of themselves, spreading from computer to computer via a variety of infection methods such as copying themselves to removable media, inserting themselves into programs, or other means. Malware authors have steadily improved on the capabilities of viruses since the 1970s when the first virus was created.

EXAM TIP

The word *virus* is often used to describe a variety of the types of malware we will discuss in this chapter. Remember that a virus is a self-replicating program, and use the features of the other types of malware to differentiate them.

Many modern viruses target users who can be persuaded to run them. Others attempt to spread via file shares and other places to which the system can write files, such as flash drives. Some viruses use email to spread, and might hijack the computer owner's own email address or webmail account, or they might send out messages pretending to be people from the owner's address book. Unlike worms, which we will look at next, viruses don't scan for other systems on a network to attack.

Real world

Ransomware

One of the nastier recent malware developments for many everyday users is the advent of ransomware, which infects a computer and then encrypts users' Microsoft Office documents, images, and other files likely to be important to the owner of the system. After the documents are encrypted and the owner is unable to access them, the ransomware then demands a payment to restore them. In many cases, this is paired with fake anti-virus software, which results in users providing a credit card number to the attackers to remove the malware they themselves created! If you encounter a system with ransomware, and it hasn't already encrypted any files, normal antivirus software can likely remove it. If files have been encrypted, some legitimate anti-virus companies provide tools that can save the day. Some ransomware would be classified as a virus, but other versions are trojans, with the malware pretending to be legitimate software.

Because viruses can't spread between machines without human interaction in most cases, their authors have had to provide them with better ways to fool people into running them. In the late 1990s and early 2000s, viruses became a common danger for instant messenger users who would receive messages that appeared to be from friends. When the user clicked the message, the virus would download, and when it was double-clicked, it would run, infecting the user's computer. The same trick has been leveraged by the proof-of-concept Commwarrior virus, which used MMS text messages to spread itself.

As malware writers developed malware, the next obvious step after writing viruses was to enable them to spread themselves over a network by using system and software vulnerabilities without human interaction. This led to the development of worms, which we'll look at next.

Worms

Worms are a form of self-spreading malware that exploits system and application vulnerabilities to move between systems. Worms have a long history, and a worm was the first piece of malware to cause a major, multisystem outage on the Internet. That worm, known as the Morris Worm (sometimes known as the "Internet Worm") took down thousands of machines in 1988 due to a mistake in how it prevented itself from being killed. The flaw in its logic caused it to make multiple copies of itself on machines as it spread, causing those systems to run out of memory, which often caused those machines to crash. After the system was rebooted, it would be virus free, but still vulnerable. In moments, it would again be infected, and given time the same issue would occur as the system was continually reinfected and the Morris Worm made copy after copy of itself.

> **IMPORTANT VIRUSES VS. WORMS**
>
> The key difference between viruses and worms is in how they spread. Worms attack vulnerabilities across a network.

Since the Morris Worm, worms have continued to rely on vulnerabilities in operating systems and applications to spread between network-connected systems. Defense against them is a relatively simple concept: the best defense against a worm is to fully patch systems, and to restrict access to systems and services to only that which is required to allow the system to do its job.

> **IMPORTANT LEAST PRIVILEGE**
>
> The principle of least privilege, which we will discuss in Chapter 11, "Identity and access control," applies here too. Systems should only have access that is required to accomplish necessary tasks. Thus, if a service needs to be accessible only to the system itself, the host firewall should prevent network access to it from other machines.

Many historical worms were designed as a proofs of concept or to prove a hacker's skills, but those that are truly malicious carry a more dangerous payload in the form of a rootkit, virus, trojan, or one or more of the other malware packages we discuss in this chapter. Modern worms have the same goal as many current viruses: the spread of tools that capture user data, usually to make the system into a zombie that can easily be controlled by a botnet.

MORE INFO **BOTNETS AND ZOMBIES**

For more details on these concepts, see the sidebar "Botnets and zombies" later in this chapter.

SQL Slammer

In 2003 a worm known as SQL Slammer was released onto the Internet. In less than 10 minutes, it had infected 75,000 systems around the world running versions of Microsoft SQL Server. As each system was compromised, it immediately began noisily and rapidly scanning the Internet for new targets. The speed of Slammer's spread set a new record for worms on the Internet and introduced a new era of rapidly spreading, highly virulent worms.

SQL Slammer targeted a known vulnerability in both Microsoft SQL Server and the desktop engine version known as MSDE. Surprisingly, a patch had been generally available for the vulnerability for almost six months. Unfortunately, many system administrators at the time did not patch regularly. Worse, many of those who had MSDE installed were unaware that it was on their systems because it was included as a component in other software. Often, even those who knew MSDE was installed didn't realize that it exposed service ports to the network it was on. Thus, thousands of machines remained vulnerable, with compromises taking seconds from the initial infection to when the infected machine would start scanning for more victims.

The Slammer worm also introduced a new issue for network administrators due to the rate at which it communicated. Many networks went offline as switches, firewalls, and routers crashed or were unable to handle the load generated by infected machines scanning the network or attempting to send traffic in and out to other systems. During the height of the infection, the Internet itself was slower than normal as routers critical to major parts of the Internet crashed or failed to find other routers, resulting in a cascade of routing updates, and thus even more traffic.

Three years later, large-scale worm outbreaks largely stopped as most major networks moved to broad use of firewalls and router ACLs (access control lists), and as system administrators began to patch on a much faster cycle. Only time will tell if we have learned our lessons well enough, because new technologies often expose similar vulnerabilities.

Trojans

Trojans, much like the Trojan horse used by the army of ancient Greece to sneak into the city of Troy, pretend to be something desirable, but are actually a means of gaining access to your PC. Trojans are often sent as email attachments or provided via file sharing sites and utilities, where they pose as legitimate software or as hacked versions of expensive commercial programs.

One of the most common types of trojan in current use is the so-called RAT (remote administration tool). After a user is tricked into installing the trojan, the RAT provides access to the computer's webcam, allows the attacker to capture the victim's keystrokes and to do things like remove the Start button from Windows. In short, the attacker has complete control over the PC on which the trojan is installed and can do almost anything he or she wants.

> **NOTE   REMOTE ADMINISTRATION TOOLS**
>
> RATs provide a great example of a tool that often has legitimate uses for system administration or security work but that can also be considered malware when used for malicious purposes. Anti-virus software often has a special category for these tools, and might not raise an alarm if they are installed, if you don't specifically set it to do so.

Trojans are reported to be the most common form of malware infection on modern computers, with widespread infections such as the Zeus Trojan directly targeting banking and other personal data.

Botnets and zombies

As large-scale infections of PCs became more commonplace, attackers began to look for a way to control all of the systems they compromised by using tools such as trojans. At first,

the infected machines, known as *bots* or *zombies*, were often controlled via Internet Relay Chat (IRC), a central text-based chat service. Zombies were designed to log into IRC and wait for commands in a chat room, known as a channel. This collection of infected systems with a central control system was called a *botnet*. As botnets grew to tens of thousands of systems and security staff became increasingly aware of them, IRC connections became an easy way to detect infected systems.

Over time, complex command and control (C&C) networks were created, with well-designed management software. Entire software packages designed to infect systems, convert them into zombies, and then maintain that control over time were created. This led to an underground economy based on control of bots and botnets where infected machines were bought, sold, and traded in large volumes. Some botnets consisted of hundreds of thousands of machines around the world, but most were far smaller, which allowed them to be used more easily.

Now botnets are often leased as tools to attackers for profit. A single botnet can be used for denial of service attacks, to perform calculations or crack passwords, or to send spam. Because botnets can be remotely controlled and updated, new software can be easily distributed, making a botnet a flexible attack tool for its owner.

EXAM TIP

Remember that a trojan pretends to be something else to get you to install or run it, then provides attackers with a way in or performs some other malicious action.

Malicious add-ons

Malicious add-ons are a specialized type of trojan. A common type of malicious add-on is the browser add-on. These browser add-ons are typically presented as helpful tools such as a search bar that is added to a web browser. When it is installed, it turns out to actually be adware, spyware, or worse, a trojan that provides access to the browser when it is running.

EXAM TIP

The CompTIA Security+ exam specifically calls out malicious add-ons as a unique type of malware. Often, these are simply called trojans or malicious browser plug-ins instead of malicious add-ons.

Rootkits

Rootkits are malware that attackers use after they have compromised a system, to help retain access and control. Rootkits are intended to conceal the existence of a compromise and typically work to conceal the presence of the intruder's software and tools.

Rootkits are often part of the payload of a worm or virus and often have a payload that they themselves deliver to the system on which they are placed. These payloads include capabilities aimed at escalating privileges and hiding malware packages such as trojans and keyloggers, and components that phone home to make the compromised system into a zombie member of a botnet.

Real world

Fighting real-world malware

In 2005, one of the authors of this book fought several attackers who were using a new rootkit protection tool called Hacker Defender. Hacker Defender was sold as a for-profit tool for hackers and included capabilities that allowed it to hide from administrators by preventing Windows from seeing it when the directory it was installed in was viewed. In addition to this ability, it was specifically designed to evade common anti-rootkit and anti-malware tools of the time, and new versions of the rootkit were tested against each update from our security tool vendors, often at the same time we were deploying them ourselves!

Fortunately, Hacker Defender did not prevent us from viewing the directory when the drive was removed and mounted on another system, or when it was accessed via a network file share. By using this technique, our organization's security team and system administrators built homemade tools that could remove the specific installations of Hacker Defender used by the groups of attackers we were facing.

We learned several lessons along the way. First, we learned to look for vulnerabilities and gaps in our opponent's rootkit design. We exploited the fact that Hacker Defender didn't conceal itself from network file share viewing, which made it easy to scan for throughout our Windows domain. Second, we learned to build flexible tools. As the attackers found that their compromised machines were being fixed, they changed their rootkit builds. By being flexible, we were able to adapt our removal tools as soon as a new infection appeared. Finally, we discovered that communications and speed of response were critical, and we worked to make sure we could take action quickly with the right information. Our large and diverse organization had to learn to share information quickly with the right people, and ad-hoc groups emerged to lead the fight.

> *MORE INFO* **DETECTING ROOTKITS**
>
> We will talk more about how to use behavior, signature, and integrity checking tools to detect rootkits and other malware in Chapter 9.

Backdoors

In addition to trojans and rootkits, another method of gaining access to a computer is via a backdoor. *Backdoors* can be broadly described as a way to enter a system that bypasses its normal authentication process. In practice, that often means a secret administrative username and password, a hidden service, or some other means of access that isn't visible to the user or administrator.

Historically, backdoors were often created by programmers who wrote them into their software for troubleshooting or support purposes. Hardware companies commonly shipped their devices with a hidden administrator user account to allow fixes when users locked themselves out of the devices. Over time, this practice has been considered more and more dangerous, and fewer developers build in a backdoor as an official part of their products. Unfortunately, some continue to build them in without the knowledge of their employers.

In addition to backdoors created by developers, many types of malware also install backdoors as part of their compromise process. Rootkits and trojans both often include a backdoor for remote access.

> **NOTE** **HARDWARE BACKDOORS**
>
> The idea of inserting a backdoor into a software package is attractive to technically sophisticated attackers, but it isn't the only way to insert a backdoor. Hardware backdoors have begun to gain more attention as national governments begin to explore cyber warfare.

> **EXAM TIP**
>
> There are two primary types of backdoor:
>
> - Those that are part of a software package or service and provide a way for the programmer or company that created the device or software to gain access
> - Those that malware creates for remote access by attackers
>
> It is important to remember that both types could be used by attackers to gain unauthorized access.

Logic bombs

A *logic bomb* is code that has been inserted into otherwise normally functioning software that will activate when certain conditions are met. This could be something as simple as a certain date or time being reached, but it could be as complex as an employee being removed from an HR database or a system receiving a specific type of packet or logon.

Logic bombs might seem like something you'd only see in a movie plot, but the concept of taking action due to a date, time, or condition has often been integrated into other types of malware. One of most famous of these was the Michelangelo virus from the early 1990s, which was designed to destroy the contents of the first part of infected systems' hard drives on March 6.

EXAM TIP

Stand-alone logic bombs are relatively uncommon, but they often appear on tests as part of a listing of malware types. Remember that logic bombs are software that will perform specific actions when a condition or conditions are met.

Dealing with APTs

Advanced Persistent Threats (APTs) are one of the most dangerous threats faced by organizations today. During the past few years, extremely sophisticated groups of attackers have begun to appear, fielding advanced malware packages and taking advantage of cutting-edge attack techniques. Their attacks are intended to gain access to systems, then retain access for long-term data theft or other purposes. These types of attacks were given their name due to their complexity and the quality of their code and capabilities, as well as the difficulty that organizations have encountered in removing them.

Many APT groups combine trojans, viruses, and/or worms to gain entry to a machine and use backdoors, rootkits, and a host of other tools to retain access to the system. They often employ unpublished exploits to target unpatched vulnerabilities, enabling them to enter machines that organizations believe to be secure. Other APT groups use sophisticated means to social engineer users into installing the malware, providing evidence that they are targeted at specific organizations.

APTs are believed to be organized groups of cybercriminals, as well as cyber warfare groups sponsored by nations around the world. This means that the tools that APTs use are typically better built, better supported, and more dangerous than ordinary malware built by small groups for profit or by individuals using ready-made toolkits.

Malware deployed by APT groups normally uses controllers that are likely to use built-in update functions to deploy more advanced versions that are harder to find each time you track down the current malware. As with most malware, reinstalling infected systems is usually the safest course of action, but a major APT attack can compromise large parts of your corporate network, making cleanup very difficult.

Organizations that deal with APTs often need to bring in specialists to beat them. Groups of security consultants have begun to track and label families of malware and attack behaviors and have learned to identify their behavior, components, and even their authors. If you suspect you are dealing with this form of attack, bringing in the experts might be your best option.

 Quick check

1. Malware that provides access for a programmer to software that programmer created is typically referred to as what?

2. What capabilities define a rootkit?

3. What is the key difference between a worm and a virus?

Quick check answers

1. A backdoor. Programmers and software companies historically often left a backdoor into their software. At times, this was simply an undocumented administrative account or password, but in some cases developers left themselves a way in without telling anyone.

2. A rootkit is designed specifically to allow an attacker to gain and retain control of a system. Rootkits combine various tools to do this and often have multiple components that are installed as part of the kit.

3. A worm spreads itself over a network by using vulnerable services or operating system vulnerabilities. A virus self-replicates, but it does not spread itself over a network by itself. A worm might leave a virus as part of its payload.

Application attacks

In addition to malware threats to machines, the applications that run on systems are a frequent target for attackers. Application attacks take many forms, ranging from attacks that cause the application to perform functions it is not intended to do to attacks that make the application display data that isn't supposed to be accessible to nonadministrative users.

In this part of the chapter, we will examine common attacks, including privilege escalation, which allows attackers to act as more trusted users. We will also explore attacks on vulnerabilities in applications such as buffer overflows, zero-day attacks, and attacks against web browsers and web servers. Finally, we will look at a series of attacks that are commonly performed against back-end services such as databases, directory services, and a range of other servers.

Privilege escalation

Operating systems typically provide users and applications with privileges to perform the tasks that they are required to accomplish. In a secure environment, applications and users typically receive very restricted privileges, which means that successfully compromising them will only provide attackers with a small range of possible actions they can take.

> **MORE INFO ACCESS CONTROL METHODOLOGIES**
>
> We cover access control methods and concepts including privileges in more depth in Chapter 11.

Obviously, attackers want to have far greater access to a system than they would get if they simply used the rights that an application has. Thus, they use attacks intended to allow them to either seize rights or to perform actions as a more privileged user. Both of these attacks are forms of privilege escalation. In fact, attackers often take advantage of existing privileges to gain additional attacks. In so-called transitive attacks, attackers take advantage of permissions on one system (A) that allow access to another system (B), which is trusted by a third system (C). Then, despite not having rights to take action on C from system A, an attacker can use a transitive attack to pass through otherwise strong security.

> **NOTE JAILBREAKING**
>
> Jailbreaking, or breaking out of the controlled vendor-provided operating systems on portable devices such as phones or tablets and gaining access to the root of gaming consoles and other devices (known as rooting) often involves privilege escalation. Jailbreaks typically take advantage of a vulnerability in the operating system, whereas console exploits have frequently used vulnerabilities in games, resulting in a continuing series of patch and exploit cycles between vendors and jailbreakers.
>
> Jailbreaking can also leave a device open to further exploits. Some of the first jailbreaks for Apple's iPhone left an open SSH (Secure Shell) server with a default password of "alpine," allowing remote logon as root (the administrative user) as part of its jailbreak process. This allowed attackers to scan for and exploit jailbroken iPhones on local networks.

Real world

Privilege escalation and the ping command

One of the most innocuous applications found on almost any network-connected system in the world is the ping utility. Pings send a simple ICMP query to a remote system to determine if the system is online, and if so, how long it takes to get a response. This is obviously a useful tool for troubleshooting, and on most systems ping has no real access controls around it so that any user who needs to can ping another system.

Unfortunately, in versions of the Solaris operating system, which was used extensively throughout the world in 2004 for critical servers and powerful workstations, ping was vulnerable to a privilege escalation attack. The privilege escalation attack allowed any local user who could access ping to gain access to the system's administrative account, known as root, and take full control of the system. In fact, the ping exploit allowed attackers to run any code they wanted to as the root user!

This simple vulnerability resulted in common exploits that allowed attackers to gain access to low-value accounts such as those of untrusted users, to quickly take full control of the machine. After they had that control, they could create new hidden accounts and use rootkits and other tools to keep access.

Sun quickly released patches for the flaw in all three current versions of Solaris, but attackers continued to exploit the ping privilege escalation attack for some time because many organizations did not have effective patching processes in place or did not want to take their Solaris systems down for the patch.

Insider threats

Insiders such as members of your own organization's staff, or others who already have privileges to access or administrate your network and systems, can use privilege escalation as well. In fact, *malicious insider threats*, or threats created by employees and other insiders who choose to target their own organization, are a major concern for organizations, because a single system administrator gone rogue can create significant amounts of damage. Even users who have been granted only low-level access can use privilege escalation attacks, install malware, or provide their credentials or data to third parties.

Application vulnerabilities

Like operating systems, applications often have vulnerabilities too. Throughout their history, both user applications and server services have suffered from a broad range of issues allowing attackers to bring them down, to cause them to perform unexpected or unintended actions, or to take them over and use them to access the systems they reside on.

Zero-day attacks

One of the most feared types of application attacks is a *zero-day attack*. Zero-day attacks gained their name because they are attacks that occur before the vulnerability is announced, thus there are zero days of warning about the attack. Unlike vulnerabilities that are announced by vendors after they have discovered the issue themselves or have been notified of it by third parties, there will be no patch available for a zero-day exploit when it occurs.

> **MORE INFO** **ZERO-DAY ATTACKS**
>
> We also discuss zero-day attacks in Chapter 8, "The importance of application security," as part of the coverage of fuzzing.

The fact that organizations don't know about zero-day vulnerabilities and thus can't patch or otherwise protect against them is why they are one of the most feared issues that an application can have. The threat that this creates is also the reason that there is an active market for finding zero-day vulnerabilities, with both legitimate and underground organizations paying money for newly discovered application issues. This drives a continued search for vulnerabilities on both sides of the market.

Real world

Stopping zero-day attacks

Many current zero-day attacks are aimed at web browsers and web browser plug-ins. Attackers combine existing exploits and one or more zero-day attacks that target Java, Flash, and other common tools, and their attack scripts try each attack in turn against the web browsers that visit sites that they have infected with their code. In several instances in the past few years, attackers have used web-based ad networks that sell advertising space. After the attackers get access by buying or stealing ad space, they then then insert their attacks in ways that look like legitimate ads when users visit the site.

Because a zero day attack doesn't have a patch available, this can quickly compromise hundreds or thousands of systems. Fortunately, when these attacks do occur, the worldwide information security community reacts quickly. This means that a zero-day exploit's threat can be limited if your organization plans ahead. Mailing list memberships, RSS feeds, and a strong network of peers can provide information early in the spread of the exploit in many cases. On the technical side, there are often short-term ways to limit the exposure of vulnerable services or applications, such as by disabling browser plugins or blacklisting specific infected sites. In addition, subscriptions via third-party vendors can provide quick protection by leveraging intrusion protection rules or anti-malware packages.

Unfortunately, if the zero-day attack is aimed at your organization before you have any warning, you might suffer a large-scale breach. Then a good incident response process and effective, tested plans are your best bet.

Buffer overflow

Buffer overflow attacks exploit the need for programs to accept input. When input is provided to a program, it is typically placed into a storage space called a buffer. In most applications, that buffer is a fixed size, because the data that is expected to be entered into it has a known maximum length.

The overflow attack happens when the data written into the buffer is longer than the buffer. This can have a variety of results: it can crash the program, it can cause the data in the buffer to overwrite other data, or it can even overwrite other program data on the system.

In the simplified example shown in Figure 5-1, a vulnerable application has a variable called *userID* and a variable called *address*. In the program's allocated memory, these two variables are contiguous, as shown in the image. This program's *userID* variable is limited to eight characters, which means that anything beyond that will go past the end of the buffer. When we provide a user name of *thisisanexploit*, the word *exploit* is written into the *address* variable. If this was executable code, or data that the user shouldn't have access to, the attacker would have successfully used a buffer overflow attack.

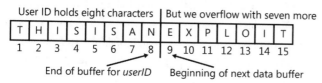

FIGURE 5-1 A sample buffer overflow attack demonstrates data that goes past the expected input.

Fortunately, there are a variety of defenses against zero-day attacks, privilege escalation, and buffer overflows:

- Applications and users should follow the principle of least privilege to limit the access that they can provide if they are exploited.

- Data execution prevention (DEP) tools can prevent code from being executed when buffer overflows place code where it shouldn't be.

- Memory address space randomization, commonly called *address space layout randomization (ASLR)* helps by making the base address of executables, libraries, and other processes random, preventing attackers from being able to figure out how much data is required in a buffer overflow to put code in specific memory locations.

- Regular patching can help prevent exploits of known vulnerabilities.

> **MORE INFO** **PREVENTING PRIVILEGE ESCALATION AND BUFFER OVERFLOWS**
>
> You can read more in-depth coverage of defenses against privilege escalation, buffer overflows, and zero-day attacks in Chapters 8 and 9.

Web attacks

The web is an ideal environment for attackers because it brings together huge numbers of client systems with web browsers and other applications running on them and a wide variety of servers, applications, and operating systems. Here we will discuss how client-side and server-side web attacks work and where they are targeted.

Cookies

Cookies, the small files left behind on workstations by websites, can be both a threat and a useful tool. Cookies are intended to be retrieved by a website to provide useful data about the user or the system that is visiting the site. This often includes things like user preferences, information about previous visits, and where users were in the site, as well as what they last did.

Because cookies can contain a lot of data about a visitor's use of the site that the cookie belongs to, they can also present a danger similar to that posed by spyware. Tracking cookies left by sites can provide information about the browsing habits of an individual, and can link that data across multiple sites, all while the person browsing the web believes he or she has some degree of privacy.

There are a variety of cookie types, including:

- HttpOnly cookies, a type of cookie intended to help combat cross-site scripting theft of cookies.

- Persistent or tracking cookies, which remain on a system until they reach their maximum age.

- Secure cookies, which can only be transferred via HTTPS. These are used for data that should only be sent securely.

- Session cookies, which only exist for the duration of a web session.

The code for the sample cookie shown in Figure 5-2 sets a username in an encoded format, shows the domain the cookie was set by, specifies that it can only be used via secure connections, and sets when the cookie was created and when it expires.

```
Name:              USERNAME
Content:           rzG0f1wvCxDSbkOkGb7d1x..
Domain:            .humongousinsurance.com
Path:              /
Send for:          Secure connections only
Accessible to script:   Yes
Created:           Thursday, March 07, 2013 6:18:50 PM
Expires:           When the browsing session ends
```

FIGURE 5-2 A cookie can include data such as a user name, time, or other information.

> **IMPORTANT COOKIES YOU CAN'T REMOVE**
>
> Both legitimate companies and attackers sometimes work to ensure that cookies can't be deleted. The cookies they create that are restored after they are removed are known as zombie cookies. Zombie cookies rely on being placed in locations that will not be wiped by web browsers that clear their cookies after being closed. Worse, many of these locations are shared amongst browsers, so using a separate browser to browse some sites won't prevent zombie cookies from reporting your behavior. Due to their location and the persistence they are able to have, they can provide long-term tracking for those who set them.

Some cookies are set by third parties as part of an ad network or due to embedded functionality in the page itself. For much of the current web these are often associated with social media sites. Because these third-party cookies travel with the browser across many sites, they also act as a type of tracking cookie, reporting to the social media sites and advertising networks about user behavior. This is particularly threatening when it is matched with the volume of data that social network sites have about the users who are browsing the web. These cookies can combine personal data with browsing data to build comprehensive profiles of the users they track.

Cookies face several threats that can result in their theft. These include packet capture, DNS cache poisoning, and cross-site scripting (XSS) and cross-site request forgery (XSRF) attacks. Packet capture can expose cookies that aren't using the secure cookie methods that send all cookie data via an encrypted channel. DNS cache poisoning, XSS, and XSRF can all result in the cookies being sent to the wrong site.

Header manipulation

HTTP headers are parts of web traffic that carry information about the client's browser, the page that was requested, the server, and software versions, cookie information, and session information. For attackers, *header manipulation* typically focuses on changing the headers sent to a web server to take over sessions. This allows an attacker to pretend to be a legitimate client who is already logged on.

Headers can be viewed and modified by using a variety of tools, including browser plugins, proxies, and other specialized tools. An attacker typically captures headers by using a packet capture tool or sniffer on an open network, by compromising a system and capturing them locally, or by performing a man-in-the-middle attack to place a system between the system he or she wants to capture from and the server that system is connecting to.

Directory traversal

Directory traversal attacks were one of the first attacks performed against web servers. Most web servers operate out of a normal directory structure such as any other found on a computer's hard drive. Attackers who visit a website often want to see content other than the content that the web server exposes to visitors, and they attempt to find other unprotected directories or to find a way to trick the web server into providing access to directories that weren't in its web directory.

Web applications that can display a file saved on the web server are a favorite target for this type of attack, because they simply need to be fooled into accepting a command that includes a path that is farther up the directory structure. You can see an example of one directory traversal attack in Figure 5-3.

Directory traversal attacks often attempt to access important system files. On a Linux or Unix system, that is often the /etc/password file. In the attack shown in the figure, the attacker has determined the relative location of the /etc/password file to the web application, and feeds the application a series of ../ commands to climb the directory structure. When the attacker gets there, the application displays the file requested, telling the attacker what user names exist on the system. Fortunately, modern Linux and Unix systems don't keep their password hashes in /etc/password, but the list of user names is still valuable. Given this information, the attacker can now avoid guessing user names and only needs to guess passwords.

A normal visitor to the page visits the page selected by the site—in this case, insurance.htm, a page about Humongous Insurance's offerings.

The attacker notices that the script directly references a file and attempts a directory traversal attack to request a file that is not normally accessible. If the web directory is two directories away from the root of the system and the script doesn't prevent this, the password file will be displayed instead of insurance.htm.

FIGURE 5-3 These screen shots show a directory traversal attack in progress.

Directory traversal attacks often take advantage of *canonicalization*, in which multiple formats for the same command can result in that command being executed. Because directory traversal requires moving through directories, various ways of encoding the "go back a directory" characters "../" are used as a canonicalization attack. Thus, %2e%2e%2f, which decodes to ../, can be used to bypass protections built into the web application that are intended to prevent directory traversal attacks.

Cross-site scripting

Cross-site scripting, often called *XSS*, is an exploitation of a web application vulnerability that allows attackers to inject scripts into the webpages that are served to visitors of a website. XSS relies on the user's trust of the site.

There are two major types of XSS attacks. The first and easiest to create is non-persistent cross-site scripting, also known as reflected cross site scripting, which is injected into a URL that the victim clicks. When the URL is clicked, the attack is executed when it is fed back to the victim's browser.

The second, often more complex attack, is a persistent XSS, also known as a stored XSS. A persistent cross-site scripting attack requires the site that is exploited to store the exploit. This is usually done by uploading the exploit code into the website or application in a way that will cause it to be displayed to visitors to the site.

In most cases, stored cross-site scripting requires the absence of user input filters that would strip the attack out from the data that attackers upload to the site. Unfortunately, that's not the only potential vector. Persistent XSS can also be created if attackers can directly access the site or application's code, or if they can otherwise cause the code to be included in what is sent to a victim's web browser. As we mentioned earlier in this chapter, this is a favorite trick of attackers who use zero-day attacks against web browsers. They simply purchase an ad that will be displayed on the target website via an ad network, then place their cross-site scripting attack inside of the ad code.

Preventing XSS

There are several common techniques that can help decrease the likelihood of successful cross-site scripting exploits. They include:

- **Stripping code out of user input**   To do this, programmers need to wrap user input in escape codes that indicate that no code inside of them should be run. When XSS was first discovered, simple defenses would just strip out the <script> tags commonly used to surround JavaScript, but there are many ways around this. Modern web application frameworks now include built-in tools to properly escape user-supplied input.

- **Validating user input**   User input is often well known and can be validated against expected data inside of the application. For example, if users are putting in a phone number, their data shouldn't include words. Any input from the user should be validated wherever possible.

- **Cookie data validation**   Cookies are typically set by a website, but that doesn't mean that malicious users can't modify them. If the site or application trusts the cookies it sets without validating them against expected inputs, attackers can place cross-site scripting attacks into the cookie data itself.

> ***MORE INFO*** **VULNERABILITY SCANNING**
>
> Obviously, testing for cross-site scripting and other attacks is a valuable tool that can help prevent exploits against your organization's web applications. We will talk about vulnerability scanning, including web application security scanners, in depth in Chapter 7.

Injection and modification attacks

Injection attacks, which insert data or commands into trusted communications or files, are another common type of attack. Injection attacks are possible in many applications and have been targeted at web-based as well as traditional PC-based applications.

Each of the attacks we will look at here relies on the attacker having the ability to insert information. For some attacks this involves a proxy, which allows the attacker to capture data sent by a client. The attacker then adds, removes, or modifies data, and sends information onward. When the server responds, the attacker can again choose what information is passed back to the client, making the changes he or she wants to as the data passes through the proxy on its way back.

Another common method of injection is to insert data into unexpected parts of an application. Some applications build database queries or other commands by using user input. Attackers can take advantage of this by fooling the application into adding their commands in addition to the legitimate commands sent to the database.

Other attacks involve man-in-the-middle schemes like those we will discuss later in this chapter, or modification of files that a system receives. In each case, injection and modification attacks insert the attacker's data into legitimate traffic or files.

SQL injection

SQL injection attacks are one of the most common attacks against web applications. As the name implies, they rely on injecting SQL (Structured Query Language) instructions into an application's input in a way that causes the application to use its privileges to run the commands against the database it uses.

In the diagram in Figure 5-4, you can see a typical web application (part of the WebGoat vulnerable web application security suite). The client connects to the web application, which resides on a web application server. From there, the application server connects to a database server protected inside the organization's data center. This separation typically helps provide protection for the database server, because the application is expected to only perform queries that its own internal logic allows. In the SQL injection attack, ' OR 1=1 has been added to the expected query "SELECT * from weather_data where station = 103". The new command is true for every station, because OR 1=1 is always true. This results in all stations being selected.

1. Our web application performs a query showing the state and temperature.

```
SELECT * FROM weather_data WHERE station = 103
```

STATION	NAME	STATE	MIN_TEMP	MAX_TEMP
103	New York	NY	-10	110

2. The normal parameter is only the station ID.

Post Parameter Name	Post Parameter Value
station	103

3. An SQL injection attack adds OR 1=1, which is true for every station.

Post Parameter Name	Post Parameter Value
station	103 OR 1=1

4. Now the application returns all stations, including those normally not shown to users.

```
SELECT * FROM weather_data WHERE station = 103 OR 1=1
```

STATION	NAME	STATE	MIN_TEMP	MAX_TEMP
101	Columbia	MD	-10	102
102	Seattle	WA	-15	90
103	New York	NY	-10	110
104	Houston	TX	20	120
10001	Camp David	MD	-10	100
11001	Ice Station Zebra	NA	-60	30

FIGURE 5-4 This SQL injection attack uses 'OR 1=1' to retrieve all data instead of only the selected data.

When SQL injection attacks are possible, attackers can perform a variety of actions:

- They can query for more data, in some cases including the full contents of the database. In fact, if multiple applications share the database and application credentials aren't well controlled, the attacker might be able to access the data for other applications.
- Attackers can delete information from the database, with results ranging from single entries being removed to an entire database being dropped.
- They can insert items into the database. Attackers might want to change a price, add their own code into pages automatically generated from the database, or add a user to a table of users.

With this broad range of potential actions, SQL injection is a major concern. Fortunately, it's relatively easy to prevent many common SQL injection attacks by using a few common defenses. These are:

- Whitelisting specific input formats.
- Removing special characters or escaping all user input.
- Canonicalization.
- Using stored procedures.
- Limiting application credentials.

> **MORE INFO** **LEAST PRIVILEGE AND SQL INJECTION**
>
> We discuss the concept of least privilege in Chapter 4, "Operational and environmental security," and Chapter 11. The same concept can be used to help reduce the impact of a successful SQL injection attack by restricting what the account associated with an application can do. SQL users who aren't properly restricted can allow attackers to access data from other databases, to write to the database when they should only allow read access, or to drop entire tables or databases!

LDAP and XML injection

 LDAP injection, much like SQL injection, relies on the attacker's ability to inject additional statements into LDAP (Lightweight Directory Access Protocol) queries. Unlike SQL injection, LDAP injection typically relies on a local proxy that can intercept the LDAP connection and modify what the application using LDAP sends or receives.

> **MORE INFO** **LDAP AUTHENTICATION AND AUTHORIZATION**
>
> We discuss LDAP as an authentication and authorization method in Chapter 11.

LDAP injection is typically aimed at privilege escalation, although it can also be used to execute commands or to modify information in an LDAP directory.

XML injection works in a similar way. XML is a markup language that is commonly used to store and send data for Internet services. Because XML uses plaintext to encode data, it can easily be changed by an attacker if the attacker can gain access to the XML files or data being sent.

> **NOTE XML**
>
> XML is used for everything from communication protocols for SOAP web services to RSS feeds to word processing document encoding. If XML is used to store user credentials or other information, attackers who gain the ability to modify the XML can take a wide variety of malicious actions.

Command injection

 Unlike LDAP and XML injection, which both target data, *command injection* uses vulnerable applications to execute system commands. Command injection attacks focus on applications that use command-line utilities to perform their functions, but it can also take advantage of applications that are poorly coded and can be forced to call a command arbitrarily.

Fortunately, simple sanitization of user input can make command injection very difficult. Developers who properly control the input that users can provide to an application can prevent it. As you might expect, avoiding applications that call system commands is also a critical part of preventing attacks.

> **NOTE COMMAND INJECTION: GRABBING A SHELL**
>
> Command injection is sometimes known as shell injection because it attempts to execute shell, or command-line, commands.

> ✔️ **Quick check**
>
> 1. An attack that adds OR 1=1 to a database query is probably what type of attack?
> 2. What is a local proxy used for when conducting an LDAP injection attack?
>
> **Quick check answers**
>
> 1. It is probably an SQL injection attack. The logical construct "OR 1=1" is always true, resulting in whatever command that follows always being executed.
> 2. The local proxy is used to intercept and modify the LDAP connection, allowing the attacker to change what is sent and received.

Network attacks

We've discussed a wide variety of malware, and the many forms of attacks that are conducted against applications and services, but what about the networks that connect all of these together? Our networks are the glue that allows the Internet to exist, and that carry all of our organizational data on a daily basis. Both wired and wireless networks are frequent targets for attackers because of the data they carry, and because without them our systems cannot accomplish much at all.

Spoofing

 One of the most basic attacks that can be conducted against a network is a *spoofing* attack. Spoofing attacks occur when an attacker provides false information on a network. This can be a false IP address, packets that have forged information in them that causes traffic to go to the wrong destination, or other false information provided to unsuspecting systems.

A few of the most common types of spoofing are:

- DNS spoofing attacks, which provide false DNS information when systems look up DNS entries. This can allow attackers to redirect systems to their own systems, allowing them to fool users into providing information or to conduct other attacks.

- Gateway spoofing, a technique that responds to other systems on a local network segment with false information about what their path to the rest of the network is. A spoofed gateway will receive all of the outbound traffic from systems that believe it is the gateway, and it can then view or modify the packets before sending them on, or it can drop the packets entirely.

- MAC spoofing, which spoofs the hardware address of a system on the network. This is a common technique when attackers want to bypass network authentication that is based on MAC addresses. In the recent past, many wireless networks relied on MAC-based filters to prohibit unauthorized machines, making MAC spoofing an effective way of gaining access to a secured network.

- Caller ID spoofing, a common attack via VoIP (Voice over Internet Protocol) networks. This can cause attackers to appear to be coming from legitimate organizations, but it can also have a much more significant impact. Caller ID spoofing has been used for SWATing, a technique that sends police to the location that a spoofed caller ID appears to be from. Typically, the call involves an emergency that will result in a significant police response, potentially causing the target to be taken into police custody.

Packet sniffing

Attackers can also target the traffic on a network itself. Although *packet sniffing* has legitimate uses, attackers can also use it for their own purposes. After an attacker has access to a system, that attacker can sniff the traffic that system has access to. This can result in access to credentials, files, and any other information that the system sends via the network.

Packet sniffing can occur in various locations on the network. As shown in Figure 5-5, it can occur at the local host (A), it can be done by a system that has access to the same subnet (B), and it can be done at a point along the path to the packet's destination (C).

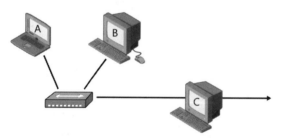

FIGURE 5-5 Packet sniffing can occur at different places on the network.

Man-in-the-middle

When attackers are able to sniff packets, they have several options for further attacks. They can read, modify, and in some cases they can even change the packets. When attackers are able to receive packets between their source and destination, the attack is known as a *man-in-the-middle* attack.

Man-in-the-middle attacks can also be conducted without the ability to sniff traffic. To do this, the attacker must persuade one computer that it should send its traffic through a system the attacker controls. This type of man-in-the-middle attack can be transparent to the system that traffic is being sent to, because the attacker can simply forward traffic with the source address matching the original system it came from.

In the diagram in Figure 5-6, system B has spoofed a response to system A, claiming that it is the gateway for the network. Now system A sends all traffic destined for the outside world (solid lines) to system B. System B is able to intercept that traffic, read it, and then send it along. In this man-in-the middle attack, system B only sees outbound traffic, and does not see responses (dashed lines) from system C to system A.

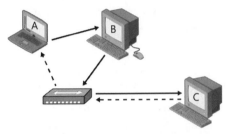

FIGURE 5-6 A man-in-the-middle attack showing system B spoofing a response to system A.

Replay attacks

If attackers have the ability to capture network traffic, they can also conduct a replay attack. A *replay attack* uses previously captured data to replay a connection, authentication, or other session. This is particularly useful if the compromised system does not expose credentials, but does send them to a remote host. If the attacker can resend the authentication sequence without the remote system noticing that it is being replayed, the attacker can then use those credentials for his or her own purposes. In a replay attack, the attacker typically cannot see the actual credentials, but only has the encoded version of them available.

Fortunately, replay attacks are easily defeated by using a simple session token or through the use of timestamps. Each session established with a remote system should use a new session token that is chosen randomly and that has a limited lifespan suitable to the length of time the authenticated session should last.

Timestamps work in a similar way and rely on both systems having their system time set properly to ensure that the packets they are sending were sent during a similar window. Replay attacks can succeed during that short time window, but attacks at a later time will be rejected.

DNS and ARP poisoning

The domain name system (DNS) that provides the glue between IP addresses and host names on the Internet is an attractive target for attackers because a simple DNS hack can redirect traffic to the attacker's system. Typically, an attacker's server is built to closely resemble the system that the unsuspecting victim expects to visit. Thus, when the victim logs on or provides data to the attacker's system, the attacker is able to capture that logon. Some particularly well done attacks will pass the credentials through to the real system and will then capture all traffic between the two, preventing the victim from noticing the attack.

DNS poisoning takes advantage of the fact that the DNS system does not have effective security controls built into it. Attackers exploit the lack of validation for DNS responses and respond with information that changes the DNS information servers cache. After the DNS response is cached by a server, it won't be updated until the cache timer is reached, which can result in users who trust that DNS server visiting the wrong system for hours.

> **NOTE   SECURING DNS**
>
> DNSSEC, the Domain Name System Security Extensions, use cryptographic signatures to determine whether DNS data is authentic. DNSSEC can counter cache poisoning attacks by preventing fake servers from being authenticated. The root domain servers for the Internet support DNSSEC and have since 2010. Unfortunately, DNSSEC is not implemented everywhere on the Internet, resulting in opportunities for attackers.

Much like DNS poisoning, ARP poisoning is a spoofing technique that provides false information in response to requests via the Address Resolution Protocol. Unlike DNS poisoning, ARP poisoning only works on a local network.

> **MORE INFO   THE ARP PROTOCOL**
>
> The ARP protocol is used to broadcast requests on a local network segment asking "who has address X?" Responses then provide the information required.

In the diagram in Figure 5-7, a normal ARP response between two systems would result in system A sending traffic to system B. When ARP spoofing occurs successfully, system A believes that system C is system B, and it sends traffic to it. System C can then respond, modify the traffic, or simply view it and then send it on to system B.

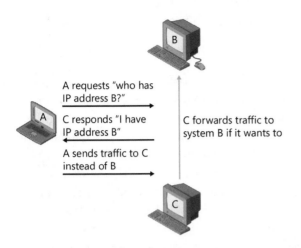

A requests "who has IP address B?"

C responds "I have IP address B"

A sends traffic to C instead of B

C forwards traffic to system B if it wants to

FIGURE 5-7 In this ARP poisoning attack, system A sends traffic to system C instead of system B.

An attacker conducting an ARP poisoning attack spoofs answers from the systems that victims are attempting to contact. If the response reaches the victim's system first, the victim's system will send traffic to the attacker's system, rather than to the legitimate system. After attackers have traffic intended for other systems coming to their PCs, they can take further action.

> **NOTE** **MITIGATING ARP SPOOFING AND POISONING**
>
> ARP spoofing and poisoning can be mitigated by using network switches and other devices that can monitor traffic and ensure that systems are not sending falsified information in response to ARP traffic.

Denial of service and distributed denial of service attacks

One of the most dangerous network attacks for modern networks is a *denial of service* (DoS) attack. Denial of service attacks come in many forms, but all have the same basic goal: to prevent a system or service from functioning properly. That goal can be reached in a variety of ways:

- Crashing or disabling the service
- Shutting down the system that runs the service
- Overwhelming the service with requests so that it cannot respond properly

- Shutting down or overwhelming a point in the path between the service or server and its clients

- Damaging or destroying systems

 Denial of service attacks that are conducted by multiple machines, and usually from several dispersed networks and IP ranges, are known as *distributed denial of service attacks* or DDoS attacks. A distributed denial of service attack allows attackers to use many machines with fewer resources to attack major sites. It also prevents system and network administrators from blocking a single system or IP address range to stop the denial of service attack.

Because denial of service attacks come in many forms, determining that one is happening can be a challenge. Often, the first signs are a network slowdown, or the inability to access a server or service. After a denial of service attack has been detected, several techniques can be attempted to stop it or to minimize its impact:

- Firewalls, switches, and routers can all be used to control access, thus limiting what systems can attack. Many have rate-limiting capabilities that can prevent systems from overwhelming protected resources as well.

- Intrusion prevention systems can block known attacks and in some cases can detect denial of service attacks as they are starting.

- Specialized DoS and DDoS prevention systems are designed specifically to prevent DoS attacks.

- Bandwidth management and application filtering systems can help to control what traffic is prioritized, thus ensuring that critical traffic makes it through to a system or service that is being attacked.

MORE INFO   MONITORING AND DEFENSE TOOLS

We discuss these tools and techniques in more depth in Chapter 6, "Monitoring, detection, and defense."

Smurf attacks

Not every attack gets its own name, but smurf attacks did. This attack, named after the children's cartoon "The Smurfs," was popular in the 1990s when computer networks were not configured to prevent their special type of network traffic exploit. In fact, the standard of the time required networks to perform exactly the set of behaviors that made smurf attacks work!

 A *smurf attack* is sent by an attacker who spoofs the IP address of the intended victim in broadcast traffic to a network. All of the systems that receive the broadcast then attempt to respond to the computer that had its address spoofed, resulting in a huge flood of traffic to that system. This was a form of denial of service attack against a single system and was quite effective against unprepared systems and networks, or those with minimal bandwidth and horsepower.

Some networks were configured in a way that allowed to them amplify the attacks even more. Those networks amplified the attacks by sending more than a single reply, resulting in a multiplied attack with no additional effort on the part of the attacker.

Xmas attacks

The *Xmas attack*, also called the Christmas tree packet, is a network packet–based attack that has every possible flag set for the protocol that is used to send it. When the term was coined, packets sent like this were imagined as being lit up like a Christmas tree due to all of the flags being "on." As you can see in the TCP packet shown in Figure 5-8, there are a variety of flags that can be set on a TCP packet, but they shouldn't all be set at the same time for a valid packet. Thus, a packet like this should never be sent under normal circumstances.

As the figure shows, TCP packets can have urgent, acknowledgement, push, reset, SYN, FIN, ECN Echo, and congestion window reduced (CWR) flags set. They can also contain information in the reserved and nonce locations. Packets shouldn't contain FIN, or end, at the same time as SYN, and many of the other combinations possible aren't compliant with the TCP protocol. In the Christmas tree listing at the bottom of the table, all flags are set to on!

Flag	Name	Binary representation
CWR	Congestion window reduced	1 0 0 0 0 0 0 0
ECE	ECN echo	0 1 0 0 0 0 0 0
URG	Urgent	0 0 1 0 0 0 0 0
ACK	Acknowledgement	0 0 0 1 0 0 0 0
PSH	Push	0 0 0 0 1 0 0 0
RST	Reset	0 0 0 0 0 1 0 0
SYN	Syn	0 0 0 0 0 0 1 0
FIN	Fin	0 0 0 0 0 0 0 1
Xmas	All flags	1 1 1 1 1 1 1 1

FIGURE 5-8 This table of TCP packet flags shows the Xmas attack.

Packets like the Xmas attack packet performed two actions for attackers. First, they tested whether the receiving system properly handled a packet that should not exist, and how it responded. Each operating system responded slightly differently to a packet like this, allowing attackers to determine what type of system they were connecting to.

The second use for an Xmas attack was to conduct a denial of service attack against systems that were underpowered or that had poorly designed network stacks that did not handle badly formed packets. A packet with all of the possible flags enabled would typically cause the system it was sent to to spend far more processing power to handle the packet or might even cause the system to crash, resulting in a denial of service condition.

> **NOTE WHY DO WE STILL STUDY XMAS ATTACKS?**
>
> Much like smurf attacks, Xmas attacks are no longer a serious concern in most modern networks. They're still covered in security books and exams to ensure that the industry doesn't have to relearn the lesson that gracefully handling something that should never exist is still a good idea.

 Quick check

1. What type of spoofing attack uses a fake hardware address?
2. Why is a smurf attack unlikely on a modern network?

Quick check answers

1. A MAC address spoofing attack uses a spoofed hardware address to gain access to a network that uses MAC address filtering.
2. Smurf attacks rely on networks allowing attackers to spoof IP addresses in broadcast traffic. Modern network equipment has built-in tools to stop this from happening.

Wireless attacks

Wireless networks have their own special set of threats and attacks beyond those that any wired network can experience. Wireless threats take advantage of two unique features of wireless networks. First, they often use the ability to intercept or interfere with wireless signals from any location within range of the network. Second, they rely on the simple fact that wireless networks broadcast traffic to their clients, and thus that traffic can be accessed anywhere that their signal reaches.

Rogue access points

One of the most common wireless threats for an organizational network is the creation of *rogue access points*. There are two types of rogue access points (often called *rogue APs*). The first and most common type of rogue access point is any wireless access point that connects to your organization's network that your organization did not intend to place. Frequently, this occurs inadvertently because laptops and cellphones automatically set up their own ad-hoc networks. If the device also connects to your wireless or wired network, a new way to access your network is created, typically without any authentication or other security in place to protect it.

Because these ad-hoc networks aren't planned, and are often automatically set up without the user's knowledge, they're likely to cause *interference* with the existing network. Most large enterprise networks use a carefully designed access point layout and channel plan to ensure that access points do not overlap in coverage on the same bands. A rogue access point can overlap with legitimate access points on the same Wi-Fi bands, resulting in interference, causing legitimate users to have problems connecting to the corporate network.

The second form of rogue access point is far less common, but it is also a more direct and subtle threat. *Evil twins*, rogue access points that pretend to be part of an organization's legitimate wireless network, are used to conduct man-in-the-middle attacks against wireless users.

Evil twins are a serious concern for organizations that don't use encrypted enterprise wireless networks. Fortunately, using an authentication system to prove the identity of the wireless network can make an evil twin attack easy to detect. In simple wireless networks, the only way to identify the correct access point is by the SSID (service set identifier), the wireless network name that the access point broadcasts. Anyone who has scanned for wireless networks knows that there can be a proliferation of networks called "Linksys" or "2Wire." Knowing which network to trust can be very difficult in a situation like that!

In some cases, an evil twin isn't necessary. Some attackers simply create an SSID called "Free Open Wi-Fi" or another innocuous name, and provide open access. After an unsuspecting user connects, the attacker can do anything he or she wants with their traffic.

> **MORE INFO**   **MAN-IN-THE-MIDDLE AND WI-FI**
>
> Remember that a man-in-the-middle attack places the attacker between the victim and a system, resource, or server the victim is trying to reach. Depending on how the attack is constructed, the attacker can often view, modify, or drop traffic sent between the systems. The same attacks we talked about earlier in this chapter can be conducted via a wireless network, too.

An example is shown in Figure 5-9, in which an evil twin pretends to be part of Humongous Insurance's network by broadcasting *HInet*, which is the same SSID as the rest of the company's corporate APs. At the same time, a user in the IT department brings in a personal laptop that automatically sets up an ad-hoc wireless network (Home) and bridges it to the laptop's wired network, which is connected to Humongous Insurance's internal network. Now wireless users are presented with three SSIDs, two of which connect to the Humongous Insurance network, and one malicious network that might fool users into connecting to an untrusted network. If they do, attackers can conduct a variety of man-in-the-middle attacks.

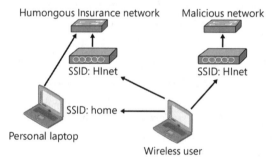

FIGURE 5-9 This illustration shows an evil twin access point and a rogue access point running on a laptop.

> **NOTE**   **PCI-DSS REQUIREMENTS**
>
> The PCI DSS (Payment Card Industry Data Security Standard) requires organizations to prevent rogue access points from being connected to networks that process credit cards. This is intended to prevent man-in-the-middle attacks from evil twins and unexpected devices accessing the network via the rogue APs.

Bluetooth attacks

Bluetooth is a short-range wireless protocol that is typically used to connect to portable devices such as phones, tablets, and headsets.

The CompTIA Security+ exam looks at two types of Bluetooth-centric exploits. The first, known as *bluejacking*, simply sends unsolicited messages to Bluetooth-enabled devices. Bluejacking received a lot of media attention when it was first reported, but hasn't become more than an annoyance for occasional users.

The second Bluetooth exploit is more serious, particularly as malware begins to target mobile devices. *Bluesnarfing*, which is the unauthorized access to data on a device via Bluetooth, is a real threat for Bluetooth-enabled devices. Unlike bluejacking, this could potentially expose all of the data on the device. Fortunately, the most effective method to prevent this is quite simple: turn Bluetooth off.

> **MORE INFO**   **HACKING AT A DISTANCE: BLUESNIPING**
>
> The CompTIA Security+ body of knowledge doesn't cover *bluesniping*, which uses a directional antenna to increase the range of Bluetooth devices. By using this type of antenna, Bluetooth signals have been received at distances of up to a mile. Bluesniping makes long-distance attacks on Bluetooth devices possible, including the potential to listen in on Bluetooth headsets and hands-free equipment. Bluesniping is a great reminder that wireless technologies can expose data at far greater distances than one might otherwise imagine!

Many owners of Bluetooth-enabled devices pair them with their cars, headsets, or other devices that they want easy access to. Thus, they're likely to leave their devices on and potentially discoverable all day. Even more dangerous is the fact that most manufacturers use an easy-to-guess code when pairing devices. In fact, many manufacturers use 0000 as their pairing code, resulting in an easy exploit for malware or attackers.

EXAM TIP

Bluetooth attacks aren't common, but the CompTIA Security+ exam covers both bluesnarfing and bluejacking. Remember that bluesnarfing implies data access, whereas bluejacking simply sends unsolicited messages.

War driving

In the decades prior to the advent of wireless networks, hackers would dial large groups of phone numbers, looking for modems that would answer and allow them to connect to unknown systems and networks. In the modern age of wireless technology, a similar tactic was employed by attackers who drove around searching for wireless networks while in a car; this technique was called *war driving*. War driving techniques typically involved using an external, high-gain antenna to pull in signals from a greater distance than the wireless card in a laptop or other portable device would normally be capable of. When software designed to map networks is combined with a GPS, a map of available networks, signal strength, SSID identifiers, and other details can be built.

> **MORE INFO   NETSTUMBLER**
>
> This technique was often called *network stumbling*, and one of the most popular tools for it was NetStumbler. NetStumbler provided the wireless network's protocol, frequency, data rate, estimated range, and a host of other capabilities that were useful when mapping networks.

Over time, a host of other network mapping techniques were named after their mode of transit: *war walking*, *war biking*, and others. One of the most interesting ideas to come out of this burst of mapping was *war chalking*. War chalkers would mark the location of wireless network access points and would include information about how they were configured with a chalk or paint marker. As shown in Figure 5-10, war chalking symbols noted whether a node was open or closed, and what type of encryption it used.

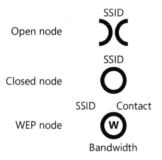

FIGURE 5-10 War chalking symbols allow hackers to notify other hackers of vulnerable nodes.

> **MORE INFO   WAR CHALKING**
>
> Though the CompTIA Security+ exam's body of knowledge includes war chalking, the practice never really became common and isn't in wide use today.

Packet sniffing and wireless networks

The protocol analyzers and sniffers discussed in Chapter 2 become even more interesting to attackers when wireless networks come into play. Because wireless networks are typically broadcast, traffic sent to every system connected to an access point is accessible in a large radius around the access point. This means that any data that isn't encrypted can be captured and analyzed with ease.

As you learned earlier in this book, WEP (Wired Equivalent Privacy), the first broadly available wireless encryption protocol, suffered from critical security vulnerabilities including problems with initialization vector attacks that made it easy to crack. The vulnerabilities in WEP serve to remind us that even encryption might not always keep our traffic secure. Fortunately, the modern WPA2 protocol has not yet suffered a significant breach, making it a viable option for organizations wanting to prevent wireless packet sniffers from being a major threat.

MORE INFO **WIRELESS ENCRYPTION TYPES**

We talked about the common types of wireless encryption called WEP, WPA, and WPA2 in Chapter 3.

Firesheep: A lesson in session hijacking

In 2010, a Firefox plug-in called Firesheep was released. Firesheep used a packet sniffer to capture unencrypted session cookies and tokens for popular websites such as Facebook, Twitter, and other social networking sites that didn't require SSL for their traffic. Because many companies that offer free Wi-Fi don't use encryption, this meant that users who were casually browsing the Internet at coffee shops, grocery stores, and other locations could easily have their sessions hijacked.

The exploit that Firesheep used was not a new technique, but it was the first time that a truly simple-to-use tool had been made widely available. The simple process of creating a session hijacking tool as a Firefox plug-in that could be downloaded, installed, and used with a few minutes of reading brought the issues with unsecured web traffic and open unencrypted wireless networks to light.

Across the world, organizations had to reassess their wireless security practices. Many popular websites at first allowed users to optionally use HTTPS for their traffic, but over time, many moved to force HTTPS for session traffic, in addition to the authentication traffic they had formerly secured. In addition to this, some organizations moved to encrypted wireless networks. Unfortunately, unencrypted open wireless networks remain easier to implement, and many smaller sites still do not require HTTPS for their traffic.

The threat that Firesheep made very visible remains an issue today. Fortunately, plug-ins exist for major browsers that attempt to force use of HTTPS wherever possible, and connecting to your organization's VPN when you use unencrypted wireless networks can prevent your sessions from being hijacked.

With wireless networks an easy target for attackers who can physically get into wireless range of an organization, it becomes even more important to ensure that appropriate protection such as encryption and secure protocols are in place for wireless traffic.

Social engineering and phishing

No matter how many technical hurdles an organization places in front of attackers, one target will remain: the organization's staff. *Social engineering* is the practice of targeting people at an organization rather than systems, software, or networks, and it is one of the most effective tactics that an attacker can use.

Social engineering can be done in person, via the phone, or even via email or social networks. All it requires is human interaction to allow attackers to persuade the people they are targeting to give them access, to help them, or to share some important piece of information.

Social engineering relies on an understanding of common human behaviors, and how those can be exploited to gain access to facilities, resources, and systems. Social engineers exploit human instincts to be considerate, to respect authority, and to trust in others. In addition, they take advantage of what scares people and what tempts them. They will use any method they can to work past the guard of staff who are otherwise trustworthy members of an organization.

> *NOTE* **SOCIAL ENGINEERING**
>
> Social engineering preparation can be as complex as researching an employee's family and work history to phone in a fake emergency involving that person's child, or purchasing a complete uniform for a well-known delivery company and posing as a delivery person to gain access to an organization. It can also be as simple as asking the person ahead of you to hold the door to the secure area that he or she is entering.

There are several common social engineering techniques:

- **Shoulder surfing**   A technique in which the attacker watches over an employee's shoulder or from another nearby location where he or she can see the employee's screen or keyboard. Shoulder surfing is a common way to steal passwords and PINs.

- **Tailgating**   A technique used to gain access to secured areas. Tailgating typically involves following a person into an area with access restrictions. This might be as simple as going through the door the authorized person just opened before it closes or speeding through a closing gate, or as complex as persuading the person to let the attacker in. Tailgating, like many of the social engineering techniques described here, often relies on common polite behavior. In this case, that behavior is holding the door for the person behind you.

- **_Impersonation_** One of the most common social engineering techniques. As the name implies, the attacker impersonates someone the employee would trust or would provide information to. Often this means the attacker poses as a technical support staff member or an executive who is out of town, but some attackers pose as a police officer or an emergency room worker.

- **_Dumpster diving_** The practice of going through an individual's or organization's trash to recover data. This has been used in the past to acquire medical records, passwords, and technical documentation. Fortunately, dumpster diving can be prevented by shredding trash, keeping trash in a secure area, and using a compactor, making trash difficult to access. Some organizations contract with third parties to take their sensitive materials offsite for secure shredding or incineration.

- **Pretexting** The art of providing an excuse, often combined with impersonation to provide a scenario in which the employee will provide information. A frequent example is to claim to be an executive in the organization who has forgotten her password or needs a file sent to an outside email address on short notice due to an emergency. This combines the desire to help and the fear of making an executive unhappy.

- **Baiting** A technique that involves placing a USB flash drive or other device or media that will be attractive to employees in an area where it might be found. The bait is created with a trojan or other malware on the device that will steal data or provide remote access to systems that the device or media is accessed from. Penetration testing companies have added this technique to their stable of techniques and will often scatter flash drives in the parking lots of companies they're testing.

- **Quid pro quo** Providing something for something. When using this technique, the attacker provides something to the user, who then feels it is safe or right to provide information to the attacker.

> **_IMPORTANT_** **SOCIAL ENGINEERING AND THE COMPTIA SECURITY+ EXAM**
> Though the CompTIA Security+ exam doesn't test you on your knowledge of pretexting, baiting, or quid pro quo, they are useful techniques to be aware of, and other social engineering attacks often use parts of these techniques to succeed.

Quick check

1. What would an attacker who is tailgating do?

2. How can dumpster diving be prevented?

Quick check answers

1. The attacker will attempt to follow an employee through a door or gate without providing credentials. This often relies on the employee being polite and allowing the attacker through.

2. Dumpster diving can be prevented or limited by crosscut shredding all documents, using a compactor, and securing the area where trash is kept.

Hoaxes

The CompTIA Security+ exam specifically includes hoaxes in its body of knowledge. Hoaxes are simply a type of social engineering that relies on gullible individuals to fall for an email message, to forward a chain letter, or to send their personal information to a scammer.

Hoaxes take many forms, and as social media sites have become ever more popular, hoaxes have moved from forwarded and chain email messages to Facebook pages that collect likes or direct users to another site.

> ***MORE INFO*** **HOAX-FIGHTING WEBSITES**
>
> There are several excellent anti-hoax sites available to help you combat hoaxes, scams, and other nuisances:
>
> - *Snopes.com*, one of the best sources for information on urban legends and hoaxes
> - *Hoaxbusters.org*, which tackles Internet hoaxes, chain letters, and scams
> - *Hoax-slayer.com*, which includes information about viruses, true email messages, hoaxes, and even humorous email messages that aren't true

Phishing

Phishing is a very specialized type of social engineering that attempts to persuade victims to provide their credentials, bank account information, credit card numbers, or other sensitive personal or organizational information to an attacker. Phishing goes beyond hoaxes to specifically target an individual's personal data. As you would expect, phishing uses many of the same basic ideas that are common in social engineering to persuade the recipients of the phishing message that they should respond.

Phishers will attempt to appear legitimate, to instill fear or worry, or to use knowledge they have gained about the person receiving the message to persuade the victim that he or she should respond because of familiarity. Phishers also often rely on fake websites that are designed to appear identical to the legitimate sites that users expect to log onto, thereby fooling them into providing credentials. Particularly well-designed phishing sites will accept credentials, then respond with a believable error message, and some even pass on credentials to the real site, displaying the proper responses to the victim.

There are several specialized phishing techniques that the CompTIA Security+ exam covers. These include:

- **Spear phishing**   Targeted phishing of individuals or companies. Spear phishers identify the targets they want to attack and carefully craft their phishing email messages, IMs, or other contacts to be appropriate to that person or organization.

- **SPIM**   A specialized form of spam sent via instant message. SPIM attacks typically send messages to many users, either attempting to persuade those users to visit a site, thus helping them engage in click fraud, which uses falsified clicks to drive revenue from ad networks, or to download a trojan or other malware.

- **Vishing**   A form of phishing also known as *voice phishing,* which relies on social engineering via the phone. Vishing is increasingly a problem for organizations as VoIP phones become more common, allowing for easier spoofing of phone numbers. Vishers often target credit card numbers by pretending to be associated with a credit card vendor, a bank, or a store the victim is likely to have interactions with.

- **Whaling**   Phishing targeted at important or high-profile targets in an organization. A phishing attempt aimed at the CEO of a company would be classified as whaling.

- **Pharming**   A combination of the words *phishing* and *farming,* coined to refer to the practice of redirecting traffic to another site for profit or to infect systems that visit it with malware.

Real world

Pharming via hosts files

Windows systems have a local DNS lookup file called the hosts file. When the system does a DNS lookup to find a site, it first checks its hosts file to see if it has a local entry. If it does, it uses the information in the hosts file rather than asking a DNS server.

Attackers have been adding entries to these for years, redirecting commonly accessed sites to sites of their choosing. This has resulted in anti-virus and anti-malware companies adding protection for the hosts file to their products, but it hasn't stopped attackers. Thus, if you find a machine that redirects traffic to the wrong site, an easy first step is to check the hosts file typically found at C:\Windows\system32\drivers\etc, as shown in Figure 5-11. Windows provides a default hosts file like the one shown in the figure. A modified hosts file will include entries pointing to different sites. If the hosts file you're viewing doesn't match this one, and it hasn't been changed on purpose, the system has probably been compromised.

```
C:\>more C:\Windows\System32\drivers\etc\hosts
# Copyright (c) 1993-2009 Microsoft Corp.
#
# This is a sample HOSTS file used by Microsoft TCP/IP for Windows.
#
# This file contains the mappings of IP addresses to host names. Each
# entry should be kept on an individual line. The IP address should
# be placed in the first column followed by the corresponding host name.
# The IP address and the host name should be separated by at least one
# space.
#
# Additionally, comments (such as these) may be inserted on individual
# lines or following the machine name denoted by a '#' symbol.
#
# For example:
#
#      102.54.94.97     rhino.acme.com          # source server
#       38.25.63.10     x.acme.com              # x client host

# localhost name resolution is handled within DNS itself.
#      127.0.0.1        localhost
#       ::1             localhost
```

FIGURE 5-11 The windows hosts file found in C:\Windows\System32\drivers\etc\hosts includes example settings like 102.54.94.96 for rhino.acme.com.

EXAM TIP

The types of phishing are relatively easy to remember just by looking at what they reference: Whales are big, vishing relates to Voice over IP, SPIM is sent via instant message, and spear phishing is targeted!

Email attacks

Email has made huge populations of potential victims available to attackers at a very low cost, both in terms of effort and of the technical infrastructure required to send bulk email. Attackers can buy large mailing lists for a low cost, send tens of thousands or millions of email messages, and can expect at least a small percentage of those who receive the messages to respond.

Email attacks often provide the social engineering front end to a technical attack that requires the user to be persuaded to fall for a sales pitch or to perform an action. The CompTIA Security+ exam covers two of these, and we'll look at both of them.

Email attachments

Malicious email attachments are a perennial favorite for attackers, and there has been a constant arms race between security professionals and email administrators who want to protect their organizations and attackers who want to get malware onto protected end-user systems.

Email attachments typically rely on persuading the person who receives the email message to open the attachment. Thus, the email message that accompanies the attachment often provides a variety of reasons why the attachment is important, ranging from a message from the IRS or a bank to pictures from a friend's last vacation. When attachments require that the reader open them, simply not clicking on them can keep users safe.

Some email attachments have gone a step farther and have used exploits in email clients or in the browsers that email clients use to display the email. This means that when those email messages are viewed, they could compromise the receiver's PC. Fortunately, this type of exploit is relatively rare.

> **MORE INFO**   **ANTI-VIRUS AND ATTACHMENT HANDLING**
>
> We talk about anti-virus and attachment handling as part of a comprehensive defensive security posture in Chapter 6, and as part of host security in Chapter 9.

Spam

Spam email, more technically known as *unsolicited bulk email*, comprises a majority of the email sent and received on the Internet today. Because spam makes up so much of the email that organizations receive, an entire industry has been created to deal with spam messages. Mail filtering tools, blacklisting organizations that track spam sites throughout the day, and a whole host of other technologies and processes have been created to fight spam.

Spam typically has one of three purposes: it might be intended to sell something, it might serve as the entry vector for a phishing attack, or it might simply be trying to get the recipient to click through to a website to drive up traffic or to get the user to infect his or her machine with malware.

> **IMPORTANT THE MANY TYPES OF SPAM**
>
> Spam isn't limited to email alone. SMS, instant message, Twitter, blogs, and any other communications medium can be used to send and receive spam.

The fight against spam constantly changes, with an ever-escalating series of anti-spam techniques countering new methods of getting spam email past common defenses. Each time a major new technology to stop spam is created, spammers find a way around it, often in a clever or creative way.

Fighting the war against spam

Starting in 2006, some spammers moved from text-based spam to image-based spam. Anti-spam technologies had advanced to a point where they used scoring and analysis to detect common spam phrases and other tricks such as changing the sender and sending from open relays. Thus, spammers needed a new way to get messages through.

Images, often of the text that had previously been sent, were the answer. Because anti-spam systems were designed to read the email and determine if there was spam content in it, removing the content allowed image-based spam to pass right through most detection systems.

System administrators took quick action, but removing images from email was problematic. A new balance was reached, and image spam continues to be used as a way to get through spam detection systems.

Images weren't the only clever way past anti-spam systems, and one technique that became common in the same timeframe was the use of compressed file attachments to deliver trojans. Processing a compressed file takes CPU time, which meant that some organizations skipped them. The spammers became even more clever, however, and used passwords on the compressed file. Recipients were instructed to open the very important attachment by using that password, and when they did, they would find themselves infected with a virus or trojan.

Quick check

1. Whaling targets what members of an organization?

2. What is the difference between SPIM and vishing?

Quick check answers

1. Whaling targets high-profile members of an organization such as the CEO, vice presidents, or other senior managers.

2. SPIM is spam sent via instant messenger and is normally targeted at click fraud or persuading recipients to download trojans or other malware. Vishing is phishing via voice and is a social engineering attack in which the caller attempts to persuade the victim that he or she should provide personal information, credit card numbers, or bank account numbers.

Chapter summary

- Adware, spyware, viruses, worms, trojans, malicious add-ons, rootkits, backdoors, and logic bombs are all types of malware. Each has distinctive capabilities that attackers use individually or in combination to gain and maintain control of systems.

- Privilege escalation attacks use accounts with limited privileges to access vulnerabilities or to exploit misconfigurations to gain enhanced rights.

- Application vulnerabilities are a popular target for attackers, including zero-day vulnerabilities that have not been announced or patched yet, and buffer overflows, which attempt to push executable code into memory by overflowing the buffers that receive user input in the application.

- Web attacks target web browsers via the cookies they store or HTTP headers that store session and other information, and via a variety of cross-site scripting and cross-site forgery exploits, as well as attacks against the browsers and their plug-ins.

- Server and application attacks often use injection to feed incorrect data to the server. SQL, LDAP, XML, and even command-line commands are all possible targets for injection attacks.

- Network attacks can steal or modify data, or they can spoof information to allow an attacker to take over a system or a user's identity.

- Smurf attacks, Xmas attacks, and other network attacks use vulnerabilities in system TCP stacks or issues with network configuration to bring systems down or to create denial of service conditions.

- Wireless network attacks create additional complexity because wireless signals are broadcast, allowing attackers to intercept them anywhere they are in range. Attackers can also create fake network access points that appear to be legitimate. These are known as rogue APs.

- Social engineering focuses on attacks that take advantage of human nature and natural tendencies. Social engineering attacks prey on fear, respect for authority, greed, and the desire to be nice and to do the right thing.

- Phishing attacks attempt to persuade victims that they should provide personal information, credit card or banking details, or passwords. Phishing relies on many of thesame social engineering techniques used in other attacks and typically is done via email, instant messaging, social networks, or even via voicemail and VoIP systems.

- Email attacks come in a variety of forms, including spam, phishing, and malicious email attachments.

Chapter review

Test your knowledge of the information in Chapter 5 by answering these questions. The answers to these questions, and the explanations of why each answer choice is correct or incorrect, are located in the "Answers" section at the end of this chapter.

1. Which type of malware spreads itself through a network by exploiting services and systems?

   A. Worms

   B. Adware

   C. Trojans

   D. Viruses

2. What type of injection attack often uses logic to attack databases?

   A. Command injection

   B. Header injection

   C. SQL injection

   D. LDAP injection

3. Attacks that occur before the vulnerability they exploit is announced are known as what type of attack?

   A. Unpatched attacks

   B. Zombie attacks

   C. Injection attacks

   D. Zero-day attacks

4. Which attack is most likely after an attacker has captured authentication session information crossing your network?

   A. Spoofing

   B. A smurf attack

   C. ARP poisoning

   D. A replay attack

5. What is a fake wireless network access point that appears to be legitimate called?

   A. A rogue access point

   B. A man-in-the-middle

   C. An evil twin

   D. A strange attractor

6. Targeted phishing attacks against specific organizations are known as what type of phishing?

   A. Vishing

   B. Whaling

   C. Spear phishing

   D. Pharming

Answers

This section contains the answers to the questions for the "Chapter review" section in this chapter.

1. **Correct Answer: A**

    A. **Correct:** Worms spread themselves via networks.

    B. **Incorrect:** Adware is a type of malware that displays ads. It is normally relatively innocuous but can be annoying.

    C. **Incorrect:** A trojans is malware designed to appear to be a desirable application, but which instead delivers a malicious payload to the system it is installed or run on.

    D. **Incorrect:** A viruses is malware that relies on humans to spread it by infecting files or copying itself to removable media.

2. **Correct Answer: C**

    A. **Incorrect:** Command injection attempts to use command-line commands injected into applications or scripts, causing them to be executed on the server.

    B. **Incorrect:** Header injection changes or replaces HTTP headers sent by clients or servers.

    C. **Correct:** SQL injection attacks a database by using logic such as *OR 1=1* to inject commands.

    D. **Incorrect:** LDAP injection attacks focus on LDAP statements based on user input and take advantage of poor user input sanitization to attempt to execute arbitrary commands such as changing permissions or changing information in the LDAP directory.

3. **Correct Answer: D**

    A. **Incorrect:** Many attacks target unpatched systems, but attacks that target systems before the vulnerability is announced will not have a patch.

    B. **Incorrect:** Zombies are part of a botnet and are remotely controlled machines.

    C. **Incorrect:** Injection attacks attempt to insert data or commands into applications or systems.

    D. **Correct:** Zero-day attacks target applications or operating systems before the vulnerability they exploit is patched or announced. This makes them even more fearsome, because there is often no way to prevent them or to know that they are coming.

4. **Correct Answer: D**

   A. **Incorrect:** Spoofing attacks work by providing false information.

   B. **Incorrect:** A smurf attack is a type of denial of service attack.

   C. **Incorrect:** ARP poisoning falsifies information about hardware addresses on a network.

   D. **Correct:** A replay attack resends previously captured data, often authentication information or transactions.

5. **Correct Answer: C**

   A. **Incorrect:** Rogue access points are access points connected to your network that should not be there.

   B. **Incorrect:** *Man-in-the-middle* is a term that refers to any attack that sends traffic through an attacker.

   C. **Correct:** An evil twin pretends to be part of a legitimate network and broadcasts the same SSID, but it is actually there to gather data from systems that connect to it.

   D. **Incorrect:** Strange attractors are part of quantum theory.

6. **Correct Answer: C**

   A. **Incorrect:** Vishing is phishing via VoIP.

   B. **Incorrect:** Whaling targets high-profile individuals such as CEOs.

   C. **Correct:** Spear phishing targets specific organizations and even specific groups of individuals in those organizations.

   D. **Incorrect:** Pharming is phishing intended to redirect those targeted by a phishing attack to another site for link farming.

## CHAPTER 6

Monitoring, detection, and defense

This chapter explores how to defend against the threats and attacks that were explored in Chapter 5, "Threats and attacks." The first step in a successful defense is to secure systems and networks by configuring them to prevent attacks. Then you need to ensure that they stay secure by providing continuous security monitoring and by keeping them fully patched and updated.

After you have learned how to secure systems from network-based-intrusions, this chapter will look at physical security practices including fences, locks, and camera systems. By the time you have finished this chapter, you will be ready to keep a system secure from the moment it is installed to the day it is retired from service.

Exam objectives in this chapter:

Objective 3.6: Analyze and differentiate among types of mitigation and deterrent techniques

- Manual bypassing of electronic controls
    - Failsafe/secure vs. failopen
- Monitoring system logs
    - Event logs
    - Audit logs
    - Security logs
    - Access logs
- Physical security
    - Hardware locks
    - Mantraps
    - Video surveillance
    - Fencing
    - Proximity readers
    - Access list

- Hardening
    - Disabling unnecessary services
    - Protecting management interfaces and applications
    - Password protection
    - Disabling unnecessary accounts
- Port security
    - MAC limiting and filtering
    - 802.1x
    - Disabling unused ports
- Security posture
    - Initial baseline configuration
    - Continuous security monitoring
    - Remediation
- Reporting
    - Alarms
    - Alerts
    - Trends
- Detection controls vs. prevention controls
    - IDS vs. IPS
    - Camera vs. guard

Securing and defending systems

The same defense in depth strategy that we have discussed throughout this book so far can be used to ensure that systems, network devices, and other organizational IT assets remain secure. To create a secure system, you first need to make the system difficult to compromise by removing access to unnecessary services, protecting necessary services, and configuring the system for greater security than it normally has when it is first built. The process of securing systems is known as hardening, and it should be one of the first things done after the initial installation when you are building a system.

Hardening

Most operating systems, applications, and devices are not secure out of the box. Performing a *hardening* process results in a more secure system than a fresh installation done without any lockdown would, and ensures that the system is deployed with as few vulnerabilities and risky configurations in place as possible. The hardening process involves locking down and securing the system through patching, configuration, and installation of security software.

Hardening can be done at each layer of the secure network and systems design we have explored so far. You can use hardening techniques on networks, network devices, servers, workstations, mobile devices, and any other device that can be patched, configured, or otherwise protected.

The hardening process can be complex, because many of the devices that organizations want to secure have dozens or even hundreds of potential security settings in their base operating systems alone. When you add on application software, user accounts, and network configuration, hardening can be a difficult task to perform. Worse, it is almost impossible to remember every possible setting, what it does, and when you should use it for every usage scenario your organization might have for each operating system and device you are likely to encounter.

Fortunately, several groups have created hardening standards, tools, and guides.

EXAM TIP

The CompTIA Security+ exam focuses on the initial baseline configuration, or how a system is secured when it is deployed. Hardening, including the techniques we discuss here, is how that initial secure configuration is done.

Hardening standards

Most major operating systems have a variety of hardening standards available. Operating system vendors often provide hardening standards for their operating systems. In addition, organizations such as the Center for Internet Security (CIS), the National Institute of Standards and Technology (NIST), and even the National Security Agency (NSA) have created hardening standards.

This creates a different issue for those who have to select hardening standards: what standard do you adopt, and why? In many cases, this will have already been decided, and your organization will have standardized on a benchmark or standard created by the manufacturer or another organization.

Real world

Handling changing hardening standards

The security hardening guidelines for operating systems are frequently not released until months, or even in some cases almost a year, after the operating system itself is available. In enterprise computing environments, this often isn't an issue because the adoption cycle for new operating systems usually trails their release due to software testing and procurement cycles. Though employees might complain about using the older version of an operating system, the ability of a support organization to avoid having to test and roll out a new operating system or software package can be a huge time saver. Unfortunately, in organizations that are moving to a bring your own device (BYOD) model, the newest operating system will show up as soon as you can buy it from retail stores.

There are two common ways to handle this issue. The first is to use the previous operating system's basic settings. These are usually close enough to get most of the new operating system's security settings right. Unfortunately, this can be problematic, as it was when Mac OS changed firewall technology between Mac OS 10.5 and Mac OS 10.6. Applying hardening standards and configuration scripts built for Mac OS 10.5 resulted in firewall settings that didn't work in Mac OS 10.6.

The other way to tackle the problem is to build your own in-house hardening standard and tools. This can be time intensive and doesn't leverage community standards, which means that your own internal expertise might be all you have to rely on. In-house development does mean that you can probably have a hardening standard done quickly, possibly before the operating system is released to consumers if you work through the manufacturer's beta program.

Most organizations choose the standards they use based on what is available at the time, whether the assumptions of a standard fit the organization's needs and usage patterns, and whether the standard provides tools, utilities, or templates that can be applied to speed up deployment of the standard. Some standards are simply written lists of settings, which are much more difficult to deploy, whereas others come with a complete toolkit.

In this chapter, we use three examples of hardening standards: Windows 7 Security Baseline, the CIS's Security Configuration Benchmark for Red Hat Enterprise Linux 5, and the NSA's guides for both Windows 7 and Red Hat Linux 5. Each of these hardening standards provides a combination of configuration baselines that provide the basic settings that every system should have, along with templates that are applied to ensure that a system meets the hardening standard. In some cases, the standards are paired with tools that automatically configure systems properly or benchmarks that test them for their compliance with the standard.

> **MORE INFO** **CONFIGURATION STANDARDS**
>
> You can find the configuration standards we discuss in this chapter at the following sites:
>
> - NSA Security Configuration Guides (*http://www.nsa.gov/ia/mitigation_guidance/security_configuration_guides/*)
> - Microsoft's Security Compliance Manager, with security baselines (*http://technet.microsoft.com/en-us/library/cc677002.aspx*)
> - The Center for Internet Security (*http://benchmarks.cisecurity.org/*)
>
> Many other security standards exist, particularly for specific operating system versions or devices. Most manufacturers provide some information about how to secure their products, although they often don't provide a full hardening standard.

Configuration baselines

A common first element for hardening standards is the creation of a configuration baseline. The *configuration baseline* defines the basic settings that any system or application that will be considered secure must have. Because the baseline needs to be broadly applicable, it will normally have only the settings that every system must have and will then rely on additional templates, standards, and add-ons to provide more detail for more complex or specialized configurations.

In the NSA's hardening guide for Red Hat Linux 5, the configuration baseline and hardening tips are a single page, with a focus on server-centric operating system installations. Thus, if implemented, the baseline would require that administrators secure machines by performing the following actions:

- Remove the X-windows graphical user interface environment, because it is unnecessary for servers.
- Use iptables, a software firewall, and TCP wrappers, which allow the use of access control lists for network services.
- Configure SELinux, a security package for Linux that provides modifications to the operating system that allow greater security for the Linux kernel and broader mandatory access control capabilities.
- Set up kernel parameters that prevent specific attacks.

- Turn on network time services to make sure the system is properly synced to a central time server.

- Configure SSH to be more secure via techniques such as preventing root, the administrative user, from logging in remotely, or disable it entirely if it won't be used.

- Disable IPv6 if it won't be used, to prevent it from being an attack vector as discussed in Chapter 3, "Secure network design and management."

MORE INFO   ACCESS CONTROL LISTS

We talked about access control lists (ACLs) in Chapter 3, and we will discuss various types of ACLs, including mandatory access control (MAC) in Chapter 11, "Identity and access control."

In comparison to the NSA's guidelines for Red Hat Linux 5, Microsoft's baseline for Windows 7 is provided as a complete package with the Security Compliance Manager, a preconfigured set of templates, and a full set of documentation for the security settings and tools included in the package. Obviously, the more complete package is easier to deploy quickly, but both require knowledge of what the settings are doing to avoid issues.

MORE INFO   WINDOWS 7 SECURITY BASELINE

You can find the Windows 7 Security Baseline at *http://technet.microsoft.com/en-us/library/ ee712767.aspx.*

Templates

Templates, sometimes known as *configuration profiles*, are intended to ease the deployment of a security baseline. Templates provide an easy-to-modify configuration that can be applied to a system. For Windows systems, this can be done via the Microsoft Security Compliance Manager, with the template applied via Active Directory Domain Services or for standalone systems, as shown in Figure 6-1. the Security Compliance Manager provides extensive templates for both operating systems and applications such as Windows Internet Explorer. The interface allows detailed customization, with large amounts of detail. Note the settings in the example for a Windows 2008 Service Pack 2 domain controller.

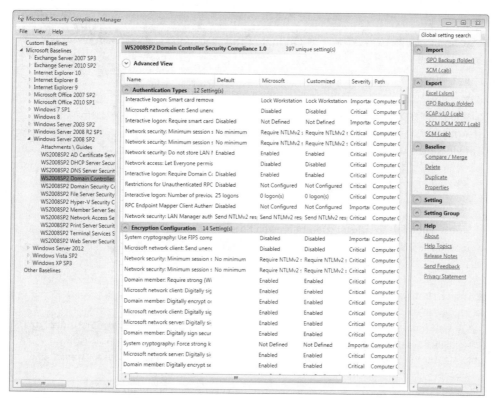

FIGURE 6-1 The Microsoft Security Compliance Manager tool provides per-setting control of security and other settings. Security Compliance Manager comes bundled with a set of prebuilt templates with policies that are ready for deployment, and that have been tested by Microsoft. This makes deploying configuration baselines easy, but most organizations will still need to review the templates they choose to use before deploying them.

Microsoft also provides the Microsoft Baseline Security Analyzer for most modern versions of Windows for both servers and workstations. The Baseline Security Analyzer provides the ability to scan for missing patches, security updates, and service packs, while also verifying some aspects of a system's security configuration. Unlike the Security Compliance Manager, it's not intended to be used as a template-based system to deploy security configuration standards as policy from a central Active Directory Domain Services server. You can see an example of the Baseline Security Analyzer in action in Figure 6-2, run on a typical Windows 7–based system. Note the options available for scans, which include checks for Windows vulnerabilities, weak passwords, IIS (Internet Information Services) and SQL vulnerabilities, updates, and the ability to set up automatic update options.

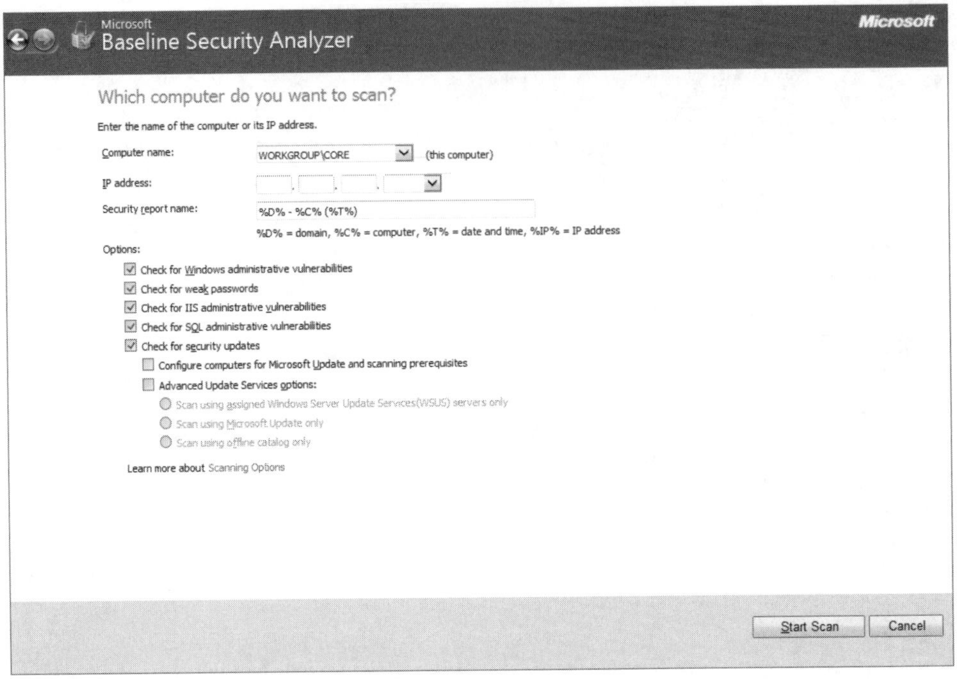

FIGURE 6-2 The Microsoft Baseline Security Analyzer allows you to configure options for scans.

After it is run, the Microsoft Baseline Security Analyzer uses a standard configuration template to assess the security of the systems it scans. In the example shown in Figure 6-3, the analyzer was used to scan a typical Windows 7–based system. The scan results note that a service pack hasn't been installed on the system, and that some accounts on the system have nonexpiring passwords. In addition, it provides details on the security of installed software, whether guest accounts are disabled, how many administrator accounts exist, and if the system properly restricts anonymous access.

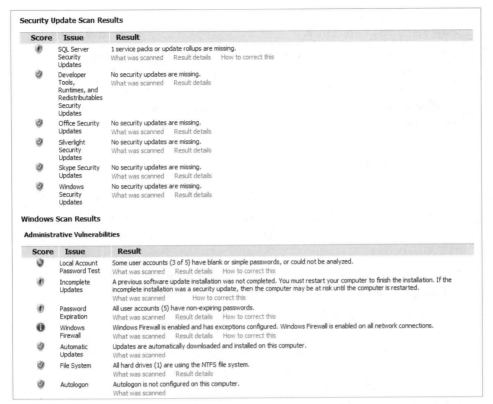

Security Update Scan Results

Score	Issue	Result
	SQL Server Security Updates	1 service packs or update rollups are missing. What was scanned Result details How to correct this
	Developer Tools, Runtimes, and Redistributables Security Updates	No security updates are missing. What was scanned Result details
	Office Security Updates	No security updates are missing. What was scanned Result details
	Silverlight Security Updates	No security updates are missing. What was scanned Result details
	Skype Security Updates	No security updates are missing. What was scanned Result details
	Windows Security Updates	No security updates are missing. What was scanned Result details

Windows Scan Results

Administrative Vulnerabilities

Score	Issue	Result
	Local Account Password Test	Some user accounts (3 of 5) have blank or simple passwords, or could not be analyzed. What was scanned Result details How to correct this
	Incomplete Updates	A previous software update installation was not completed. You must restart your computer to finish the installation. If the incomplete installation was a security update, then the computer may be at risk until the computer is restarted. What was scanned How to correct this
	Password Expiration	All user accounts (5) have non-expiring passwords. What was scanned Result details How to correct this
	Windows Firewall	Windows Firewall is enabled and has exceptions configured. Windows Firewall is enabled on all network connections. What was scanned Result details How to correct this
	Automatic Updates	Updates are automatically downloaded and installed on this computer. What was scanned
	File System	All hard drives (1) are using the NTFS file system. What was scanned Result details
	Autologon	Autologon is not configured on this computer. What was scanned

FIGURE 6-3 Microsoft Baseline Security Analyzer scan results show issues, configuration problems, and correct settings.

Secure system configuration and management

After an organization has hardened a system to meet security standards, either by using a template, a central management and policy tool such as the Microsoft System Center Configuration Manager (SCCM), or manually, it is important for the organization to ensure that it remains secure by managing the system in a secure way. This is done by ensuring that a secure system configuration is maintained and monitored. Part of that maintenance and monitoring is *remediation*, or restoring systems to compliance if they deviate from them.

There are several underlying concepts that hardening standards and long-term security maintenance share. These include keeping software and operating systems up to date, patching and implementing patch management, disabling unnecessary ports and monitoring ports that are in use, and implementing administrative interface security, host firewalls, and password and account management.

Fail safe vs. fail open

One of the important choices that must be faced by organizations that are designing security controls is whether security controls and systems should fail safe (also sometimes referred to as *fail secure*) or fail open. This critical choice is often made based on the effect that the system's failure mode would have on the organization and its employees.

Systems that fail open are designed to allow access when they fail. A common example of a fail open design choice is that made with electronically controlled access doors. In the event of a fire, many organizations have security doors that are designed to fail open: when a fire alarm goes off, the fire doors unlock, allowing occupants to escape and letting firefighters in. This makes fires a potential security risk, but the safety risk to employees outweighs the security risk to the organization.

A system that fails to a safe mode will continue to provide security when the underlying system fails. Bank vaults typically fail safe, meaning that they remain locked during a power outage. Unlike in areas that use security doors, in banks, employees typically are not in a vault with the vault door closed, making the risk of a fail closed design acceptable.

Similar considerations apply for networked security devices. A fail open authentication mechanism might be preferable for low-value applications that need to be online and always available. Failing closed is much more common than failing open for all but the least sensitive network devices and operating systems.

Unfortunately, failing open or closed isn't always a decision that is made with the input of security staff. One of the authors of this book encountered a software package used for authentication on a large-scale research network that failed open instead of closed. The research network users relied on the authentication software as a primary security mechanism without knowing that the developers had opted to allow authentication to be accepted even if certificates in use by users failed to be accepted. The developers had made the decision that failing to log users on when an error occurred wasn't acceptable because research might be impeded. Unfortunately, this also meant that the entire authentication mechanism couldn't be trusted. Multiple institutions were required to install replacement authentication software throughout an enormous research network. In the end, hundreds of hours of staff time were lost due to a security decision that the administrators of the network weren't even aware had been made without them.

Updates and patches

After a system has been configured to meet baseline security standards, it needs to have software *updates* known as *patches* installed, and it needs to remain patched on an ongoing basis to stay secure. Other updates, such as those that add functionality or that update software to newer versions, might not be necessary for security reasons but might be desired by users or the organization. Because vulnerabilities are constantly being discovered in both operating system and applications software, patch management is a key part of securing systems. In addition, patch management is an important part of staying within configuration baselines and remaining compliant with security standards.

> **NOTE PATCHES, UPDATES, AND WORKAROUNDS**
>
> Some organizations make a distinction between patches, which fix flaws, and updates, which add functionality, but it isn't an industry-wide standard. It's also worth noting the other way to address a problem if a patch isn't available: a workaround, which might or might not be vendor supported but which can prevent or help prevent a problem.

Companies responsible for software packages typically release advisories about security issues with their software or hardware. The bar chart in Figure 6-4 shows the rate at which the three vendors responsible for the operating systems we are using as examples in this chapter have released advisories and related patches.

The table lists the total number of advisories released by Microsoft for Windows, Apple for Mac OS, and Red Hat for Red Hat Linux Enterprise 5, from 2007 to 2012. It is worth noting that although this gives some insight into the relative patch rate, simply comparing rates like this can lead to misconceptions. Here, Microsoft's patches include multiple Office patches; Apple's patches cover more than one version of Mac OS; and Red Hat Enterprise Linux 5 patches can be quite specific. In addition, this table does not include re-releases of patches, which occurred for all three vendors at various times. You can find full data about these patches, including details of what they affect, at the original sources:

- Microsoft's security patch bulletin archives at *http://technet.microsoft.com/en-us/security/bulletinarchive?y=2007&m=1*

- Apple security updates list at *http://support.apple.com/kb/ht1222*

- Red Hat Linux Server 5 patch list at *https://rhn.redhat.com/errata/rhel-server-errata-security.html*

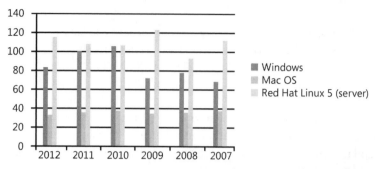

FIGURE 6-4 This chart shows advisories per year for major operating system vendors.

Patching in a production environment has its own set of dangers. Patches can introduce new issues with existing software, and some patches have caused significant issues for the systems they are installed on. Patch issues such as the problem found with MS13-036/2823324, which resulted in crashes when Windows 7–based systems restarted make system administrators reluctant to patch immediately after a patch is released.

Updates can also cause issues, even when they appear relatively innocuous. In 2006, McAfee released a virus definition (DAT) file for their VirusScan product that improperly identified files for many popular programs as malware. Organizations that had their anti-virus products set to delete viruses rather than quarantine them found that their workstations had deleted their productivity software, resulting in significant issues for their staff.

By now you're asking yourself how you can balance the need for quick security patching against the potential dangers that patches and updates can create. That's why organizations and vendors have developed a variety of patch management methodologies.

Patch management methodologies

Because so many patches are released each year, patching systems consistently and in a way that can be centrally monitored and controlled is important for most organizations. Fortunately, there are a variety of ways to manage patches.

Most modern operating systems and devices, and even many applications, have an automated patch management system built in, which means that personally owned devices have a fighting chance of being up to date. Unfortunately, many device owners don't patch, or delay patches for convenience. If patching is left in the hands of individuals, it often doesn't happen, or it fails and isn't detected.

> **NOTE INSTALLING PATCHES OFFLINE**
>
> One of the safest ways to install patches on a newly built system is to install them offline. In fact, systems that are being installed should be built either offline or on a secure network segment where they can be protected from attacks. Many operating systems do not come fully locked down by default, or the installation media or package might be out of date, making them vulnerable to attack out of the box.

Because a single unpatched machine can provide attackers with an attractive way into a network, enterprises usually want a centralized patch management capability. Centralized patch management and reporting allows administrators to decide when patches are released and which workstations and devices receive them, and it also allows them to track whether patches have been installed properly and report on where issues might exist.

Patch management tools are provided by most major operating system vendors for desktop and server operating systems, but third-party add-on patch management systems are necessary for tracking patches for most other applications. Patch management tools usually have a combination of a policy-based patching system with an in-depth status and compliance reporting capability. Because patch management systems often cover a broad range of operating systems and applications, they can provide a single view of your organization's patch and update status.

Real world

Protecting unpatched systems

One of the authors of this book experienced the pain of online patching first hand. An employee was assigned to rebuild a Windows XP system and was given media for an unpatched version of Windows XP with known network vulnerabilities. The employee proceeded to install the operating system with his workstation on the network, and before the installation had completely finished, the system had been attacked and taken over due to a vulnerable service.

The compromised system was detected when it connected to a botnet controller, and the system was conveniently just down the hall from the security office. A security staff member walked down the hall to talk to the surprised employee, and told him to rebuild the system offline. He did, and then he plugged the system back in when the installation was complete, but before patching. The system was immediately compromised again, and again the attack was detected. The security staff member took another walk down the hall, this time with a thumb drive of patches—and this time, he took the employee's Ethernet cable away and left the thumb drive with him, with instructions to come retrieve the network cable when he was done patching.

This entire scenario could have been avoided with a simple personal firewall device, or even a protected network with access out to patching sites, but no access in to the unprotected system. Unfortunately, the organization had not provided those tools.

Disabling unnecessary services and ports

Operating systems provide a variety of network services that they use to allow connections from other machines. File sharing, print sharing, and other services are common on workstations, and servers must provide services to perform their duties as servers. In addition to these desirable services, systems also expose services for administration, remote control, and a host of other functions.

Because services allow remote connections to the system, they're also a popular target for attack. Without exposed services, worms and other network-aware malware would have nothing to attack. If attackers couldn't reach services, they would be limited to attacking client software such as web browsers. Thus, limiting the services that are available on a system, and the service ports that can be reached by systems connecting to the system, is a valuable practice for security administrators.

The set of services that a server or workstation starts out with after a fresh installation are known as the system's default services. These often include services that might not fit the system's role or that are not desirable to the person or organization to which the system belongs. Part of security baselining, which we discussed earlier in this chapter, is to define what default services should be enabled for each operating system.

As shown in Figure 6-5, Windows services can be set to automatic start, delayed start, manual start, or disabled. In most cases, services are either set to automatic or disabled, depending on the security baseline settings applied to the system. Fortunately, modern Windows, Linux, and Mac OS systems tend to come with their more dangerous services disabled rather than enabled by default.

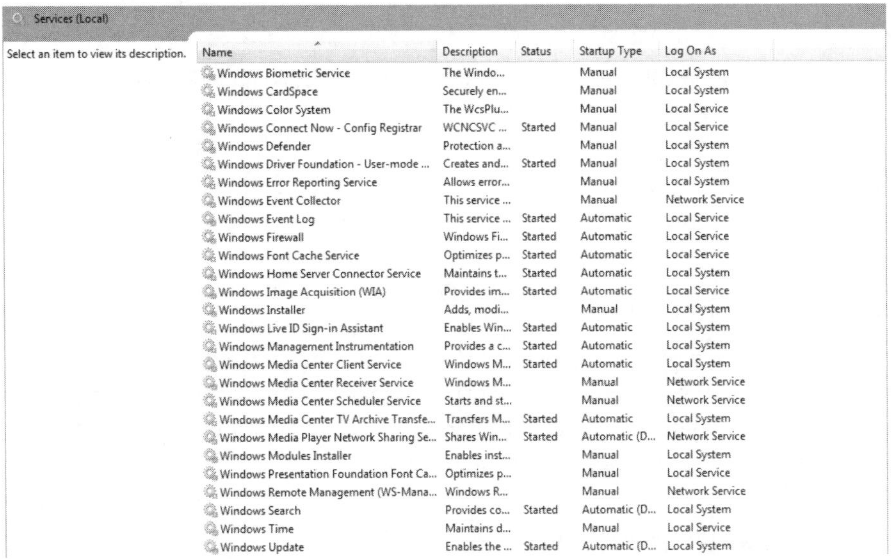

FIGURE 6-5 Windows 7 Services Control Panel allows you to set options for services.

NOTE **CHECKING RUNNING LINUX SERVICES**

Linux has a variety of ways to check running services. For many current Linux systems, the command *service –status-all* will show all running services.

One common problem with services is ensuring that they remain in the state you want them to be in. If a service is disabled, detecting that it has been re-enabled is important for the security of the system. At times, vendor updates, patches, or new software installations can change the enabled status of a service. Attackers often turn services on for their own purposes, as well.

Fortunately, there are several ways to keep services under control. As with other controls, a defense in depth strategy helps:

- Use centralized policy enforcement to control security baselines and configurations via policy.

- Use vulnerability or port scanning tools to periodically check that systems aren't exposing unexpected services.

- Deploy firewalls to protect systems by blocking services and ports that aren't necessary for the systems behind the firewall to expose.

> **MORE INFO**   **VULNERABILITY SCANNING**
>
> You can read more about vulnerability scanning in Chapter 7, "Vulnerability assessment and management."

One final way to help protect services is to change the port that the service uses. This is often considered a form of security through obscurity, or attempting to provide security for something by making it hard to find, and it works by assuming that attackers will only look for the service on the port on which it normally appears. Despite security by obscurity's shortfalls as a strategy, this frequently does work against automated attack tools and worms that only look at default service ports, such as SSH scanners. Simply changing the SSH port on a system to something other than port 22 can prevent many scanners from ever seeing the service. Unfortunately, this does mean that all users for the system must make sure that they change their SSH client configuration to use the proper port.

> **MORE INFO**   **COMMON SERVICE PORTS**
>
> We covered common service ports in Chapter 3.

> **Quick check**
>
> 1. What are two ways that you can use to identify services running on a system?
> 2. Why must you check service status and the list of available services on a regular basis?
>
> **Quick check answers**
>
> 1. You can identify services running on a system by checking the system's internal list of running services or by performing a port scan on the system. Port scans might not always identify every running service, particularly if the full range of potential service ports is not scanned or if a firewall is in place that blocks the scan.
> 2. Many services are modified by patches, and some might be enabled or re-enabled when an update or patch is installed. In addition, attackers might compromise a system and start a service. Both of these are good reasons for regularly reviewing the services that a machine is presenting to the network.

Host firewalls

Many hardening standards rely on a host firewall to provide an additional layer of security after unnecessary services have been disabled. Host firewalls provide an effective part of a defense in depth strategy because they can block access to services that might accidentally be configured on a system, and they can also block outbound access from systems that should not be able to access other systems on the network.

Host firewalls typically offer a limited set of features, with some providing only basic packet filtering or stateful packet filtering capabilities. As shown in Figure 6-6, the Windows host firewall can be set to block programs that aren't on a list of allowed programs, it can have different settings depending on what network it is connected to, and it can notify the user of the PC when a new program attempts to connect. The Windows host firewall identifies both private trusted networks and public networks, allowing different firewall settings for both environments. By default, it blocks inbound connections and allows all outbound connections, and it can be set to notify users when a new program tries to send traffic to other systems.

> **MORE INFO** **FIREWALL TYPES**
>
> We discussed the different types of firewalls, including stateful and packet filtering firewalls, as well as the differences between host and network firewalls, in Chapter 3.

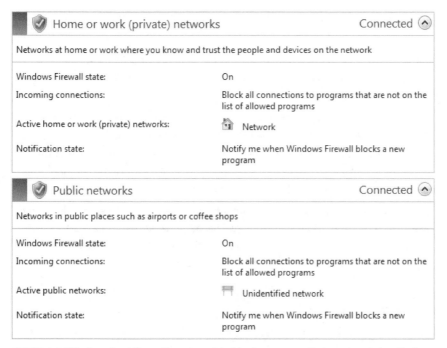

FIGURE 6-6 Windows host firewall can be set to block programs that meet certain criteria.

Many enterprises use a centrally managed firewall either because they require more capabilities from their firewall or because they want to take advantage of central reporting and configuration. Enterprise firewall settings are normally configured via a central policy management system such as Microsoft's Active Directory Group Policy. This allows enterprise system administrators to ensure that predictable firewall rules are in place for many systems. More advanced firewall settings and reporting can be achieved with commercial host firewall products, which are often paired with host IPS (intrusion prevention system) software.

Protecting management interfaces and applications

Network devices, appliances, and servers each have some form of administrative interface. Network devices and appliances are increasingly using web-based management interfaces, but most also retain a command-line interface via SSH.

> **MORE INFO** **MANAGEMENT INTERFACES**
>
> We talked about Telnet, SSH, HTTP, and HTTPS in Chapter 3.

Management interfaces are an attractive target for attackers because they provide control over the entire system and are often not properly secured. Many management interfaces come equipped with a default user name and password out of the box, and it's not uncommon for an administrator to forget to change the defaults. Unfortunately, sometimes they're purposely left unchanged.

Useful strategies for protecting management interfaces are similar to those for any other service:

- Disable the service if it isn't needed. Removing the unencrypted Telnet service and unencrypted web service that many devices provide, but leaving SSH and HTTPS, is a common practice.

- Change default administrator account passwords, or replace the accounts entirely to prevent password-guessing attacks against a known account.

- Make sure that the administrative console or interface is fully patched. Because the services often rely on a web server or SSH server, you might actually be running one or more services you don't consider during your normal patching.

- Finally, many organizations choose to create a distinct network for their administrative interfaces, which requires additional security. This might require using a trusted host from which to log on, or an incoming VPN connection for all network users to a secure network segment that doesn't connect to the Internet.

Real world

Nonsecure management interfaces

Old network devices frequently don't provide encrypted connections for their management interfaces by default. This means that you're likely to see Telnet and HTTP services exposed by default, and because the protocols are unencrypted, any passwords or other management data you send to that service will be able to be sniffed off the wire. If you run into old devices, you should check to see if you can replace Telnet with SSH, and enable certificates for SSL or TLS services for any web interfaces. If you can't, you'll have to isolate the management interfaces and networks to keep them secure.

Password protection

After you have disabled unnecessary services and ensured that access to services that you want to provide is secured, the final layer of protection is often the passwords associated with administrative and user accounts. Hardening systems through password protection is important, and many systems and devices have poor password security out of the box.

Default passwords are insecure by default

admin:admin, root:password, administrator:blank—each of these is a common user name and password pairing that is the default administrative user credential on a network device or appliance. One of the easiest ways an attacker can gain access to a device or system is by using one of these or a host of other default user names and passwords.

Most appliances and network-connected devices come from the factory with a default administrative account set up, often with a very simple password. Enormous lists of these user name and password pairings exist on the Internet, and many are posted on the support sites for the devices themselves. At worst, a few minutes with the device's manual will usually reveal how to log on.

You might think this wouldn't be a frequently encountered issue, because it's a simple matter to change the user name and password, but it is very common. Thus, it's a common best practice to perform an audit of default user names and passwords for anything connected to a network on a periodic basis. Scanning tools such as Nessus, HP's WebInspect, and many others automatically scan for common default user names and passwords and can help you find vulnerable systems.

MORE INFO   **MORE DETAIL ON PASSWORDS**

In Chapter 11 we will talk about passwords and password practices in more detail.

Hardening techniques involving passwords are relatively simple. Most hardening guidelines provide advice that mirrors the following list:

- Change default passwords.
- Set password complexity settings, if they exist.
- Ensure that no accounts exist that do not have a password set.

These simple settings will prevent the most common attacks against password-protected accounts and services, but monitoring for attacks against passwords is still important, and we discuss it later in this chapter as part of the exploration of monitoring techniques.

Unfortunately, the instructions in this simple list can't always be followed. One of the most troublesome types of password is the firmware or hardware password found on many embedded devices and appliances. These devices come preconfigured with passwords set by the manufacturer. PCs, Macs, and other systems can also have firmware passwords set to protect their BIOS< which provides the basic foundation that starts the system. PCs typically don't have a BIOS password set when they arrive, but organizations sometimes set the BIOS password to prevent attackers from tinkering with drive boot order or to keep BIOS-level security tools safe.

Real world

Unchangeable administrative passwords

Some devices have passwords that can't be changed, either due to the fact that they're a permanent setting for the device or because a vendor doesn't allow for password changes in its software. In fact, one device that one of the authors of this book ran into re-set its default administrative user name and password to admin:admin any time it restarted. Much to our chagrin, the device was directly connected to the Internet for research and was regularly compromised.

Fortunately, it is relatively rare to run into cases like these. If you do encounter a situation like this, alternate means of protecting the device or system might be required, such as installing a hardware or software firewall, limiting access to a management network or only from specific trusted IP addresses, or even removing the device from the network entirely.

Disabling unnecessary accounts

In addition to the default user names we talked about earlier, many systems come with one or more unnecessary built-in accounts enabled by default. In Windows, the guest account might be enabled and can allow access to a Windows-based system without a password. Fortunately, newer versions of Windows disable the guest account by default, as shown in Figure 6-7. It is very simple to disable the Windows administrator and guest accounts and rename guest accounts in Windows 7. The security policy snap-in can be run by typing *secpol.msc* at the Run prompt or it can be accessed via Control Panel.

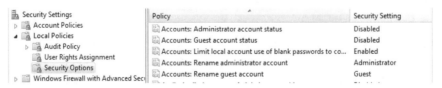

FIGURE 6-7 These Windows account settings show that the administrator and guest accounts are disabled by default.

Another common practice is to rename default accounts with different user names to avoid password-guessing attacks. As with many other configuration changes, this can provide some security through obscurity by making it harder to guess the name of an important account such as root or administrator, but it doesn't stop attacks from occurring. Many hardening standards still suggest changing the default administrator account for the same reasons that default service ports might be changed: it makes it harder for dumb malware to force its way in.

Real world

Renaming accounts

In 2006 a talented group of system administrators built a large Active Directory Domain Services domain with thousands of systems that were managed by the central domain controllers. They used password best practices that were common at the time and required their users to change their passwords on a regular basis.

Unfortunately, one user in the domain installed a trojan that stole their system's local password database when it was installed and sent it to a group of hackers. These hackers cracked the passwords in the local database and found out that the administrators of the domain had changed the local administrator for the machine to a different name and had equipped it with a strong password. Unfortunately, the administrators had also used that same local administrator account and password on every system in the domain.

The attackers exploited their knowledge to compromise hundreds of systems until they finally stumbled across one of the domain administrators' workstations. There they deployed tools that allowed them to capture the administrator's domain administration credentials, allowing them to seize control of the domain controller itself.

In the end, the administrators didn't get much benefit out of renaming their accounts because they left them remotely accessible and used the same password everywhere. The tradeoff between ease of local administrative access didn't work out, and when they rebuilt their domain they used a different local administrative password for each machine.

Network device hardening

All of the techniques we've discussed for system hardening are part of common network device hardening standards as well. In addition, there are a few network device–specific port security techniques that the CompTIA Security+ exam specifically focuses on. They are MAC (hardware network address) limiting and filtering, including port security; the 802.1x standard; and disabling unused ports.

MAC limiting and filtering

Every network device on a TCP/IP network has one or more physical hardware addresses known as MAC addresses. One way to filter the systems that can connect to a wired or wireless network is to filter the MAC addresses that the switch or wireless access point will allow to connect to it. The technique used for Cisco switches is called port security, although other manufacturers might refer to it by slightly different names.

MAC filtering is vulnerable to attackers who change their MAC addresses, a relatively trivial operation under many circumstances. Port security and similar tools fight this by limiting the number of MAC addresses that can connect to a single port and the number of addresses that a port can have connect to it over time. This still doesn't prevent an attacker from cloning a valid MAC address, but it can decrease the chances of a casual connection attempt succeeding.

802.1x

Port security, as well as 802.1x, are both useful for limiting who connects to your network. Network jacks are often available in rooms that might be accessible to an intruder or even an unauthorized employee. Using port security to limit the systems that can connect, or authenticating users at the port, makes sense for any area where those risks might exist.

Disabling ports

The final technique that the CompTIA Security+ exam covers for preventing unauthorized connection to a network is quite simple. Disabling ports is as simple as it sounds, and many organizations disable any port that isn't registered to a known PC. If your switches and other network devices don't allow ports to be enabled via a management interface, this can also be as simple as unplugging a network cable from the device and ensuring that users can't plug it back in.

Though disabling network ports is a simple technique, it can be labor intensive, and the balance between time spent maintaining a large network with a default configuration that includes disabled ports and the ease of setting up a new machine up can be difficult to determine.

Monitoring and reporting

Monitoring and reporting are key elements in an organization's security plan. Monitoring focuses on tracking items such as system logs, event logs, and security device notifications, including those from intrusion detection and prevention system, anti-virus management platforms, firewalls, and a host of other devices. Reporting systems then take the mass of data that a complex monitoring infrastructure can generate and make the data more easily accessible. Thus, both elements are necessary to a successful information security practice.

Continuous security monitoring

One of the most important concepts in information security is monitoring. Although we have focused on attacks and defenses thus far, the ways in which we detect those attacks, and how we ensure that our defenses are working, are equally important. *Continuous security monitoring* is the process of using tools and human intelligence to watch over a secure environment on an ongoing basis.

> **NOTE** **NIST AND SECURITY MONITORING**
>
> NIST standard 800-137 defines continuous monitoring as "maintaining ongoing awareness of information security, vulnerabilities, and threats to support organizational risk management decisions."

In this part of the chapter, we explore system logging, including how logs are monitored, what logs contain, what is worth logging and how to determine when and what to log, and the differences between Windows and Linux/Unix logs. It's worthwhile to note that Mac OS is built on top of a Unix operating system, which means that we can cover Mac OS logging at the same time we explore Linux log concepts.

System log monitoring

One of the first things that comes to mind when security professionals look at monitoring and reporting is system logging. Workstations, servers, and even mobile devices all have the ability to generate logs of information about what they are doing, what users have done or failed to do, what services are running, and whether applications are performing their functions correctly.

System logging can be a complex topic because of the variety of logs and the sheer number of log events that can occur. It is important to know what you want to log, and why you want to log it, but it is also critical to actually look at the logs you generate. Many organizations log massive amount of event information but don't have a usable process to filter through those events to detect problems. In fact, many system and application administrators cannot answer the question, "What logs does your system or application generate, and which indicate that something is wrong?"

Now we'll dive into what you need in a good logging environment, and we'll start with something that makes logs useful: time.

Time stamps and log rotation

One of the key elements of monitoring and logging is capturing the time that the log event occurred, and ensuring that it is accurate. For most modern systems, this is relatively easy. You simply point the system to a system that provides network time via the *network time protocol (NTP)*. This can be one of a large number of public NTP servers. Many organizations use GPS technology to sync to satellites that provide accurate time, thus ensuring that their servers are all recording time and thus logging properly.

Real world

Time sink

When you don't have system time set accurately, you can spend hours chasing multiple attacks. You might then find out that it was the same attack at the same time on servers that didn't have their time synced! One of the authors of this book found that four servers that were being investigated after a compromise were each set to different times, despite being in the same room and run by the same administrator. One was using Coordinated Universal Time (Greenwich Mean Time), another was set to the local time zone, and two others were each between 10 and 20 minutes off from the actual time. Nobody involved in the investigation noticed the issue at first, leading to hours spent on a wild goose chase for more information about the attacks we saw logged five hours apart! Simply setting the servers to use NTP, the network time protocol, and knowing what time zone they were set to, would have avoided the issue entirely, and that change was identified and implemented as part of our incident response remediation process.

MORE INFO **NTP**

You can read about NTP, including lists of public time servers, at *www.ntp.org*.

Another key part of log management is *log rotation*. Log rotation is a process intended to keep logs from filling entire system drives as they log event after event for the life of the system. Instead, operating systems and applications typically have a log rotation setting with multiple options, allowing you to make the logs rotate based on several things. Typical options include rotation of the logs at a certain size or based on how old entries are. Rotation also often includes settings that allow you to compress old log files and to keep them for a certain amount of time.

Organizations that are building a configuration standard also need to set a logging standard based on how the systems are used and what the logs might be used for. For a single user workstation, retaining authentication logs for months on end might not be particularly useful. On the other hand, if you provide hosting services for websites, your authentication logs for hundreds or thousands of users might be one of the most important logs you have, if you need to prove that a certain user was logged on at a specific time.

Log rotation is also important when logs fill up. Some malware can fill logs with useless data, making it difficult to detect the actual actions taken by an attacker.

Quick check

1. Why is having a consistent time setting across multiple machines important?
2. What is the technique for replacing old log data with new log data called?

Quick check answers

1. Time synchronization via the Network Time Protocol (NTP) is important because it results in logs that have the same time stamp for events that occurred at the same time. If system time isn't synchronized, events can appear to have happened at widely different times, making incident investigation much more difficult.

2. Log rotation is used to replace old logs with new logs. Various systems provide different capabilities, but most offer a choice between replacing old log entries with newer entries as they come in or archiving old logs for a set amount of time. Most log rotation systems also offer the ability to choose either a time-based or size-based log rotation capability.

Windows vs. Linux logging

Windows logs differ from most Linux and Unix logs in several ways. Windows logs events to a central logging system, which stores a variety of logs including application, security, setup, and system logs in a single location. Linux and Unix systems and services generally place logs into a directory such as /var/log, but this can vary depending on the application that is providing the log. In Figures 6-8 and 6-9, you can see an example of Linux and Windows authentication logs for root and administrator, the administrative users for each operating system, respectively. Figure 6-8 shows a Linux logon entry for a local logon. In the Linux example, there is the entry note that a user with a user name of root logged on, and that it was on /dev/tty1, a local console logon via the keyboard on the system.

```
Apr 27 17:34:42 bt login[31483]: pam_sm_authenticate: Called
Apr 27 17:34:42 bt login[31483]: pam_sm_authenticate: username = [root]
Apr 27 17:34:42 bt login[31483]: pam_unix(login:session): session opened for user root by root(uid=0)
Apr 27 17:34:42 bt login[31504]: ROOT LOGIN  on '/dev/tty1'
```

FIGURE 6-8 These Linux authentication log entries for root show a local logon on a terminal.

Figure 6-9 shows a Windows example in which a system called Core, which is part of a stand-alone workgroup, has an account called CORE logging onto it.

An account was successfully logged on.

Subject:
        Security ID: SYSTEM
        Account Name: CORE$
        Account Domain: WORKGROUP
        Logon ID: 0x3e7

Logon Type: 5

Log Name:	Security		
Source:	Microsoft Windows security	Logged:	4/27/2013 5:29:20 PM
Event ID:	4624	Task Category:	Logon
Level:	Information	Keywords:	Audit Success
User:	N/A	Computer:	Core
OpCode:	Info		
More Information:	Event Log Online Help		

FIGURE 6-9 This Windows authentication log entry shows Core logging on.

Linux and Unix logs are frequently captured in a format known as syslog, and syslog data is designed to be sent to remote syslog servers for analysis and storage. Syslog is a plaintext protocol that has been in use since the 1980s and is widely supported by everything from network devices, servers, and printers to embedded systems.

Syslog messages include information about a facility such as cron (a time-based system for running scripts), syslog (a Unix/Linux logging facility), or auth (an authentication handler log), and include a severity such as Alert, Critical, Notice, or Error, as well as the message content. This allows them to be easily accepted by standardized syslog-handling systems.

Modern Windows logs are captured in an XML format, which allows them to be more easily accessed by a variety of tools. Like Linux and Unix logs, Windows logs can be sent to a central location; however, this must generally be a Windows domain controller or workstation, and unlike syslog, the Windows logging format is not a broadly adopted standard. Many organizations choose to deploy a syslog tool for Windows to allow Windows-based systems to send syslog-formatted messages to the same central servers that their other devices send logs to.

Reading logs: log parsing

Historically, logs were a challenge to monitor due to the variety of formats that they used. Without standardization, log analysis required specialized tools and often ended up relying on home-built utilities to find specific log events. Over time, this has improved as Windows moved to its XML format, and as syslog became a recognized standard.

Log analysis is still a complex topic due to the variety of applications and events that are logged in a typical enterprise network. Fortunately, a variety of tools have been created to read and sort logs, from the SIM and SIEM tools we will discuss later in this chapter to tools like Splunk and Sawmill, which are designed to accept a broad array of log files. After these tools receive the logs, they can then be sorted and analyzed by using powerful built-in tools.

Manual review of logs remains a useful skill, particularly when you are conducting incident response. Thus, you'll find it useful to be aware of where to find Linux, Mac OS, and Windows logs, and the basics of what they contain.

Event logs

Windows-based systems use a tool called the Event Viewer to show information from several different specific *event logs* in one place. The Windows Event Viewer is the easiest way to understand what the system has logged in a single place, as shown in Figure 6-10. The Windows Event Viewer provides access to and control over configuration of Application, Security, Setup, and System logs, as well as events received from other systems. You can change how logs are rotated, their maximum size, and how events are received from systems (known as Subscriptions) via the Event Viewer.

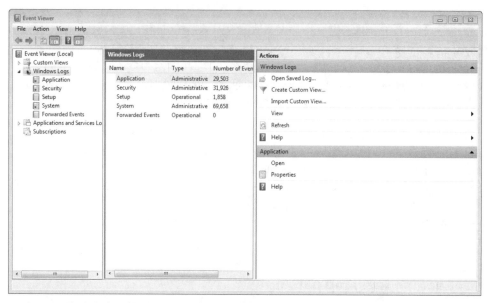

FIGURE 6-10 The Windows Event Viewer displays a variety of event types.

Event logs in Windows include five types of events. These are:

- Application events, which are generated by programs the system is running.
- Forwarded events received from other systems.
- Security events, known as audit logs.
- Setup events, which log entries about software installation and updates.
- System events such as service startup and shutdown events.

Audit logs

 Audit logging is a general term for the collection of logs that provides a way to track the actions of users. Often auditing is enabled for specific events that involve the use of privileges that specific users or accounts have, but auditing can also be used for broader monitoring.

Audit logs need to track the user or service that performed an action, the time and date at which the action occurred, the action that was performed, and whether it succeeded or failed. In addition, the log needs to include information about whether the user was a local user, accessing the system from a keyboard, or if the user was a remote user. If the user is a remote user, the system should log the IP address that the connection came from.

As you explore the specific types of logs available in Windows, Linux, and Mac OS systems, bear in mind the need for auditable log entries. We will discuss how each of these entries could be used for auditing purposes as we review each type.

> **NOTE   HELP! THERE ARE TOO MANY WINDOWS LOG EVENT TYPES!**
>
> There are hundreds of Windows log entries, and keeping them all straight can be a challenge! You can find a list of all of them, along with descriptions, the versions of Windows that generate that log, a list of fields, and examples at *http://www.ultimatewindowssecurity.com/ securitylog/encyclopedia/Default.aspx*.

Success vs. failure

Most audit logging systems have two basic events that they can record: success and failure. Each provides useful information, but deciding when to log success, failure, or both is not only important, but often challenging.

Audit logs of successful actions are particularly useful when it is important to know what users have done, or when they are using a system. This means that when use of credentials is important, success should be logged. Success doesn't reliably inform you of when attacks are being attempted, because most success logs will be legitimate users performing actions that they have rights to do.

Success logs can also be useful when you are attempting to ensure that activities and events are occurring when and how they are supposed to. Thus, monitoring for success can be important to make sure services start, or that an application shuts down properly. Here, failure can also be useful, and both log events might be combined to tell the full story of a system's health.

Audit logs of failure events are very useful when used to detect inappropriate access attempts. This can be as simple as detecting a user who is attempting to install software that he or she not allowed to install, or who is attempting to log on to a system that he or she has no rights to. It can also be far more complex, because a subtle series of failure events can indicate that an attacker has ensured that critical services such as anti-virus protection don't start on a machine as a rootkit locks it down for the attacker's convenience.

Fortunately for security administrators, operating system and device vendors often provide guidelines for which success and failure events to monitor. Microsoft notes that system events should be logged with both success and failure enabled because system events are relatively fewer in number, and the information is of relatively high value. Conversely, they only suggest logging success in policy changes on domain controllers

This advice would make intrusion detection harder, because failures for logons and policy changes might be related to an attack. In most cases for an Active Directory Domain Services environment in a secure organizational network, the great majority of failures are going to be accidental due to typos by users or due to an improperly made change to domain policy.

> *MORE INFO* **AUDIT LOG SETTING RECOMMENDATIONS**
>
> You can read more about Microsoft's audit log–setting suggestions, including the reasoning behind each change, at *http://go.microsoft.com/fwlink/?LinkId=92229*. Note that although this says that it applies only to Windows Server 2003, Microsoft continues to point to it from their Windows Server 2008 documentation. The basic concepts and advice provided is still good, and the thought process is a great model for how to make decisions about audit settings.

Real world

When the logs are gone

During an incident one of the authors of this book was involved in, a group of Linux systems were compromised by a hacker who was quite familiar with how to exploit them. The systems were heavily used and very important to one particular group of the organization's staff, which meant that the compromise gained a lot of attention, and the cause of the exploit needed to be identified quickly.

Unfortunately, the attacker knew enough to wipe the system logs for the machines, which were found in /var/log, as well as several other locations that contained information about their activities, such as the console history for the accounts the hacker used. This meant that all of the information about who had logged onto the system, what the attacker did, and any useful information from the application logs about errors that might have pointed out how the intruder made it in, was all gone.

Because there was no information about what had occurred on the system, we created an image of the drives and imported it into forensic software, and then used that software to create a timeline of the files on the machine. We were able to locate the point in time when system files and applications started to be replaced, and worked in each direction from there, assessing whether file changes were part of the intrusion. In the end, we discovered that our intruder had exploited a service that one of our users was running on a single system, then used that user's credentials to move through the rest of the systems by using privilege escalation attacks to gain root access.

The organization learned from its mistakes: all of our Linux systems were soon set to log to a central location, allowing us to have a secure copy of the logs the next time an intruder broke in. Our lesson learned was that it's rare to have systems that can't be compromised at some point in their lifespan in a large organization, but it is possible to have secure, useful logs to work from when a compromise does happen.

Now that we've looked at the types of log information that can be collected and why they might be used, it's time to take a deeper look at each of these types of events. We will also look at their Unix/Linux equivalents. As you review each of these log types, pay attention to what they capture and how they might be used to monitor for attacks as well as day-to-day operational problems for an organization.

Application logs

Application logs in Windows contain information logged by or about applications that are run on the system, as shown in Figure 6-11.

There are five primary types of log entries captured by the Windows Application log:

- **Information**   Describes successful operations such as a service startup or completion of a task
- **Warning**   Can provide information about problems
- **Error**   Describes major problems such as service failures
- **Success**   Audits for logons that succeed
- **Failure**   Audits for logons that fail

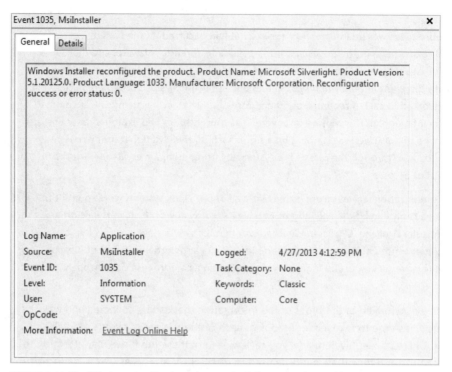

FIGURE 6-11 The Windows Application log contains information logged by or about applications.

The Windows Application log can provide data about application installation, configuration changes, and updates. In the log entry in Figure 6-11, the Windows Installer service has modified Microsoft's Silverlight plug-in, a tool frequently used for streaming services. This is an information log and is logged as SYSTEM, which means that the operating system itself logged the entry. Note that the date and time are shown, and that an event ID is captured, allowing for events to be searched for and analyzed based on when they happened and what type they are.

Security logs

The Windows *security log* records a variety of system activity including logon and logoff events, privilege use, and system events. The security log for Windows systems, particularly domain controllers, can be one of the most frequently written logs. This can make the security log a challenge to audit, but it is also one of the most important logs to audit for Windows systems.

Security logs can contain:

- Account logons
- Account management events
- Directory service events

- Object access details
- Policy change logs
- Privilege uses
- Process (application information) logging
- System event information

The Windows security log contains logon and logout information, as well as the events that are configured to be logged via the Windows audit policy. In the example shown in Figure 6-12, a special logon (4672) occurred and was logged. This event denotes an administrative user logon. The previous entry was a normal user logon event.

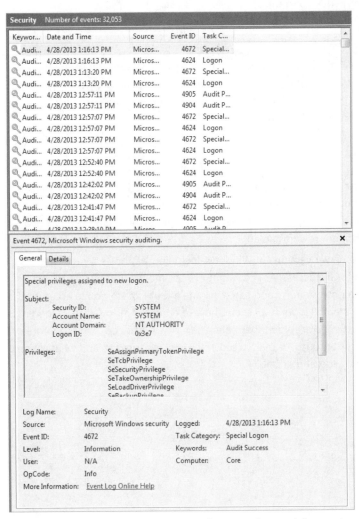

FIGURE 6-12 This sample Windows security log entry shows privilege assignment.

Red Hat Linux records security information as well as other information in a specialized audit log stored in /var/log/audit/audit.log. This information can include logons, privilege use, and a variety of other audit log information similar to the Windows security log, and much like in Windows, what is logged is up to the system administrator.

Access logs

Access logs are logs that track when a file, system, or server is accessed. Access logs can take many forms, from the information recorded by web servers to detailed file access logs retained by file systems. The ability to track access to a file or a server can be an important part of a security monitoring and incident response plan.

Fortunately, some of the newer versions of Windows, including Windows 7, provide the ability to set audit logging for file access. As you might expect, monitoring many files for when they are accessed can be very noisy and can consume a lot of space, so file access auditing is not turned on by default. Figure 6-13 shows how to enable Windows access logging. To do so, simply right-click the file or folder, then select Security, Advanced, and then Auditing. You can select which users, groups, or built-in security principals to audit, and what actions should be audited when they succeed or fail.

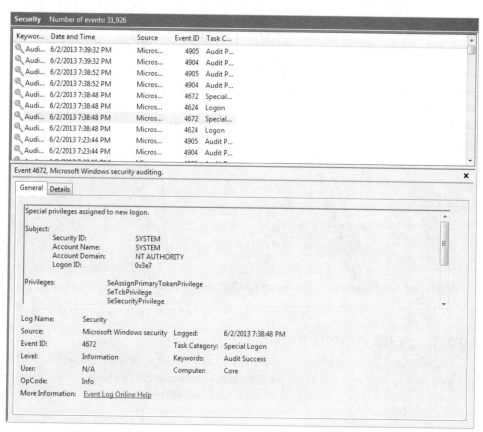

FIGURE 6-13 Windows access logging records logons and other security access events.

In addition to operating system access logging, applications and hardware devices also often provide access logs. The information contained in these logs varies, with some applications and devices supporting syslog and others simply logging to a file or their own custom logging system.

> **NOTE** **MODIFY/ACCESS/CHANGE INFORMATION**
>
> In Linux and Mac OS, individual files also often maintain information about creation, modification, and access times as part of their file information. You can see an example of a Linux MAC (modify/access/change) entry in Figure 6-14. In the figure, you can see the Linux modify/access/change information available via the *stat* command. Note that this file was changed shortly after it was accessed. Over time, this information would change as the file was modified at later dates.

```
[demo@localhost ~]$ stat demo.txt
  File: 'demo.txt'
  Size: 16         Blocks: 8         IO Block: 4096    regular file
Device: fd02h/64770d    Inode: 410757    Links: 1
Access: (0664/-rw-rw-r--)  Uid: ( 1001/    demo)  Gid: ( 1001/    demo)
Context: unconfined_u:object_r:user_home_t:s0
Access: 2013-04-28 14:23:07.274714051 -0400
Modify: 2013-04-28 14:23:07.274714051 -0400
Change: 2013-04-28 14:23:07.295712915 -0400
 Birth: -
```

FIGURE 6-14 This screen shot shows a Linux modify/access/change log.

Reporting and monitoring

We've discussed logging a variety of events, and we have looked at how those events can be useful for ensuring that security events are detected. In environments that have more than a handful of systems that can send system logs, it is very important to have some form of reporting system.

Reporting on logged events, whether from system logs or other sources, requires knowing what is worth reporting on and monitoring for. This is defined by a threshold—the level at which an event sets off an alarm, sends an alert, or causes an automated action to be performed.

> **EXAM TIP**
>
> The CompTIA Security+ exam focuses on alarms, alerts, and trends. Remember that alarms are set to occur when a threshold is reached or a specific event occurs. Alerts are sent to notify administrators about specific conditions, and trends help to indicate the direction of events.

After logs are properly configured for systems, applications, and devices, adding some means of central reporting and monitoring is typically the next step, as shown in Figure 6-15.

During the past few years, the concept of a security information management system has become increasingly important to the security monitoring and management of organizations around the world.

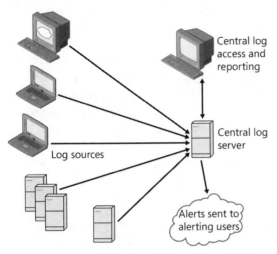

FIGURE 6-15 A central logging design receives data from multiple log sources.

In the central logging design shown in the figure, a variety of workstations, servers, and network devices send logs to a single central log server. This central log server is usually in a very protected part of the network, ensuring that it retains a secure copy of the log in case of compromise. Security administrators access the log server to perform reporting and analysis, and the server is configured to send alerts and alarms to specified users when events occur that match specific criteria. In addition, the server monitors specific log types for trends and at set thresholds will send alarms or take preprogrammed action.

SEM, SIM, and SIEM devices

One of the biggest changes in automated log analysis and event management has been the adoption of security event and information management systems. These are variously called *security event management systems (SEMs), security information management systems (SIMs),* or *security information and event management systems (SIEMs).* As the industry has progressed, most event management systems have added information, and vice-versa, so most devices are now full SIEM systems.

SIEM systems are designed to do live analysis of log and event information. They apply rules to the logs, events, and other data they receive, and then perform automated actions based on those rules. In many cases, that response is a notification, but SIEM systems often have advanced capabilities allowing scripting and even active responses to attacks.

In addition to their analysis capabilities, SIEM system are typically designed to provide long-term storage and reporting capabilities, allowing organizations to analyze logs over time, and to preserve them in the event that the system that generated the log originally is compromised and its logs are wiped. The ability to search through logs from a user-friendly interface, and to then sort through them, can be very powerful. Even better, most SIEM devices have built-in correlation capabilities, allowing them to provide some automated analysis that security staff can use to dig even deeper into events.

The dangers (and benefits) of automated response

Many SIEM devices provide the ability to apply automated responses to events. This can be very desirable in organizations that have specific security reactions that should occur when a particular event occurs, such as a firewall rule being enabled to block a system if it scans the organization's network.

Automated responses can also be dangerous if they are not well designed, or if attackers figure out how to cause them to react in ways that aren't in the organization's best interest. This is frequently discovered at an inopportune time, as an organization that one of the authors of this book worked with discovered when deploying an IPS system with automated response capabilities in a data center.

The IPS software allowed servers to automatically defend themselves against intrusions, which system administrators in the organization found very attractive. Unfortunately, the IPS software was not properly tuned, and it identified normal traffic as an attack. Soon, server after server responded to what they perceived as an attack by blocking legitimate traffic. In short order the organization's central infrastructure was offline, including the administrative remote access that would have allowed control over the IPS software. Administrators had to go to the data center to gain physical access to the misbehaving systems, and quickly uninstalled the IPS software.

As with any other security control, a system with automated responses should be carefully considered before it is deployed. If an automated response could prevent your organization from carrying on its normal business, then you will have to carefully design the restrictions under which it can happen. Sometimes, having a human in the loop is the best option!

Alerts and alarms

Earlier in this section we touched on the difference between *alerts*, which are sent to notify administrators about specific events, and *alarms*, which notify administrators when a specific threshold has been hit or an event has occurred. As you've seen, logging systems can generate huge volumes of data, and because of this, alerting for logging systems usually requires some form of automated log analysis system such as the SIM, SEM, and SIEM devices discussed earlier. Alerting systems usually monitor for a threshold to be hit, or for a specific event or event type that must result in an alarm or notification. Alerting can consist of any of the following:

- Alerts to a console where operators or administrators monitor for alerts in real time
- Email-based alerts to individuals or mailing lists when events occur
- SMS (text message) alerting, which has become increasingly popular because it can provide detail and speed, and can reach handlers even when email systems are down
- Phone-based alerts with automated calling systems

Alerting systems face a difficult balance because they must alarm when necessary, but they can't overwhelm responders with an incessant set of alerts and alarms that require response. Owners of the alerting system have to work with responders to determine when alerts should be sent, how they should be sent, and when alerts should be escalated to other responders.

Trends and thresholds

One useful way to look at log information is to look at *trends* in the log data being received by the log server. Trends can indicate if a specific account is being attacked more often than normal, if disks are filling up, and a variety of other loggable issues. Logs can generate enormous amounts of data, and a visual representation of trends is often available via SIEM systems, allowing security staff to quickly notice that something has changed.

Thresholds can help alarm on trends. Setting a threshold beyond what an organization typically sees for a particular trend with an appropriate alarm or alert set can provide early notification that an event or issue is occurring.

Real world

The problem with trends

One of the authors of this book has operated an organization-wide anti-virus monitoring and logging system for several years. With a few thousand systems spread across a diverse environment, the central console provides a view of what malware is infecting systems, whether updates are being properly installed, and whether systems are checking in as they should be.

The console for the malware management system provides a view that displays the current number of malware infections for the organization, which should make it easy to see when a malware outbreak occurs. Unfortunately, upward trends tend to be because a single system cannot properly remove a virus or trojan. This results in that single system reporting an infection and error at regular intervals, driving what looks like a spike in infections.

There are a few ways to handle this, if your trend reporting system has the right abilities, but it also highlights an issue with trends: you need to understand why the trend is occurring to make sure that it actually is a trend! It also means that you need to understand your environment, and what normal is for the environment. If you don't know what to expect, you'll never know if the trend is out of the ordinary or not.

Physical security design and concepts

No matter how well you have configured your network, and no matter how many layers of security you have implemented, weak physical security can allow an intruder to take total control of systems and networks.

The CompTIA Security+ exam tackles a few very specific areas related to physical security, including access lists, locks, mantraps, fences, and proximity readers. Each of these elements needs to be considered in the context of a complete physical security plan, much like the layered network defenses we discussed earlier in this book.

Hardware locks

Locks are frequently used to provide access control to areas. Because most locks don't have the ability to report unauthorized access, they primarily act as a deterrent. Unauthorized attackers can bypass most locks given sufficient time and resources, and many locks are relatively easily bypassed by using lockpicks or even simpler means.

Hardware locks are available in many forms, and much like the other security controls we have covered, they have a variety of strengths and capabilities. Locks aren't only used to secure doors. They help provide access control for utility panels, buildings, server racks, and a host of other items that are important to an organization. Their broad range of uses is one of the reasons that security is often represented by a picture of a lock.

There are several types of locks you should be familiar with:

- **Preset locks**   Typical door locks used for houses, businesses, and many other locations. Older locks typically had to be changed if the keys needed to be replaced, but newer models with "programmable" cylinders allow a master key to set a new key to unlock the door.

- **Cipher locks**   Locks that are opened with a programmable keypad. Some cipher locks are network enabled and track when they are opened, but many simply accept a code and unlock. Cipher locks offer the advantage of not requiring keys, and they're also easier to change than a traditional keyed lock.

- **Biometric locks**   Locks that use unique parts of the user's physiology such as the person's fingerprint, hand geometry, or retina to validate people who want access.

- **Multi-criteria locks**   Locks that use more than one of these three types of locks.

In addition to these common lock types, cable locks and padlocks are frequently used to secure devices and items that need to be prevented from being removed from a location.

 EXAM TIP

These terms for locks may seem odd, but they're easy to remember when you think about what they do. Preset locks are only set to allow a specific key; cipher locks accept a code; and biometric locks use the same biometric factors frequently used for authentication.

MORE INFO   **BIOMETRIC LOCKS**

Biometric locks work on the same biometric technologies we will discuss in Chapter 11.

Proximity readers

 Another way to authenticate users is through the use of *proximity readers*. When used for physical security, proximity readers read *proximity cards* when they are in range, and check them against a known access list of allowed cards. If the card is valid, a door is unlocked, a gate is opened, or another form of access is provided.

NOTE   **MORE ABOUT PROXIMITY AND SMART CARDS**

Proximity cards are also used for payment systems, including the tap-to-pay capabilities built into key fobs and some credit cards. We discuss smart cards in Chapter 11.

Proximity cards, like the one shown in Figure 6-16, come in a variety of forms, from traditional credit card–sized cards to key fobs and labels. When cards require more range, they can be equipped with batteries that allow them to create their own signal, rather than simply being passively read by a reader. Proximity cards are typically based on RFID (radio frequency ID), although other proximity card technologies do exist.

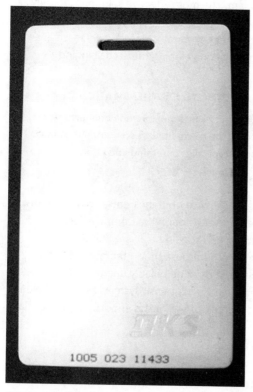

1005 023 11433

FIGURE 6-16 A traditional proximity card is the size and shape of a credit card.

Proximity cards are read at relatively short distances and are used as part of an access control system. If proximity cards aren't paired with a PIN or other identification factor, all they ensure is that the person accessing the facility has a proximity card.

> **NOTE   READING PROXIMITY CARDS**
>
> Proximity cards operate in both the older 125-kilohertz (kHz) and the more modern 13.56-megahertz (MHz) contactless smart card bands. This means that matching your technology to the cards that you deploy is important, and that not all cards can be read by all readers.

Proximity cards can be vulnerable to cloning if they don't provide some form of security for the data they provide when queried by a reader. Many cards simply provide a card ID number, sometimes with a version or sequence number in case a card has been reissued. Obviously, this is easy to clone and won't provide much security if a member of your staff loses his or her card and an attacker can make a copy. Fortunately, proximity card vendors have implemented several solutions to this problem. The most effective solutions typically include a card ID number and a unique ID number, which are then encrypted by using a key that the reader is equipped with. As long as the secret key is not exposed, reverse-engineering ID numbers and sequence numbers is difficult, making cloning more challenging.

> **MORE INFO** **USING PROXIMITY CARDS FOR TWO-FACTOR AUTHENTICATION**
>
> Even with techniques such as these in place, proximity cards only provide one factor for authentication: something you have. In Chapter 11 we discuss two-factor authentication. For a more secure environment, a second factor—typically something you know, such as a PIN or password—is a good best practice to implement.

As organizations have grown to require more intelligence from their entry access systems, contactless smart cards have begun to be more popular. Though the CompTIA Security+ exam doesn't explore their use for physical security, you should be aware that they can include more intelligence than a simple proximity card because they integrate a chip that can perform cryptographic functions, allowing the cards to be reliably uniquely identified. Contactless smart cards are already used in a variety of mass transit systems as stored value access cards, where the ability to be sure of the identity of the card is important for financial reasons.

Access lists

Proximity readers and other security controls are often paired with *access lists*, or lists of authorized individuals who can access a facility or room. Access lists can be stored electronically as part of an access control system or can be paper records used by guards or others who control access to a facility.

Fences

The first layer of defense for many organizations is its exterior *fence*. In fact, one of the most common ways to implement physical security for a building or other location is through the use of fences. There are many types of fences, from the common chain-link fences that are frequently used, with or without barbed wire on top to dissuade climbers, to razor wire or electric fences.

Fence design, much like the design of other physical security tools we have discussed, has more depth to it than might be immediately obvious. Many organizations simply put a chain-link fence in place, but a simple chain-link fence is only a minor deterrent at best.

Guards

Security guards are another common physical security control. Guards act as a preventive control by monitoring secure areas, providing access control, and ensuring that only the activities that should occur in an area are occurring there. The CompTIA Security+ exam doesn't specifically mention guards as a topic on its own, but it does consider the difference between what a guard can do and what a camera can do. The key concept it tests is the idea of detection vs. prevention.

Detection vs. prevention

We have looked at a variety of detection methods, including the logging techniques discussed earlier in this chapter as well as intrusion detection systems, anti-virus software, and a multitude of other ways to detect attacks and exploits. Each of these is considered a detective control, rather than a preventative control.

Prevention goes a step further and attempts to stop attacks before they occur, rather than simply detecting their effects. Earlier in this book (in Chapter 3) we discussed network and host intrusion prevention systems that work to stop attacks in progress; in this part of Chapter 6 we will look at the differences between cameras, which can detect an issue, and guards, who can help prevent it.

The CompTIA Security+ exam requires that you know the difference between a preventative control and a detective control. Remember that a preventative control attempts to stop the attack, whereas a detective control only records it or detects it in progress.

Both types of controls are an important part of layered security design, and your security design isn't complete unless you have considered both types of controls as well as where and why they should be deployed.

Cameras and video surveillance

Cameras serve as a detective control for organizations. Although the presence of a *video surveillance* camera can dissuade attackers simply by suggesting they might be caught on camera, they aren't considered preventative controls by themselves. This doesn't mean that they aren't frequently used as a deterrent—this is the reason that there is an entire industry that sells fake cameras, which are found everywhere from stores to school buses. The glowing red LEDs and fake ceiling-mounted camera bubbles have a crime deterrence capability by themselves.

Real cameras provide an element of a comprehensive physical security monitoring and detection system. In the past, cameras required dedicated operators to watch banks of cameras constantly to provide a monitoring function, but modern camera systems have the ability to detect and alarm on movement or specific behavior by themselves.

Cameras are available in a broad variety of types, with capabilities that include night vision, pan, tilt, and zoom support, as well as both analog and digital connections.

Mantraps

Another simple type of physical security mechanism is the mantrap, as shown in Figure 6-17. A *mantrap* is simply an entrance with a pair of doors, one after the other. After a visitor has entered the first door, it locks. This requires the visitor to unlock the second door, usually via a biometric or code-and-card access system. Mantraps are designed to trap unwanted visitors in the secured area, while allowing legitimate access.

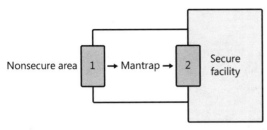

FIGURE 6-17 A mantrap uses two interlocked doors to provide additional security.

Mantraps help prevent piggybacking, which occurs when an unauthorized person attempts to enter with an authorized visitor. A small mantrap will only have room for one person to enter at a time, but larger mantraps still make it obvious that others are piggybacking into the facility.

> **MORE INFO   BYPASSING PHYSICAL SECURITY: IN-PERSON IMPERSONATION**
>
> In Chapter 5, we talked about a social engineering technique called *impersonation*, where an attacker acts like a person in authority or a legitimate member of the staff of an organization. Impersonation is a frequent technique in person, too, but a mantrap entry that requires a biometric sign-in or a card and PIN to enter can help stop the impersonator completely.

Quick check

1. What type of defense is used as a perimeter defense to deter intruders from entering an area?

2. What type of physical security defense is intended to stop piggybacking?

Quick check answers

1. Fences are often used to deter intruders from entering areas. They provide a physical barrier and help with the perception that the area is off-limits. Unfortunately, fences won't stop a determined intruder, because they are passive defenses.

2. Mantraps are designed to prevent piggybacking by only allowing users through doors after they have authenticated themselves. This prevents someone from simply following a legitimate member of the organization through a single open door that the first user unlocked.

Chapter summary

- Hardening standards provide guidelines and templates for how systems should be secured prior to deployment. Vendors and third-party groups provide hardening standards, templates, and other guidance for securing operating systems, appliances, and applications.

- Lockdown best practices include removing default passwords, disabling unnecessary services and accounts, and protecting management interfaces and applications.

- Organizations need updates and patching to ensure that their systems are not vulnerable to known exploits and issues. Unfortunately, installing patches can introduce new issues or break existing functionality. Central patch management tools help to secure the enterprise by ensuring that systems are at the same level of patch compliance.

- Security event logs and auditing allow security and operations staff to monitor the health of security of systems, applications, and networks. Key elements to log and monitor include event logs, application logs, security logs, and access logs. Windows, Mac OS, and Linux each have logging capabilities; however, what they log, how they log, and how their logging systems work differ.

- A key part of centralized reporting in many organizations is a SIM, SEM, or SIEM device, which provides a security operations capability for reporting and analysis of logs and events. An alternative solution is a central log host. Both solutions can help provide a secure copy of log data in the event of system compromise.

- Alerting systems often use thresholds and trending to assess changes in the state of a system or network, and when certain levels are hit, alerts or alarms are sent. Logging systems frequently use both alerts, which notify administrators that a set event has occurred, and alarms, which notify administrators when thresholds are reached.

- There are two types of controls: detective controls, which provide information when an event happens, and preventative controls, which seek to stop the event from occurring.

- Common physical security controls include access lists, mantraps, fencing, proximity readers, cameras, and locks.

- There are several types of physical locks: preset, cipher, biometric, and multicriteria locks. Preset locks are traditional key-style locks; cipher locks accept code input; biometric locks use unique physical characteristics such as fingerprints; and multicriteria locks require more than one of these methods.

Chapter review

Test your knowledge of the information in Chapter 6 by answering these questions. The answers to these questions, and the explanations of why each answer choice is correct or incorrect, are located in the "Answers" section at the end of this chapter.

1. What is the difference between fail open and fail safe?

    A. Fail open fails to a secure mode.

    B. Fail safe is always the proper failure mode.

    C. Fail safe fails to a secure mode.

    D. Fail open is always the proper failure mode.

2. Which of the following techniques is not part of a typical hardening process?

    A. Disabling unnecessary services and accounts

    B. Protecting management interfaces

    C. Upgrading the operating system

    D. Changing default passwords

3. What security techniques can be used to prevent access to network ports by attackers?

    A. MAC limiting, 802.1x, and disabling unused ports

    B. BIOS passwords

    C. Using a hardening standard and patching

    D. ACLs and a SIEM

4. Which Windows log contains logon information?

    A. The application log

    B. The setup log

    C. The system log

    D. The security log

5. What type of physical access control system is designed to prevent attackers from following legitimate staff through to access a secure area?

   A. A mantrap

   B. Gates

   C. Locks

   D. Fences

6. What type of hardware lock uses codes to allow access and can be reprogrammed?

   A. Preset

   B. Cipher

   C. Biometric

   D. Multifactor

Answers

This section contains the answers to the questions for the "Chapter review" section in this chapter.

1. **Correct Answer: C**

   A. **Incorrect:** Fail open fails to an "open" mode, allowing continued access in a failure scenario.

   B. **Incorrect:** Fail safe is not always the proper failure mode. Fire doors and other systems must fail open to save lives.

   C. **Correct:** Fail safe fails to a secure mode, ensuring that in a failure security is maintained.

   D. **Incorrect:** Fail open is not always the proper failure mode. As an example, a bank vault should not fail open in the event of a power failure.

2. **Correct Answer: C**

   A. **Incorrect:** Disabling unnecessary services and accounts is part of a typical hardening process. This prevents the services from being compromised and limits the accounts that attackers can attack.

   B. **Incorrect:** Management interfaces are a frequent target for attackers, and most hardening processes include techniques to protect them.

   C. **Correct:** Operating system upgrades are not typically part of a hardening process. Most hardening processes do emphasize proper patching.

   D. **Incorrect:** Changing default passwords prevents attackers from using them to access the system and is therefore part of a normal hardening process.

3. **Correct Answer: A**

   A. **Correct:** MAC limiting prevents hardware addresses that have been prohibited from accessing the network from connecting. 802.1x requires authentication before allowing access to the network, and disabling ports prevents unused ports from being used by attackers.

   B. **Incorrect:** BIOS passwords are the firmware passwords used for PCs and will not help protect a network port.

   C. **Incorrect:** Using a hardening standard and patching can help protect network devices but won't protect the network from an intruder who wants to plug in to a physical port.

   D. **Incorrect:** Access control lists (ACLS) provide security for network devices by limiting what traffic passes through the network device they are deployed on allows through. A SIEM accepts logs and events, and many SEIMs can take active action, but neither will protect physical network ports from unauthorized access.

4. **Correct Answer: D**

   A. **Incorrect:** The application log contains logs from application software.

   B. **Incorrect:** The setup log contains information about installed software.

   C. **Incorrect:** The system log contains information about system events.

   D. **Correct:** The security log contains information about logons, privilege use, and other auditable security events.

5. **Correct Answer: A**

   A. **Correct:** A mantrap is designed to prevent attackers from following legitimate users through to a secure area. The first door in a mantrap locks behind the person entering, and the person must provide a PIN or other access method before he or she can enter the second door. This helps legitimate users detect intruders.

   B. **Incorrect:** A gate is used to prevent physical access to an area, but it does not prevent an intruder from following a legitimate staff member.

   C. **Incorrect:** A lock is used to limit access to an area but does not prevent an intruder from following a legitimate staff member.

   D. **Incorrect:** Fences are frequently used as deterrents, but they do not prevent an intruder from following a legitimate staff member.

6. **Correct Answer: B**

   A. **Incorrect:** Preset locks are traditional keyed locks and require physical changes to be re-keyed.

   B. **Correct:** Cipher locks use a code to provide access and are easily reprogrammed without hardware changes.

   C. **Incorrect:** Biometric locks use biometric information rather than codes.

   D. **Incorrect:** Multifactor locks require more than one of the preceding types of information to unlock.

## CHAPTER 7

Vulnerability assessment and management

The CompTIA Security+ exam covers common techniques used to identify risks and vulnerabilities. Organizations frequently assess their risks and vulnerabilities by using both formal and informal techniques, as well as technical tools.

In this chapter, we will explore how you can find exposed services and vulnerabilities on systems and devices by using port and vulnerability scanning tools. We will discuss vulnerability assessment methods, as well as ways to identify vulnerabilities by using both technical and nontechnical means. Finally, we will explore the art of penetration testing, including common techniques, types of penetration tests, and best practices for performing them.

Exam objectives in this chapter:

Objective 3.7: Implement assessment tools and techniques to discover security threats and vulnerabilities

- Vulnerability scanning and interpret results
- Tools
    - Protocol analyzer
    - Sniffer
    - Vulnerability scanner
    - Honeypots
    - Honeynets
    - Port scanner
- Risk calculations
    - Threat vs. likelihood

- Assessment types
  - Risk
  - Threat
  - Vulnerability
- Assessment technique
  - Baseline reporting
  - Code review
  - Determine attack surface
  - Architecture
  - Design reviews

Objective 3.8: Within the realm of vulnerability assessments, explain the proper use of penetration testing versus vulnerability scanning

- Penetration testing
  - Verify a threat exist
  - Bypass security controls
  - Actively test security controls
  - Exploiting vulnerabilities
- Vulnerability scanning
  - Passively testing security controls
  - Identify vulnerability
  - Identify lack of security controls
  - Identify common misconfiguration
- Black box
- White box
- Gray box

Vulnerabilities and vulnerability assessment

Vulnerabilities are weaknesses in systems, networks, applications, and other elements of an organization's security environment. Vulnerabilities can include a range of issues such as:

- Operating system issues that allow privilege escalation.
- Services that allow denial of service attacks.
- Poor coding that allows a web application to be susceptible to a SQL injection attack.
- Process issues that allow an intruder to enter a building without proper identification.

A typical server has the potential to have vulnerabilities in its operating system; in the third-party application software that it runs, including backup, remote administration, and other software; in its hardware components or the firmware that makes them work; or in the management and administration practices used by the support staff who work with it. Further vulnerabilities might exist in the network switches and routers the server uses to communicate to the outside world, as well as the power and cooling systems it relies on to function. With this broad range of potential vulnerabilities, it can be almost impossible to be sure that all known vulnerabilities are being appropriately handled via updates, workarounds, or other fixes at any point in time.

Attackers know that a software vulnerability is often the best way into a system, and they specifically target vulnerable applications and operating systems by using malware and other attack tools. Due to this, entire exploit testing packages such as the Metasploit Project have been created to provide an easy way for testers to use a variety of attacks against known vulnerabilities, providing both security staff members and attackers with a powerful tool. In other words, organizations focus on assessing vulnerabilities as part of their security program, and that is why vulnerability assessment is an important part of the CompTIA Security+ body of knowledge.

MORE INFO **WHAT IS METASPLOIT?**

The Metasploit Project resulted in the Metasploit Framework and other related commercial tools. Metasploit includes exploits, payloads that are delivered via exploits, and a complete set of tools to manage attacks against systems. More detail on Metasploit can be found at *www.metasploit.com*. We will look at Metasploit's capabilities later in this chapter when we discuss penetration testing.

Organizations conduct vulnerability assessments by using many different methods and tools in an attempt to track and avoid the risks that they face. In this chapter, we will examine vulnerability assessment concepts and methodologies, including those used for system vulnerability and threat assessments. Using the risk assessment concepts explored earlier in this book, we will look at technical means to identify vulnerable systems and services. Finally, we will delve into penetration testing, the art of breaking into systems and networks to test their security.

Risk-based vulnerability assessments

The first element of a vulnerability assessment program is a risk assessment. Of course, first you need to understand what a risk is. In this context, you can take the definition of *risk* from Chapter 1, "Risk management and incident response," as "the intersection of a threat and a vulnerability," and look at a risk as the potential that a threat will exploit vulnerabilities of a system, network, or other asset, resulting in harm. Here, threats are dangers that could result in an incident or breach.

> **MORE INFO   RISK ASSESSMENTS AND RISK MANAGEMENT**
>
> We discussed risk assessments and risk management as a discipline in Chapter 1.

A wide variety of threats have to be taken into account when you are performing risk assessments. In a full assessment, physical threats such as fires, floods, and tornados would be assessed at the same time as information security threats such as information exposure, system compromise, and outages. For the CompTIA Security+ exam, we will focus on threats that affect the confidentiality, availability, or integrity of systems, networks, and other assets.

> **NOTE   DEFINING THREATS**
>
> The National Institute of Standards and Technology (NIST) defines a threat as "any circumstance or event with the potential to adversely impact organizational operations (including mission, functions, image, or reputation), organizational assets, or individuals through an information system via unauthorized access, destruction, disclosure, modification of information, and/or denial of service. Also, the potential for a threat-source to successfully exploit a particular information system vulnerability." in the Federal Information Processing Standards (FIPS) 200 publication.

Threat assessments

Threats are defined in several ways by various organizations, but in general, a *threat* can be defined as a possible danger that might exploit a vulnerability, resulting in harm to the organization. Threats are aimed at weaknesses, which are protected by controls, as shown in Figure 7-1.

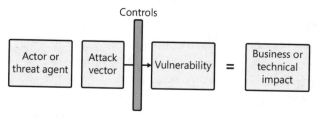

FIGURE 7-1 Threat agents attack vulnerabilities via attack vectors such as an exposed service, resulting in business or technical impact to the organization.

Threats require an actor, a vulnerability or weakness, and a motivation. This can be as simple as a tornado taking down power lines, or as complex as a group of criminals targeting vulnerable web applications in the banking industry to steal money from ATMs.

The threats an organization faces aren't always the result of attack, and most organizations assess threats that include physical threats such as fires, storms, and floods, as well as power outages, in addition to technical threats and human factors. Threat assessments build a list of the threats to an organization, allowing the organization to think coherently about what the threats it faces are.

Note that a threat may be included in a risk assessment, and in fact a threat assessment is often used as part of a risk assessment.

> **MORE INFO   OWASP'S GUIDE TO ASSESSING RISKS AND THREATS**
>
> OWASP, the Open Web Application Security Project, provides a useful example of assessing risk and threats to application security at *https://www.owasp.org/index.php/ Top_10_2010-Main.*

Vulnerability assessments

Vulnerability assessments specifically look at flaws and weaknesses in security systems, processes, controls, and designs. Thus, vulnerability assessments are targeted at the actual implementation of security, rather than considering who or what might attack, or what the impact of the threat being realized is. Vulnerability assessments tend to follow risk and threat assessments, because they provide information about what the threats that an organization faces could result in. Performing a vulnerability assessment without performing some form of risk assessment is likely to lead to wasted effort, because low-risk areas can absorb significant amounts of time during their vulnerability assessment.

Assessment techniques

There are a variety of ways to assess vulnerabilities, ranging from code reviews that consider the source code of applications to architecture and design reviews that validate the structure of systems and applications. The CompTIA Security+ exam covers a number of common vulnerability assessment techniques. Among them are:

- *Code reviews*, which use manual or automated review of source code for programs and applications to find vulnerabilities. Code review can expose flaws that cannot be found by a vulnerability scanner, including issues with internal logic. Many organizations perform code review before releasing application code into production, but code reviews are also performed as part of vulnerability assessments, penetration tests, and after attacks as part of a remediation process.

- Determining the *attack surface* of organizations and systems. The attack surface is the collection of services, applications, and other elements of a system or organization that are exposed to potential threats. Many organizations carefully design their network to minimize their attack surface, and vulnerability assessments will verify that the actual exposed elements match the design.

- *Architecture* and *design reviews*, which focus on the architecture of applications and services. These terms are often used interchangeably because the architecture of the application or service is typically part of its design. Design reviews consider how the service was designed to work internally, including how traffic flows, where data resides, and what servers, workstations, and other network and system elements work together to provide the service or to access it.

- *Baseline reporting*, a technique that relies on the baseline security standards discussed in Chapter 6, "Monitoring, detection, and defense." Baseline reports check current settings against the baseline, then provide information about what differences, if any, exist. Baseline reporting is very useful for day-to-day monitoring of system configuration because it can easily point out issues with how security standards are applied. In some cases, changes from the baseline may mean that a system was compromised!

> ***MORE INFO*** **APPLICATION SECURITY AND BASELINING**
>
> We will discuss application baselining in Chapter 8, "The importance of application security," as part of our coverage of application security.

Risk calculations: threat vs. likelihood

With these assessment methodologies in hand, you still need a way to decide which threats, risks, and vulnerabilities to pay attention to. Thus, in addition to the risk calculations explored in Chapter 1, you need one additional calculation, which is key to the CompTIA Security+ exam: the calculation of risk as the product of likelihood and impact. The equation is simple:

$R = L \times I$

Here, the likelihood is based on whether the threat appears and if it can exploit the vulnerability it is aimed at. The impact takes into account what harm the organization would experience if the threat succeeded, and should take into account the value of the assets involved.

> **IMPORTANT** **PROBABILITY AND LIKELIHOOD**
>
> In many risk assessment methodologies likelihood is called probability, and it isn't uncommon to see this equation as $R = P \times I$, rather than $R = L \times I$.

In many risk calculations, these values are simply rated as high, medium, and low, although there are many variations in ratings and scales. Some organizations rate risks in more complex ways, with scales from 1 through 10 covering multiple impact factors to finances, business operations, and reputation, while others rate everything based on the detailed calculated value of each asset.

We can use the imaginary company, Humongous Insurance, to examine this process in more depth. For Humongous Insurance, a successful denial of service attack against their website is a significant threat because it could result in lost revenue for the company. If we assume that Humongous knows that they face a real threat from a group of attackers who want to disable their site, and assuming that they have some controls in place but think they might not work, Humongous might rate the likelihood of the threat appearing and succeeding as a medium.

If we assume that Humongous Insurance makes $100,000 every 15 minutes through their website sales of insurance products, and that loss of that amount of money for hours or even a day is a significant loss to the company, we can easily calculate the impact of the risk they face. Here we will call the impact to the organization high, because they might lose customers and revenue, and suffer reputational damage.

The calculation would then be:

$Risk = Medium\ Likelihood \times High\ Impact$

Most organizations that use this calculation use a chart similar to the chart shown in Figure 7-2, where each level of impact has been given a number from 1 through 3, with low levels listed as 1, medium as 2, and high as 3, with the values multiplied by the likelihood to give a final score. Note that a risk with a high impact and a medium likelihood would be considered a high risk (6) and would receive prompt attention.

	High	3	6	9
Impact	Medium	2	4	6
	Low	1	2	3
		Low	Medium	High
			Likelihood	

FIGURE 7-2 A Risk chart shows the intersection of likelihood with impact.

Example: Humongous Insurance

We can also look at Humongous Insurance for a discussion of their assessment process. For this example, Humongous wants to assess the risks, threats, and vulnerabilities to their new web application environment, which allows customers to manage their insurance products online.

First, Humongous performs a risk assessment scoped to the new environment. They will consider what risks the organization would face if the new environment was compromised, if it was offline, or if it had another failure. Their assessment of the risks involved will likely require a threat assessment, which they will base on knowledge of what threats they have seen and what their competitors have dealt with. With that knowledge in hand, Humongous can more effectively choose where to spend their time assessing vulnerabilities.

 Quick check

1. What type of assessment is intended to determine flaws that might be exploited by attackers?

2. What type of vulnerability assessment involves looking at the source code of the programs being assessed?

Quick check answers

1. A vulnerability assessment focuses on the flaws or weaknesses in systems, services, anapplications that could be exploited by attackers.

2. Code review is an assessment technique that uses manual review or automated tools to find vulnerabilities in source code and its internal logic.

Vulnerability scanning

Vulnerability scans serve several purposes for organizations. Not only do they help organizations identify vulnerabilities, they also help point out when security controls have not been properly put in place, or when an attacker or misconfiguration has disabled them. They also help organizations find common misconfigurations such as default usernames and passwords, default directories and scripts that can be dangerous, and a host of other, similar issues.

Organizations typically conduct vulnerability scanning one of two ways: by using internal tools to passively scan for vulnerabilities by checking version numbers and configurations, and by active scanning using a vulnerability scanning tool. We've already discussed security baselines, which can provide *passive identification*, , so this chapter takes a look at active vulnerability scanning tools.

Vulnerability scanning tools

A key part of assessing vulnerabilities is scanning for them. This is done by using a variety of tools, including packet sniffers, port scanners, vulnerability scanners, and specialized tools such as web application vulnerability scanners. Each of these tools has a role to play in a vulnerability assessment, and they are often used together or in sequence to help provide a faster, more accurate result.

We will examine each of these tools in the order in which they are frequently used to scan systems and networks. The process typically starts with a sniffer and a port scanner, which are used to look for hosts that provide services on the network. From there, vulnerability scanners are used to find vulnerable services and systems. Finally, if you discover web applications, you might want to use a web application vulnerability scanner's specialized abilities to test it.

Protocol analyzers and sniffers

In Chapter 2, "Network security technologies," we looked at protocol analyzers and sniffers, tools that allow you to view and analyze network traffic on the wire. The capabilities that make these tools useful for detecting attacks and analyzing attack traffic also make them a useful part of vulnerability assessment.

There are a few ways in which sniffers are frequently used during vulnerability analyses and during penetration tests, which include:

- Capturing data during port scans and vulnerability scans to provide additional information about what data is being sent and received. This provides a log that penetration testers find useful to demonstrate what occurred and when. Capturing network activity can also provide more information about specific responses, allowing manual analysis if needed.

- Providing insight into the actual content of traffic sent by an attacker or attack tool, thus allowing security professionals to assess the significance of a threat. If the payload of the packets is an attack that your organization is vulnerable to, it is far more of a threat than a random attack that uses a tool you're not susceptible to.

- Analyzing the results of your own attack traffic when testing a system. This uses the same concepts as watching a third-party attack traffic but can be used inside of a network to monitor your own testing.

- Capturing traffic to determine whether network controls such as an IPS, firewall, or proxy work. A sniffer deployed at each point along the path between the sender and receiver can provide in-depth information about what traffic is permitted, and whether the network security devices are making changes to the traffic. This process is very similar to the process that many network and security professionals use when diagnosing network connectivity issues, but it changes the focus from making traffic flow to ensuring that controls work.

As you can see, sniffers are a critical part of your arsenal of tools when you are conducting vulnerability scans and penetration tests. The process for penetration testing, including the selection of tools from those discussed here, is covered in the "Penetration testing" section later in this chapter.

Port scanners

One of the first tools that a security professional uses from his toolbox when starting to assess a network is a *port scanner*. Port scanners provide a quick and easy way to assess the services that are exposed on a network and can help analysts quickly get an idea of whether an organization's systems are well maintained and secured or if there are problems throughout the network.

Port scanners attempt to connect to services hosted on systems and devices on a network, and then they monitor responses. In their simplest form, they check to see which ports respond, but they can provide a variety of capabilities beyond that if they analyze the responses from the systems they receive data from.

> **MORE INFO   NMAP SCANNING**
>
> Over the years, port scanners have added a range of capabilities intended to allow them to be more effective. A quick read through the Nmap guide to port scanning techniques can help you explore how many ways there are to scan a network. You can find the full list of techniques at *http://nmap.org/book/man-port-scanning-techniques.html*.

One of the major advantages of port scanners is that they can be quite fast. Unlike the vulnerability scanners we will discuss next, a port scanner is focused on a very limited set of information about systems, which helps it provide a quick list of ports and services, often with basic operating system identification thrown in. Most vulnerability scanners also limit themselves to a set of default ports, rather than scanning the full set of 65,535 ports that could be exposed to the world. Of course, scanning only part of the range of ports means that services that run on different ports might be missed!

> ## Real world
>
> ### Nmap
>
> The network mapper Nmap is an open-source security scanner that is one of the most popular port scanners in the world. Nmap provides the ability to discover hosts, identify which ports are accessible and what state they are in, perform service identification for the services running on those ports, and determine the likely operating system of the host (see Figure 7-3). Versions of Nmap have been created for most major operating systems, making it a common choice for most security professionals who need to conduct a port scan.
>
> In the scan shown in Figure 7-3, Nmap also identified that the scan was run against a Linux system that appeared to be running a 2.6.x branch of Linux, and that the host itself appears to be a VMWare virtual machine. You now know much more about the system, but you don't know if these services are vulnerable.

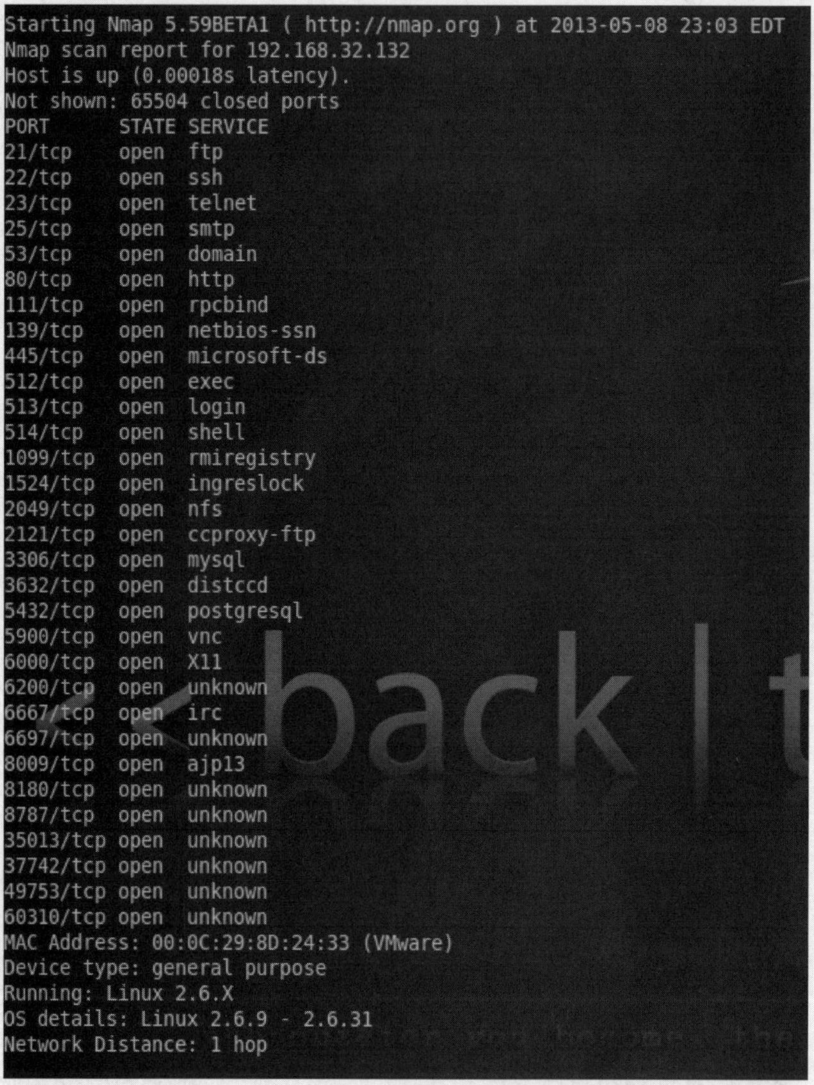

```
Starting Nmap 5.59BETA1 ( http://nmap.org ) at 2013-05-08 23:03 EDT
Nmap scan report for 192.168.32.132
Host is up (0.00018s latency).
Not shown: 65504 closed ports
PORT       STATE SERVICE
21/tcp     open  ftp
22/tcp     open  ssh
23/tcp     open  telnet
25/tcp     open  smtp
53/tcp     open  domain
80/tcp     open  http
111/tcp    open  rpcbind
139/tcp    open  netbios-ssn
445/tcp    open  microsoft-ds
512/tcp    open  exec
513/tcp    open  login
514/tcp    open  shell
1099/tcp   open  rmiregistry
1524/tcp   open  ingreslock
2049/tcp   open  nfs
2121/tcp   open  ccproxy-ftp
3306/tcp   open  mysql
3632/tcp   open  distccd
5432/tcp   open  postgresql
5900/tcp   open  vnc
6000/tcp   open  X11
6200/tcp   open  unknown
6667/tcp   open  irc
6697/tcp   open  unknown
8009/tcp   open  ajp13
8180/tcp   open  unknown
8787/tcp   open  unknown
35013/tcp  open  unknown
37742/tcp  open  unknown
49753/tcp  open  unknown
60310/tcp  open  unknown
MAC Address: 00:0C:29:8D:24:33 (VMware)
Device type: general purpose
Running: Linux 2.6.X
OS details: Linux 2.6.9 - 2.6.31
Network Distance: 1 hop
```

FIGURE 7-3 In this Nmap scan, a vulnerable Linux system provides a huge number of services, including FTP, SSH for remote access, SMTP email, DNS, a web server, and many other ports.

Of course, port scanning alone cannot provide a full understanding of the vulnerabilities that a system might have. When your scan completes, you will probably have useful information about potential targets, and you might even have some ideas about which systems might be vulnerable. With that data in hand, the next step for most security professionals is to scan the systems identified by a port scan with a vulnerability scanner.

Vulnerability scanners

Vulnerability scanners are the next step up in the scanning process. There are two common types of vulnerability scanners: network vulnerability scanners and web application vulnerability scanners. We'll explore each in turn.

Network vulnerability scanners

Network vulnerability scanners are designed to scan for vulnerable systems through a network. After they are provided with a target, which can be a single system, a network, or a whole range of addresses, they scan for and connect to services. This allows them to gather information about the version of the application or service running and to check it against a database of known vulnerable versions. More advanced vulnerability scanners also conduct tests to determine if specific vulnerabilities exist, either by testing for specific signs, or querying information on the system for details of what is installed. Some vulnerability scanning tools even allow you to embed administrative credentials that allow the scanner to log into systems they're scanning to verify software versions and other system settings directly.

In Figure 7-4, a scan was conducted against a sample vulnerable system by using Nessus, apopular vulnerability scanning package, resulting in a list of vulnerabilities. As you can see, the sample vulnerability selected from the scan is classified by its risk level based on the significance of the issue that would be created by exploitation of the vulnerability.

In this example, Nessus found 156 results, and the figure shows a high-security issue from that list that involves the SUDO command in Ubuntu Linux. Note that Nessus provides a description, a solution suggestion, links to details on the vulnerability itself, and information about when the vulnerability was discovered.

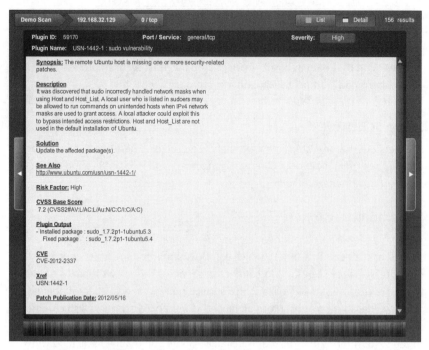

Synopsis: The remote Ubuntu host is missing one or more security-related patches.

Description
It was discovered that sudo incorrectly handled network masks when using Host and Host_List. A local user who is listed in sudoers may be allowed to run commands on unintended hosts when IPv4 network masks are used to grant access. A local attacker could exploit this to bypass intended access restrictions. Host and Host_List are not used in the default installation of Ubuntu.

Solution
Update the affected package(s).

See Also
http://www.ubuntu.com/usn/usn-1442-1/

Risk Factor: High

CVSS Base Score
7.2 (CVSS2#AV:L/AC:L/Au:N/C:C/I:C/A:C)

Plugin Output
- Installed package : sudo_1.7.2p1-1ubuntu5.3
  Fixed package   : sudo_1.7.2p1-1ubuntu5.4

CVE
CVE-2012-2337

Xref
USN:1442-1

Patch Publication Date: 2012/05/16

FIGURE 7-4 Nessus provides detailed vulnerability information for each vulnerability it discovers.

Web application vulnerability scanners

Web applications are the face of most organizations, and those applications can have a wide range of vulnerabilities, such as to the cross-site scripting, SQL injection, and faulty logic issues we discussed in Chapter 5, "Threats and attacks." Each application can respond differently to its users, and the way applications display data, accept input, and interact with back-end database servers can vary greatly. This means that web application assessment is a relatively specialized discipline. Until recently, most network vulnerability scanners did not have strong web application vulnerability assessment capabilities, leaving a niche for a variety of specialized *web application vulnerability scanners* (sometimes called *web application security scanners*). This is slowly changing, and major products are starting to add increasingly useful web application scanning tools to their existing vulnerability scanning products.

Web application vulnerability scanners act like an attacker might, and feed web applications bad input, change what forms send back to the application, and attempt to inject SQL statements, along with other specialized techniques. They also check for common misconfigurations, sample files and scripts, and vulnerable versions of the underlying software for websites such as their scripting engines and web servers.

In Figure 7-5, you can see a simple open-source web application and server vulnerability scanner called Nikto. Nikto's primary focus is on web servers and common vulnerabilities in known web applications, which means it is a useful tool to check for known vulnerabilities. Unlike more complex scanners, Nikto doesn't provide an in-depth scanning tool for custom applications.

```
- Nikto v2.1.4
---------------------------------------------------------------------
+ Target IP:          192.168.32.128
+ Target Hostname:    192.168.32.128
+ Target Port:        80
+ Start Time:         2013-05-12 14:44:30
---------------------------------------------------------------------
+ Server: Apache/2.2.8 (Ubuntu) DAV/2
+ Retrieved x-powered-by header: PHP/5.2.4-2ubuntu5.10
+ Apache/2.2.8 appears to be outdated (current is at least Apache/2.2.17). Apache 1.3.42 (final release) and 2.0
.64 are also current.
+ DEBUG HTTP verb may show server debugging information. See http://msdn.microsoft.com/en-us/library/e8z01xdh%28
VS.80%29.aspx for details.
+ OSVDB-877: HTTP TRACE method is active, suggesting the host is vulnerable to XST
+ OSVDB-3233: /phpinfo.php: Contains PHP configuration information
+ OSVDB-3268: /doc/: Directory indexing found.
+ OSVDB-48: /doc/: The /doc/ directory is browsable. This may be /usr/doc.
+ OSVDB-12184: /index.php?=PHPB8B5F2A0-3C92-11d3-A3A9-4C7B08C10000: PHP reveals potentially sensitive informatio
n via certain HTTP requests that contain specific QUERY strings.
+ OSVDB-3092: /phpMyAdmin/: phpMyAdmin is for managing MySQL databases, and should be protected or limited to au
thorized hosts.
+ OSVDB-3268: /test/: Directory indexing found.
+ OSVDB-3092: /test/: This might be interesting...
+ OSVDB-3268: /icons/: Directory indexing found.
+ OSVDB-3233: /icons/README: Apache default file found.
+ 6448 items checked: 1 error(s) and 13 item(s) reported on remote host
+ End Time:           2013-05-12 14:45:12 (42 seconds)
---------------------------------------------------------------------
+ 1 host(s) tested
```

FIGURE 7-5 This Nikto scan identified the system as an Ubuntu Linux server running Apache 2.2.28 with PHP 5.2.4, which is outdated. In addition, Nikto identified multiple vulnerabilities listed in the Open Source Vulnerability Database (OSVDB) that could be issues or misconfigurations.

More complex scanners include internal logic that can analyze custom web applications and can identify vulnerabilities in how they handle input and user interaction. In Figure 7-6, the open-source Web Application Attack and Audit Framework (w3af) scanner has been run against a vulnerable application. Unlike Nikto, it explored the full application and attempted to feed it a variety of input.

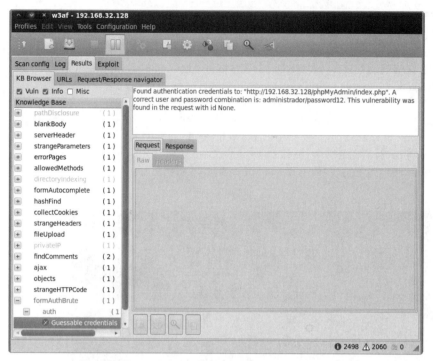

FIGURE 7-6 w3af provides far more information about vulnerabilities in the application than Nikto does.

In the example scan shown in the figure, you can see a list of issues with descriptions. Theselected vulnerability that is marked by red text provides more information, including the user name and password for a vulnerable phpMyAdmin installation on the target system.

> **NOTE WHEN AUTOMATED TOOLS AREN'T ENOUGH**
>
> Automated tools provide many features and don't get bored while scanning, but in many cases it takes a human to fully understand the internal logic of a web application. Thus, although web application scanning tools are a useful part of a vulnerability management program, you may still want to engage a talented web application assessment tester if it is absolutely critical that your web applications are secure.

No matter what type of vulnerability scanner you use, you should bear in mind that scanners are rarely 100 percent accurate. Vulnerability scanning is a useful tool as part of a strong vulnerability management program, and is a key part of a defense in depth strategy, but it isn't enough protection on its own.

Quick check

1. What type of tool would you use to monitor the traffic sent by a vulnerability scanner?

2. How do web application vulnerability scanners differ from network vulnerability scanners?

Quick check answers

1. A sniffer or packet analyzer is typically used to monitor the packets sent by a vulnerability scanner or port scanner. This allows you to see what is sent and received by the scanning system, providing useful information about what systems were scanned and how they responded.

2. Web application vulnerability scanners focus on internal logic, vulnerabilities in how applications handle user input that allow attacks such as cross-site scripting, SQL injection, and similar problems. Vulnerability scanners typically look for vulnerable services and configuration issues and typically don't understand how the applications themselves work or handle user input.

Honeypots and honeynets

 The CompTIA Security+ exam looks at two types of systems designed to lure attackers into targeting them: *honeypots* and *honeynets*. Honeypots are specially designed systems and applications that expose tempting interfaces and vulnerabilities to potential attackers. Often they will provide a complete copy of a legitimate vulnerable system, but will be designed in a way that prevents attackers from gathering actual data or performing further attacks. Instead, they gather information about what the attackers do and how they do it. Most honeypots log every action taken on the system, and many also keep copies of files and tools that attackers bring with them.

Honeypots are often classified into one of two types:

- Low-interaction honeypots, which provide a few commonly targeted services and are focused on studying the most heavily attacked applications and systems
- High-interaction honeypots, which emulate an entire operating system or application, allowing attackers to perform the actions they normally would on a compromised system

Honeynets work much like honeypots do, but on a much broader scale: they are entire networks of systems designed to lure attackers in. This means that some honeynets can detect attacks in a variety of locations or attacks aimed at a variety of systems on a network.

Network honeypots are often called *sinkholes*. Much like honeypots, sinkholes are designed to absorb attacks safely while providing researchers and security professionals with a chance to study malicious traffic.

> **MORE INFO** **THE HONEYNET PROJECT**
>
> Information security researchers around the world contribute to the Honeynet Project, a collaborative network of honeypots run through a nonprofit coordinating body. More information about the Honeynet Project can be found at *www.honeynet.org*.

Organizations might deploy honeypots or honeynets for research, allowing them to understand new threats, or for production use, to help detect attacks and new threats on their own internal networks. In addition to the honeynets and honeypots the CompTIA Security+ exam focuses on, two other common security tools exist, with related uses: darknets and tarpits.

Darknets

Darknets are segments of unused network space that host no servers and provide no services. Thus, no traffic should be sent to them, because they don't advertise anything that should result in connections. This means that any network traffic sent to the darknet IP addresses is suspect and is likely to be of interest to security professionals.

Darknets typically host one or more systems that collect all network traffic sent to the network. When the traffic is captured, it can be analyzed to detect port scans such as those discussed earlier in this chapter. Darknets have been used to detect worm outbreaks, misconfigured systems, and a host of other abnormal network traffic.

> **MORE INFO** **REAL-WORLD DARKNETS**
>
> Team Cymru, a nonprofit security research organization, runs an extensive darknet to capture probes, malware, and other attacks that randomly attack IP addresses on the Internet. More details on the Darknet project can be found at *www.team-cymru.org/Services/darknets.html*, where you can access full instructions on how to set up your own darknet server.

Tarpits

In addition to detecting scans, some organizations prefer to slow down scanners. Tarpits are the answer. A *tarpit* is a system specifically configured to delay network connections such as those made by a worm that is scanning for new systems to compromise, or a network vulnerability or port scanner that is searching for services.

Tarpit implementations can be as simple as an increased delay for connections to an email server, and as complex as a dedicated server that responds to every connection to a subnet with a variety of connection messages, resulting in scanners taking hours to scan, only to return a list of fake services and systems.

> **IMPORTANT WHY TARPITS AND DARKNETS?**
>
> Though the CompTIA Security+ exam doesn't cover darknets, tarpits, or sinkholes, the concepts behind them are useful for security professionals to keep in mind when learning about how attackers can be monitored, stopped, and studied.

> **EXAM TIP**
>
> The CompTIA Security+ exam covers honeypots and honeynets. Simply remember that ahoneypot is a single system, and that a honeynet is more than one system, typically deployed in various network locations.

 Quick check

1. What type of network security tool is designed to allow attackers to break in and interact with the operating system so that security professionals can learn about their behavior?

2. Why might you deploy a honeynet?

Quick check answers

1. A high-interaction honeypot is designed to provide a simulated, safe target for attackers that reacts like a real system would.

2. Honeynets are useful for detecting attacks that are distributed across a network or that occur in more than one location. Honeynets can help security professionals determine the scope and size of a scan or attack by capturing traffic in a variety of locations.

Penetration testing

Penetration testing is the process of attacking an organization to test its technical security, practices, procedures, and other defenses. Penetration tests are conducted by, or for, organizations that want a real-world test of their security. Unlike actual attacks, penetration tests are conducted with the knowledge of the organization, although some types of penetration tests occur without the knowledge of the employees and departments being tested.

Penetration tests are typically used to verify threats or to test security controls. They do this by bypassing security controls and exploiting vulnerabilities, using a variety of tools and techniques, including the attack methods discussed earlier in this book. Social engineering, malware, and vulnerability exploit tools are all fair game when it comes to penetration testing.

> **IMPORTANT**   **PENETRATION TESTING AND THE COMPTIA SECURITY+ EXAM**
>
> The CompTIA Security+ exam focuses on the use of penetration testing for these purposes. Penetration tests actively test security controls by exploiting vulnerabilities and bypassing security controls, and this helps to verify that a threat exists.

Penetration tests are often classified as overt or covert and as internal-perspective or external-perspective tests. Overt penetration tests are intended to be visible to members of the organization being tested, and use techniques that are likely to be detected by security tools, system administrators, and security professionals. Covert tests better simulate more stealthy attacks and attempt to evade detection. Tests with an internal perspective or view are conducted from inside an organization's security perimeter, whereas external-perspective tests are conducted from outside that perimeter. Note that the designation of a test as an internal-perspective test does not imply that the testers were allowed past that perimeter. One common technique for penetration testers is to bypass external security perimeters physically by placing devices inside an organization.

Real world

My Little Pwnie Plug

Pwnie Express (pronounced "Pony Express") is a company that specializes in penetration testing hardware. Among their products are penetration testing aids known as the Pwn Plug and the Power Pwn (see Figure 7-7), which are designed to help bypass security perimeters.

FIGURE 7-7 The Pwn Plug looks like a common power adapter.

The Pwn Plug resembles a common "wall wart" power adapter but conceals a small Linux computer complete with flash memory, network adapters, and penetration testing software packages preloaded. The Pwn Plug shown in Figure 7-7 is an innocuous device that penetration testers can plug into any power outlet in buildings to which they can gain access. Once there, it can connect to wireless and wired networks, perform vulnerability testing with a variety of built-in open-source tools, and provide an encrypted tunnel in for penetration testers. The device even includes a set of stickers intended to make it look more like a common power adapter. Most of the staff in your organization would probably not think twice about a Pwn Plug.

Devices such as the Pwn Plug aren't the only way in for penetration testers. Other recent techniques include seeding parking lots with USB flash drives that contain malware that phones home to the testing team after they're plugged into a workstation, using social engineering techniques to persuade staff members into allowing the penetration testers themselves to access their PCs, and a host of other techniques.

Types of penetration tests

The CompTIA Security+ exam divides penetration tests into three major types of testing, classified by how much information the testers have. The categories are black box, white box, and gray box testing. We'll take a look at each of them, and then we'll explore how they are performed.

Black box penetration testing

 Black box penetration tests, sometimes called *blind penetration tests*, are conducted with no knowledge of the environment. They are much more difficult to conduct than white box or gray box vulnerability tests, because they require the penetration testers to gather any information they need about an organization by themselves.

This makes black box penetration tests a far better test of what an actual attacker might manage to do. Because black box testing is as close to a real-world attack as possible, some organizations opt to use black box penetration tests to test their own defenses against attackers. As you might imagine, a black box penetration test is typically far more expensive in terms of both time and effort than tests that provide attackers with more knowledge. Worse, black box testing can leave entire sections of an IT infrastructure alone if the attacker misses them when scanning for targets.

White box penetration testing

 White box penetration tests provide the most information to the penetration testing team. Because white box testing provides a complete and unobstructed view of the environment tothe attacker, it is sometimes called *crystal box penetration testing*.

White box penetration testing provides several advantages:

- More focus is placed on the test itself, rather than on gathering information.
- More in-depth testing can be accomplished, because everything that can be tested is exposed.
- Attacks against known systems and services are more likely to be the right attack and to demonstrate true issues with the systems and services.

White box testing can be very helpful in identifying vulnerabilities that might be missed by a black or gray box test, but they can add additional cost because of the broader scope that total visibility can create.

EXAM TIP

If you can't recall what information is available during a penetration test, remember that the color of the box tells you all you need to know. You can't see through a black box, but the white (crystal) box shows you everything.

Gray box penetration testing

Gray box penetration testing is a middle ground between black box testing and white box testing. Gray box testers typically receive partial information about the subjects of their testing but don't have access to every detail of the target. Gray box testing can help avoid some of the problems with black box testing by ensuring that important parts of the target aren't missed. It can also prevent the common white box testing issue of not replicating an actual attack scenario.

> *NOTE* **GRAY BOXES: PARTIAL KNOWLEDGE TESTING**
>
> Gray box testing is sometimes called "translucent box" testing, a halfway point between white box testing's "crystal box" and black box testing's "blind" testing.

> ### ✔ Quick check
>
> 1. A penetration that that is performed with full knowledge of the systems, network, and defenses of a target is known as what type of penetration test?
> 2. What are the advantages and disadvantages of a black box penetration test?
>
> ### Quick check answers
>
> 1. A white box, or crystal box penetration test provides full knowledge of the environment being tested to the attackers. This allows them to more fully test the environment, but it does not simulate a real-world attacker's view of the systems.
> 2. Black box penetration tests provide a real-world test by providing no internal knowledge of the organization or systems that are being tested. This can result in systems being missed due to lack of knowledge.

Conducting a penetration test

After you have decided on the type of penetration test that will be conducted, a complex process still awaits. Thorough penetration testing can be very involved, and using a standard process can help keep the test from causing issues or breaking down midway through.

A typical penetration test will use most of the following steps:

1. Documentation of the request for the penetration test, including the authority under which it will be performed, its scope, and who the audience for the results will be

2. Planning and design

3. Identification of the targets of the test

4. Selection of methods and tools

5. Vulnerability testing and validation against the target and/or security assessment of the target

6. Reporting

7. Remediation of issues discovered during the penetration test

> **IMPORTANT PENETRATION TESTING AND PERMISSION**
>
> Penetration testing should only be done with appropriate authorization. Many penetration testers and security professionals refer to this as a "Get out of jail free card," because having the right permission ensures that security testing won't get the tester fired!

Next we will explore each of these steps, including what each requires, what it involves, and what you need to know to execute each step.

Authority, scope, and audience

Three key elements to understand before you begin a penetration test are the authority under which you are conducting it, the scope of the penetration test, and who you are preparing the results for.

Penetration tests should be authorized by an appropriate member of the organization engaging the penetration tester. Often this means the CEO or CIO of an organization, or an equivalent member of management. Equally important is to have written authorization for the test.

The person or group that authorizes the test is typically the sponsor within the organization. The sponsor of a penetration test plays a key role, which usually includes coordination within the organization. In addition, the sponsor can help handle issues that arise during the penetration test, particularly if it is a black box test that staff members in the organization are not aware of.

The sponsor or sponsors of the penetration test will also help to set the scope of the test. Properly scoped tests will include appropriate systems and networks. If scope isn't well defined, or if the scope includes the wrong systems, penetration tests can cause outages or other issues. Obviously. penetration tests bear some risk even at the best of times, but proper scoping can keep those risks within the risk appetite of the organization. Scoping also helps penetration testers estimate how much effort and time they will need to complete the test, which can ensure that appropriate resources are used.

During the scoping process, testers will also typically set the rules of engagement for the penetration test. These should clearly state what the testers are allowed to do, as well as what they are prohibited from doing. If testers are not allowed to use social engineering, or cannot seed the parking lot of the facility with flash drives filled with malware, they need to know this as part of the rules. This means that the penetration testers need to carefully explain what they will be doing to the sponsors, because sponsors are unlikely to realize the full impact of what they may authorize if they are not told.

Finally, penetration testers need to know who their report will be provided to. Often, penetration tests include both a high-level executive summary suitable for senior management as well as a more technical, in-depth report. The executive summary must provide key information about the testing and what issues were found without venturing too far into esoteric technical data. The in-depth report typically includes far deeper detail on what actions were taken, what resulted from the actions, and how vulnerabilities were verified.

If these three initial elements aren't well understood, a penetration test can fail before it starts!

Penetration test planning and design

In order to perform a thorough penetration test, you need a plan. Fortunately, several organizations provide documentation on penetration testing methodologies, including NIST's SP 800-115 Technical Guide to Information Security Testing, the OWASP (Open Web Application Security Project) guide to web application penetration testing, and the Institute for Security and Open Methodologies' (ISECOM's) Open Source Security Testing Methodology Manual, or OSSTMM.

> **MORE INFO   PENETRATION TESTING METHODOLOGIES**
>
> You can find these methodologies the following sites:
>
> - NIST (*csrc.nist.gov/publications/nistpubs/800-115/SP800-115.pdf*)
> - OWASP (*www.owasp.org/index.php/Web_Application_Penetration_Testing*)
> - ISECOM (*www.isecom.org/research/osstmm.html*)
>
> Other methodologies exist, allowing you to choose the methodology or elements that best fit your organization's needs.

Whether you select a third-party methodology, use one to develop your own, or simply create one in house, a thorough penetration testing plan can help avoid problems. Plans help you identify tools and infrastructure, needed information and skills, and when and how the test will be conducted. A well-designed plan can reduce the potential negative impact that attacking an organization's infrastructure can have, while still allowing you to gather useful information.

Target identification

The way targets are identified for a penetration test depends on the type of test being conducted. A white box test will usually be accompanied by a list of targets, including systems, applications, and security procedures that need to be tested. Black and gray box tests provide far less information, leaving identification of targets to the penetration testing team.

Target identification without full knowledge starts with gathering information about the organization. Public information includes public websites, information from web forums, and postings that employees have made about the company. With that information in hand, the penetration tester can gather more detail, including IP address ranges, domains, and other information that can help narrow the list of potential targets.

After the penetration testers have identified a list of potential targets, they will typically conduct information-gathering exercises such as DNS queries, port scans, and sometimes vulnerability scans. Each of these can provide more detail about the systems their target exposes to the world.

MORE INFO **EXPLOIT AND VULNERABILITY DATABASES**

Knowledge is also a key component of testing for vulnerabilities. Most vulnerability assessment tools provide links to known vulnerabilities, but knowing where to find more information is important. Fortunately, large-scale exploit databases exist that can provide information about vulnerabilities, often including working exploit code and details about which versions of software packages have the vulnerability.

Some of the most popular vulnerability resource and reference sites are:

- The Common Vulnerabilities and Exposures (CVE) dictionary run by MITRE (*cve.mitre.org/index.html*)
- The Exploit Database (*www.exploit-db.com/*)
- The Open Sourced Vulnerability Database (*www.osvdb.org/*)
- The National Vulnerability Database (*nvd.nist.gov/*)

Simply entering an application's name into these reference sites can be a very informative exercise.

When they are done, penetration testers will have a list of targets with information about each. From there, they can build a list of penetration testing goals and tasks that will drive the rest of their assessment. In order to complete the assessment, they need to determine what methods and tools they will use to meet their penetration testing goals.

Methods and tools

Penetration testing methods include many of the same attacks discussed in earlier chapters but are intended to determine if a vulnerability exists, rather than to disable the organization. Thus, attacks tend to focus on vulnerability verification, with exploits used to prove that the vulnerability exits or to gain further access to allow deeper testing. Most penetration tests avoid conducting denial of service attacks, although it is possible that an organization may include them in the scope.

Methods for testing are often selected in the planning phase of the penetration test to meet the scope of the assessment. After targets have been identified, those methods can be refined based on information gathered about the targets. If the targets are web servers, then web application testing tools and techniques would be chosen, whereas a Windows domain would require the selection of tools that focus on Active Directory and common Windows vulnerabilities.

A broad variety of tools exist for penetration testers to choose from, ranging from commercial tools to open-source packages, and those that have both commercial and open-source versions, such as the Metasploit Framework. A key part of penetration testing is selecting appropriate tools for the targets of the test.

MORE INFO **LINUX PENETRATION TESTING DISTRIBUTIONS**

In addition to commercial tools, a variety of prepackaged open-source penetration testing tools are available. Some of the most popular include:

- BackTrack Linux (*www.backtrack-linux.org/*)
- Kali Linux, a recent replacement for BackTrack Linux: (*www.kali.org*)
- InGuardians Samurai Web Testing Framework (*samurai.inguardians.com/*)
- Knoppix Security Tools Distribution (STD) (*s-t-d.org/*)
- BugTraq (*bugtraq-team.com/*)
- BackBox Linux (*www.backbox.org/*)

Penetration testing toolkits are constantly being created, and each has its strong points, so it is worth reviewing what toolkits are being actively updated at the time you need to conduct your test. If you prefer to test your skills, distributions such as Metasploitable, a product found at *http://sourceforge.net/projects/metasploitable/files/Metasploitable2/*, provide a playground for penetration testers to attack in a safe lab environment.

Vulnerability testing, validation, and assessment

The full details of how to conduct a penetration test could fill a book on their own. For our purposes, it is important to know that a penetration test should be conducted in accordance with the rules of engagement that the sponsor helped set when the assessment was scoped, and that the tester or testers must be careful to not go beyond that scope without approval.

During a penetration test, the testers will use a variety of scan, attack, and analysis tools. All of the data that is collected should be carefully logged, including notes on when each attack is conducted, what target or targets it is aimed at, and what data was gathered from the attack.

Careful logging and analysis is important, and if a team is conducting the penetration test, a method to keep the team coordinated is very important. Penetration tests can be expensive and dangerous to an organization's business and infrastructure if they are not carefully conducted, so care and diligence are critical.

Reporting

After a penetration test has been completed, a report needs to be prepared for the sponsor or sponsors. In many cases, additional technical reports will also be required for the areas in which issues were identified, because the report to the sponsor of the penetration test is typically a high-level report.

> **IMPORTANT TARGETING YOUR REPORTS**
>
> High-level reports should prioritize issues. Penetration tests can provide massive amounts of information, and understanding what your sponsor is looking for and how to best provide that data to the sponsor is key!

Reports should include the scope, the targets, the tools and methods selected and used, and information about what vulnerabilities were found and successfully validated. Reports should also include details on any vulnerabilities that were identified but that testers were unable to exploit, particularly if they were not exploited due to constraints set by the scope or rules of engagement of the test.

Reports typically include technical information as an appendix or as an additional document. This allows the sponsors to provide detail to system administrators or security staff, which will allow them to put in place appropriate controls or fixes for the issues observed during the test.

Remediation

The final stage of a penetration test is remediation. After the sponsor and those who have a stake in the test have read the report, the issues that were reported must be prioritized and acted on. In most cases, penetration tests find a variety of issues, and not all of them will be remediated due to costs, time constraints, or other reasons.

When remediation is finished, long-term monitoring and maintenance is necessary. The network monitoring techniques we discussed in Chapter 6 are important to implement to ensure that ongoing monitoring occurs. Many organizations choose to perform penetration tests on a recurring basis, and some standards and laws require them.

> **MORE INFO PCI –DSS AND PENETRATION TESTING**
>
> Requirement 11.3 of the Payment Card Industry Data Security Standard (PCI-DSS) credit card standard requires penetration tests at least annually, as well as any time a significant change is made to the credit card processing environment. In fact, the PCI Security Standards Council provides guidance that notes that all upgrades and modifications of the environment should be penetration tested! Their guidance document also suggests that the method and results should be documented to ensure that information about the testing is available. Details of this requirement can be found at *www.pcisecuritystandards.org/pdfs/infosupp_11_3_penetration_testing.pdf.*

Quick check

1. Who authorizes a penetration test?

2. What information should a penetration test report contain?

Quick check answers

1. A senior administrator such as a CEO or CIO should authorize a penetration test. Penetration tests should only be conducted with full authorization from a person who has the authority to permit them, and documentation of the authorization and scope should be retained as part of the test.

2. Penetration test reports should include the scope, methods used, and information about the issues discovered. Typically, reports should include both an executive overview and detailed information for technical staff who need to remediate vulnerabilities found during the test.

Chapter summary

- Risk is used to determine organizational priorities. You can use the equation *Risk = Likelihood × Impact*, to rate risks based on how often they occur and how much harm they would result in.

- Threats leverage vulnerabilities via attack vectors, resulting in business or technical impact. The relationship and differences between risks, threats, and vulnerabilities is important to remember: a risk is the potential that a threat will exploit vulnerabilities of a system, network, or other asset, resulting in harm. A threats is an actor that might exploit a vulnerability.

- A broad range of tools can be used for vulnerability assessment, including protocol analyzers, sniffers, port scanners, and vulnerability scanners. Protocol analyzers and sniffers are used to monitor traffic sent by other tools, and to look at responses. Port scanners and vulnerability scanners are used to actively scan systems and devices.

- The reasons for conducting vulnerability scans including identifying vulnerabilities, verifying security controls, checking for missing controls, and finding misconfigurations.

- Port scans identify accessible services, operating system versions, and other basic information about a system. Vulnerability scans check for service versions and other information about a system and compare that data to a list of known vulnerabilities. Penetration tests often take advantage of both by first scanning for open ports and then targeting specific services.

- Honeypots and honeynets are security tools that invite attackers to break in, and allow security professionals to learn their techniques and tools by capturing them.

- Organizations use assessment techniques such as baseline reporting, which checks current settings against those defined in a security baseline or template; and code review, which explores the source code of an application to ensure that it doesn't contain bugs, mistakes, or other flaws to monitor for new vulnerabilities and risks to their systems and software.

- Design and architecture review, which takes advantage of knowledge of how services, networks, and systems are put together to determine whether they are vulnerable. This also helps to assess the attack surface, which is the part of the design that is accessible to attackers.

- Penetration tests are a hands-on way to test actual vulnerabilities. Penetration tests typically follow a process that starts with authority to conduct a test, then moves through setting a scope, selecting tools, and then performing a penetration test. They typically conclude with a report, followed by application of controls or fixes to identified issues.

- Penetration test view, include black box penetration testing, which provides no data to the tester; gray box testing, which restricts available information; and white box testing, which provides full detail and visibility of the environment to those who are testing it.

Chapter review

Test your knowledge of the information in Chapter 7 by answering these questions. The answers to these questions, and the explanations of why each answer choice is correct or incorrect, are located in the "Answers" section at the end of this chapter.

1. A security tool that is designed to allow attackers to attack a simulated system and thatgathers information about the attackers' tools and techniques is known as what?

   A. A vulnerability detection system

   B. A port scanner

   C. A darknet

   D. A honeypot

2. What type of vulnerability review focuses on how systems are put together?

   A. A penetration test

   B. A vulnerability scan

   C. A design or architecture review

   D. A code review

3. The potential that a threat will exploit vulnerabilities is known as what?

A. A risk

B. A vulnerability

C. A threat

D. An exploit

4. The equation to calculate risk is:

A. *Risk = Likelihood × Vulnerability*

B. *Risk = Impact × Vulnerability*

C. *Risk = Vulnerabilities × Threats*

D. *Risk = Likelihood × Impact*

5. What type of penetration test provides partial visibility into the details of the environment to the testers?

A. Red box

B. White box

C. Gray box

D. Black box

6. What type of testing would you perform to identify services and accessible ports via a network?

A. A port scan

B. A penetration test

C. A vulnerability scan

D. A ping sweep

Answers

This section contains the answers to the questions for the "Chapter review" section in this chapter.

1. **Correct Answer: D**

   A. **Incorrect:** Vulnerability detection system is a made-up term.

   B. **Incorrect:** Port scanners are tools used to scan for open services.

   C. **Incorrect:** A darknet is an unused network set up and instrumented to detect attacks—any traffic sent to a darknet is suspect, because no valid systems should exist there.

   D. **Correct:** A honeypot is designed to allow attackers to compromise a fake system, providing the opportunity to study their actions.

2. **Correct Answer: C**

   A. **Incorrect:** A penetration test tests a broad variety of security controls by attacking systems and networks to attempt to gain access.

   B. **Incorrect:** A vulnerability scan scans for vulnerabilities by using a scanning tool.

   C. **Correct:** A design or architecture review investigates the design of a system, network, or application.

   D. **Incorrect:** A code review targets the source code of an application or service to check it for vulnerabilities and bugs.

3. **Correct Answer: A**

   A. **Correct:** A risk is the potential that a threat will exploit vulnerabilities.

   B. **Incorrect:** A vulnerability is a weakness in a system or asset that can be exploited.

   C. **Incorrect:** A threat is a possible danger that might exploit a vulnerability, resulting in harm to the organization.

   D. **Incorrect:** An exploit is a successful attack against a vulnerability, or a known method of attacking a vulnerability successfully.

4. **Correct Answer: D**

   A. **Incorrect:** Likelihood is important to risk, but vulnerability isn't used in the calculation.

   B. **Incorrect:** Impact is important to risk, but vulnerability isn't used in the calculation.

   C. **Incorrect:** Neither vulnerability nor threats are used in the calculation of risk.

   D. **Correct:** Risk is calculated by multiplying likelihood and impact. This makes higher-impact or higher-probability risks more important.

5. **Correct Answer: C**

   A. **Incorrect:** Red box is not a term associated with penetration testing.

   B. **Incorrect:** White box or crystal box penetration testing allows full visibility and knowledge of the penetration test target.

   C. **Correct:** Gray box penetration testing provides partial knowledge of the target.

   D. **Incorrect:** Black box testing provides no knowledge of the testing target.

6. **Correct Answer: A**

   A. **Correct:** A port scan provides information about open ports, helping to identify services on a network.

   B. **Incorrect:** A port scan is often part of a penetration test, but you are unlikely to perform a complete penetration test to identify services.

   C. **Incorrect:** Vulnerability scans search for vulnerable services but are not the best way to identify them.

   D. **Incorrect:** A ping sweep tries to ping a series of machines to see if they are online and responding to pings—something that most modern operating systems don't do by default.

## CHAPTER 8

The importance of application security

The issues around application security are of utmost importance if there is to be any possibility of reliable data and host security. Application security starts with the programmer during the design and creation phases, and then responsibilities shift to the administrators and users of the environment where the software is employed. However, even with the best intentions, administrators and end users cannot compensate for insecure coding practices. Bad programming leads to vulnerabilities and exploitations. A solid foundation of security managed software creation leads to reliable application security in deployment, management, and use.

Exam objectives in this chapter:

Objective 4.1: Explain the importance of application security

- Fuzzing
- Secure coding concepts
    - Error and exception handling
    - Input validation
- Cross-site scripting prevention
- Cross-site Request Forgery (XSRF) prevention
- Application configuration baseline (proper settings)
- Application hardening
- Application patch management

Fuzzing

Application security is key to the long-term success of any IT endeavor. With well-designed defensive applications, organizations have a fighting chance of standing up to a wide range of attacks and exploitation attempts. However, reliable secure coding practices and solid design management are not as widespread as we would prefer, hence the widespread availability of hacks and attacks against software products.

Vulnerable and flawed software includes operating systems, services, client applications, general software, network protocol stacks, and add-ons and extensions to base products, as well as updates and patches. Even firmware (on-device–stored software) and BIOS (firmware on a mainboard) often have flaws and vulnerabilities. No software product type or category is excluded from having issues or flaws.

New attacks and exploits are constantly being developed by malicious programmers. As security researchers and system managers uncover new exploits, an attack is initially labeled as a zero-day attack. A zero-day attack is simply any new attack or form of compromise against which there is initially no specific defense. The term is derived from the idea that the victim is given zero days' notice of the impending compromise or the fact that a vulnerability is present. After a new attack is examined and countermeasures are developed, it loses the zero-day moniker and becomes known by its name and malware categorization. For example, Citadel, a form of malware that extorts money from victims, was initially labeled as a zero-day attack, but it now has a name and is categorized as a malware delivery/injection toolkit that can be used to plant other malware, such as ransomware. Ransomware is an attack that locks, freezes, or encrypts data or an entire computer, then displays messages that attempt to extort the victim into paying money to have the system released.

In Chapter 5, "Threats and attacks," several common application attacks were described in detail, including cross-site scripting, SQL injection, command injection, and buffer overflow. It is common knowledge among programmers and developers that there are probably one to five flaws, errors, or defects (on average) in every 1,000 lines of released programming code. It stands to reason that often compromises are made possible in software because of errors in the software's code.

But how does a hacker find an error, bug, flaw, or defect in software code if the designers, developers, programmers, managers, and QA analysts missed it before releasing a product for public use? And how do hackers find flaws to write exploits for, even when the vendors attempt to keep that information hidden? There are at least three different techniques that can be used: source code review, patch analysis, and fuzzing.

Source code review is the tedious process of reading and interpreting source code line by line by line. This is a challenging task, but many expert programmers, both ethical as well as malicious, often review code in detail looking for mistakes. Hackers can gain access to open-source code or stolen proprietary code, or they can use decompilers. Open-source code is software that is released in its original form so the public can review and alter it before compiling it into an executable form. Many free software projects are open source.

EXAM TIP

Open-source software has not been found to be any better or worse than commercial closed-source software in relation to security design or errors in the code (see "A Tale of Four Kernels" by Diomidis Spinellis at *http://www.dmst.aueb.gr/dds/pubs/conf/2008-ICSE-4kernel/html/Spi08b.html*).

Most proprietary and commercial code is compiled into ready-to-execute form before a new software product is released for licensed customers. This is done to minimize access to the code in order to protect patented processes and intellectual property. However, hackers are sometimes able to breach the security of an organization and steal copies of the original noncompiled code. Another option for hackers is to decompile an executable product back into raw code. Although the results of decompiling are not exactly the same as the original code, they are a representation of that code, which is often close enough to reveal flaws and defects. This technique is sometimes referred to as reverse engineering rather than source code review.

If adversaries are unable to access the source code, another option is to examine the patches, hotfixes, and updates released for a target product. By focusing on the code altered or replaced by patches, hackers can focus their attention on flaws already known to the software vendor. At first, it might seem a bit counterintuitive for a hacker to want to develop an attack based on a flaw that already has a patch available for it. However, so many systems remain unpatched for a significant period of time that there is often still a large window of opportunity in exploiting patchable vulnerabilities. To see this in effect today, visit the attack tracking site at *http:// atlas.arbor.net*. The site includes a section on global attacks and threats for the past 24 hours. You are likely to find that one or more of the top ongoing attacks is against a vulnerability discovered and patched 2 to 12 years ago.

 A third way hackers discover errors or flaws in code is through *fuzzing*. Fuzzing or *fuzz testing* is a software evaluation technique that attempts to uncover errors in coding through stressing the input processing of a targeted application. A fuzz-testing tool, or fuzzer, generates invalid, abnormal, unexpected, out-of-bounds, and often random input data sets and watches how the target application responds or handles the odd inputs. After discovering an input that causes an abnormal reaction, such as a delay in response, unauthorized access, data displays or dumps, crashes, exposure of memory leaks, or verbose error messages, the fuzzer logs the input and continues to perform more testing. The hacker inspects the output log from time to time, hoping that the fuzzer locates attack gold quickly. However, fuzz testing only has the potential to discover flaws in applications; there is never a guarantee. And the testing can last for weeks or months with no results.

Fuzz testing or fuzzing has become a staple in the software development and quality assurance fields, as well as in criminal hacking. Fuzzing is a form of black-box testing where the internal logic and structure of a target is unknown and the attacker or tester must discover everything through submitted inputs and examination of outputs, responses, and behaviors. The brute-force mechanisms of fuzz testing are often able to stress test a product far beyond what a normal or typical use environment would be able to do. Additionally, fuzz testing includes abnormal, unexpected, and invalid inputs in its testing parameters to simulate some of the analysis methods used by hackers to discover flaws.

It is important to remember that any flaws discovered through source code review, patch analysis, and fuzzing were left there by the programmers. With higher quality coding practices, many of these flaws could be discovered and addressed before a software product is released for use. In fact, development companies can run fuzz testers against their own products during development and as a final hardening procedure before release. Then they should continue to search for issues after release in order to roll out patches to fix any remaining issues as they are uncovered.

 Quick check

1. What are the three techniques hackers can use to discover coding flaws?

2. Who can employ fuzz testing?

Quick check answers

1. Source code review, patch analysis, and fuzzing

2. Anyone with access to software can perform fuzzing, but those who are most likely to use fuzzers are hackers and programmers or developers.

Secure coding concepts

Fuzz testing is only one of the threats to the security of applications. Many other examples were discussed in Chapter 5, such as cross-site scripting, SQL injection, command injection, and buffer overflow. Often these attacks are made possible by the coding practices of the programmer and the development environment.

Crafting software code is a skill that a growing number of people are cultivating. Most who write programming code often learned just enough to create functional software, but little more. Others might have been trained on secure coding practices, but due to time constraints, cost limitations, perceived difficulty, or simply oversight and laziness, left out defensive mechanisms. It does require specific focus and intent to embed into software defensive elements that mitigate common vulnerabilities and attack methodologies. Secure coding practices need to be more widely adopted by all programmers. The best protection against attacks to software starts with well-written defensive code.

Although individuals can learn to be defensive programmers, often it takes an organization with various levels of management, supervision, auditing, assessment, and quality assurance in order to consistently implement the more effective secure coding practices. Consistency in creating secure software takes significant time, focus, and effort. When properly achieved, secure code is much more resistant to traditional attacks and exploitation attempts (see *http://www.owasp.org/index.php/Secure_Coding_Principles*). Secure coding does not guarantee the security of an application, but it gives the application a strong starting position when compared to other, less-secure coding alternatives.

The collection of processes and methodologies employed to produce a more consistently secure and reliable coding environment is a component of a well-thought-out software development life cycle (SDLC). Also known as a *systems development life cycle*, SDLC defines a framework for the planning, oversight, and control of the programming process with a focus on secure coding practices. SDLC often includes elements that range from mandating defensive coding practices to the development of end-user training.

SDLC can be implemented in many ways, and there are several methodologies for how it should be used. However, those details are well beyond the scope and focus of the CompTIA Security+ exam.

For the CompTIA Security+ test, only a few of the scattered elements of SDLC are actually relevant to the exam content. These include the following:

- Design from a standpoint of implicit denial and the principle of least privilege.
- Perform design reviews before starting coding.
- Perform code reviews throughout the programming process.
- Perform threat modeling and address any identified significant risk.

- Review compiler logs for errors and warnings.
- Control error messages to prevent fault disclosure to users.
- Sanitize output to minimize data loss or disclosure to unauthorized users.
- Define the intended audience and develop appropriate control interfaces and training.
- Design a test plan and simulated data sets.
- Perform user acceptance testing before locking the code base.
- Take advantage of operating system security features, such as data execution prevention (DEP) and address space layout randomization (ASLR).

EXAM TIP

DEP is a security mechanism used to protect against arbitrary code being executed from random locations in memory. DEP is primarily a defense against buffer overflow attacks where injected executable code can take over a system. DEP separates memory into executable and nonexecutable regions. Any code not in an executable region is prevented from executing. ASLR is used to randomize the memory locations of core system components during their initial loading phase at startup. This prevents malware from finding where components, code, drivers, or sensitive values are located. Malware known as Frankenstein malware attempts to construct malicious code from existing system components through the use of memory address references. If those components are located in random locations, the Frankenstein malware fails.

In addition to this list of general elements found in SDLC for secure coding practices, the CompTIA Security+ objectives list points out two specific concerns: error and exception handling, and input validation.

Error handling and exception handling

It is important to control error messages to prevent fault disclosure to users. Although programmers might strive to write the best code possible, there are often numerous errors, typos, and mistakes. Some are even errors in data flow or code design or procedure. Quality assurance and code review practices seek to locate these concerns, but many often still remain in the final product. However, when a user performs an action that encounters a programming issue, the message delivered to the user about the problem needs to be securely controlled with *error handling* and *exception handling*.

Often when a program fails, it reveals sensitive details to the user. These details might disclose specifics of the program, database interfaces, supporting services, identities, data structures, path and file names, and more. To the typical end user, such an informative error message is of no value, because most of the contents have no meaning to them. However, if a hacker can trigger a verbose error message, the details of such a message can often assist in the targeting of a exploit.

Error and exception handling is a key component in secure coding practices. Verbose error messages leak information and details to hackers, so limiting error messages to simple statements can reduce this concern. It is also important to remember that error and exception handling can refer to the idea of designing in a general default operational response to errors, such as freezing operations, halting processing, or rebooting. These potentially fail-safe, fail-secure, or fail-close options might prevent an accident or attack from gaining unauthorized access to resources or data due to an application error.

Not all errors are caused by poor coding or design practices. Some error messages are caused by abnormal or out-of-bounds input. Such input could simply be a mistake on the part of a user, but it could also be the intended probing of a hacker seeking out flaws or details to exploit. In any case, verbose error messages need to be stored in a log file that is only accessible to administrators or system managers. End users only need to be told that an error occurred and what action they should take next, such as trying again, coming back later, or contacting technical support. Providing any other details, other than maybe a nondescriptive reference code to be provided to technical support for context, is only going to lead to either end user confusion or increased intrusion and compromise activity.

Proper error message handling therefore focuses on pre-crafting the error messages that are to be displayed to a user. This also requires the creation of an exception-handling or fault-handling mechanism. Leaving error handling up to the operating system or execution environment often leads to oversharing of database details. When a programmer includes his or her own error-handling and exception-handing subroutines, the messages of and about errors are under control and cause less leaking of security-related information.

Input validation

Input should be considered potentially harmful until it has been validated and sanitized. Suspect input could lead to intrusion and other forms of security compromise. Many forms of compromise and attacks are made possible by the lack of input validation, including buffer overflows, CGI scripting attacks, injection attacks, command injection, SQL injection, XML injection, Lightweight Directory Access Protocol (LDAP) injection, cross-site scripting (XSS), and cross-site request forgery XSRF). It is important to make sure that all input is in compliance with what your program was designed to process. Blindly trusting the dynamic input from users is a recipe for security failures.

Input validation is the inspection, analysis, parsing, and filtering of data before it is accepted for use. (Note that most inputs are stored in memory, then pulled from memory to be processed.) However, input validation is not just looking for invalid input. Creating a master filter list of specific examples of malicious input is not possible. Hackers are adept at crafting new payload constructions that do not match existing pattern filters. It is often more effective to create a filter to check that input is legal and within defined boundaries.

Some inputs are easily limited to only a small set of valid values, such as input expecting only numbers or items selected from a provided set of options (such as sizes or colors). Other forms of input are a bit more challenging, such as strings (arbitrary text, such as a comment or question from a user), file names, locations, dates, URLs, and email addresses. But each of these is still an example of input that can be limited to a set of known values, ranges, constructions, and character options. Filters for these types of input are known as boundary or domain limitations.

Attempting to create a master blacklist of all possible invalid or illegal inputs is unrealistic. However, there are some specific invalid or undesired inputs you could still focus on. For example, metacharacters received in input could result in command injection attacks or scripting execution. A metacharacter is any character that has been assigned a special programmatic meaning by a programming language or execution environment. Common metacharacters include quotations, plus signs, equal signs, less-than and greater-than signs, semicolons, dots or decimals, ampersands, and dashes or minus signs (", ', +, =, <, >, :, ., &, and -). However, the special meaning or function of metacharacters can be avoided by escaping them Escaping is the use of an escape character, often the backslash (\), just before the metacharacter, which causes the string or statement to "escape" from the meaning or function of the metacharacter that follows.

In certain situations, having a short list of explicit denial filters might make sense. For example, blocking script calls or SQL expression statements from being accepted in input to a web server is often a good defensive measure. What is important is not to get caught up in creating an exhaustive list of filters for the undesired input. Instead, focus on defining the finite range of allowed input and check to see that what is received falls within that context.

The buffer overflow attack is a common and popular attack against software targets. A buffer overflow attack can be performed both over the Internet and in localized on-system attacks. A buffer overflow is often made possible by the use of unbounded functions from a programming language. This allows for arbitrarily large inputs to be sent to a vulnerable program, which results in the allocated memory area (the buffer) being filled, after which the additional input is allowed to flow into the next sections of memory. Such an occurrence can cause system crashes, compromise data stored in memory, or lead to arbitrary code execution. Most buffer overflow attacks can be prevented through the use of an input limit check.

An input limit check is a filter that verifies that received input is within an expected valid range or length of data. If the input is outside the specified size requirements, it is rejected. In other words, it is not allowed to enter memory, so its unwanted consequences are prevented.

In addition to escaping metacharacters, performing input limit checks, and implementing boundary and domain definition, there are many other forms of input validation, such as:

- **Allowed character confirmation**   Ensures that only the intended characters are contained in the input
- **Batch total check**   Detects missing records or skipped activities due to the batched or combined results not equaling an expected total

- **Cardinality check**   Verifies that the specific number of items or records exists
- **Check digits validation**   Calculates an additional digit from the original number and then adds it to the end
- **Consistency check**   Cross-checks related or dependent values to ensure that they are linked or consistent, such as that a title value of Mrs. matches a gender value of Female.
- **Data type check**   Ensures that only expected data types (such as numbers or letters) are received
- **Format check**   Ensures that data is of the proper format structure, often by using a regular expression filter such as checking dates with MM/DD/YYYY
- **Language check**   Verifies that the expected language is used, such as English versus Spanish
- **Logic check**   Verifies that input does not result in a logical error
- **Presence check**   Ensures that needed data is present
- **Spelling and grammar check**   Verifies that spelling and grammar rules are being followed
- **Uniqueness check**   Ensures that the input is unique

EXAM TIP

The topic of input validation and sanitation can become quite technical in a hurry. The CompTIA Security+ exam does not typically dive into detail on programming topics, because it is more concerned with the general idea of secure coding practices. For the exam, remember that checking the length and the type or format of content are elements of input validation.

Input validation can take on many forms. It is an essential part of secure coding practice and is essential for maintaining defenses against a wide range of security compromise and intrusion.

 Quick check

1. Where should detailed error messages be sent?

2. What attacks might be prevented when input validation is used?

Quick check answers

1. To a secured log file for administrators and system managers

2. Buffer overflow, CGI scripting attacks, injection attacks, command injection, SQL injection, XML injection, LDAP injection, XSS, and XSRF

Cross-site scripting prevention

Cross-site scripting (XSS) attacks are an exploitation of a user's trust in a website. However, the technical flaw that is exploited is usually the lack of input sanitization on the web server. By giving a hacker the ability to inject scripts into an otherwise safe or typical website, website designers and programmers are playing a dangerous game with their visitors. Often the symptoms of an XSS attack are not evident until after the harm has been caused to the client.

Cross-site scripting attacks have become one of those most common forms of web server attacks in recent history, rivaling the occurrence rates of SQL injection and buffer overflow. XSS exploits are a favorite of hackers because of their effectiveness, the extent of damage or access possible, and the ease by which they can be implemented. The general idea of an XSS exploit is to send attack code to a vulnerable web server in order to plant altered content. This altered content is then sent to subsequent visitors, on whose systems the client-side execution of the injected malicious code takes effect.

> **MORE INFO** **LOOK BACK TO XSS**
>
> More information on XSS was presented in Chapter 5.

The focus of this section on XSS prevention. However, there are several varieties of XSS attacks, as well as uncountable actual versions of XSS exploit code. Thus, simple or universal prevention of XSS from the web server's perspective is not always possible. Often, a countermeasure focuses on one specific form of XSS or blocks a particular mechanism employed during either the initial injection or subsequent distribution of compromised material.

Fortunately, for clients, there is a simple fix: disable all scripting or execution support for all forms of mobile code. Often the primary culprit in malicious scripts is JavaScript, but there have been attacks using other scripting and mobile code languages and platforms, so XSS is not exclusively JavaScript based. However, disabling all scripting and mobile code support will cause most websites to stop functioning properly (as perceived by the client). So, though this is a sure defense against XSS, it is a difficult solution to live with. Without client-side execution, most popular and even essential web services (such as those that are work-related or financial) will no longer be useable. Most users would rather live with some risk and still have access to these sites, rather than be fully cut off from them.

> **EXAM TIP**
>
> The CompTIA Security+ exam will likely focus more on the elements of web server prevention techniques than on prevention on the client. The client-side protections are the standard cautions to avoid risky behaviors and disable scripting.

So the onus often falls back onto the website's owners, managers, designers, and programmers. In fact, as discussed previously, the original programmers have the greatest responsibility to create reliable, secure defensive code. Only with defensive code can most of the common exploits and attacks be prevented.

The primary means by which a website can defend against or prevent XSS is to filter and sanitize input from visitors. The exploit code from a cross-site scripting attack can be injected into the web server by the hacker directly or through a transitive exploitation of an innocent client. If an innocent client clicks on a hyperlink from an email message or other website that is crafted to inject the exploit script to the target website, then the client is inadvertently made the delivery agent for the attack.

A web server's filtering and sanitization of input is not a simple function enabled by the click of a mouse. It takes some adroit programming skills. Generally, this is implemented by using a whitelisting concept where all input is rejected by default unless it satisfies the filter requirements of items or rules on the allowed list. Other important additions to whitelisting include escaping metacharacters from input, using an anti–cross-scripting coding library, and being cautious about how web documents and forms are constructed. There are many specific details about how to implement these defenses that we are not including here, mostly because they change over time and they are too detailed for the CompTIA Security+ exam.

> **MORE INFO**   **HOW TO STOP XSS**
>
> If you would like to learn more about web server XSS prevention, see *https://www.owasp.org/index.php/XSS_(Cross_Site_Scripting)_Prevention_Cheat_Sheet*.

 Quick check

1. XSS is an attack that is an exploitation of what?

2. What is the best defense against XSS for a client? What is best for a server?

Quick check answers

1. Cross-site scripting (XSS) attacks are an exploitation of a user's trust in a website. However, the technical flaw that is exploited is usually the lack of input sanitization on the web server.

2. A client's best defense is to disable scripting in his or her browser. A server's best defense is to perform input sanitization.

Cross-site request forgery (XSRF) prevention

 Cross-site request forgery (XSRF) is an attack that takes advantage of a server's trust in an authenticated user account or user's system. The attack can be waged by malicious code infecting a client's machine, which stays dormant or stealthy until a connection to the target server is established. This attack could also be waged via a scripting mechanism where the client is tricked into clicking a hyperlink that injects a script to the server. In either case, the client is unaware of the attack event, because it piggybacks on the authenticated session without affecting the normal operation, function, or result of the connection.

EXAM TIP

It is easy to get caught up in the technical details in relation to XSS and XSRF, but here are the basics:

1. Both are based on scripting attacks.

2. Both are possible due to a lack of input sanitization on the part of the web server.

3. XSS attacks start on the web server, whereas XSRF attacks start on the client.

4. Both attacks can harm the client's system or modify the client's account on the web server.

One of the more insidious aspects of an XSRF attack is its ability to harm a server or a client's account or session on a server even across a fully authenticated and encrypted connection. It is important to realize that the flaw or vulnerability being exploited is a server's inability to distinguish forged transactions from legitimate commands and requests coming from an authenticated client. With a client system that has already been infected by malware or a user who is tricked into clicking a malicious hyperlink, the attack is able to interact with the server over an otherwise secured connection. All encrypted communications have two weak points—namely, the endpoints or entrance and exit anchors of the encrypted tunnel. Side attacks of the transaction might be prevented, but attacks can still enter into one end of an encrypted tunnel in order to attack the system on the other end.

End users have a responsibility to keep their systems from being compromised locally to prevent XSRF and other types of attacks caused or perpetrated by malware. They are responsible for avoiding risky behaviors that might expose them to malware infection. Advice to users for reducing their risk of exposure to XSRF include these cautions:

- Be suspicious of all hyperlinks, especially of those sent via email, instant messaging, or through social networks.

- Always use the logoff function to leave a site or web application.

- Do not allow the browser to store logon credentials.

- Do not allow websites to "remember" your logon details.

- Use separate browsers (or operating systems) between financial sites and general personal web access.

- Make use of security plugins, such as ScriptNo and NoScript.

- Disable client-side scripting, such as JavaScript, Java, and ActiveX.

However, XSRF exploitations ultimately depend on a design and/or coding flaw in the target server.

Because XSRF takes advantage of a server's lack of input sanitization and verification, it is mostly the responsibility of the server's designers and programmers to address any issue that an XSRF attack could exploit. Servers that accept commands or instructions to perform sensitive operations without reverifying the identity of the user are at risk for XSRF attacks. It is important to differentiate between requests from the actual user versus the browser or other software being manipulated by malicious code. Because the command will be received through the same authenticated connection whether the issuance is from a malicious source or the user, it is up to the server to differentiate. This is usually accomplished by asking for a reverification of authentication credentials before taking action on a sensitive or risky operation. To repeat, XSRF attacks are dependent on target servers that fail to verify that a request action is actually from the user, and not just received through the established connection.

Numerous major websites have been discovered to have XSRF flaws, including banks, social networks, shopping sites, video sites, news agencies, and more. Many web programmers and designers are often caught off-guard when investigative users or security scans detect XSRF vulnerabilities in their sites. Many XSRF vulnerabilities exist not because of bugs or errors in design and coding, but because programmers lack an understanding of how such exploitations work and don't include specific defenses against it.

An XSRF attack is limited by the level of access or power the victim user has on the target system. The user's role or privilege level on a service limits the depth and scope of damage that an XSRF attack can cause. When the user is a typical end-user with limited capabilities, only the user's data within a service is at risk. However, even end-user–level access can be significant when related to an e-commerce or e-banking site. An XSRF attack could potentially drain a bank account (as in the case of the Zeus banking trojan) or make false charges on a credit card stored in an online retail site. If a user's role on a site is of a more powerful nature, such as manager, moderator, administrator, or root, then the XSRF attack could potentially compromise the entire web service or application as well as other aspects of the host operating system.

There are several techniques for reducing or potentially eliminating the risk of XSRF. Many of these are fairly advanced session and cookie management mechanisms far beyond the scope of the CompTIA Security+ exam. Generally, they include the exchange of a secret random code in webpages, forms, objects, and double submit cookies (that is, using a hidden form value and a cookie with the same pseudorandom session ID), which must be returned intact in order for the request to be accepted as valid. Because most compromises of the client system that result in XSRF attacks craft their own response/reply values independent of any content actually received by the browser, they would not include the random value.

MORE INFO   **MORE ON XSRF**

For a more in-depth look at these options, see *https://www.owasp.org/index.php/ Cross-Site_Request_Forgery_(CSRF)_Prevention_Cheat_Sheet* or just *http://www.owasp.org* and search using "CSRF" or "XSRF".

In addition to a random value exchange, almost any of the human detection mechanisms could be employed to reduce XSRF vulnerabilities. These are tools and techniques to detect that responses or communications from a connected session are under the control of a human and are not automated responses produced by robot software, especially malicious code software that could be attempting an XSRF attack. Most of these techniques are considered a form of challenge-response and are designed specifically to be difficult for an automated tool to be able to solve. They include:

- **CAPTCHA (and reCAPTCHA)**   Ask the user to type in an answer from viewing a distorted word, phrase, or random characters. ReCAPTCHA is also used to automatically perform OCR on scanned books and manuscripts (see *http://www.google.com/ recaptcha*).

- **Task activities**   Ask the user to perform simple drag-and-drop tasks, such as matching or reordering; these activities can also include simple games such as tic-tac-toe.

- **Image tasks or interpretation**   Ask the user to type in a response to a question about an image, such as, "What is on the table?" or "What is the girl doing?" when the image is of a breakfast table with a girl reading a book. Alternatively, you can have the user click an area of an image based on a question, such as "Where is the waffle?"

- **Audio questions**   Have the user listen to an audio clip and type in the words or letters heard.

- **Math operations**   Have the user provide an answer to a complex or simple math problem.

- **Trivia questions**   Ask simple questions, such as, "What do you call frozen water?" or "What is the color of the sun?"

- **SMS or text message verification**   Send a code or word SMS/text message to a user's phone or messaging account, then ask for that code/word to be typed back into the interface.

- **Secondary confirmation page**   Have an additional confirmation page after a form field submission, asking the user to review the received data before proceeding.

- **Timing detection**   Users require time to type in information in form fields, but bots can perform the task instantly. If a form is submitted too quickly, it is likely not under the control of a user.

- **Hidden field test**   Include an unnecessary but common field (such as email address, phone number, or county) in a form, then use CSS or other methods to hide the field from display to the user. A bot would still see the field and would fill it in with information, whereas a user would not and would thus leave it blank.

- **Advertisement interpretation**   Show an advertisement image or banner, then ask a simple question about the product, company, or slogan.

Another XSRF prevention technique is to simply prompt the user to reauthenticate before performing a sensitive task, such as changing a password, altering shipping information, making a purchase on a store credit card, or scheduling a money transfer.

 Quick check

1. What is the concept of exploitation by an XSRF attack?

2. What general technique can be used on a web server to reduce XSRF attacks?

Quick check answers

1. XSRF or cross-site request forgery is an attack that takes advantage of a server's trust in an authenticated user account or user's system.

2. Verify that commands are from a user and not an unauthorized third party.

Application configuration baseline (proper settings)

A baseline is the written documentation of minimal requirements for a computer system. An *application configuration baseline* outlines the essential proper settings and configurations for software. In many organizations, there are several different security baseline policies defined for the various computers and their specific roles. Although there are often many common elements in the various baseline definitions, there are often distinct requirements based on a system's function or purpose. There should be separately defined baselines for desktop workstations, mobile notebook systems, tablets, smartphones, data and resource servers, border devices, DMZ/extranet servers, domain controllers, remote access servers, VPN servers, and so on.

One purpose of a baseline is to ensure consistency in deployment across an organization. Every new system must be constructed and configured in compliance with the baseline before it is installed into production. Every production system needs to be assessed in relation to the baseline to confirm ongoing operational compliance with the baseline. As the baseline is improved and adjusted based on changing security conditions, threats, or business tasks, all systems need to be adjusted to close any compliance gaps.

Baselines often include hardware and software requirements. This can include firmware versions, startup settings, operating system versions, patch levels, security add-ins (such as firewalls, antimalware, and IDS), and productivity applications. In addition to the required hardware and software, a baseline should also define the desired configuration and settings as well.

The task of setting up a new system to be in compliance with a baseline can be quite extensive, time consuming, and tedious. A common process to simplify the task is to spend the effort once to build a template system, then create an image clone of its storage devices. This baseline image can then be applied to other systems with compliant hardware to quickly install all of the software and settings. Periodic updates to the baseline image can be created when the number of updates begins to be significant.

Baselines are used to standardize system deployment and ensure security compliance. The use of a baseline can reduce the time and costs associated with rolling out new equipment. Customizations and one-off constructions can still be crafted when necessary, but these should be minimized to avoid straying from the preferred security stance.

Many organizations implement new systems into a lab, testing, or piloting environment before approving them for deployment into the production network. If a system doesn't meet the requirements of the baseline due to mistakes, oversights, or installation or configuration errors, it is important to protect the production systems from potential exposure to compromised computers. As a new system is being set up, it can be isolated from production. After it has been confirmed to be in compliance, it can be approved for deployment into a position for productive use.

Baselines can also be established for business tasks, procedures, multidevice systems, and users. Many business operations require specific steps to be performed in order and in specific ways to accomplish a goal but also prevent security violations. By defining training and operational baselines, an organization can maintain quality of tasks and processes. Multidevice systems and solutions are often very complicated. Even when every individual machine is baseline compliant, there can still be issues in data exchange or distributed processing. Establishing a baseline for systems and solutions that employ numerous elements to perform essential business operations can help to ensure greater uptime and availability. Baselines for users often focus on general security awareness as well as job-specific training. Educational efforts often provide direct benefits of increased productivity and reduced security violations.

Application hardening

Hardening is a security management process that includes two primary steps or phases:

1. Remove unnecessary components.

2. Secure that which is a necessary component.

At first this might seem like a simple concept; however, the implementation of hardening is often anything but simple. The process of hardening often involves repeated application of these two phases. Every update or change can lead to extraneous elements, which in turn leads to new vulnerabilities that need to be secured.

EXAM TIP

The two primary steps of hardening—removing unnecessary components and securing that which is a necessary component—do not need to be implemented in any specific order. In fact, real-world hardening sometimes requires removal first, but other times requires securing first. However, on the exam, if you are prompted about which is an earlier or later step in hardening, keep the number order listed here in mind.

Hardening can be somewhat simplified by breaking it into smaller areas of focus or concern. These separated operations could include system hardening, platform hardening, operating system hardening, network hardening, application hardening, and possibly others. Hardening appears twice in the CompTIA Security+ official objectives list. The first mention is in objective 3.6 as the term *hardening*. Objective 3.6 is discussed in Chapter 6, "Monitoring, detection, and defense." The second mention is in objective 4.1 as the term *application hardening*, which is what is covered here. There is usually significant overlap in the various focused efforts of hardening, and there is also some repetition of the coverage of hardening between this section and the discussion in Chapter 6.

Application hardening, as well as every other hardening focus, should be driven by standardized company policies, procedures, and guidelines. It is a very good habit to have all security management steps written down so they can be followed, such as in a step-by-step checklist. This is especially true of the activities of hardening. However, hardening might require that some steps or entire procedures be repeated several times, because later actions (especially updating software, installing patches, or implementing security solutions) could result in new extraneous components, elements, or features. Thus, hardening policies need to be thorough as well as flexible.

The function of hardening is to reduce the attack surface of a system, network, and/or organization. As fluff or additional elements accumulate, the number of vulnerabilities increases as well. Hardening assists with the overall goal of security, which is to prevent compromise and misuse. With the potential of errors or flaws in code, leaving unnecessary software active or accessible on a production system simply increases the risk of compromise. Most organizations understand that the primary task of IT is to maintain the ability to perform business tasks (the mission-critical business functions). Failing to remove all unnecessary risks will lessen an organization's ability to remain viable and operational.

When a hardening process is being applied to a specific system, it is essential to document every step along the way. Every update, every uninstall, every setting change, every disabled element, every alteration should be recorded into an activity log. This log will be helpful in keeping track of what has and has not been accomplished. It allows an auditor to check or review the work of security personnel and compare the final results of the procedure to the claimed expectations. A hardening log also helps the organization understand the complexities of the process and assists IT in developing better procedures for future implementations. The hardening documentation can also be used as a basis for training new employees on the steps employed.

Hardening should initially focus on the native features and security services of an application. Additional supporting security services and mechanisms can be added to supplement any insufficient native capabilities. When designing, architecting, or coding a new solution, it is important to consider the implementation and hardening issues that production or the marketplace will face. Including core security features in new products will assist with making new applications more secure natively, but it also will reduce the burden of hardening and reduce the need for supplemental security solutions. This will not only save money, but time and effort, while usually providing for more reliable security.

Some common elements in a hardening process, especially related to application hardening, include:

- Considering installation of the most current version of software from the vendor or programmer (see the section "Application patch management," later in this chapter).
- Installing all available updates and patches.

- If possible, performing a code review.
- Disabling unnecessary features.
- Deleting example files or sample data.
- Changing default account credentials.
- Considering every default setting and adjusting for the organization's specific needs and environment.
- Updating device drivers for relevant hardware.
- Disabling plain-text access to management interfaces, requiring encrypted connections.
- Blocking any unused or unneeded ports.
- Synchronizing system clocks and time zones.
- Configuring auditing and logging.
- Configuring performance monitoring.
- Establishing a performance, security, and use baseline.
- Using a file system that supports authorization control, auditing, and other security features.
- Implementing the principle of least privilege on all accounts.
- Compartmentalizing administrative accounts via separation of duties.
- Disabling last user account display.
- Installing local filtering.
- Considering the use of a proxy.
- Implementing a firewall.
- Using malware scanners.
- Requiring multifactor authentication.
- Configuring account lockout.
- Displaying a legal warning banner against unauthorized use and access.
- Configuring backups.
- Running a vulnerability scanner against the system.
- Performing fuzz testing.
- Implementing the system initially in a test or pilot system.
- Getting approval of assessment results before deployment into production.

This is a great list of hardening elements to remember for the exam. Many of these are repetitions of other exam topics and objectives. However, do keep in mind that this is only a representative sample and not an exhaustive list of all possible real-world activities performed during hardening.

When designing the steps or elements of a hardening procedure, it is important to consider the known existing vulnerabilities, the needed business functions, potential threats, and costs. Evaluate all potential sources or causes of compromise, including:

- Intrusions.
- Compromises that might initiate from outside threats as well as from the inside.
- Intentional damage as well as accidental damage.
- Use by trained professionals as well as fumbling by ignorant users.
- Targeted and focused attacks as well as broad and diffused efforts.
- Physical, logical, and social attacks.

It is also important to consider attacks from both a software/application perspective as well as from hardware and networking perspectives. Hardening is a customized operation for each organization and for each major type of system, computer, network, or software. Hardening is often used as a process to implement or achieve system compliance with organizational baselines.

✔ **Quick check**

1. What are the two primary steps in hardening?
2. What is the function of hardening?

Quick check answers

1. Removing unnecessary components and securing that which is a necessary component
2. The function of hardening is to reduce the attack surface of a system, network, and/or organization.

Application patch management

Application patch management is an essential part of application and system hardening. As such, it is an element of sound security management. In general, the most currently updated version of software is the most secure version. This is not absolutely always true, but most updates and patches focus on fixing security issues and closing vulnerabilities. So it is reasonable to assume that for most situations, updates are beneficial. However, in those cases where an update interferes with a business task or introduces new problems, such as instability or new vulnerabilities, the update might not be as desirable.

Thus, to deal with the possibility that an update that is intended to improve an application actually causes problems, a formal system of patch management is needed. Patch management might be referred to as update management, configuration management, or change management. Though these terms are not strictly synonyms, they are similar in nature and seem to be used interchangeably on the exam. No matter what the formal label, the idea is generally the same: Any update or change that is to be applied to a production system needs to be formally evaluated before being installed.

An update, service pack, hot fix, patch, or whatever a vendor or programmer calls the new code he wants to apply to an installed application is a change. Changes can cause problems. In fact, unmanaged changes have the potential of causing unexpected conflicts and security reductions. Thus, a formal patch management system is needed to oversee changes. Only those changes that are shown to cause little or no significant negative results are eventually approved for installation onto production systems.

EXAM TIP

Patch management is an important part of security. However, traditional patch management mandates significant manual attention by administrators. Fortunately, automated solutions have been developed. Some implementations of NAC (network access control) are automated. (NAC is covered in Chapter 3, "Secure network design and management").

An application patch management system should always ensure that only valid and original updates from a vendor are applied. Patches should only be obtained directly from the vendor and not through a third party. Patches should be verified by file name, change data, size, hash value, and digital signature when available. These verification procedures will eliminate the possibility of installing the wrong patch, a corrupted patch, or a maliciously modified patch.

Before any updates or patches are installed, the current system and application should be backed up. This could include both file-by-file forms of backup as well as a storage device imaging backup. It is also useful to extract or export a configuration or setting file. The purpose of a backup is to ensure that there is a rollback or backout potential in the event that an update still causes unexpected results even after formal testing is performed and approval attained.

All patches and updates should be applied to systems in a lab or pilot environment for initial testing and evaluation. The systems in the lab or pilot should be clones of the production system or as much like that system as possible. Systems should be tested and evaluated on performance and security before and after patch application. The results of these tests should be compared to gain an understanding of the effects and consequences of an update. These findings should then be reviewed by a separate auditor or change approval board. Only upon written approval should a tested update be installed into a production environment.

Updates should be scheduled to occur at the start of a known periodic or scheduled time frame of reduced workload or downtime. For many organizations this is either the typical weekend or might be a scheduled day or two once a month. Scheduling patch applications during less intensive operational time frames reduces the chance of a failed update process or unintended consequences causing significant business interruptions.

The entire application patch management process should be clearly defined in a formal security policy and procedural guide. This policy should be followed every time an update is needed. When a standard procedure is followed, the results of patch management will be more consistent and predictable. A standard procedure ensures consistent security over time, which is much better than allowing random changes to unintentionally diminish security.

EXAM TIP

There are a few "standard" answers on CompTIA exams, specifically on the CompTIA Security+ exam. Instructions and orders are to come from senior management; this is known as the top-down approach. Always document every security action or activity. Always protect human life and safety first. And always follow a policy when performing any security task.

All actions and activities undertaken as part of application patch management should be documented. This documentation allows for an auditing review of the ongoing practices of the management personnel. Documentation helps auditors identify deficiencies in the application patch management process. A record of patch management activities helps support security decisions in the event of a legal entanglement challenging the security structure and stance of the organization.

 Quick check

1. What is a benefit of application patch management?

2. What are the means to ensure that the correct patch is applied?

Quick check answers

1. Prevention of unintentional downtime or security reduction due to uncontrolled changes

2. Patches should be verified by file name, change data, size, hash value, and digital signature when available.

Chapter summary

- Application security is key to the long-term success of any IT endeavor.

- New attacks and exploits are constantly being developed by malicious programmers.

- A zero-day attack is simply any new attack or form of compromise against which there is initially no specific defense.

- Ransomware is an attack that locks, freezes, or encrypts data or an entire computer, then displays messages that attempt to extort the victim into paying money to have the system released.

- There are at least three different techniques that can be used to find an error, bug, flaw, or defect in software code: source code review, patch analysis, and fuzzing.

- Fuzzing or fuzz testing is a software evaluation technique that attempts to uncover errors in coding through stressing the input processing of a targeted application.

- A fuzz testing tool generates invalid, abnormal, unexpected, out-of-bounds, and often random input data sets and watches how the target application responds or handles the odd inputs.

- Any flaws discovered through source code review, patch analysis, and fuzzing were left there by the programmers.

- Secure coding practices need to be more widely adopted by all programmers. The best protection against attacks against software starts with well-written defensive code.

- SDLC (software development life cycle, also known as systems development life cycle) defines a framework for the planning, oversight, and control of the programming process. SDLC often includes elements that range from mandating defensive coding practices to the development of end-user training.

- When a program fails, it often reveals sensitive details to the user. These details might disclose specifics of the program, database interfaces, supporting services, identities, data structures, path and file names, and more.

- Proper error message handling focuses on pre-crafting the error messages that are to be displayed to a user.

- Input should be considered potentially harmful until it has been validated and sanitized.

- Many forms of compromise and attacks are made possible by the lack of input validation,. These attacks include buffer overflows, CGI scripting attacks, injection attacks, command injection, SQL injection, XML injection, LDAP injection, XSS (cross-site scripting), and XSRF (cross-site request forgery).

- Input validation is the inspection, analysis, parsing, and filtering of data before it is accepted into memory.

- Escaping metacharacters, performing input limit checks, and defining boundaries and domains are examples of input validation.

- Cross-site scripting (XSS) attacks are an exploitation of a user's trust in a website. However, the technical flaw that is exploited is usually the lack of input sanitization on the web server.

- The general idea of an XSS exploit is to send attack code to a vulnerable web server in order to plant altered content. This altered content is then sent to subsequent visitors, on whose systems the client-side execution of the injected malicious code takes effect.

- The primary means by which a website can defend against or prevent XSS is to filter and sanitize input from visitors.

- XSRF (cross-site request forgery) is an attack that takes advantage of a server's trust in an authenticated user account or user's system.

- One of the more insidious aspects of an XSRF attack is its ability to harm a server or a client's account or session on a server even across a fully authenticated and encrypted connection.

- End users have the responsibility to avoid risky behaviors that might expose them to malware infection.

- Because XSRF takes advantage of a server's lack of input sanitization and verification, it is mostly the responsibility of the server's designers and programmers to address any issue that an XSRF attack could exploit.

- A baseline is the written documentation of minimal requirements for a computer system. An application configuration baseline outlines the essential proper settings and configurations for software.

- One purpose of a baseline is to ensure consistency in deployment across an organization. Every new system should be constructed and configured in compliance with the baseline before it is installed into production.

- Baselines are used to standardize system deployment and ensure security compliance.

- Hardening is a security management process that includes two primary steps or phases: removing unnecessary components and securing that which is a necessary component.

- Application hardening, as well as every other hardening focus, should be driven by standardized company policies, procedures, and guidelines.

- The function of hardening is to reduce the attack surface of a system, network, or organization.

- Application patch management is an essential part of application and system hardening.

- Any update or change that is to be applied to a production system needs to be formally evaluated before being installed.

- The entire application patch management process should be clearly defined in a formal security policy and procedural guide.

Chapter review

Test your knowledge of the information in Chapter 8 by answering these questions. The answers to these questions, and the explanations of why each answer choice is correct or incorrect, are located in the "Answers" section at the end of this chapter.

1. Fuzz testing is used to send _____ input to a target in order to detect programming flaws.

    A. Standard

    B. Abnormal

    C. Bounded

    D. Predictable

2. Which of the following is not a typical element of SDLC with respect to secure coding concepts?

    A. Design from a standpoint of implicit denial and the principle of least privilege.

    B. Perform code reviews throughout the programming process.

    C. Focus on completing the code on deadline in order to be first to market.

    D. Sanitize output to minimize data loss or disclosure to unauthorized users.

3. Which of the following is not considered a secure event in relation to error and exception handling?

    A. Providing users with complete details of faults and errors as they are encountered

    B. Controlling error messages to prevent fault disclosure to users

    C. Creating a default fault-handling mechanism or response for the application to use rather than relying on the host operating system to handle failures

    D. Recording error details into a log file for administrative use

4. Which of the following is not an example of input validation?

    A. Escaping metacharacters

    B. Performing input limit checks

    C. Accepting arbitrary responses

    D. Setting boundary and domain restrictions

5. Which of the following statements is true with respect to XSS?

    A. An exceedingly large amount of data is sent to a vulnerable web server.

    B. A client is tricked into clicking on a hyperlink, which takes the user to a spoofed version of a website.

C. Sessions encrypted with SSL/TLS (Secure Sockets Layer / Transport Layer Security) can be used to reduce the risk of XSS.

D. Attack code is sent to a vulnerable web server in order to plant altered content. This altered content is then sent to subsequent visitors, on whose systems the client-side execution of the injected malicious code takes effect.

6. An XSRF attack is able to bypass what common security mechanism by infiltrating the client before attacking a targeted server?

A. Input sanitization

B. TLS sessions

C. Hashed passwords

D. Auditing

7. Which of the following are potential solutions to eliminate or reduce XSRF vulnerabilities? [Select all that apply]

A. Use a challenge-response dialog.

B. Limit the length of input.

C. Set a time out on sessions.

D. Require a re-authentication process.

8. Which of the following is not an element of application configuration baseline security management?

A. Crafting a written document

B. Making a digital image of a pilot system

C. Configuring access to external public wireless networks

D. Reviewing production systems for compliance

9. Which of the following is more likely to be an early step in the process of application hardening?

A. Installing updates and patches

B. Training users

C. Reviewing audit logs

D. Performing compliance testing

10. Which of the following is a part of application patch management?

A. Filtering abnormal input

B. Re-authenticating users

C. Ensuring a rollback path

D. Setting ingress filter rules

Answers

This section contains the answers to the questions for the "Chapter review" section in this chapter.

1. **Correct Answer: B**

   A. **Incorrect:** Standard inputs are not used in fuzz testing, because nonstandard or unexpected input has greater potential of uncovering flaws.

   B. **Correct:** Fuzz testing is used to send abnormal input to a target in order to detect programming flaws. This is used to detect flaws triggered or accessed by atypical or unexpected input.

   C. **Incorrect:** Bounded or limited input is not used in fuzz testing, because unbounded or out-of-bounds input has the greater potential to uncover flaws.

   D. **Incorrect:** Predictable input is not used in fuzz testing, because unpredicted or unexpected input has the greater potential to uncover flaws.

2. **Correct Answer: C**

   A. **Incorrect:** Designing from a standpoint of implicit denial and the principle of least privilege is an element of SDLC.

   B. **Incorrect:** Performing code reviews throughout the programming process is an element of SDLC.

   C. **Correct:** The goal or focus of completing the crafting of new code in order to meet a deadline is not directly related to secure coding practices. In fact, bounding coding by hard deadlines often reduces the focus on checking and verifying security, especially when coding activities take longer than expected.

   D. **Incorrect:** Sanitizing output to minimize data loss or disclosure to unauthorized users is an element of SDLC.

3. **Correct Answer: A**

   A. **Correct:** Disclosing details of errors to users can often assist in the targeting of an exploit by a hacker.

   B. **Incorrect:** Controlling error messages to prevent fault disclosure to users is an example of secure error and exception handling.

   C. **Incorrect:** Creating a default fault-handling mechanism or response for the application to use rather than relying on the host operating system to handle failures is an example of secure error and exception handling.

   D. **Incorrect:** Recording error details into a log file for administrative use is an example of secure error and exception handling.

4. **Correct Answer: C**

   A. **Incorrect:** Escaping metacharacters is an example of input validation.

   B. **Incorrect:** Performing input limit checks is an example of input validation.

   C. **Correct:** Accepting arbitrary responses is the problem that input validation is intended to address.

   D. **Incorrect:** Defining boundaries and domains is an example of input validation.

5. **Correct Answer: D**

   A. **Incorrect:** This statement is not related to XSS; instead, it relates to buffer overflow attacks.

   B. **Incorrect:** This statement is not related to XSS; instead, it relates to phishing and spoofing attacks.

   C. **Incorrect:** Encryption is not a valid protection against XSS, because this exploit can take place over secured connections.

   D. **Correct:** This is a true statement of a means of implementing XSS. Attack code is sent to a vulnerable web server in order to plant altered content. This altered content is then sent to subsequent visitors, on whose systems the client-side execution of the injected malicious code takes effect.

6. **Correct Answer: B**

   A. **Incorrect:** If a web server was performing input sanitization, some forms of XSRF attacks would be prevented. This is not the reason XSRF attacks focus initially on clients.

   B. **Correct:** In order to bypass or subvert the protections provided by TLS, namely authentication and encryption, an XSRF attack infiltrates the client before attacking a targeted server so it can piggyback on the client's authenticated and secured connection to reach the server.

   C. **Incorrect:** Hashed passwords are not the secure mechanism XSRF intends to circumvent; instead, the targets are the authentication and encryption processes of a TLS connection.

   D. **Incorrect:** XSRF does not attempt to subvert auditing; in fact, the audit logs on the server will show that all malicious actions taken were from the authenticated client.

7. **Correct Answers: A and D**

   A. **Correct:** Challenge-response dialogs can reduce XSRF vulnerabilities.

   B. **Incorrect:** Input length limitations do not reduce XSRF vulnerabilities.

   C. **Incorrect:** Session time-outs do not reduce XSRF vulnerabilities.

   D. **Correct:** Requiring a re-authentication process can reduce XSRF vulnerabilities.

8. **Correct Answer: C**

   A. **Incorrect:** Crafting a written document is an element of application configuration baseline security management.

   B. **Incorrect:** Making a digital image of a pilot system is an element of application configuration baseline security management.

   C. **Correct:** Connecting to external public wireless networks is often a compromise or a violation of a baseline and of good security management.

   D. **Incorrect:** Reviewing production systems for compliance is an element of application configuration baseline security management.

9. **Correct Answer: A**

   A. **Correct:** Installing updates and patches is usually an early step in the process of application hardening.

   B. **Incorrect:** Training users often occurs much later in the process of hardening and system deployment.

   C. **Incorrect:** Reviewing audit logs often occurs much later in the process of hardening and system deployment.

   D. **Incorrect:** Performing compliance testing often occurs much later in the process of hardening and system deployment.

10. **Correct Answer: C**

   A. **Incorrect:** Filtering abnormal input is related to input validation.

   B. **Incorrect:** Re-authenticating users is to prevent XSRF attacks.

   C. **Correct:** Ensuring a rollback path is a part of application patch management.

   D. **Incorrect:** Setting ingress filter rules is related to firewall configuration.

## CHAPTER 9

Establishing host security

The focus of this chapter is on the host security subset of this domain. Host security includes the issues related to operating system and application security from an implementation and operational perspective. Host security also includes hardware-related security topics. When precautions are taken and appropriate procedures followed, reliable host security can be established. However, this requires a directed effort and the use of compatible hardware and software security solutions. In every organization, the weakest link in a network's security is that of the desktop or workstation system in use by a human operator. The end user's ability to interact with a computer puts that host and potentially the entire network at risk. Taking proper precautions against host compromise is essential.

Exam objectives in this chapter:

Objective 4.2: Carry out appropriate procedures to establish host security

- Operating system security and settings
- Anti-malware
  - Anti-virus
  - Anti-spam
  - Anti-spyware
  - Pop-up blockers
  - Host-based firewalls
- Patch management
- Hardware security
  - Cable locks
  - Safe
  - Locking cabinets
- Host software baselining
- Mobile devices
  - Screen lock
  - Strong password

- Device encryption
- Remote wipe/sanitization
- Voice encryption
- GPS tracking
- Virtualization

Operating system security and settings

Operating systems are large, complex collections of code. Even the smaller operating systems, such as those on smartphones, still contain millions of lines of code. Some of the largest server operating systems have more than 100,000,000 lines of code. This massive amount of code allows for bugs, mistakes, typos, errors, and design flaws to be overlooked or lost in the bulk of the program. As discussed in the previous chapter, these flaws represent potential attack points or vulnerabilities. Though many operating system vendors have implemented security initiatives and redesigns, and have even re-created operating systems, there are no perfectly secure and flawless operating systems.

Operating system security and settings are the collection configurations and mitigations that improve upon the out-of-the-box security of a base operating system. This topic is listed on the CompTIA Security+ objectives list to highlight the importance of establishing a secure foundation upon which to construct a reliable computer system. Assessing the vulnerabilities of an operating system and then establishing a configuration baseline are key components of carrying out the appropriate procedures to establish host security.

In years past, there was some buzz and uproar caused by arguing about which operating system was more or less secure than another. Though there are those who still make these arguments, most no longer consider any operating system to be significantly better than any other. They all have flaws. Every operating system has numerous known exploits that target its vulnerabilities, and every operating system will continue to face future compromises as new zero-day attacks are developed. Ultimately, every operating system needs security management.

Real world

No perfect operating systems

Every operating system has flaws. There are no perfectly secure operating systems. Instead of trying to find the most secure operating system, pick an operating system based on your organization's functional needs. Then use security management to implement sufficient security protection on that operating system.

Security management is the focus on governance of the security controls, countermeasures, and configuration of an operating system (or any hardware or software product) with the goal of tuning and improving security over time. Most security management systems include several core elements:

- Patch management
- Removal of unnecessary components
- Configuration baselining
- Monitoring of performance trends
- System hardening
- Anti-malware protection
- Installation of countermeasures, such as firewalls and IDS/IPS (Intrusion Detection System/Intrusion Prevention System)

By keeping track of the security needs of a system and regularly updating, improving, and evaluating the technologies implemented, an organization can reasonably maintain security against the majority of compromise attempts, especially against known attacks.

Patch management was discussed at the end of Chapter 8, "The importance of application security," in the section "Application patch management." Though the focus in that section was on applications, all of the aspects of patch management for applications apply to the operating system and the hardware's firmware as well. If you keep software of all types and forms as current as possible, you have the best chance of defending against attacks. Although not all updates from vendors are in a business's best short-term interest, because some updates interfere with existing business tasks, it is important to revise the business task to adjust to the more secure form of the software. In order to minimize unintended consequences of a patch or update to an application, always test new code in a lab, test, or pilot environment first. Only after the ramifications of the new code are understood and approved by a production manager should an update be implemented onto production systems.

Removing unnecessary components was covered in Chapter 6, "Monitoring, detection, and defense." This activity reduces a host's attack surface by getting rid of anything that is not essential to the business. This slimming down of the capabilities of a host also makes other aspects of security management easier. When there are fewer things to consider and lock down, then more time and focus can be spent on the critical components.

Operating systems, applications, and hardware all have a plethora of configuration settings that might need to be manipulated to create a more secure operational stance. Often the default settings of a system are not the most secure settings. It is important to avoid the tyranny of the default—the assumption that the defaults are good enough. They never are good enough. The defaults are often set for ease of installation and to cause the least number of problems, such as incompatibility or connectivity issues, during initial implementation. Always review and consider every available setting, especially those that obviously have security ramifications. After setting and configuration choices have been made, these should be documented in a configuration baseline or configuration policy. This baseline should be used to compare and confirm settings on hosts into the future.

MORE INFO **MORE ON BASELINES**

Configuration baselines are also discussed in Chapter 6.

After a host has been configured and deployed, monitoring it for its performance levels helps administrators detect when problems are occurring. Performance levels can reveal when there is a bottleneck to performance levels (perhaps caused by a growth trend). Some bottlenecks can be resolved to allow for greater throughput or processing. Performance levels can reveal misconfigurations, hardware errors that could lead to device failure, unauthorized or inappropriate activities of end users, or the presence of malicious code or an intrusion. Keeping track of performance measurements over time allows for trending to be discovered. An understanding of the trending of various performance levels of a host can disclose when greater capacity is needed to handle increased productivity or when unwanted or malicious events are taking place.

System hardening was discussed in Chapter 8 in the section "Application hardening." Again, most of the discussion there applies to all aspects of a host, not just software applications. Removing that which is unnecessary and locking down what remains is a key security maxim that should be applied throughout an organization and its infrastructure.

Anti-malware protection and the installation of other countermeasures, such as firewalls and IDS/IPS, are discussed later in this chapter.

These are just some of the elements or aspects of managing host security as related to operating system security and settings. Every organization will need to tune and focus its security efforts based on its assets, threats, risks, and vulnerabilities. Although some general guidance will apply to many organizations, no specific set of steps applies to every organization.

 Quick check

1. Name at least three elements of security management.

2. What are at least three examples of how performance monitoring can relate to security?

Quick check answers

1. Most security management systems include several core elements, including patch management, removal of unnecessary components, configuration baselining, monitoring of performance trends, system hardening, anti-malware protection, and installation of countermeasures, such as firewalls and IDS/IPS.

2. Monitoring can detect growth trends, misconfigurations, hardware failures, unauthorized or inappropriate activities of end users, the presence of malicious code, or an intrusion.

Anti-malware

Malware has become a serious concern for everyone using a computing device. This includes global enterprises as well as SOHO (small office/home office) networks, Malware affects servers, clients, home computers, tablets, and smartphones. Malware exists for every operating system and every platform. Malware is prevalent everywhere.

There is a wide range of malware forms, including viruses, worms, trojans, rootkits, backdoors, logic bombs, botnets, adware, and spyware. All of these forms of malware were discussed in detail in Chapter 5, "Threats and attacks." However, this is not an exhaustive list of the forms of malware. There is also ransomware, keyloggers, exploits, buffer overflows, URL injectors, DNS changers, and many, many more. Here are some brief descriptions of these additional malware examples:

- **Ransomware** This type of malware locks a system, often by encrypting the drives, to prevent the user from accessing his data or the system in general. Then it displays a fake law enforcement warning about suspected malicious/illegal activities and demands payment to avoid prosecution.

- **Keylogger** A keylogger can be classified as a form of spyware, but it is usually much more specific and focused. A keylogger collects the keystrokes from the local keyboard. This log of typed material can be saved to a file for later retrieval or uploaded to an Internet service (such as FTP or an email service).

- **Exploits** An exploit is any software code written to take advantage of a vulnerability, flaw, or weakness in software or hardware.

EXAM TIP

An exploit is any malicious code written to cause harm by taking advantage of vulnerabilities, flaws, or weaknesses in hardware or software. A zero-day exploit is any exploit against which there is no specific defense. The term is derived from the statement or concept that a victim has no (that is, "zero") notice of an impending attack. A zero-day exploit might be hours or years old. When a new zero-day exploit is discovered in the wild, security experts analyze its code and how it works. This enables the other security experts to write filters, update signatures, develop patches, and otherwise develop defenses against the discovered attack. After defenses exist for a zero-day exploit, it is no longer considered a zero-day attack. Instead, it is just a classified and labeled exploit based on its primary malicious function or action.

- **Buffer overflow** This is a specific type of exploit that takes advantage of poor input management on the part of a software's programmers. Because the code fails to limit how much input is accepted and stored into memory, hackers are able to inject sufficient data to abuse execution functions, allowing them to arbitrarily run their own code.

- **URL injectors** A URL injector changes the link a user clicked on to an alternate URL. This might be performed by adware-like or spyware-like tools in order to track activity or redirect users to marketing materials, or this might be performed to hijack a website and direct users to a hacker-controlled version of a website.

- **DNS changers** DNS changers alter the domain name to IP resolutions requested by a system. DNS changers might hard-code false resolutions into the local DNS cache (by poisoning the HOSTS file that is read into memory upon startup). Some DNS changers alter the DNS server addresses in the IP configuration so that queries are sent to a hacker-controlled DNS server, in order to feed the victim false IP addresses and redirect the victim's traffic to unintended, often malicious locations.

It is important to remember that hackers who write malicious code do not typically plan to specifically or intentionally write a worm or a backdoor. Instead, they decide upon some form of harm or some method of interaction or choose a means of distribution, and then they write code to accomplish those tasks. The labels *worm*, *virus*, *logic bomb*, *trojan*, and so on are applied to malware after it is discovered by security professionals in an attempt to classify and understand the malware. Don't assume that just because a specific instance of malware is assigned a certain label that it is exclusively exhibiting the features or characteristics of that label. Most malware exhibits features of a wide range of malware forms (these are also know as *blended threats*). Newly discovered malware is often labeled by the first detected feature or its most significant feature. To gain a full understanding of what any example of malware can do, read up on the full report offered by the major malware-defending software vendors, such as Symantec, McAfee, and F-Secure.

 When planning host security, it is essential that you include *anti-malware*. Every computer, no matter what its purpose or its platform, needs malware protections. Malware protections include a variety of technology, including anti-virus, anti-spam, and anti-spyware solutions, pop-up blockers, and host-based firewalls. All of these are discussed in detail in the sections that follow. However, even with the best anti-malware technology, users continue to exhibit risky behaviors, and infections from new and zero-day malware will continue to occur.

Anti-malware technology is still mostly dependent upon a continuously updated database of patterns and signatures of known and discovered malicious code. Unfortunately, even with the most current database updates, unknown zero-day attacks are still undetectable. There are attempts to include anomaly and behavioral-based detections in order to potentially detect previously unknown malware. Although these technologies are improving the ability to detect new threats, they are neither foolproof nor perfect.

 EXAM TIP

The methods of malware detection, including the methods used by IDS and IPS systems, include anomaly detection and behavioral detection. Anomaly detection is performed by defining a set of rules or boundaries that distinguish desired activities from potentially undesired activities. Behavioral detection is based on a period of recorded activity against which future events are compared.

User behavior modification is just as important as implementing the latest and greatest anti-malware technology. The main goal of modification of user behavior is to have users avoid risky activities. These include blindly opening email attachments, downloading files from the Internet, following hyperlinks from social networking, using P2P (peer-to-peer) file sharing services, and using portable storage devices (especially between secure and insecure, company and personal, or private and external environments). After users are made aware of the consequences of their unthinking actions and the steps they can take to reduce the risk, the level or rate of exposure to zero-day malicious code is significantly reduced.

An overall better solution to the issue of zero-day malware is to replace our current computing concept of "allow by default and deny or filter by exception" with the opposite approach—namely, deny by default and allow only by exception. The current standard or normal computer system allows everything to be executed under a user's privileges. Though some users might be prohibited from installing new device drivers or installing new software, they are often allowed to execute any standalone application or utility. This freedom of execution allows for malware of all types to be launched by unsuspecting users. By blocking everything from executing except for those few specifically necessary applications, no foreign or unknown code will be allowed to run. This is known as *whitelisting*. There have been attempts to implement whitelisting in tablets and smartphones in the past few years, with mixed results. Application whitelisting by file path or digest has been available in Windows for years but has rarely been used. We would not be surprised to find a major operating system release soon that supported a default-enabled whitelist mode for business systems.

 Quick check

1. What type of systems can be affected by malware?

2. In addition to implementing anti-malware technology, what other protection should be used?

Quick check answers

1. Malware has become a serious concern for everyone using a computing device. This includes global enterprises as well as SOHO networks. Malware affects servers, clients, home computers, tablets, and smartphones. Malware exists for every operating system and every platform. Malware is prevalent everywhere.

2. User behavior modification to train users to avoid risky activities that expose them to malware threats is just as important as implementing the latest and greatest anti-malware technology.

Anti-virus

Anti-virus products are essential security tools for every computer. Malicious code is one of the most prevalent threats to computers and networks. Every computer needs protection against malicious code. The term *anti-virus* was coined years ago when the primary form of malicious code was the virus. Now that there are a plethora of forms of malware, including worms, trojans, logic bombs, backdoors, remote access, keystroke loggers, rootkits, and botnets, the products labeled as anti-virus are often capable of scanning for, removing, and preventing infection from a wide range of malware types. A more appropriate label might be *anti-malware* instead of *anti-virus*. However, the names of these products are still consistently anti-virus, even when the vendors describe their products as malware protection.

EXAM TIP

Familiarity with the various types and forms of malware will be important for the exam. Knowledge of their basic descriptions should be sufficient. Malware types were discussed in Chapter 5 as well as earlier in this chapter.

The concern that every system needs anti-virus protection is that although some operating systems, such as Unix, Linux, and derivatives, have few traditional viruses directed at them, there are many other forms of malware that can infect these systems. As discussed previously in this chapter, anti-virus technology is only one part of a complete anti-malware solution; user behavior modification is also necessary.

An effective deployment of anti-virus products is often more complicated than it might at first seem. Some anti-virus products are more capable and reliable than others. It is essential to evaluate each anti-virus product you are considering before making a final choice. The decision is not straightforward, either. Though you can view the reviews from trusted technology evaluation sites and blogs, such as *www.cnet.com* and *www.pcmag.com*, depending on someone else's perspective on security to satisfy your specific security needs is not always prudent. Use the guidance of technology reviews as a starting point rather than a final decision point.

The most overlooked and misunderstood aspect of anti-virus products is the forms or types of targets they scan for and report about. Although of course most detect malware, what is important is understanding the vendor's definition of malware versus your expectations of what malware is being detected by any specific product. Not all anti-virus products scan for rootkits, and some don't scan for spyware. It is also the case that many anti-virus products do not scan for hacker tools or administrator utilities that can be put to malicious purpose. If you expect your anti-virus product to detect port scanners, password crackers, sniffers, encryption crackers, remote access tools, and other common hacker and administrator tools, then you need to make sure those types of targets are included in the detection dataset of your anti-virus product.

The problem with these other forms of unwanted programs and tools is that they are not necessarily malicious in and of themselves; they can be used for malicious purposes by an unscrupulous hacker or legitimately by an authorized administrator. Many vendors clearly indicate when they include these in their target set, but not all of them are so forthcoming. Some vendors post their detection database online as a form of malicious code encyclopedia (see *www.symantec.com* and *www.mcafee.com* for examples). If a vendor provides easy access to their detection database, then you can look through it to see what categories of targets it includes, and can even look for specific examples of tools or utilities you are concerned about.

One method to confirm that an anti-virus product is able to detect and report on hacker tools is to perform direct tests. This can be accomplished in at least two ways. First, you could set up a lab system as a virtual machine (for example, by hosting the operating system in VMWare or VirtualBox), then install the trial version of an anti-virus product. Copy into the lab system samples of tools, then run a full system scan (be sure to turn on all detection features and classes). Based on the anti-virus's report, you'll know whether it includes those particular tools in its detection database.

Second, you can use an online in-browser scanning system that accepts uploaded files and then scans them with a set of anti-malware tools. One such site is *www.virustotal.com*. This site is very useful in determining whether a suspicious file is potentially malicious. By using this site to scan known forms of malware as well as examples of hacker tools, you'll quickly see a side-by-side comparison of the various scanning products (on a per scan basis) as to which products detect the offered item as a potentially malicious target and which ones don't.

EXAM TIP

An important tip for the exam is to remember that everything needs to be tested before deployment. Never trust or assume that new software will work as claimed. Creating a test lab where new products, configurations, or versions can be put through various stresses to determine whether or not they will be beneficial to your environment is an excellent security procedure. Test, don't trust.

Unless you work in this security arena already, you might be at a loss for what to use as samples in either of these product testing procedures. Here are some suggestions to consider. However, be sure to only download this first list on systems that you have set up specifically for testing, because these are (mostly) active malicious code. Getting examples of actual malware can be a challenge for most of us, but a site that offers this specifically is *www.offensivecomputing.net*. Here you can search by using the name of the malware and then view descriptions and links to download examples. Again, visit this site and download malware only on a virtual lab system. Examples of viruses to search for and use for testing include:

- Klez
- Doom
- Sality
- Toal
- Virut

- Conficker

- SQLslammer

- Storm

- Netsky

- Love

Another option is to use the safe testing string known as EICAR. This is a standardized test for anti-virus products. You can download various samples of EICAR embedded into files at *www.eicar.org/85-0-Download.html.*

Any anti-virus product you consider must at least be able to detect the actual malicious code on the previous list as well as pass the EICAR test. Otherwise, stay away from it. However, most of us assume that anti-virus products also include hacker tools in the detection database. This is not always the case. So be sure to test your narrowing list of anti-virus product options on hacker tools. Here is a list of several tools you should test against and where you can find them:

- Nmap (*nmap.org*)

- Netcat (nc) (*netcat.sourceforge.net*)

- Cain and Abel (*www.oxid.it*)

- John the Ripper (*openwall.com/john*)

- TCPDump (*www.tcpdump.org*)

- WinDump (*www.winpcap.org/windump*)

- Ettercap (*ettercap.github.io/ettercap*)

- SuperScan (*mcafee.com/us/downloads/free-tools/superscan.aspx*)

This is just a sampling of popular scanning, enumeration, and sniffing tools that can be used by malicious hackers or by authorized administrators. However, these should give you a good idea whether or not a particular anti-virus product is able to inform of the presence of unwanted tools in addition to actual malicious code. When performing your evaluation, you should consider numerous aspects of the product before making a final decision.

Anti-virus products abound in both paid commercial versions as well as free and/or open-source versions. Often the paid versions bundle in more features or other security tools, such as IDSs, firewalls, and spam filters. Generally, both the free and paid versions of anti-virus products (from the same vendor) are able to detect the same targets, because both versions usually use the same detection database. However, the ability to detect various forms of malware and hacker tools can vary greatly between vendors and products (hence the reason for the test evaluation processes discussed earlier).

Anti-virus protection should generally be a resident live or active-scan technology. This means that it is always monitoring the system in the background. Live or real-time detection is essential to catch new infection attempts as they occur. Scanning should include all inbound and outbound network connections, but it should also cover new storage devices, email attachments, and contents of webpages. An anti-virus product that performs real-time scanning will provide a constant layer of protection against known malicious code.

In most cases, only a single anti-virus product that performs real-time or live scans can be installed onto a single system. If two real-time scanning products are installed on the same system, each usually detects the other product's sample database as malware and attempts to quarantine it. This usually results in system failure. Thus, even though it might seem desirable to use multiple anti-virus products simultaneously, it is usually not possible.

However, there are many scan-on-demand anti-virus products. It might be possible to have one or more of these types of anti-virus tools available and/or installed, to supplement your real-time, resident anti-virus product. Be sure to read the documentation for all of the anti-virus products you want to use together, to see if they indicate whether or not this is even possible or supported. You should also search the Internet by using the two (or three) product names as keywords to discover any complaints, comments, or suggestions. Then, always test your planned deployment on a lab system (a virtual system would be the best choice), just to confirm that the products actually will operate without interfering with each other.

EXAM TIP

Keep in mind that any malware that makes its way onto your system while that malware is still unknown (in other words, a zero-day attack) will be overlooked by the live or real-time scanning as long as it stays dormant in a file, even after the detection database is updated to include its identity (that is, after it is detected by the vendor). Run scheduled on-demand scans of the entire storage system to ensure that newly detectable malware hiding in storage is dealt with sooner rather than later.

Due to the limitations of only running a single real-time scanner on any one system and the fact that any single anti-virus product might not detect the full range of malware and suspect tools that your organization is concerned with, you might want to consider a multi-vendor approach. This can be accomplished by installing one vendor's product (often your top-choice product) on your clients, a second product on internal servers, and finally a third product on external servers. This would ensure that all communications heading inbound or outbound will be scanned by at least two anti-virus products. This would give your organization the best foundation against malicious code.

There is a third option for anti-virus products, in addition to real-time and on-demand scanning: offline scanning. Offline scanning is a malware scan that occurs while the target system is not running. This is often performed by rebooting the computer with a USB drive or an optical disc that is hosting an offline scanner product. There are many of these available, many from the same anti-virus product vendors you know, but one that you might be surprised about is Windows Defender Offline.

Windows Defender Offline is a great option from Microsoft that scans for malicious code on Windows operating systems. It is easily downloadable from Microsoft's website, but the URL is long, so search for it by using *Windows Defender Offline*. You could even add in *64* as a search term if you want the 64-bit version of this tool. The scanner is very thorough and can download updated malware definitions if the network interface on the computer can be operated by using a generic NIC driver included in the boot system of Windows Defender Offline. The benefit of an offline scanner is that it can prevent the malware from loading into the operating system, where it might be able to disguise itself and make detection more difficult.

Technically there is a fourth method to scan for malicious code, and that is to submit a suspicious file to an online scanner, such as *www.virustotal.com* (which was mentioned earlier). However, this is a file-based scanner rather than a system-wide scanner. There are a few anti-virus vendors who offer system-wide scanners as in-browser downloads. These forms of online scanners execute from within the browser. If you are unable or unwilling to install anti-virus software into your system, this could be another option to consider. But because it requires that you visit the website every time you want to run the scan, it is inconvenient and might be inaccessible when you really need it.

After you have selected an anti-virus product, you will want to make sure that you keep the software current. This means that you must upgrade to the latest scanning engine each time the vendor revises its code. This is sometimes performed automatically at the same time that the detection database is updated. However, when vendors change versions, which are usually based on the year of release, you might need to manually force the update, or you might be forced to purchase the new version. It is always the best course of action to be running the most current version of a scanning engine in order to have the best and most current detection technology on your system. In most cases, the anti-virus product's version should be the same year as is on your current calendar.

EXAM TIP

Don't rely upon yourself or your users to remember to update the anti-virus detection database manually on a daily basis. You need an automated system to ensure that this critical step is performed. If your detection database is out of date, then you don't have the protection you need or assume you have.

The second part of keeping anti-virus software current is to update the detection database. This should be done at least once per day. If your product supports it, you might be able to schedule multiple update checks per day. Anti-virus products are only as useful as their detection database is current. The typical anti-virus product is most capable of detecting known threats, but only if the pattern or signature of the threat is in the current local detection database. One potential downside of free anti-virus products is that they might require manual detection database updates rather than performing that crucial activity automatically. If your preferred product does not automatically update, then you should continue searching for another solution.

In addition to real-time scanning, you will also want your anti-virus product to perform scheduled system-wide scanning. Real-time scanning only detects concerns that make their way into the areas being monitored, such as memory, execution space, the browser or email client interface, and network connections. However, anything residing in a file or other storage structure that is not active or accessed will not be detected by a real-time or live detection system. A system-wide or storage-level scan should be performed to detect any hidden or inactive malicious code. It is possible and likely that malware will have made its way onto your system before it was known and included in the detection database. If malware does not become active, a real-time scan will never detect it while it stays dormant in storage. A system-wide or storage-level scan will evaluate every item on the connected storage devices in order to detect these inactive and previously unknown targets.

Many current anti-virus products are able to detect infections as they are attempted as well as after they have occurred—at least for any malware for which a definition exists in the local detection database. After an infected file (or other host) is detected, it can be quarantined until the user responds to the threat. The user can choose to ignore the threat (in the event of a tool that does not pose a current risk) or to remove the threat. Some forms of malware can be cleanly removed and any damages caused by the malware repaired. However, there are some forms of malware that cause damage to an extent that cannot be easily repaired. In such cases, the infection can still be removed, but the damaged files will need to be restored from backup. Thus, even malware protection benefits from a reliable backup solution.

It is also important to address two additional threats in relation to anti-virus protection and viruses in general—namely, hoaxes and fake antivirus software. A hoax is a false or misleading message that attempts to trick people into taking actions that damage their computers or reduce the network's security. Some hoaxes use the threat of malware, known as a *virus hoax*, to persuade victims to alter their system, often deleting files, in the attempt to clean up an infection or prevent an infection. Both "reasons" are false and are simply a ruse to socially engineer people into harming their own systems. Never follow any instructions that are not solicited, and still try to get several corroborating sources to verify the accuracy of incident response actions.

Fake anti-virus protection is another serious risk to watch out for. Often fake anti-virus applications are offered or installed by websites, but they can also be "marketed" through email messages or messaging systems (including Facebook, Twitter, and SMS). Never accept or install any unsolicited offering of an anti-virus product or other security tool. Always go directly to a vendor's website to download valid anti-virus software. As discussed in the "Pop-up blockers" section later in this chapter, some websites will display pop-ups that look like local software interfaces and displays. They might show an animation that looks like an anti-virus product scanning your system. The scan is fake, but the website will claim to have discovered malicious code on your machine that the site happens to be able to remove with a free anti-virus product ready to download with just one click. Do not fall for this. A fake anti-virus product will infect your system. At first, you might not experience anything negative, but over time this "product" will "find" new malware, this time claiming that the free version will not address the issue and that you need to pay to upgrade to a more full or professional version. If you fail to pay, your system will experience degraded performance, ultimately resulting in system failure or lockup. This is just a social engineering scam to extort money from you in exchange for not harming your system.

Anti-virus protection is an excellent tool that every system needs to protect against malicious code. However, because only known examples of malware are in the detection database, the protection offered only goes so far. Avoiding the risky activities that expose your system to zage devices, will reduce the risk of new zero-day malware infecting your computer.

EXAM TIP

When it comes to security, humans will often trump technology. This is especially true in regard to malware infection. Current blacklist anti-virus technology is only as good as it is current and up-to-date, and it will still be unable to detect new zero-day threats. However, humans can continue to perform risky activities and expose their systems to infection to these yet-to-be-discovered threats. Human behavior modification is essential to the long-term security of any environment.

As mentioned in the introduction of this malware section, the best defense against malicious code is with whitelisting. Anti-virus protection is traditionally a form of blacklisting. Everything is allowed until it is discovered or recognized as being malicious, then it is added to a block list. Unfortunately, there is an infinite variety of malicious code, and thus it is impossible to keep up with the onslaught of new malware being released daily. As of April 2013, more than 22.5 million examples of malware have been discovered, and the rate of discovery is increasing. The alternate concept of whitelisting assumes that nothing should be allowed to run unless it is on the preapproval list known as the whitelist. Because there will be a finite number of executables that users should be launching, and that list will remain rather static, the mechanism of whitelisting is more effective as well as being more efficient at blocking malware of all forms.

 Quick check

1. What are the forms or types of anti-malware scanning or protection?

2. What is the most effective approach to malware protection?

Quick check answers

1. Real-time or live, on-demand, offline, uploading suspicious files to test services, and online in-browser scanning services

2. The most effective approach is to use whitelisting; however, most environments cannot or will not commit to an exhaustive whitelisting system. Thus, the next-best option is to use a current anti-virus scanner in conjunction with user behavior modification.

Anti-spam

Spam is a serious problem that everyone with an email address has to face. Although most spam is simply digital junk mail, there are malicious elements encountered in email messages from time to time. Spam is formally called *unsolicited commercial email.* (UCE) or *unsolicited bulk email* (UBE). But no matter what you call it, it is a nuisance we all deal with.

For the most part, spam just wastes resources. It consumes some server resources as email servers process and forward messages to destination inboxes. It consumes bandwidth while it traverses the Internet and while being downloaded to your device—whether you view your inbox in a web browser, a standalone email client, or your smartphone. It consumes some of your time, attention, and effort in having to notice that a received message has no value to you, and then to delete it.

 One question that is commonly asked is, "Where does spam come from?" The answer might be surprising. The majority of spam is sent from computers that have been taken over by hackers who are using a remote agent known as a *spambot.* There are hundreds (if not thousands) of variations or versions of spambots, and there are millions of systems worldwide that are infected by spambots. A spambot is able to distribute billions of email messages daily to the world. A spambot operates without the consent of the system's owners, nor does it offer the victims any compensation. Instead, hackers controlling spambots are stealing system resources, network connectivity, and electricity in order to blast the world with spam.

> **MORE INFO** SPAM AND SPAMBOTS
>
> For some interesting statistics about spam and spambots, see *https://www.trustwave.com/support/labs/spam_statistics.asp.*

Those controlling the spambots often sell off their ability to send out massive numbers of email messages as a service to marketing outfits. The hackers often create a false front for their spam business so that marketing companies believe they are purchasing a legitimate service. Often, the hackers earn a percentage of the sales triggered by spam, are paid for each click-through, or are paid a flat fee for the message distribution to a specific number of recipients. The selling of bulk email transmissions and the subsequent return on services rendered has earned some hackers thousands of dollars per day. Thus, this is an attractive activity for hackers, because it has great potential to earn them cash.

 One of the most common ways of dealing with spam is to use a spam filter. Most of the email service providers that individuals and companies use include spam filtering as a standard feature of their email services. However, the spam filtering provided by your email provider might not be good enough. If not, then installing a spam filter or *anti-spam* software on a user's system is often the next step. However, client-side spam filtering tools are only effective if three things are true:

- The client is using a local email client and downloads messages to the local system
- The spam filtering product is current
- The definition database of the spam filter is up to date

Many spam filtering tools allow end users to mark messages as spam in order to fine-tune their own local results as well as share new spam characteristics with the spam-filtering vendor.

Real world

One vendor, multiple products

Many of the full-featured anti-virus suites include anti-spam technology. If you are already invested or interested in a particular anti-virus vendor, be sure to check out their other product offerings. Sometimes, if anti-spam is integrated into the other elements of a product suite, you might gain better protection than using an anti-spam solution from a different vendor.

For web-based email, only the email provider's spam filtering can be easily used. There are some online or Internet-based spam filtering services. However, these require that you have your own domain name; for example, *genericuser@contoso.com* rather than *genericuser@gmail.com*. Then you configure your DNS settings to forward all inbound message to the spam filtering provider, who then filters your messages and finally forwards all non-spam messages to your actual inbox. One such provider of this type of spam filtering service is MailRoute (*mailroute.net*).

Just as with malicious code, new spam is created on a regular basis. Most anti-spam filters will not be able to stop new spam; therefore, most users will still need to deal with some amount of spam in the email inboxes. There are a few actions that users can take to further reduce the amount of spam they receive.

First, whenever signing up for a new service or website, especially one that is new or that you will be testing for a while before committing to it, use a secondary email address rather than your primary work or personal email address. With the wide variety of free web and on-line email services; such as *gmail.com*, *outlook.com*, and *mail.yahoo.com*; you can sign up for additional accounts whenever you need them. After you commit to a site or service, you can always update your contact information to include your primary email address.

Second, be sure to run current antimalware scanning tools in order to minimize the chance that adware or account hijacking attacks can occur from your system. If malicious code can monitor your email communications or record your keystrokes, then it is possible for you to be targeted for more spam.

Third, consider using a temporary or disposable email address for trial offers or other one-time-use sites and services, especially when you already know or suspect that they will either be a hard-sell annoyance or might leak your contact information. There are dozens of temporary email services, most free, that can be discovered easily with a web search by using the keywords *temporary email*.

Although we will have to deal with spam for years to come, at least there are some options of anti-spam technology and behavior changes than can reduce the burden.

 Quick check

1. What is spam?

2. Who sends the most spam?

Quick check answers

1. Spam is unwanted digital junk mail.

2. Spam is sent mostly by hackers using spambots.

Anti-spyware

Spyware is any software that monitors or tracks activities and then reports the findings back to its management center. Spyware is often classified as software that runs without the knowledge or consent of the system's owner. However, legitimate forms of spyware exist and are often clearly disclosed in license agreements or other documentation. Because most end users fail to read license agreements and supporting documentation for software, they consent to anything listed in those virtual contracts by default. (Hence, this is a good reason to take the time to read license agreements—less spyware!)

Legitimate spyware is used by product vendors and marketing firms to learn more about their customers. This information can be used to improve products or change marketing strategies. Sometimes vendors provide products for free, in exchange for the user's consent to be monitored or tracked. However, even legitimate spyware can seem intrusive and a violation of privacy.

Most spyware is illegitimate. Such spyware makes its way onto a system without the knowledge or consent of the user. This form of spyware monitors the activities of a system and its users for malicious purposes, such as the falsification of advertisements, DNS resolutions, or website spoofing. Spyware might collect keystrokes and launched applications, monitor web activity, embed malware into transferred files, read email messages and messages from other services, read files on hard drives, record via the microphone or webcam, and potentially much more. Any information collected by spyware might be used in real time to modify or alter a user's system or online experience, but it can also be uploaded to the Internet for hackers to use in furthering attacks, launching false websites, targeting social engineering attacks, attempting identity theft, and much more. Obviously, spyware needs to be addressed on the same level that malware in general is addressed.

EXAM TIP

Adware is any software that generates or displays advertisements for the benefit or revenue of the software's author or vendor. Adware can be freeware that is "paid for" through advertising. However, some adware is installed in conjunction with spyware. Such adware is then driven by the data collected by the spyware tool and is thus often considered illegitimate as well. Most anti-spyware scanners include this form of malicious adware in their detection database.

Anti-spyware tools often exist independently of anti-virus tools. Though many forms of spyware can easily be classified as malware, not all are malware. Some simply gather generic metrics of activity, performance, and habits to further marketing strategies or improve software. Many anti-virus products often include the malicious forms of spyware in their detection databases. However, it is still important to have a separate anti-spyware scanning tool.

An anti-spyware tool can be used to monitor a system in real time as well as perform a system-wide scan on a periodic basis. Essentially, a spyware scanner operates much like an anti-virus product, but with a few different means of detection for its brand of targets and a detection database of spyware. And just like anti-virus tools, current anti-spyware tools are better than older ones, and the detection database needs to be updated regularly.

There are several commercial, free, and open-source anti-spyware products. To select one that is right for you, search for *best spyware tool*. When you learn of some potential options, visit *www.cnet.com* and *www.pcmag.com* in order to read reviews of the products you discovered. Only consider products that have been reviewed and achieved a recommended rating. You can also check with your anti-virus and anti-spam vendor to see if they offer an anti-spyware product as well.

EXAM TIP

Although your anti-virus product includes spyware in its database, always assume that it is generic protection. You should supplement that generic protection with a specific anti-spyware tool in order to get the best-of-breed protection you need.

Spyware, as with many forms of unwanted or malicious software, might present detectable symptoms of its presence. Though the lack of symptoms does not ensure that nothing unwarranted is occurring, the existence of the symptoms should prompt you to perform further research or perform deep scans of your system. Some of the common symptoms of spyware include:

- Numerous pop-ups from a web browser that are not related to web activity.
- Changes to settings, such as the designation of a new default search engine or home page.

- An overly sluggish or unresponsive system, especially related to web activity.

- Additional toolbars or icons present in a web browser.

- An increase in spam related to recent activities (that is, if you were shopping for a baseball glove and sports-related spam starts to show up in your email inbox).

- Applications freezing, failing to launch, or having a significant delay when launched.

- Difficulty accessing Internet resources.

- A noticeable increase in network traffic not related to any user activity.

- Search results being provided by a different search engine than the one you attempted to use, or selected search results redirecting you to alternate destinations other than that which was clicked.

- The discovery that firewalls, anti-virus tools, and other security tools are disabled.

If you suspect that you have been infected by any form of malware or you have detected one or more of these symptoms, perform a full system scan with your anti-spyware and other security tools. You might even consider using an offline scanner, such as Windows Defender Offline (as mentioned earlier) to ensure that results are not tampered with by live malware.

Beware of fake anti-spyware software. Hackers know that their spy tools are often the intended target of security scanning products. In an attempt to counterbalance legitimate spyware discovery and removal tools, hackers have developed fake anti-spyware software. Effectively, a false anti-spyware tool is a trojan horse that acts like a spyware scanner but often does nothing but present the user with an interesting display of false activity of scanning, while installing additional spyware onto the system. Fake scanning products are often encountered via pop-ups that attempt to use scare tactics or general social engineering techniques to trick users into accepting their false tools as legitimate. Never accept unsolicited security software from pop-ups.

 Quick check

1. Does all spyware have obvious symptoms?

2. What is the suggested defense against spyware?

Quick check answers

1. No, not all spyware causes symptoms that a typical user will see or notice.

2. Because spyware is often just another form of malware, using a current and updated scanning technology in combination with user behavior changes is recommended. It is also a good idea to read license agreements.

Pop-up blockers

A *pop-up blocker* blocks websites from being able to open new browser windows or tabs without the consent of the user. Pop-ups were originally a unique way for a web designer to grab the attention of the visitor to display promotions, alerts, special messages, and advertisements. Though pop-ups can still be used for legitimate purposes, they are also a common vector of exploitation. A pop-up can be used to upsell to a customer, misdirect visitors to other sites (often to the benefit of the initial site's owner), or trick users into downloading malicious software.

Some sites still design pop-ups into their architecture for the specific purpose of using them to manipulate visitors. However, pop-ups planted onto an otherwise non–pop-up site appear on a user's system in the exact same way as valid pop-ups. The problem is that there is usually no easy way to tell whether a pop-up is safe or malicious. Most traditional pop-ups appear over the current browser as new but smaller display windows. These windows are rendered by the browser but can be configured to hide toolbars, menus, and the address bar. This means that pop-ups can appear without any information as to their source.

It is also the case that some pop-ups have been crafted to be completely visually false. In a standard pop-up, the browser renders a window control frame around the displayed content. This control frame often includes a red close button in one of the upper corners and can be resized by clicking and holding on a side or corner of the pop-up window. Hackers and website designers can use special coding tricks to prevent the browser from showing a control frame and just display a raw clickable image (also known as an image map). Unscrupulous designers and hackers might include a graphic representation of a standard control frame in their image in order to trick users. The displayed pop-up seen by the user looks just like a typical pop-up; however, the control frame is false, and clicking anywhere on the pop-up will trigger a malicious action. Even Close, No, or Cancel buttons are false and will still trigger the malicious response if clicked.

EXAM TIP

Most forms of malware, including those that trigger malicious pop-ups, inherit the privileges, permissions, and access of the user account under which they gained initial access to a system. All too often, users are logged in as administrators. This allows malware, such as pop-ups, to gain full access to the system. Users should always be logged onto a limited or restricted account in order to reduce risk.

There are several options to take in order to reduce the risk to you and your computer in regard to pop-ups. First, never trust that a pop-up is legitimate just because it happened to appear while you were at a site that you think is trustworthy. If there is something shown on a pop-up that you have an interest in, write it down and then go to the vendor's site and search for it, or just search by using a Internet search engine.

Second, always close pop-ups safely by using keystrokes, such as Ctrl+C or Alt+F4. If that fails, locate the browser in your taskbar, right-click its icon, and close the whole process (you can also close or terminate the process from the Windows Task Manager). If that still fails to remove the pop-up, reboot your system. This final option might seem a bit drastic, but you would not think so if malware destroyed your system or helps hackers steal money or your identity. Most legitimate or moderately malicious pop-ups will be closed by the keystroke option. If that fails, taking more drastic steps is warranted.

Third, use a modern browser that employs tabbed browsing. Then configure the settings to block pop-ups generally and to open pop-ups in other tabs. So far, hackers have been unable to take over the tab control mechanism as they have on the control frame rendering, so the close function on a tab will still work safely even on a malicious pop-up opened as a tab.

Fourth, if your browser does not offer a pop-up blocking feature, install a plug-in or extension for your browser that adds support for pop-up blocking or use a pop-up blocker from an anti-virus or anti-spyware vendor. As with any form of security software, look up reviews first, then if a favorable recommendation is given, consider installing it.

Fifth, avoid installing software from odd sites, offered to you from social networks, obtained from unethical or illegal sources, or accessed from an anonymous provider via a peer-to-peer file sharing service. If you don't know that a vendor, software provider, or person is trustworthy, then don't assume that the software obtained from them is. Software from unknown sources is much more likely to include malicious code that could trigger pop-ups.

Generally, once you have a pop-up blocker, most pop-ups will no longer automatically open, including valid and safe ones. When a site that you consider safe needs to open a pop-up, often holding down the Ctrl key will allow the pop-up to open. Some browsers can configure their pop-up blocking feature to allow pop-ups on a site-by-site basis.

 Quick check

1. Do pop-up blockers prevent just malicious pop-ups?

2. Is it possible to click the red close button on a pop-up to safely close it?

Quick check answers

1. No, pop-up blockers block all pop-ups by default. Some blockers can be temporarily bypassed by using Ctrl, whereas others can be configured to allow pop-ups on specific sites.

2. Not always, and it is not possible to know when the red close button is safe to use. Always close pop-ups with Ctrl+C or Alt+F4.

Host-based firewalls

A final component in this list of technology related to anti-malware protection is the host-based firewall. A *host-based firewall* is a software firewall installed directly onto a computer. This is distinct from a network firewall, hardware firewall, or appliance firewall, which are independent, dedicated devices that function exclusively as firewalls for a network. A host-based firewall is a software-based filtering system for an individual computer. A host-based firewall does not replace a hardware firewall; instead, it is a supplemental countermeasure against a wide range of internal threats.

Host-based firewalls were primarily third-party products only a few years ago. In order to obtain a software firewall, users or network managers had to purchase or obtain free firewall products and install them on top of their operating systems. Today, most computer operating systems include a software firewall. However, the native firewall can be replaced or superseded by a third-party firewall if desired.

Most organizations and nearly every home user should have a host-based firewall installed on every computer system, because the threats that could compromise a system are rampant and are not just encountered on the Internet. There are numerous threats within private networks, including company networks, SOHO environments, and home networks.

EXAM TIP

A host-based firewall will assume that network connections or inbound or outbound communication attempts are not allowed by default. This deny-by-default stance is the security foundation that modern firewalls are built on. However, it can also be a hindrance when the default or current settings interfere with an essential business task, process, communication, or application. Take the time to perform the full gambit of essential business functions when you are first setting up a new host-based firewall. Be sure to intentionally allow only those actions that are essential and leave the denial setting enabled for all undesired or nonessential events.

A software firewall provides an additional layer of protection both for the computer onto which it is installed and also to the network to which the computer is connected. If malicious activity is coming from the network, a host-based firewall might be sufficient to prevent it from compromising the computer. If malicious activity originates on the computer and attempts to reach out to the network, a host-based firewall might be able to block it from reaching another network target. A host-based firewall will ensure that more ports are closed or are harder to access from the network, especially for clients. A host-based firewall also maintains a list of programs that are allowed to communicate with the network and will notify the user when a new program attempts network communications.

When you install a new host-based firewall, it might take you a while to get the firewall configured so it supports and allows intentional, benign activity entering or leaving the system. After this initial configuration is completed, the firewall will remain as a protective barrier to the system and only demand the attention of the user when a new unknown event or connection is being attempted.

Patch management

Patch management is the process of becoming aware of new updates to a system, testing those updates, the installing the updates that pass an approval process. This concept of managing patches was discussed in Chapter 8, in the "Application patch management" topic. The only difference between these two concepts is that application patch management focuses on updates for installed software, whereas general patch management covers anything and everything, including the operating system and hardware firmware, as well as installed software. So you might notice that the discussion here is similar to that from Chapter 8, because the only real difference is focus, not methodology. We have included this again here for completeness and compliance with the official objectives list.

EXAM TIP

The ideas related to patch management are fairly consistent, whether the focus is on the operating system, installed software, or hardware firmware. When you understand the overall idea, the use of any related term on the exam should not cause confusion.

Patch management is a foundational part of any security endeavor. It is part of the process of system hardening. Only with the most current and complete version of code from the vendor is there a chance of reliable functioning and protection. Although it is not a guarantee of security, using updated code is always more secure than using out-of-date code or versions of software. Good security management practices include a means by which new software updates are tested in a lab or simulated environment. Such testing reveals the most likely outcomes, consequences, or ramifications of implementing new updates into the production environment. Not all updates will be installed into the production network, because some updates will interfere with essential business tasks. Any new version of software that is discovered to cause severe interruptions to work processes or that introduces new vulnerabilities should be held back until a compensation technique is discovered or crafted.

A systematic process of patch evaluation before deployment is needed to minimize the risk of downtime, compromise, or reduced productivity due to newly installed patches. This process can be called patch management, update management, configuration management, or change management. However, the overall process is the same no matter what an organization calls its particular process. The gist of this idea is that all updates need to be fully tested and approved before they are installed into a production network.

An update, service pack, hot fix, patch, or whatever a vendor or programmer calls the new code he wants to apply to an installed application is a change. Changes can cause problems. In fact, unmanaged changes have the potential of causing unexpected conflicts and security reductions. Thus, a formal patch management system is needed to oversee changes. Only those changes that are shown to cause little or no significant negative results are eventually approved for installation onto production systems.

All patch management processes should verify that any updates to be applied are the original updates from the vendor. Updates should never be obtained from a third-party site or service. Only updates directly from the vendor can be considered reliable. Always confirm that you have the proper updates by confirming the file name, size, hash value, date of release, and digital signatures (when available). This will minimize the chance of installing a fake or modified update.

Most updates include an uninstall procedure. However, most uninstall procedures are not as elegant or exhaustive as they should be. Therefore, never depend upon the uninstall process; instead, make your own preinstallation backups. Making your own backups of a system before updates or other changes are applied ensures that you have a reliable path back to a working data set in the event of a problem with an applied patch. Without the ability to roll back to a previous working state, an update can be a one-way path to significant downtime and productivity loss.

Patches that are tested in a lab environment should be evaluated by a third party before being installed into a production system. An approval process is necessary to ensure that sufficient testing and evaluation has been performed and any detected or potential downsides to patch installation have been addressed. Often those doing the testing need to generate a formal findings report, which is then reviewed by the approval group. Only those updates that are authorized by the change approval board should be installed into the production network.

Updates can be released by a vendor at any time. Some vendors attempt to release updates only on a specific monthly or quarterly schedule. However, even vendors who have established a reliable release schedule have had to release updates out of cycle for the most serious or mission-critical–rated patches. Organizations that apply patches should establish their own schedule for testing, approving, and installing updates. However, they also need to be flexible in order to respond to out-of-cycle releases that are too important to delay until the next scheduled test and release process. Though testing and approving should never be skipped, it can be initiated on the fly when necessary, and in some cases the procedure can be streamlined to shorten the time window to application. Often, streamlining of the process involves using more machines in the test environment and using more personnel to perform the evaluation. The important thing is not to skip any steps in the testing process.

After an update is approved for release, a schedule should be set for its application. Generally, installing updates during time frames of lower workload is the best choice. It is also desirable to install updates just before an expected time of downtime or reduced productivity, such as a weekend, holiday, or seasonal load reduction. This should help minimize any negative effects caused by issues or errors during the patch installation process. For example, it is usually a better plan to install updates on Friday afternoon rather than Monday morning, in order to keep downtime to a minimum.

Every component, step, and responsibility in the patch management process needs to be prescribed formally in a written procedural document. This patch management policy should be used as a step-by-step guide each time an update becomes available. More standardized and predictable results from patch management can be achieved by following a set policy. Consistency in security management helps to reduce unintentional security reductions due to unexpected consequences.

 Quick check

1. When can an update be installed immediately after being released by a vendor?

2. Does update testing eliminate the potential for downtime caused by patch installation?

Quick check answers

1. Never, if that means skipping the testing and approval process

2. No, but it does significantly reduce the chance

Hardware security

 Another important area of host security is *hardware security*, which is essentially the physical security of a computer or device. Physical security is often an overlooked aspect of a security solution. Often the focus is on new technology or some form of update or configuration change to the operating system or applications. Although these are important areas to consider and address, they should not cause you to overlook other essential areas of vulnerability and weakness.

Every security management effort needs to address logical or technical concerns, and personnel or social engineering concerns, as well as physical or environmental concerns. Failing to address each area of risk sufficiently will leave a gap in the overall implemented security structure.

Physical host security requires the implementation of several real-world elements to provide a reasonable defense against loss, damage, or compromise. Many physical security issues for the network as a whole were addressed in Chapter 6. Here we want to focus on those efforts related to protecting individual hosts against physical threats.

The physical threats of concern to a host computer include physical access by an outsider or unauthorized user, loss, theft, and damage due to environmental concerns. The official objectives list points out the concepts of cable locks, safes, and locking cabinets. These are each addressed later in this section. However, there are many other considerations for both the real world and the certification exam.

Peripherals represent a serious threat to a host. Storage device peripherals, such as flash drives or USB-attached external hard drives, can be used to extract data from a host or bring in malicious code from outside. Such peripherals place the user and the data on a computer at risk. The convenience and the usefulness of portable storage devices need to be evaluated in light of the consequences of their misuse and abuse. Keep in mind that flash drives are now available in ever-larger storage capacities, all while their overall physical dimensions are shrinking. For example, a microSD card with a capacity of 128 gigabytes (GB) is about the size of a dime. Also, many storage devices are now disguised as other objects, some for fun but some for subversive purposes. These could include pens, toys, and other novelties. Such devices are difficult for a security guard or an employee to recognize as a potential malicious tool.

EXAM TIP

Data loss prevention (DLP) is the security policy aimed at reducing the threat of private or internal data being leaked to outsiders. The most common method by which data loss occurs is through USB drives. Often a worker will use a USB drive to move files between systems, then forget that the files remain on the drive. If the USB drive is then lost or stolen, the files on the drive are potentially exposed to unauthorized access. A growing number of organizations are banning the use of USB drives that do not have hardware-enforced encryption.

Monitors and notebook displays put data at risk of shoulder surfing or allowing someone to take a photograph of the screen. Monitors should be positioned to minimize the ability of a personal walking by an office or workspace to easily see the contents shown on the screen. This type of visual surveillance reduction can be enhanced with the use of a privacy screen film. A privacy screen film is a thin material placed over the display that is transparent when viewed directly or nearly directly perpendicular to the screen, but that is opaque when viewed from a greater angle. This limits the useful viewing range to the typical location of the user directly in front of the screen.

Disposal of broken, old, or unused devices should be planned out carefully before discarding the equipment. Tossing a device into the trash only exposes the organization to information leakage. Even broken computers or other equipment might contain readable storage devices. At the very least, the presence of a specific piece of equipment in a dumpster reveals that the organization is using such equipment. This might indicate to a dumpster diver that the broken device could have been replaced by a similar or identical product or that other similar products are still in use. This is known as *intrinsic information* and is commonly overlooked when organizations discard devices, their manuals, old software, and even boxes and packing materials. All of these items should be shredded or incinerated beyond recognition to eliminate the risk of intrinsic or stored data theft. This might be an extreme measure for most organizations, but it should be seriously considered by those with sensitive information, in order to prevent data leaks.

 Quick check

1. What is the risk of throwing away the box, packing materials, and manuals after unpacking a newly purchased device?

2. What are two forms of risk that a portable storage device represents?

Quick check answers

1. Disclosure of the intrinsic information that a specific device is now present in your organization

2. A portable storage device can be used to leak data out of the organization, or it can be used to bring malicious code into an organization.

Cable locks

Cable locks can be used to reduce the risk of device theft. Cable locks have been a well-known security tool for notebook computers, but they can also be used on a wide number of devices. The most common or recognized type of cable lock is a locking mechanism on the end of a reinforced tethering cable (see Figure 9-1). The tethering cable is looped or anchored to an immovable or at least difficult-to-move object. Then the locking mechanism is attached to the device to be protected. The standard means of connecting a cable lock to most notebooks is to use the K-slot built into the notebook's chassis.

FIGURE 9-1 A typical cable lock uses the K-slot on a notebook.

The K-slot, or Kensington Security Slot, was designed by the Kensington Computer Products Group. A wide number of devices, including notebooks, desktop computers, keyboards, monitors, game consoles, networking devices, projectors, and even some tablets have the K-slot built into them. The K-slot can be used to secure a device by using a K-slot locking mechanism. Kensington manufactures and sells many such cable lock products, but there are also many other vendors of compatible cable locks.

The K-slot is not the only means to secure a computer or other device; there are locking mechanisms that can attach securely to other peripheral ports, such as the VGA port, serial port, or parallel or printer port. Some larger devices include a metal locking loop point to which a strapping cable or a padlock can be connected to provide physical security.

In many cases, these types of locks, especially a cable lock connected to a K-slot, are not designed to be completely impervious. Instead, they are designed as a deterrent. With enough effort, the plastic or thin metal components that are connected to the locking mechanism can be forcibly broken. However, this will cause noticeable damage to the device and might render the device unusable (it might crack the screen or break the motherboard).

EXAM TIP

Using a cable lock will minimize the random opportunistic theft of portable devices. When you have your device secured to a table or chair when you are in a restaurant or meeting room, anyone who might have considered a swipe-and-run caper will often look elsewhere for an easier target, if your device is obviously securely cabled.

Cable locks can be based on a key or a combination. They are used to secure devices that are to remain in a single location at all times., but that might be exposed to a large number of workers or the public in general. Cable locks are also commonly used on portable devices. For traveling or simply using a device in a public place, cable locks can provide an extra level of physical security. Restaurants, hotels, libraries, coffee shops, and conference rooms, might be great places to use a portable device, but they also provide the opportunity for device theft, especially when you could be easily distracted.

 Quick check

1. What is the purpose of a cable lock?

2. When should a cable lock be used?

Quick check answers

1. To discourage theft of a device.

2. Whenever there is a greater risk of theft, such as when a device is in a public place.

Safe

A *safe* is a strong, lockable container, also known as a *strongbox* or *coffer*, that is used to protect valuable objects against loss, damage, or theft (see Figure 9-2). Safes are often constructed out of thick metal or plastic. Most safes have a hinged door or lid that can be secured closed with a locking mechanism involving keys, number pads, or twist combination locks. Safes can be small enough to fit in a desk drawer or large enough to be an entire room (such as a bank's vault).

FIGURE 9-2 A safe provides physical security for devices.

Safes can be used by individuals and organizations to physically secure devices and media. Notebooks, tablets, smartphones, storage devices, and other smaller items could be secured in a drawer safe or portable safe in any standard office environment. Larger safes could be used to house extremely valuable or sensitive equipment.

EXAM TIP

A safe is not just for storing the family jewels; it can also be used to secure sensitive paperwork and storage devices against damage or theft. You might also want to consider keeping backup media secured onsite and offsite in a safe rather than just in boxes or on shelves in a parts closet.

Safes are not necessarily a required physical security device for every environment, but when the protection they provide is needed, they can represent a valuable tool in providing reliable physical security. Safes can provide various levels of protection against fire as well as physical theft. Safes are rated based on the levels of protection provided, such as time of fire resistance, ability to maintain a stable internal maximum temperature, water resistance, and resistance to forcible entry with various tools. Be sure to evaluate your protection needs when selecting a safe. Then select a safe that meets or exceeds your security needs.

 Quick check

1. What can be stored in a safe?

2. What does a safe protect against?

Quick check answers

1. Anything that will fit inside and still allow the door or lid to close and lock. This can include computers, equipment, storage devices, and paperwork.

2. Depending on the safe, it could protect against theft, fire damage, and/or water damage.

Locking cabinets

A *locking cabinet* is another useful physical security component for both the home user as well as any company or organization (see Figure 9-3). There are a wide range of assets, resources, and supplies that do not mandate the need for a safe, but that do require greater levels of protection than just being left in the open in a home or office. A safe is often expensive by comparison, and might not have sufficient storage capacity to contain the less-than-highly valuable items.

FIGURE 9-3 Locking storage cabinets provide a lower level of physical security than a safe.

A locking cabinet is a great place to store general-purpose office documentation, blank media, replacement parts, and installation discs for operating systems and applications. These types of resources should not be left out in the open where they could be lost, misplaced, or stolen, but should be kept under a reasonable level of physical access control. A locking cabinet is usually sufficient security to protect blank media and generic installation discs.

EXAM TIP

When using a locking cabinet, be sure to designate a few trusted employees who will have a copy of the key or knowledge of the combination. A locking cabinet should keep out intruders, but it should not keep you out when you have a legitimate need for what's inside.

It might be a good idea to keep a running inventory of the contents of locking cabinets. The inventory should be updated and adjusted every time items are added or removed. A librarian could be assigned to manage access and track the cabinets' contents. Workers would then need to check out equipment and return it at the end of the day or project. This will help ensure that resources taken from a cabinet are not overlooked, misplaced, or wasted.

Quick check

1. Why choose a locking cabinet over a safe?

2. What materials are appropriate to store in a locking cabinet?

Quick check answers

1. A locking cabinet is likely less expensive and might provide greater storage volume than a safe.

2. Only items that do not contain valuable information or that are easy to sell for cash. Blank media, installation discs, and general office documentation are good examples of appropriate materials to store in a locking cabinet.

Host software baselining

Host software baselining is effectively the same concept as application configuration baselining, which was discussed in Chapter 8.

Host software baselining is the establishment of the essential requirements of the operating system and all applications installed onto a host system. This written document of minimal settings and configurations is to be used to establish consistent implementation across multiple computers. It can also be used to check compliance and consistency over time by comparing a current configuration to a desired or required configuration. For most organizations, multiple baselines are defined for the various and disparate purposes of different computers and equipment. Each system's specific purpose, function, or role mandates different operating system and application configurations. In larger environments, dozens of different host baselines have to be established in order to properly manage the software on systems, including desktop workstations, mobile notebook systems, tablets, smartphones, data/resource servers, border devices, DMZ/extranet servers, domain controllers, remote access servers, and VPN servers.

With clearly defined host software baselining requirements, organizations can achieve a higher level of consistency across the network. Consistency in configuration causes fewer problems, reduces downtime, and increases security. Consistent configurations ensure that security is properly enabled across all devices.

As new systems are brought into the organization, they should be set up in compliance with the appropriate host software baseline. Only when it is in full compliance with the baseline should a system be allowed onto the production network. Systems already in production should be periodically reassessed as to their compliance to the appropriate baseline. Over time, baselines will need to be adjusted in response to new threats, changes in the environment, and the availability of new tools, features, and capabilities. As baselines are updated, deployed systems should be adjusted to be in compliance with the new baseline versions. Any system that fails to be in compliance introduces a security gap that needs to be recognized and addressed promptly.

A host software baseline should include all aspects of software relevant to the type of system. This should obviously include the version of operating system and installed applications, but should also include firmware updates to hardware, any add-ons or extensions to applications, device drivers, patches, updates, and security improvements. The baseline should include details on what is to be installed, in what order, and the configuration settings to make. The baseline should also include items specifically not to install and configure, as well as a list of items to remove, disable, or block from the operating system or installed applications.

 EXAM TIP

Baselining of host software is an excellent way to ensure consistent deployment. However, being consistent is of little value when current security improvements are not added to established configurations. It is essential to revise baselines each time a new security improvement is available.

A host software baseline is initially a written document. However, after it is defined, a baseline can be implemented in technology. Often a sample system is constructed in full compliance with the baseline, and then an image of its storage device can be applied to other devices to quickly bring them into compliance as well. This image cloning process is very fast, efficient, and effective in rolling out large numbers of duplicate systems.

Security compliance and the standardization of new system deployments are improved through the use of baselines. Use of baseline documentation as well as baselined images can significantly reduce the time and cost of new system deployment. However, not every system is a clone of another. One-time configuration might be necessary for some devices and equipment. It is important to establish at least a documented baseline even for singular systems.

 Quick check

1. True or false: software baselining is a substitute for patch management.
2. Host software baselines should be used to manage what types of systems?

Quick check answers

1. False. Software baselining is used to establish a secure and consistent starting point for systems. Patch management is still important in maintaining current code and defenses against compromises discovered after initial deployment.

2. All systems should be managed with host software baselines, including those with numerous clones as well as individual unique devices.

Mobile devices

Mobile devices have become so commonplace that they seem to be everywhere. Notebook computers, netbooks, tablets, smartphones, audio players, and digital cameras are just some of the portable technology that we use in our personal and professional lives. However, the security implications of mobile devices need to be carefully considered before they should be allowed in locations where they might pose a serious risk.

Most mobile devices include some type of native or expandable storage. If a mobile device is connected to a computer by a cable or by Bluetooth or another wireless option, the mobile device might appear on the computer as a storage device. This enables a mobile device to carry data out of an organization as well as bring malicious code in. Effectively, any mobile device that can be used as a means or method of storage when connected to a computer is essentially the same as a USB thumb drive, a flash card, or a burnable optical disc.

EXAM TIP

CompTIA seems to intertwine the risks and security issues of mobile devices (such as smartphones and tablets) with those of peripherals (such as USB thumb drives and wireless keyboards). So don't be too hard-lined on attempting to keep these two groups of devices in separate categories when answering exam questions.

The ubiquity of mobile devices has also made us complacent. Mobile devices seem just like part of our work outfit or one of our standard accessories. This can cause them to be overlooked by security guards when people are entering or leaving a building. Every company needs to take a closer look at the risk that mobile devices pose in their ability to easily move data in or out of an organization. When those mobile devices are owned by employees, as personal devices rather than corporate assets, it can be difficult to control the contents or use of the devices and potentially complicate any legal search of devices for unwanted material. Thus, the increasing BYOD (bring your own device) policies or freedoms offered by companies is a much bigger concern than most realize.

In addition to the risk related to data leakage or malware infection are the risks of access by unauthorized individuals, loss, theft, eavesdropping, cloning, and improper disposal.

Mobile devices are often shared with others, left on tables, borrowed by friends and co-workers, or simply lost or stolen. When these devices are in the hands of someone else, the content of the mobile devices might be exposed to unauthorized disclosure. Few mobile devices have content, folder, or app-specific security controls. There is often an overall security assumption on mobile devices that if you have physical possession of the device and you can log into the device, everything on the device is of the same level of value and access. If a device is exposed to use by someone other than yourself, then only fully public data should be kept on the device in order to prevent disclosure to unauthorized individuals.

Mobile devices are susceptible to loss or theft. By their very nature, they are small and thus vulnerable to being misplaced, dropped, or taken by someone. When your device is out of your control, anything on the device can be accessible to whomever found or took your device.

Making voice and video calls is no longer limited to devices specifically designed as mobile phones or smartphones. Many tablets and audio players with Wi-Fi connectivity can run apps that enable voice and video call capabilities. Unfortunately, though the calls and connections made over our devices might be encrypted (although not always), there is always the risk that someone nearby can overhear at least one side of the conversation, if we are in a public location such as on a sidewalk or in a coffee shop.

Eavesdropping is not limited to hearing someone's voice but can also be performed against the digital and radio-wave data exchange that is taking place. Most of the public wireless networks that mobile devices are connected to are not secured with encryption. This means that data is vulnerable to sniffing and analysis.

EXAM TIP

Mobile devices with Wi-Fi or wireless carrier connections might be able to share their connection with a standard computer. This sharing process is known as *tethering*. When tethered, the wireless connection allows for unfiltered access to the Internet. This type of connection is just another risk that could allow data loss or malware infection.

Mobile devices that use mobile phone providers might be targeted for cloning. *Cloning* is the process of duplicating the identification elements of a phone onto another blank or reprogrammable phone. The electronic serial number (ESN), mobile identification number (MIN), and International Mobile Station Equipment Identity (IMEI) could be read from a victim's phone and then programmed into a hacker's phone. SIM (subscriber identity module) cards can be copied or duplicated. If a phone hacker (known as a *phreaker*) has a few moments alone with a target phone, he might be able to duplicate its identity. This would allow the clone to make calls on the account of the original phone.

Another risk that needs to be addressed is that of improper disposal of mobile devices. Many people simply throw away, give away, or sell their mobile devices without properly sanitizing them of their personal data. This exposes that data to disclosure and could result in identity theft, access to online accounts, or extra charges on service bills.

All of these issues are serious concerns, but most of them have reasonable countermeasures and safeguards that can be implemented by individuals and companies to improve mobile device security. Some of these safeguards include the use of screen locks, setting a strong password, using on-device encryption, enabling remote wipe or sanitization, using voice encryption, and employing GPS tracking. These are each discussed in this section.

However, there a few other supplements to this list in addition to the official objectives. These include training, policy, and understanding the device.

As in most situations where security is at stake, the more a person understands about the value of the assets at risk, the types of threats that exist, and the vulnerabilities present in mobile devices and how they are used, the more that person will start adjusting his or her behavior to avoid risks and make more security-conscious choices regarding his or her devices. Training is the best tool available to help reduce risk through the modification of user behavior. By avoiding risk, users reduce the potential and the severity of security breaches.

EXAM TIP

The CompTIA Security+ exam places an emphasis on training. It is called out with the terms *awareness*, *training*, and *education*. Training is a key defense against social engineering as well as against falling into common security traps or mistakes. However, don't forget that though training is essential, there has to be something to be trained upon. Training can only happen when security policies have been defined. So although training is an important mechanism for securing personnel, training has to be based on the company security policy.

Organizations need to develop mobile device–specific policies. By clearly outlining what is and isn't allowed in terms of mobile device software, hardware, use, applications, and so on, organizations can reduce many of the common risk factors. When the use of security tools is mandated and use of software from untrusted sources is limited, mobile device security can be significantly improved. Without corporate direction on the use and function of mobile devices within the organization and in communication with company IT services, both the company and the individual are put at risk.

More often than not, many of the security problems related to mobile devices are related to a lack of understanding or an ignorance of the native security features built into the phone or available through add-on applications. Spending the time and effort to become familiar with the security features and available security apps for a mobile device will be well rewarded with fewer breaches and occurrences of data loss.

 Quick check

1. What are the risks of connecting a mobile device to a computer?

2. What are the general means by which eavesdropping can take place against a mobile device?

Quick check answers

1. Data loss or leakage from the computer to the device and then to the outside, as well as malware infection into the computer from the device obtained from outside.

2. Eavesdropping is not limited to hearing someone's voice but can also be performed against the digital and radio-wave data exchange that is taking place.

Screen lock

A *screen lock* on a mobile device is similar to a password-protected lock screen or screen saver on a typical computer (see Figure 9-4). A screen lock is a useful feature for several purposes. First, it reduces the occurrence of accidental access to the phone function or apps (for example, if you sit on your phone). However, a screen lock that is just a swipe to unlock is not actually a security protection. Only with a password, PIN, or nonobvious gesture to unlock the screen can a screen lock feature be considered secure.

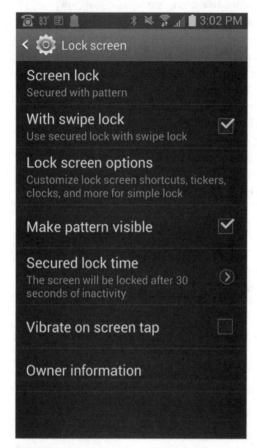

FIGURE 9-4 An Android smartphone has several screen lock settings.

EXAM TIP

Implementing the basic security measure of a password-based or PIN-based lock screen will prevent most casual accesses to your mobile device. When someone has just a few moments of access to your device while you are away or distracted, if the screen is locked with a password, that person won't have enough time to attempt any more involved methods of gaining unauthorized access to your device.

Strong password

When a password is used on a mobile device, it is recommended that you follow *strong password* policies, as shown in Figure 9-5. Good password rules include the following:

- Do not duplicate another current or previous password.
- Do not use a single word or obvious phrase as a password.
- Use a mix of characters, such as uppercase, lowercase, numbers, and symbols.
- Use a long password rather than a short one. Consider 12 characters a minimum, but try to use more (or at least up to the maximum allowed by the device).
- Do not write the password down in an obvious location.
- Do not share your password with anyone.

FIGURE 9-5 You can use LastPass to create a secure password on an Android smartphone.

For some devices, an additional benefit over any other form of lock screen bypass method is gained when you assign a password: the USB port is locked when the screen is locked. This prevents a connection cable from being used to bypass the screen and interact with the storage on the device without first unlocking the screen.

EXAM TIP

When you are making up a password, weird is often easier to remember than compli-cated. Consider selecting three to five unrelated words, then stringing them together in a nonsense sentence. Sprinkle in case changes, numbers, and symbols, and you might have developed an easy-to-remember but difficult-to-guess password.

For most devices, the screen lock password is the only line of defense, either because the device simply does not support any other security feature or that is the only feature configured and enabled. When there is an option, pick a mobile device that offers a wide range of security features. Then make the effort to configure all security features supported by your device.

Device encryption

Encryption is often touted as a magic potion in relation to security (see Figure 9-6). Unfor-tunately, encryption is not a perfect solution, and improper use of encryption can lead to false security while leaving glaring vulnerabilities. Encryption is a great tool to defend against confidentiality violations (that is, unauthorized disclosure) during data storage or communica-tions—but only when the attacker does not have access to the encryption keys. When a device is stolen or otherwise in the hands of someone else, if that person is able to interact with the system, often he or she will also have access to the encryption keys for any stored data or com-munication channels. Thus, for encryption to provide any security assistance, it must be used in combination with other solid security measures. Most notable is strong authentication.

Any mobile device that connects to a wireless carrier network will be able to participate in that carrier's encrypted services (if and when they are available). Thus, phone calls and data exchanges over a provider network might be encrypted at a respectable level. However, when Wi-Fi networks are used, only those networks with WPA-2 encryption should be considered secured. Open Wi-Fi networks communicate in cleartext; WEP-encrypted wireless networks can be compromised in less than 60 seconds, and WPA-encrypted wireless networks can be compromised in only a handful of hours. Only WPA-2 encryption currently stands up to attack.

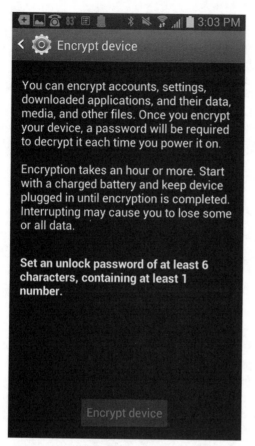

You can encrypt accounts, settings, downloaded applications, and their data, media, and other files. Once you encrypt your device, a password will be required to decrypt it each time you power it on.

Encryption takes an hour or more. Start with a charged battery and keep device plugged in until encryption is completed. Interrupting may cause you to lose some or all data.

Set an unlock password of at least 6 characters, containing at least 1 number.

Encrypt device

FIGURE 9-6 An Android smartphone has a device encryption configuration page.

A growing number of devices also now include on-device storage encryption. Such a feature might be able to encrypt all of the content on the phone or potentially just the user data. In either case, it should be implemented or enabled on the device. This will provide an additional barrier against unauthorized data or system access to the mobile device, especially when the lock screen is enabled.

EXAM TIP

The CompTIA Security+ exam seems to have the perspective that on-device encryption is a rare security feature on mobile devices. Though this may have been true in 2011, when the last CompTIA Security+ exam revision took place, in 2013 the majority of new devices include this feature as a standard native capability of their core operating systems. Although it is usually not enabled by default, it is not typically a complex procedure to turn it on.

Remote wipe/sanitization

The ability to *remote wipe* or perform a *sanitization* on a mobile device can be a safety net for when devices are lost or stolen. A remote wipe is the ability to trigger a deletion of on-device data after a device is no longer in your possession (see Figure 9-7). The triggering of a remote sanitization function is done via an online service or through a mobile carrier. However, the device has to "check in" with the remote wipe service in order to receive the signal to clean off the system. If the device's wireless interfaces are disabled or it is otherwise unable to make a mobile carrier or Internet connection, the device will not receive the command to wipe its storage.

FIGURE 9-7 This Android smartphone shows the data wipe (remote wipe) option of the Lookout Mobile Security app.

Remote wipe is a common feature in many mobile devices, but for those devices whose operating systems do not include a native remote wipe feature there are numerous apps that can be used to add this capability. In some cases, app-based remote wipe can be installed and initiated even after the device has been lost or stolen.

Voice encryption

Voice encryption can be used to provide an additional layer of protection around audio communications and potentially video conferencing as well. When you are using a mobile carrier's voice network, the protections of the phone call are only those provided by the carrier. Some technologies transmit voice calls in clear form, whereas some provide moderate or strong encryption. If the security of a communication is too important to leave up to the carrier who might or might not be providing sufficient encryption, there are numerous apps that can provide data communication–based alternatives with encryption as well.

Many of the Voice over IP (VoIP) apps for mobile devices can provide fully encrypted conversations of audio only or video conferencing between two devices running the same (or compatible) communications software over a data connection. If the other end of the conversation is using a more traditional cell phone or land line, then VoIP services will encrypt the first portion of the call from the mobile device to the VoIP provider's servers. After the communication reaches the bridge point between the VoIP provider and the traditional carrier service, the conversation reverts to the often plaintext form that the receiver's phone is able to accept.

GPS tracking

Mobile device *GPS tracking* is another security concern. Many mobile devices, especially smartphones and tablets, have native GPS as well as wireless and cellular radios (see Figure 9-8). This allows for at least three different forms of location tracking. Though location-based services— such as navigation or location-specific discount shopping or dining offers—can be very beneficial, those location services can be used in unexpected ways. An unreasonable number of apps require or request access to your location data; this data might be used to provide location-based service benefits, but IT could just as easily be collected for demographic tracking purposes. Tracking information could also be used maliciously by apps designed to track users and then use that information for unethical purposes, such as stalking or targeting someone for a theft.

If tracking is of concern, you can gain moderate protection by disabling the GPS and Wi-Fi adapters on a mobile device. However, the mobile carrier antenna is still able to detect your general location via tower triangulation. Turning off the carrier antenna will further reduce the ability to track a device. However, there are some mobile phones that maintain a connection to mobile carrier towers unless the battery is removed. Thus, for the best protection against tracking, not having a mobile device in your possession is the only assured means.

However, GPS tracking is not just a potentially creepy risk, it can also be used for device recovery. With remote-enabled GPS tracking, if your mobile device is lost or stolen, the device can report its GPS coordinates back to a centralized monitoring service. With this information, you can trace your steps back to recover a device, or direct law enforcement officials toward potential criminals.

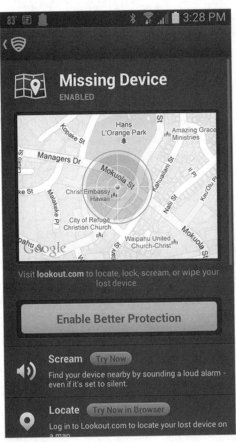

FIGURE 9-8 The Missing Device GPS location feature of the Lookout Mobile Security app is enabled on an Android smartphone.

Real world

GPS tracking tradeoff

Geolocation services are growing in popularity. Some services assist with finding restaurants, getting reviews and recommendations, finding your friends in a crowd, offering discounts or specials, or providing navigation services. However, these geo-location service benefits are gained by trading the details of your physical location and other interests. Tracking is not inherently malicious, but you should consider the rewards and consequences of giving up your privacy in relation to your location. Also keep in mind that when something is offered to you for free through your mobile device or on the Internet, what is being sold is you.

 Quick check

1. What two security features depend upon a device's connectivity?

2. What two security features, when used in concert, provide the best protection against use or access into your device when it is lost or stolen?

Quick check answers

1. Remote wipe and GPS tracking depend upon a lost or stolen device being able to connect to the Internet or carrier network.

2. A strong password and device encryption used in combination are the best de-fenses. If the device is inaccessible through both the locked screen as well as the USB port, then the only option for the hacker/thief is a full hardware wipe. In ad-dition, passwords and on-device encryption are effective even without network connectivity.

MORE INFO **VIRTUALIZATION**

Virtualization is formally listed by CompTIA as a topic in this section of the objectives list, but it does not actually fit with the overall focus of the other items discussed in this chap-ter. Thus, we have discussed this topic fully elsewhere. Virtualization and cloud computing are discussed in detail in Chapter 3, "Secure network design and management."

Chapter summary

- Operating systems, applications, and hardware all have a plethora of configuration settings that might need to be manipulated to create a more secure operational stance.

- Always review and consider every available setting, especially settings that obviously have security ramifications. After setting and configuration choices have been made, these should be documented in a configuration baseline or configuration policy. This baseline should be used to compare and confirm settings on hosts in the future.

- Performance level tracking can reveal when there is a bottleneck to performance levels (due to a growth trend).

- Every computer, no matter what its purpose or its platform, needs malware protection.

- Anti-malware technology is still mostly dependent upon a continuously updated database of patterns and signatures of known or discovered malicious code. Unfortunately, even with the most current database updates, unknown zero-day attacks are often still undetectable.

- User behavior modification is just as important as implementing the latest and greatest anti-malware technology. The main goal of modification of user behavior is to have users avoid risky activities.

- Anti-virus protection is an essential security tool for every computer. Malicious code is one of the most prevalent threats to computers and networks. Every computer needs protection against malicious code.

- Anti-virus protection should generally be a resident live or active=scan technology. Such a product is always monitoring the system in the background. Live or real-time detection is essential to catch new infection attempts as they occur.

- Offline scanning is a malware scan that occurs while the target system is not running. This is often performed by rebooting the computer with a USB drive or an optical disc that is hosting an offline scanner product.

- In addition to real-time scanning, you will also want your anti-virus product to perform scheduled system-wide scanning.

- A virus hoax is a false or misleading message that attempts to trick people into taking actions that damage their computers or reduce the network's security.

- Fake anti-virus applications are offered or installed by websites, but they can also be "marketed" through email messages or messaging systems (including Facebook, Twitter, and SMS). Never accept or install any unsolicited offering of an anti-virus product or other security tool.

- Spam is a serious problem that everyone with an email address has to face. Though most spam is simply digital junk mail, there are malicious elements encountered in email from time to time.

- One of the most common ways of dealing with spam is to use a spam filter. Most of the email service providers that individuals and companies use include spam filtering as a standard feature of their email services.

- Spyware is any software that monitors or tracks activities and the reports the findings back to its management center. Spyware is often classified as software that runs without the knowledge or consent of the system's owner.

- Spyware might collect keystrokes, launch applications, monitor web activity, embed malware into transferred files, read email messages and messages from other messaging services, read files on hard drives, record via the microphone or webcam, and potentially much more.

- An anti-spyware tool can be used to monitor a system in real time as well as perform a system-wide scan on a periodic basis.

- A pop-up blocker blocks websites from being able to open new browser windows or tabs without the consent of the user.

- Though pop-ups can still be used for legitimate purposes, they are also a common vector of exploitation.

- Never trust that a pop-up is legitimate just because it happened to appear while you were at a site that you think is trustworthy.

- A host-based firewall is a software-based filtering system for an individual computer. It does not replace a hardware firewall; instead, it is a supplemental countermeasure against a wide range of internal threats.

- Patch management is the process of becoming aware of new updates to a system, testing those updates, and then installing the updates that pass an approval process.

- Patch management is a foundational part of any security endeavor. It is part of the process of system hardening.

- Physical security is often an overlooked aspect of a security solution.

- Physical host security requires the implementation of a number of real-world elements to provide a reasonable defense against loss, damage, or compromise.

- The physical threats of concern to a host computer include physical access by an outsider or unauthorized user, loss, theft, or damage due to environmental concerns.

- Cable locks can be used to reduce the risk of device theft.

- A safe is a strong, lockable container, also known as a strongbox or coffer, that is used to protect valuable objects against loss, damage, or theft.

- A locking cabinet is another useful physical security component for both the home user as well as any company or organization. There are a wide range of assets, resources, and supplies that do not mandate the need for a safe, but that do require greater levels of protection than just being left in the open in a home or office.

- Host software baselining is the establishment of the essential requirements of applications installed onto a host system. This written document of minimal settings and configurations is used to establish consistent implementation across multiple computers.

- If a mobile device is connected to a computer by a cable or by Bluetooth or another wireless option, the mobile device might appear on the computer as a storage device. This enables a mobile device to carry data out of an organization as well as bring malicious code in.

- Mobile devices are more susceptible to loss or theft than traditional desktop or notebook computers.

- Mobile devices that use mobile phone providers might be targeted for cloning.

- Organizations need to develop mobile device–specific policies. By clearly outlining what is and isn't allowed in terms of mobile device software, hardware, use, and applications, they can reduce many of the common risk factors.

- A screen lock on a mobile device is similar to a password-protected lock screen or screen saver on a typical computer.

- Passwords used on mobile devices should follow strong password policies.

- Encryption is a great tool to defend against confidentiality violations (unauthorized disclosure) during data storage or communications.

- The ability to remote wipe or perform a sanitization on a mobile device can be a safety net for when devices are lost or stolen.

- Voice encryption can be used to provide an additional layer of protection around audio communications and potentially video conferencing as well.

- Many mobile devices, especially smartphones and tablets, have native GPS as well as wireless and cellular radios. This allows for at least three different forms of location tracking.

Chapter review

Test your knowledge of the information in Chapter 9 by answering these questions. The answers to these questions, and the explanations of why each answer choice is correct or incorrect, are located in the "Answers" section at the end of this chapter.

1. Which operating system is inherently more secure than the others?

   A. Windows

   B. Linux

   C. Macintosh

   D. None

2. Which of the following is false?

    A. All configuration settings should be customized for a specific environment.

    B. The default settings of an operating system are often preferred.

    C. Default settings are often designed with ease of use in mind.

    D. Default settings are often insecure.

3. A typical malware scanner is unable to detect and prevent what type of unwanted activity?

    A. Installation of spyware

    B. Infection with a rootkit

    C. An unauthorized user attempting to guess an account password

    D. Compromise by a trojan

4. What platforms need anti-virus products?

    A. Servers

    B. Linux

    C. Database hosts

    D. All of the above

5. The biggest reason why is it unsafe to attempt to close a pop-up by using on-screen visible controls is what?

    A. Social engineering

    B. Malware infection

    C. False advertising

    D. Better deals on sales are available elsewhere

6. Which of the following is not a primary benefit or purpose of using patch management?

    A. Minimizing the risk of downtime

    B. Reducing administration responsibilities

    C. Diminishing the threat of compromise

    D. Reducing productivity loss due to bad or interfering code

7. What should not be kept in a locking cabinet?

    A. Blank media

    B. Replacement parts

    C. Operating system and application installation disks

    D. Private data of customers

8. What is an important goal of host software baselining?

   A. Keeping systems in compliance with stated security policies

   B. Reducing hardware failures

   C. Training users

   D. Implementing open-source software

9. Which of the following statements is false?

   A. Mobile devices are more susceptible to loss or theft than traditional desktop or notebook computers.

   B. The increasing BYOD (bring your own device) policies or freedoms offered by companies is a much bigger concern than most realize.

   C. A screen lock is sufficient security against data loss in the event of a device theft.

   D. Many tablets and audio players with Wi-Fi connectivity can run apps that enable voice and video call capabilities.

10. According to CompTIA, which type of mobile device security is the least likely to be on a mobile device?

   A. Storage encryption

   B. Remote wipe

   C. GPS tracking

   D. A screen lock

Answers

This section contains the answers to the questions for the "Chapter review" section in this chapter.

1.   **Correct Answer: D**

   A.   Incorrect: Windows is not necessarily more or less secure than any other operating system.

   B.   Incorrect: Linux is not necessarily more or less secure than any other operating system.

   C.   Incorrect: Macintosh is not necessarily more or less secure than any other operating system.

   D.   Correct: No operating system is inherently more secure than any other. They all have flaws and all need security management.

2.   **Correct Answer: B**

   A.   Incorrect: All configuration settings should be customized for a specific environment. This is a true statement.

   B.   Correct: The default settings of an operating system are not preferred, because they were not designed with a specific environment in mind. Instead they were designed to minimize problems during installation.

   C.   Incorrect: Default settings are often designed with ease of use in mind. This is a true statement.

   D.   Incorrect: Default settings are often insecure. This is a true statement.

3.   **Correct Answer: C**

   A.   Incorrect: An anti-malware scanner might be able to detect the installation of spyware.

   B.   Incorrect: An anti-malware scanner might be able to detect infection with a rootkit.

   C.   Correct: A typical anti-malware scanner is unable to detect the unwanted activity of a user, such as guessing a password. Strong password policies, technical controls that lock accounts after too many failed attempts, and logging and monitoring to detect excessive failed password attempts would be better suited for that purpose.

   D.   Incorrect: An anti-malware scanner might be able to detect compromise by a trojan.

4. **Correct Answer: D**

   A. **Incorrect:** Every system might need an anti-virus product, including servers.

   B. **Incorrect:** Every system might need an anti-virus product, including Linux systems.

   C. **Incorrect:** Every system might need an anti-virus product, including database hosts.

   D. **Correct:** Every system might need an anti-virus product.

5. **Correct Answer: B**

   A. **Incorrect:** Pop-ups can be a vector of social engineering, but the bigger risk is malware infection.

   B. **Correct:** The biggest reason it is unsafe to close a pop-up by using on-screen visible controls is malware infection. Hackers can falsify the controls so that any click on the pop-up triggers an installation of malicious code.

   C. **Incorrect:** Pop-ups might have false advertising, but the bigger risk is malware infection.

   D. **Incorrect:** Pop-ups might not offer the best deals, but the bigger risk is malware infection.

6. **Correct Answer: B**

   A. **Incorrect:** Minimizing the risk of downtime is a benefit of patch management. Without patch management, unpatched systems are more likely to experience a breach resulting in downtime.

   B. **Correct:** Patch management does not reduce administration responsibilities—it might make the process of patching more efficient, but it is still a necessary task.

   C. **Incorrect:** Diminishing the threat of compromise is a benefit of patch management. With the application of updates, known vulnerabilities will be protected against compromise.

   D. **Incorrect:** Reducing productivity loss due to bad or interfering code is a benefit of patch management. Patch management will keep optimal code in use to support productivity.

7. **Correct Answer: D**

   A. **Incorrect:** Blank media can be kept in a locking cabinet.

   B. **Incorrect:** Replacement parts can be kept in a locking cabinet.

   C. **Incorrect:** Operating system and application installation disks can be kept in a locking cabinet.

   D. **Correct:** Private data of customers should not be kept in a locking cabinet, but in a safe.

8. **Correct Answer: A**

   A. **Correct:** A primary goal of host software baselining is keeping systems in compliance with stated security policies.

   B. **Incorrect:** Host software baselining does not typically assist with reducing hardware failures.

   C. **Incorrect:** Training users is important, but it is not part of host software baselining.

   D. **Incorrect:** Implementing open-source software is not a goal of host software baselining; however, any type of software should be managed by using host software baselining.

9. **Correct Answer: C**

   A. **Incorrect:** Mobile devices are more susceptible to loss or theft than traditional desktop or notebook computers. This is a true statement.

   B. **Incorrect:** The increasing BYOD (bring your own device) policies or freedoms offered by companies is a much bigger concern than most realize. This is a true statement.

   C. **Correct:** A screen lock is not a sufficient security measure in any situation.

   D. **Incorrect:** Many tablets and audio players with Wi-Fi connectivity can run apps that enable voice and video call capabilities. This is a true statement.

10. **Correct Answer: A**

    A. **Correct:** Storage encryption is considered the least likely security feature to be present on mobile devices.

    B. **Incorrect:** CompTIA considers remote wipe a common feature.

    C. **Incorrect:** CompTIA considers GPS tracking a common feature.

    D. **Incorrect:** CompTIA considers a screen lock a common feature.

## CHAPTER 10

Understanding data security

Data security is concerned with the protection of the confidentiality, integrity, and availability of data. A wide range of tools, techniques, and policies are used to control access to data. However, the most prevalent is encryption. Chapter 12, "Cryptography," discusses the details of cryptography algorithms, whereas this chapter focuses on the application of cryptography to operational activities.

Exam objectives in this chapter:

Objective 4.3: Explain the importance of data security

- Data Loss Prevention (DLP)
- Data encryption
  - Full disk
  - Database
  - Individual files
  - Removable media
  - Mobile devices
- Hardware based encryption devices
  - TPM
  - HSM
  - USB encryption
  - Hard drive
- Cloud computing

Data loss prevention (DLP)

Data loss prevention (DLP) is both a company policy and a product available on the technology market. As a company policy, DLP focuses on implementing defenses against data loss and theft. As a product, DLP is a technology solution that can assist with the fulfillment of a company's DLP policy.

Data loss is a serious risk to any organization. Data loss due to outright theft or loss due to accidental misplacement can both be disastrous events for a company. Data loss involves situations in which unauthorized personnel, competitors, outsiders, or others gain access to private, personal data or proprietary, trade-secret, corporate data. When information disclosure occurs, the damage that results could be just a minor inconvenience or could be something more significant, such as identity theft or the closure of an organization. Organizations everywhere need to take the loss of control of valuable data seriously.

The goal of DLP is to focus on the potential for data to be lost or disclosed, and to implement preventions. DLP can also include defenses and detections to make the act of data theft more difficult to perform. DLP is often implemented by using many other common elements of a general security solution, but with the primary focus on preventing data loss. These elements include training, system design and architecture, and hardware and software tools.

It is fairly common for DLP to be a central part of any security solution. The typical company security policy always includes elements that can be labeled as preventing the loss or disclosure of data to unauthorized parties.

 A DLP system is intended to detect potential and occurring data breaches. Any occurrence of *data exfiltration* is unwanted, and DLP attempts to thwart such events by using an approach based on monitoring, detection, and interruption of unwanted data activities. DLP can monitor events taking place at endpoints, such as a data file being opened by a user or accessed by an application (known as in-use events). It can also monitor transmission events as data is moved between locations on the network or between networks (known as in-motion events). DLP can also monitor data at rest in storage, whether the location is local online storage or remote archival storage (known as in-place events).

Data loss or leakage events can occur either by means of malicious intent or accidental mistakes. In either case, DLP can reduce the likelihood of actual data exposure by detecting and interrupting the unauthorized data flow. Various DLP implementations, such as in-use, in-motion, or in-place implementations, can be combined to establish a broad detection and prevention matrix for an organization.

 EXAM TIP

The terms *data loss* and *data leak* are often used as synonyms, but in fact they are different. Data loss occurs when information is lost or otherwise inaccessible to the authorized owner. The loss of a USB drive or a backup medium are examples of data loss. A data leak occurs when data is obtained by an unauthorized third party. A data loss can lead to a data leak, which is why they are often seen as interchangeable terms. A DLP solution attempts to address both loss and leakage.

DLP solutions are often an important part of maintaining compliance with government regulations, industry standards, or contractual obligations against data loss. For example, HIPAA (Health Insurance Portability and Accountability Act) compliance requires DLP. Similarly, the PCI DSS (Payment Card Industry Data Security Standard) requirements necessary to be allowed to process credit cards often include DLP implementation.

There are a wide number of DLP products available in both open source as well as commercial form. One example of an open source DLP solution is MyDLP (*www.mydlp.com*). Examples of commercial DLP products include Microsoft Forefront (*www.microsoft.com/forefront*) and Symantec Data Loss Prevention (*www.symantec.com/data-loss-prevention*). Several other DLP products are also available on the market.

 Quick check

1. What types of data situations can DLP solutions monitor?
2. Must DLP be implemented by using a dedicated third-party product?

Quick check answers

1. DLP solutions can monitor data in use, in motion, and in place.
2. No. Although a wide range of third-party products are available, DLP can be implemented into an overall security strategy by using DLP-focused policies and procedures to craft a home-grown solution.

Data encryption

 One of the most important tools in the protection of data security is encryption. *Data encryption* is a key technology in preventing unauthorized disclosure of information as well as preventing corruption or intentional integrity changes. However, encryption is not foolproof and does not protect against everything. For example, encryption does not provide protection for availability. This chapter addresses the uses and applications of data encryption in relation to data security. Keep in mind that although the focus is on data security, many of these issues apply to servers, mobile devices, and many other systems and situations. This chapter does not focus on the algorithms of encryption or the actual implementation and management of cryptography. Those topics are discussed in depth in Chapter 12.

Encryption is the technology that converts or transforms original data into a chaotic and seemingly random, and thus unintelligible, form. In cryptographic terms, the original usable data is called *plaintext* or *cleartext*. It is important to realize that this does not mean to imply that all data is text, but rather that it is in its original, usable form. The secured form of data is known as *ciphertext*. The process of converting or transforming from plaintext to ciphertext is encryption. The process of reverting back to plaintext from ciphertext is decryption.

The processes of encryption and decryption are managed by a complex set of mathematical operations known as an *algorithm*. Most modern algorithms use a random initial value and a key. The random initial value is known formally as the *initialization vector (IV)*. The IV is a random number incorporated into the plaintext just before the actual encryption process starts. The key is the secret number used to lock the ciphertext so that only the intended recipient is able to decrypt the data back into plaintext. Both a key and an IV are needed by the recipient to perform decryption. It is essential that the key and IV be exchanged securely so that no unauthorized third parties have access to those values. All real-world data encryption solutions address these concerns and implement them around a specific individual algorithm or a set of algorithms. Again, the details of specific algorithms and key management are discussed in Chapter 12.

Data encryption is used to provide security protection for data. Primarily, data encryption provides protection for the confidentiality of data. Because only those in possession of the correct key and IV for a specific ciphertext can decrypt it into plaintext, the content of the data is protected against unauthorized disclosure—assuming a reasonably strong algorithm, a reasonably difficult-to-guess key, and the use of reasonable security for *key exchange*.

EXAM TIP

Cryptography is an excellent security tool, but only for the purposes for which it is effective. Cryptography protects confidentiality. However, that protection is not guaranteed, only reasonably assured. The issue is that encryption is like a lock. If someone is skilled at lock picking, that person might eventually get lucky and figure out the key. Cryptography is constantly being pushed forward as attacks get better. More complicated algorithms and longer keys help cryptographic efforts stay in front of hackers' attempts to breach the protection. But because attacks are always getting better, the great encryption of today will eventually be the poor security of yesterday.

Within the realm of cryptography is another concept known as *hashing*. Hashing is used to detect violations of integrity—in other words, changes to data. Hashing works by creating a representative number from data. When a hash value is created, it marks the identity of data at that specific instant in time. At some future time, the data can be hashed again. If the second hash value matches the initial hash value, the data did not change during the interim time period, and thus its integrity was maintained. However, if the two hashes are not exactly the same value, then integrity was violated because something about the data changed during the interim time period. Thus, hashing detects integrity violations but does not prevent them.

Hashing has another benefit: it provides protection simply because of how hashing algorithms work. Hashing algorithms are one-way functions. This means that they can be calculated or run in a forward direction, but it is not possible to reverse them. Thus, after a hash value is calculated, it is not possible to decrypt or reverse the hash back into the original data. This is because hashing algorithms are based around *lossy mathematical operations*. A lossy mathematical operation is one that discards or drops data as it performs calculations. A common example of a lossy mathematical operation is that of modulo or mod. Modulo is a division function that keeps the remainder but discards the quotient. This one-way nature of hashing prevents data re-creation by reversing the hashing function.

EXAM TIP

A great way to think of hashing is to equate it with taking a photograph. By taking a snapshot of someone, you now have an image of them that you can use to recognize them in the future. However, with that image you are unable to create a clone of that person, because the photo does not include enough data about them, such as their DNA.

But wait, isn't there a big issue with password hashes being cracked to steal passwords? Yes, there is, but it is not decrypting the hash that is the problem here. The problem is that passwords are relatively short (most are fewer than 10 characters) and are created from common characters (such as lowercase letters only, or the standard options on a typical keyboard, such as uppercase or lowercase characters, numbers, and symbols). Hackers can crack passwords by either guessing or crafting potential passwords (input data) and then creating a hash from the result. Each potential password is then compared to the target in hopes of finding a match. If a match is found, then the crack has revealed the original password. Again, this is not decrypting the hash value, it is instead guessing the original password characters. A good defense against password cracking for end users is to use longer and more complex passwords, thus making it much less likely that a quick password crack will be successful.

Most data encryption tools use a combination of encryption processes and hashing processes to provide a complete security service for the data being protected. It is important to prevent data from falling into the wrong hands, and it is important to make sure that data is not changed or modified.

When you are selecting a data encryption solution, it is important to consider some of the features, options, or specifications of the available products before making a purchase and implementing the solution:

- Consider only products that offer strong algorithms, such as those vetted for use by the US federal government under FIPS (Federal Information Processing Standard) 140-2. If the product features only older algorithms, look for something more current.

- Be sure the solution includes integrity checking.

- Be sure the product offers options for the longest keys available for the algorithms supported.

- Favor products that ask for user input or activity to assist in the generation of random encryption key values (see Figure 10-1).
- Select products that indicate that they use secure storage of keys, credentials, and other elements of identification and access.

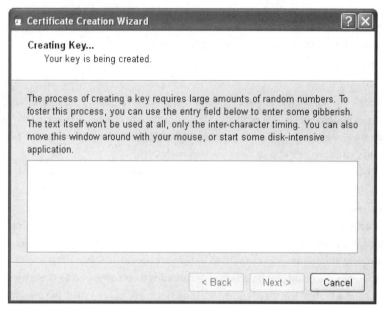

FIGURE 10-1 In the random key generation dialog box of the Gpg4win tool, the product asks for random keyboard input to use as a seed for generating more unpredictable (that is, more secure) keys.

Data encryption can be implemented to provide protection for a wide variety of data management situations, including full-disk, database, individual file, removable media, and mobile device encryption. All of these implementation scenarios are discussed in the following sections.

 Quick check

1. What are the benefits and potential drawbacks of data encryption?
2. What is the difference between encryption and hashing?

Quick check answers

1. Data encryption can offer reasonable protection in specific circumstances. However, if the key is ever guessed or stolen, then the protection is lost.

2. Encryption is the conversion of plaintext into ciphertext to prevent disclosure. Hashing is the function of creating a representative value to use to determine whether or not integrity has been violated.

Full-disk encryption

Full-disk encryption is the application of data encryption technology to an entire storage device. Though most full-disk encryption is focused on encrypting the standard or traditional spinning internal hard disk, it can also be used to encrypt solid-state disks, external disks, and removable disks.

Full-disk encryption can be provided natively by the operating system or through an installed third-party product. In addition to software solutions, there are also hardware devices that can provide encryption for entire storage devices; these include special versions of the storage devices themselves as well as some controller cards.

Full-disk encryption operates transparently to the end user after it is properly installed and configured. At least, it is transparent during normal activities. The user might be prompted upon startup to provide an additional set of credentials to unlock the encrypted storage device. Though multiple sets of credentials might be required for multiple configurations—for example, if an organization encrypts its data disks as well as its main operating system disk and external disks—the inconvenience is minimal and is not a significant burden to normal activities. After it is configured, full-disk encryption ensures that everything saved, copied, or moved to the storage device is automatically encrypted. Additionally, when the master unlock credentials are provided, all data on the disk is decrypted on the fly as it is read into memory by an application or any file management tool.

Full-disk encryption can be applied to the main operating system startup disk or to data disks. The encryption can be set to secure every disk in a system, or only disks containing sensitive information. Encrypted disks can be configured to be automatically unlocked upon startup or logon, or they can remain protected until a user specifically requests access to the secured disk. These are just some of the many options available with full-disk encryption.

Full-disk encryption offers several benefits over other forms of storage encryption, specifically when compared to file encryption. File encryption is discussed in detail in a later section. File encryption only encrypts individual files on a per-file request basis. The drawback to the file encryption approach is that metadata is not protected. When temporary copies of the file are made by applications or when some of the file's data located in RAM is paged off into the virtual memory swap file, those additional copies or versions of the data are not encrypted by the original file's encryption. All of the data on a storage device is encrypted when full-disk encryption is in use. Every file, all metadata, every temporary file, every swap file, everything on the storage device is protected with full-disk encryption.

A drawback to full-disk encryption is that a single master encryption key is used to encrypt the contents of the disk. If that one key is ever lost, corrupted, or stolen, it could be disastrous. A lost or corrupted key could result in legitimate users being blocked from gaining access to data on the protected storage device. A stolen key could allow someone to gain access to the data on the storage device. Thus, precautions should be taken to minimize these risks.

Full-disk encryption is never a substitute for a reliable backup system. Only backups are insurance against data loss or corruption. Full-disk encryption is potentially a protection against data loss or data leakage, but if the disk is damaged, lost, stolen, or otherwise becomes inaccessible, only with a backup can you regain access to the hosted data. Always back up all data, even if it is stored on a storage device hosting full-disk encryption.

EXAM TIP

The CompTIA Security+ exam claims that full-disk encryption will cause a significant delay in the startup process and can cause performance degradation for typical activities. And though this could be an issue, it rarely is one with relatively modern equipment. Most CPUs are now equipped with an onboard dedicated encryption chip that offloads the complex work of encryption from the main processor. This not only speeds up encryption operations but also relieves the CPU to use all of its computation cycles for other work. Thus, on most modern systems, full-disk encryption will not cause any noticeable delay in startup or reductions in performance or responsiveness. But do keep in mind that the exam still considers full-disk encryption to be a performance sink.

Implementing full-disk encryption

The process of implementing full-disk encryption is not usually overly complex, but neither is it a completely obvious or simple process. It is important to remember that the act of converting a disk from standard or normal plaintext form into an encrypted form can render the hosted data unusable if anything goes wrong during the process. *Always* make a backup of all files on a storage device before attempting to implement full-disk encryption.

The first step is to determine whether you are using the native full-disk encryption feature of your operating system (such as BitLocker for Windows) or a third-party add-on product (such as TrueCrypt). If you are using the native operating system feature, you will work from the configuration app provided by the operating system. If you are installing a third-party product, follow the instructions to install the software, and then access the full-disk encryption software's configuration tools.

Second, determine which disk is to be converted into a full-disk encryption device. Be sure that everything on the disk is protected in a backup. If you are not sure about whether or not you have a recent backup, go ahead and make another backup *now*! The process of setting up full-disk encryption can take a significant amount of time, especially if data is already resident on the target device. It is usually possible to encrypt data in place without any consequences other than that it might take much longer. When possible, consider converting a blank storage device to a full-disk encryption device, then copy your data onto the now-encrypted disk. This is almost always the faster operation.

Real world

An experience with disk encryption

In the time frame of about six weeks, one of the authors had the opportunity (or the misfortune?) twice to create a storage device hosting full-disk encryption. In both cases, the disks were 500 gigabytes (GB) in capacity with about 300 GB of data in place. The first time he performed the operation, the data was already resident on the target hard disk. The process of converting the disk from plaintext to encrypted format took nearly 18 hours. The second time, he had a blank disk to start with, and the conversion from plaintext to encrypted disk took less than 1 hour. Then the transfer of 300 GB of data took less than three additional hours. So, in this experience, in-place data conversion to full-disk encryption took more than four times as long as performing the conversion on a blank disk and then moving the data onto the secured target.

The third step in implementing full-disk encryption is to select the encryption algorithm, define the key, and make other configuration setting selections. Always read the documentation and instructions for your product before proceeding. It is not really possible to give specific recommendations on what you should do or select here. However, some general recommendations are:

- Select a modern encryption algorithm, such as AES (Advanced Encryption Standard), over older options.

- Select longer keys over shorter encryption keys—although longer keys could cause performance lag.

- Encryption keys should never be shorter than 128 bits for general or personal data, and at least 192 bits for corporate or organizational data.

- Consider multiple algorithms or multiple passes of encryption, but realize that these will cause noticeable performance delays on most systems.

- Always select an integrity checking method. SHA (Secure Hash Algorithm) options are preferred over MD5 (Message Digest).

- If prompted to provide user input to increase the entropy of the random number creation, provide as much as possible (some systems automatically terminate the request session after they get enough) or continue providing input long after you think it is enough (that is, spend 3 minutes instead of just 10 seconds).

- Define a long and complex master unlock password or passphrase. Be sure it is one you can remember and reproduce. If not, you will be locking yourself out of your own data.

- Consider auto-unlock and multifactor credential options if they are offered (we'll talk more about this soon).

After the setup or configuration process for applying full-disk encryption to a disk is complete, you will then need to wait until the conversion or encryption process is done before you can perform any other action. It is usually a good idea to leave the system alone until the process is complete. Attempting to use the computer for other tasks, including surfing the web, reading email, accessing documents, or playing back audio or video content, could at best delay the conversion or at worst interfere with the operation. If you happen to open a file that is in the process of being encrypted, it could cause a corruption. If you need to use the system soon, then plan on performing the full-disk encryption implementation process at a later time when you can leave the system alone for hours.

Decommissioning an encrypted device

 Another important issue to keep in mind in relation to full-disk encryption is the chance that your specific encryption product might not offer a deconversion or *decommissioning* process. If you need to convert from a full-disk encryption device back to a plaintext device, the process might be easy or it might be complicated. The easy process would be if your encryption solution offered a decryption process. It will simply decrypt the disk with data in place, returning it to a nonencrypted state without any data loss or corruption. However, many encryption products do not offer a seamless or simple decommissioning procedure. Instead, you will have to perform your own manual reversion. Manually reverting back to a plaintext disk requires that you back up or make a copy of every file on the encrypted device to another storage device, delete the partition or volume on the encrypted device, create a new volume, format the new volume, and then copy all the data back onto the now plaintext device.

Decrypting an encrypted device

Full-disk encryption is a security technology designed to prevent unauthorized access to electronically stored data. However, that security is dependent upon the management software used, the selected algorithm, the key in use, and most importantly, the master set of credentials used to gain access to the encrypted data. Most encryption products allow the use of a password or passphrase to be used directly (or indirectly) to decrypt a disk. However, there are potentially several other options, including the use of a TPM (Trusted Platform Module, which is covered in a later discussion), a USB device, and combinations of these.

From the user's perspective, the potential means of unlocking a storage device hosting full-disk encryption can range from automatic and transparent to complex, multifactor, and multistep. The methods could include (but would not necessarily be limited to) the combinations listed here, in order from least to greatest user inconvenience:

1. TPM only

2. User password with TPM

3. USB only

4. USB with TPM

5. User password with USB and TPM

The following list explores these options in depth.

1. **TPM only**   The easiest option from the users' perspective is to allow the system itself to automatically unlock encrypted disks upon system startup This is made possible if the computer has a motherboard that includes a TPM chip. The TPM (Trusted Platform Module) is a special chip designed for use by encryption solutions as a secure and tamper-proof storage location for encryption keys. If a full-disk encryption system is configured to use the TPM, the disk's master encryption key will be stored in the TPM. Upon startup, the TPM provides the master key to the encryption software and the disk is automatically unlocked for the user. This configuration is fully transparent to the user; however, it provides no protection in the event that the system is accessed by an unauthorized person. The only protection provided by this configuration is if the hard disk itself is the only item stolen by a hacker. Without the TPM, the disk will not be able to be unlocked by reasonable means.

> **NOTE   WHERE OH WHERE IS THE TPM?**
>
> The TPM is a chip that is located on a system's motherboard. However, this is not a chip found on every motherboard. It is most often found on portable devices, such as notebooks. More and more motherboards are featuring the TPM chip, so it might be found on tablets, desktops, smart phones, and servers. However, if you plan on using the TPM, be sure to consult your systems specifications to ensure that the TPM chip is actually present.

2. **User password with TPM**   A variation on the TPM-only method is to require a password upon startup or user logon in order to unlock the TPM. Without the password, the TPM will not disclose the master encryption key for the storage device. This is an improvement on the TPM-only process, but only in the event that the system is encountered by an unauthorized person when it is turned off or in a locked state. If the storage devices have already been unlocked, then no protection is actually being provided against an at-the-keyboard attacker.

3. **USB only**   This credential option requires that the user insert a USB key or other USB device when prompted in order to unlock the secured storage device. The USB device contains a file hosting the encryption key. This encryption key is loaded by the encryption software from the USB drive, then used to unlock the local storage device. If the USB key is lost, access to the disk is prohibited. An additional level of protection is gained if the file hosted on the USB key requires a password to be opened.

4. **USB with TPM**   This credential option requires that the user insert a USB key when prompted in order to unlock the TPM. In this case, the storage device's master encryption key is stored in the protection of the TPM. The USB key simply hosts an unlock code that is used to access the contents of the TPM. This technique is considered a more secure option than using USB only because the encryption key is not stored on

a USB drive where it might be more accessible and instead is stored in the tamper-resistant TPM vault.

5. **User password with USB and TPM** This credential option requires the user to insert a USB key and type in a password to unlock the TPM, which in turn unlocks the encrypted hard disk. This option requires the most of a user—a physical device and a password—but it also provides the best protection against unauthorized access, especially when the system is turned off when it is encountered by an unauthorized person.

It is always important to consider all credential options before making a decision. This is a decision you should make before starting the plaintext-to-encrypted-storage conversion process. If you don't understand the credential options, then you will not be able to make an informed decision. The options listed here are just some of the more common examples of credential sets for full-disk encryption. Read the documentation for your specific encryption software to find out what it actually offers and make your selections based on that information.

Recovery options

Another important consideration to think about before selecting a full-disk encryption product is what recovery options are available. A recovery option gives you the ability to regain access to an encrypted disk if you forget your master password or lose your master USB key. Often a recovery procedure uses a recovery disk built at the time of disk encryption initialization. It is used to recreate an access key for the encrypted disk. Not all encryption products offer a recovery mechanism. And even if the feature is part of your encryption product, you might choose not to set up a recovery option. The recovery process can be performed by a hacker just as easily as by the authorized user, especially if the hacker is able to steal both the encrypted disk and the recovery disk. You might consider taking a no-hope-of-recovery perspective on full-disk encryption. For full-disk encryption, if you forget your master key, you should not be able to regain access. This will also help to ensure that full-disk encryption is not treated as a backup option. Disk encryption is not a substitute for backups. If you do not configure a recovery option, a backup will be the only means by which access to the data can be regained.

Full-disk encryption vulnerabilities

Full-disk encryption provides protection for data stored on the disk, but only in specific circumstances. If the encryption uses password-only credentials, then a hacker could steal just the hard disk and have the chance of brute-force guessing the key over time, although this form of attack is highly unlikely to succeed. If the encryption uses the TPM, then both the hard disk and the motherboard must be stolen to give the hackers a chance at gaining access. Similarly, if a USB drive is involved in the credentials, then the USB drive must also be obtained by the hackers to attempt to circumvent the encryption. In these situations, full-disk encryption is likely to provide reasonable protection.

However, there are circumstances in which full-disk encryption does not provide sufficient protection—specifically, if a hacker is able to access the physical system while the computer is active. An active computer is a fully started system with a user logged on with an open and accessible desktop; it could also be a system that is locked with a screen saver, requiring a password, as well as a system in sleep mode. Sleep mode is a low power–consumption mode in which process execution is suspended but in which the contents of memory stay in RAM. In each of these active computer situations, one flaw is always present. That flaw is the fact that full-disk encryption uses a single master symmetric encryption key to encode the stored data, and that single encryption key is stored in memory in plaintext form. Attacks that are able to access and read the specific area of RAM will be able to learn the encryption key. These include DMA (direct memory access) attacks over FireWire ports as well as attacks that restart the system from a USB drive and dump the memory contents to a disk. The RAM used in a typical computer does not instantly become empty; instead, the memory-resident data decays over time. On a typical system, it could take 45 seconds for all data in RAM to dissipate. If a system is just restarted, RAM will retain its contents, allowing for a memory dump to capture everything stored there, including a full-disk encryption key. If a system cannot be restarted from a USB device, then another approach called the *cold boot attack* might be possible. This attack requires the RAM chips to be supercooled to slow down the rate of data decay. Often, an upside-down can of compressed air can be used to quickly reduce the temperature. The cold RAM chips can be removed and placed into a memory reader to extract the contents. For more details on the cold boot attack, see the research from Princeton University at *https://citp.princeton.edu/research/memory/*.

A wide range of products are available to implement full-disk encryption. These include operating system–native tools such as Windows BitLocker, Apple's FileVault, and the Linux dm-crypt+LUKS. There are also many third-party options, such as Symantec's PGP Whole Disk Encryption (a commercial product) or TrueCrypt (an open source product).

✔ **Quick check**

1. What is the least secure form of credential configuration for unlocking full-disk encryption?

2. If a user forgets or loses his or her encryption credentials, what options are available for data recovery?

Quick check answers

1. Using just the TPM is the least secure form of credential because the disk will auto-unlock at system startup.

2. If a recovery option was configured during initialization, then a recovery procedure can be attempted. Otherwise, only a backup of the data will provide access to the secured data.

Database encryption

Database encryption has quickly become an essential security issue as organizations realize how much damage and loss can occur due to a breach of a mission-critical database. It is also the case that many regulations and contracts now require organizations to implement database encryption in order to stay in compliance. However, database security is not as straight-forward and simple as file or disk encryption. The main difficulty with database encryption is implementing the proper key management solution.

The interactions with a database by users and applications within an organizational network are quite complex, much more so than those of a shared file system on a network share. This complexity causes serious complications when it comes to managing encryption keys. If the encryption is done incorrectly, the keys might be inaccessible to authorized users or might become accessible to unauthorized entities, neither of which is a desirable outcome. Often a centralized key management system is needed. This could be a software-only solution or could involve various HSMs (Hardware Security Modules) to support large-scale key management.

It is important to ensure that the encryption keys used to protect any data, but especially data stored in a database, are not stored alongside or in an obvious place relative to the data. A separate key storage and key management system is essential. The practice of comingling secured data with its encryption keys is the equivalent of locking your front door and then hiding the key under the doormat. Usually, a distinct key storage database will provide a much more reliable means of key retention.

Database encryption can range from individual cell encryption to full table encryption, as well as any other intermediary division (such as rows or columns). When the encryption is on a table or database level, there are many fewer keys to manage than when each individual data cell has its own unique key. Often, choosing a less granular key assignment scheme makes key management more streamlined.

EXAM TIP

Although database encryption is important for organizations and online services, is does not seem to be a major topic on the CompTIA Security+ exam. Simply knowing that database encryption exists and that its use is important is likely sufficient.

As mentioned previously, encryption is not a substitute for backups. This is equally true in relation to encrypted databases. However, it is important to encrypt the backups as well as the original data. Failing to encrypt and protect the backups of a database will simply shift the focus of breaches and compromises towards those backups. Always assume that the backups and the originals are equally vulnerable to intended or accidental compromise.

Another potential and common problem with database encryption is using out-of-date encryption technologies and algorithms. Many organizations invest decades in their DBMSs (database management systems). Although a DBMS from the previous decade might be sufficient for storing and organizing the data of the database, often the encryption from the previous decade is not strong enough to withstand modern attacks. Be sure to update or supplement the encryption scheme of older databases with modern solutions.

 Quick check

1. At what level can a database be encrypted?

2. What is the risk of using an older DBMS?

Quick check answers

1. A database can be encrypted as a whole entity (similar to full-disk encryption), on an individual data cell basis (similar to file encryption), or potentially based on other database divisions, such as tables, rows, or columns.

2. Old DBMSs might have outdated encryption technology.

Individual file encryption

 The encryption of individual files is implemented in a completely different fashion than full-disk encryption. The main distinction between *individual file encryption* and full-disk encryption is that each individual file can be encrypted by using its own unique encryption key. This is definitely the case for native file encryption features such as EFS (Encryption File System), which is part of the Windows NTFS file system. EFS, instead of storing and managing an increasingly large number of encryption keys in some form of master key-ring mechanism, stores each encryption key on the file it encrypts. This is implemented by using a public key cryptosystem in which the public key of the user is employed to envelop or encrypt the file's symmetric encryption key. This enveloped key is then stored on (or with) the encrypted file. When the user needs to regain access to the file, he or she returns with his or her private key to unlock the public key envelope and regain access to the symmetric key, which in turn is used to decrypt the file. Each time a file is decrypted by using this process, when the file is closed or saved back to the disk, a new randomly selected symmetric encryption key is selected and used to encrypt the file, and then that new symmetric key is enveloped by the user's public key for storage. This system allows the user to keep track of just a single private key rather than a growing number of symmetric keys. Not all individual file system implementations use this specific technique. However, the CompTIA Security+ exam uses this as its primary example of this concept.

This process might seem complicated, but can be broken down in to a series of steps (see Figure 10-2):

1. A random symmetric key (K1) is selected for the target file.

2. K1 is used to encrypt the target file.

3. The user's public key (Pu) is used to encrypt (envelop) the file's symmetric key (K1) and then is stored on or with the encrypted file. At this point, the file is secured.

4. When the user returns to gain access, the user's private key (Pr) is used to decrypt the envelope that is encrypted with the public key (Pu) to extract the symmetric key (K1).

5. The symmetric key (K1) is used to decrypt the file.

6. When the user closes or resaves the file, a new symmetric key is generated (K2), and the process is repeated.

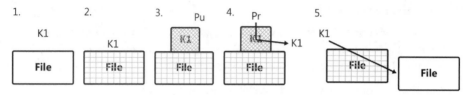

FIGURE 10-2 The steps for individual file encryption involve public and private keys.

There are a few concerns related to individual file encryption. First, this type of encryption does not protect metadata or temporary copies of open files. Only the original file itself is secured by individual file encryption. The other data created by the operating system or applications that interact with the file might expose the content to disclosure. Second, if the user's private key is ever lost or corrupted, this would prevent the user from decrypting files. A mechanism known as the *KRA (key recovery agent)* could be used to provide an alternate access path to the encrypted files.

A key recovery agent is a trusted administrator or group of administrators who can be called upon to decrypt files when the user's private key is lost or corrupted. This is made possible by storing additional copies of the file's encryption key in encryption envelopes made by using a key recovery agent's public key (see Figure 10-3). Thus, the key recovery agent's private key can be used to access the additional stored copy of the file's symmetric key. The key recovery agent mechanism creates an additional recovery strategy not available when only the individual's public key enveloping is used. However, the use of a KRA should be considered carefully, because it creates a backdoor that a malicious user might take advantage of.

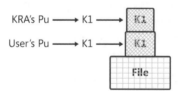

FIGURE 10-3 An additional copy of a file's symmetric key can be stored by the key recovery agent.

File encryption can often be used on folders as well as files . Using file encryption on a folder would effectively "archive" the folder's contents into a container that is encrypted. In order to access any of the folder's contents, a user would have to decrypt the whole folder.

Individual file encryption might not always be the best choice for protecting data., because only those files that are intentionally encrypted have any protection, and then only the original files, not their metadata, are secured. Users of file encryption often only encrypt important files and not mundane files. Thus, hackers know to focus their efforts on the encrypted files because they contain the most useful or valuable information.

An often-overlooked benefit of individual file encryption is that files from multiple users can be stored on the same shared network storage device without conflict. Each user would only be able to decrypt his or her own files using his or her own private key. When full-disk encryption is used on shared storage devices, each user is given a copy of the single master key. Although this retains protection against outsider access, it does not differentiate access between those with possession of the master encryption key.

 Quick check

1. What is and is not protected with individual file encryption?

2. If a user loses his or her private key, can he or she regain access to encrypted files?

Quick check answers

1. Only the original file is encrypted, not file metadata or temporary copies of the file created by the operating system or applications

2. Only if a key recovery agent is defined or if the user has a backup

Removable media

Removable media presents its own set of risks and threats to an IT infrastructure. The two main risks related to removable and portable media are data leakage and loss, as well as malware infection. *Removable media* includes a wide range of technologies and devices, including:

- USB flash drives
- Portable hard drives
- Optical discs, such as CDs, DVDs, and Blu-ray disks
- Tapes
- Memory cards, such as SD cards
- Floppy disks

USB flash drives seem to be the most prolific in terms of causing problems for organizations—so much so that many have banned their use on company equipment and might even outlaw their presence on company property. This type of security policy and company stance reduces the risk of removable media by not allowing these drives in or out of the organization. Though this policy could be considered an extreme measure, it is often a justified measure.

Users are notorious for leaving important files on removable and portable media. This often occurs when a user uses a portable drive to move files between computers, and then after the files are copied to the destination computer, forgets that the files remain on the portable drive. If users fail to maintain respect for the files and the drive, they will often drop the drive into a drawer, leave it on a desk, drop it in their pocket, or allow other workers to borrow it. This situation leaves the drive open to being misplaced, lost, or stolen. If that occurs, whoever gains access to the drive in the future will now have access to those important files copied onto the drive. This is an all-too-common data loss scenario that can be prevented.

The primary means by which this form of data loss or data leakage can be prevented is through on-device encryption. This can be accomplished by using one of several currently available encryption technologies, such as individual file encryption, full-disk encryption, or on-device hardware encryption. The first two options would be applied to the removable media by encryption software on the computer. Thus, the same encryption software would need to be present on any other computer that the drive will need to connect to. The third option is encryption provided by the portable drive itself. This is only available if the specific make and model of portable device provides this feature. There are several manufacturers that offer encrypted USB drives. These drives are usually more expensive than the nonencrypted versions, but the additional security provided by the drives might be worth the extra expense in some situations.

For the best protection, automated or forced encryption is better than encryption that you have to remember to implement. Hardware-provided encryption or full-disk encryption automatically encrypts anything copied to the portable device. Individual file encryption does not usually encrypt new files automatically, so you will have to remember to manually trigger the protection. Also, don't forget that metadata and temporary file copies will not be protected by individual file encryption.

Another risk of removable media is that of malware infection. When portable media devices are allowed to exit the building, they are exposed to compromise in the outside world. If a compromised portable medium is then returned into the organization, it can be a vector for malware infection. Additionally, even "new" portable devices can be vectors of infection. Just because a media device is sealed up by the manufacturer does not guarantee that it was not infected at the manufacturer's own facility. This has occurred and will probably occur again. This, in fact, has own name: the shrink wrap attack.

It is even more likely that any media device that is "found" will be a means by which malware infests an organization. Hackers often use the social engineering trick of planting USB drives in public places, such as parking lots, waiting rooms, bathrooms, or break rooms. Such a planted storage device might seem like a windfall to a worker who does not realize that it is a trick to get the user to plug the device into his or her work machine, where auto-launching malicious apps can grant hackers access to the network.

Although using encryption will not fully eliminate the risk of malware infection from a removable media device, it will significantly reduce it. If storage device is secured, only when it is unlocked will there be an opportunity for malware to gain access to it. Cautious users who know that this window of opportunity exists will be careful about their use of these devices. And if the organization only allows encrypted removable media, those devices brought in from outside that don't meet the security requirements will not be used on the network.

For this latter statement to be fully enforced, organizations cannot depend exclusively upon users to abide by the written policy. Instead, they should use technology to enforce the approved-devices-only rule. This can potentially be accomplished by the setting the

CMOS and BIOS settings on motherboards to either fully disable all USBs or just disable the connection of storage devices. For a more flexible solution, many operating systems now offer the ability to block the class of general portable storage devices while allowing specific devices by serial number or model number. Thus, only the approved, encrypted storage devices will be allowed to connect, while all other devices will be automatically disabled and ignored because the operating system will not allow their relevant device driver to load.

A few other good security practices in relation to removable media are:

- Don't leave removable media attached to a computer; instead, remove them as soon as their use is completed.
- Check computers for attached removable media before every startup or restart process.
- After using a removable media device to transfer files, perform a media sanitization process to delete and scrub the drive clean of all data remnants.

- Use a precleaning process (a *"sheep dip"*) to "verify" new removable media devices before allowing them to be used in the organization.

EXAM TIP

The term *sheep dip* is sometimes used to describe a stand-alone anti-malware scanning system that is intended to be used as a precleaning tool for removable media devices before they are connected to the production environment. A sheep dip system needs to have scanner updates manually transferred to it daily. The use of this precleaning methodology will reduce malware infections via removable media.

Removable media, portable media, and external storage devices are neither perfectly safe nor unable to be secured. However, it does take considerable effort to establish a security policy, and it requires user practice to improve the security around removable media devices and reduce the risks they pose against an organization.

✔ **Quick check**

1. What are the two primary risks that removable media pose to an organization?

2. What are tools to reduce these risks?

Quick check answers

1. Data leakage and loss, and malware infection

2. Banning the devices, encryption, precleaning, and training

---

Mobile devices

Mobile device encryption is another important tool in the toolbox of the security manager whose job it is to protect an organization against data loss and security breaches. Many of the security issues related to mobile devices, including mobile device encryption, were presented in Chapter 9, "Establishing host security." For clarity, we have reframed the encryption discussion for this chapter.

What are *mobile devices*? Generally, the phrase is used to refer to smart phones, feature phones, and other forms of mobile phones. But the term is not strictly related to phone devices. The exploding category of tablets is also included in the concept of a mobile device. And to be thorough, don't forget about audio players, digital still and video cameras, mobile hotspots, portable projectors, and media sharing devices. Those devices that might be considered miniature computers, such as smart phones and tablets, are often exposed to the same risks as traditional computers. Other less powerful, less capable, or less flexible forms of mobile devices might not have as many threats against them, but such a device can be just as big of a threat against individual computers or an organization's network.

One of the big issues with mobile devices of all types is that they can often be connected to a computer by a USB cable, via Bluetooth technology, or through a wireless network, and they appear on the computer as storage devices. This requires security professionals to treat mobile devices like removable media, as discussed in the previous section. Any mobile device that has any form of data storage ability can be used to perform intentional or accidental data leaks, data loss, and/or malware distribution. Thus, precautions must be taken to avoid and when possible eliminate this risk.

One option is to implement an organization-wide ban on mobile devices. However, this is a challenge to implement due to the popularity and convenience of these devices. Plus, even with a restrictive policy on mobile devices, users will sometimes accidentally or intentionally bring them into the workplace. So mobile device prohibition will not be effective without other security measures.

A second option is to implement a *BYOD (bring your own device)* policy. This sets up a bit of freedom for users to bring in their own devices but establishes minimum security feature requirements that users will have to comply with in order to use their own devices on or with the company's IT infrastructure. Some BYOD policies even list specific makes and models of devices that are allowed, and ban all others not on the list. Such policies should focus on encouraging employees to use mobile devices with security features and set up and configure those features properly, and the organization should provide user training to assist in reducing risky activities and behaviors.

One of the most important on-device features to be recommended for mobile devices is encryption. On-device encryption for mobile devices has only recently become a fairly standard feature. However, most devices that support on-device encryption do not have the feature enabled by default. So it is important to not only select devices that support encryption but to actually implement the feature.

When selecting a device with encryption features, be sure to take note of what type of data is and is not encrypted by the device. Some devices only encrypt the native software and not user data, some encrypt only user data and not native software, and still others might encrypt everything stored on the device. Some devices will encrypt the built-in storage but not encrypt expanded storage, such as that provided by memory cards.

For mobile phones supporting encryption, the screen lock feature should be enabled with a password or other secure credential in combination with device encryption. This will prevent a hacker from being able to use a connected cable to access the contents of the mobile phone when the screen is locked. Only when the screen is unlocked is access granted through the USB port to the storage volumes of the mobile phone.

If a mobile device does not provide native or on-device encryption and if the device can be mapped as a storage device on a computer, it might be possible to implement individual file encryption or full-disk encryption on the device. However, this could also prevent the device from working normally when it is not connected to the computer hosting the encryption software. Perform testing before making this a standard practice. If you only encrypt the user data on such devices and avoid encrypting any system files, this should not cause a problem for normal device operation.

It is important to reiterate that encryption is only a partial solution to data loss or malware distribution. Many other security elements must be implemented both in policy, on the device, and in user practice.

Hardware-based encryption devices

Hardware-based encryption devices offer the security of strong encryption with the ease of minimal configuration and platform interoperability. Any device that provides onboard encryption can be categorized as a hardware based encryption device. However, these types of devices are not always a form of storage device; many other nonstorage-specific devices can provide onboard or hardware-based encryption.

Hardware encryption can offer several benefits beyond those provided by software encryption. These include faster algorithm processing, tamper-proof or tamper-resistant key storage, and protection against unauthorized code.

When software encryption is in use, the system's resources (such as the CPU, bus, and RAM) will be partially consumed by the operations of encryption and decryption. These are finite resources, so using a portion of them for cryptographic functions will reduce the resources available for other operations, calculations, and functions. Thus, software encryption often causes a reduction in performance, including delays in processing, laggy response, and longer timeframes for computation. The more cryptography becomes a part of regular activities, the more of a drain the algorithm calculations place on the system. When hardware-based encryption is implemented, the workload of cryptography computation is offloaded to dedicated hardware processors, freeing up the general system resources for other use. This results in faster cryptographic processing as well as an improvement in overall system performance.

Hardware encryption devices often have the ability to store encryption keys and other sensitive items in highly protected areas of RAM or flash memory. Although they are not completely write-proof or change-proof, these storage locations often have restricted and limited access methods and pathways so that only the encryption hardware can interact with data stored there. These forms of secured storage are excellent for temporary and potentially prolonged encryption key storage. This is usually a significant improvement over allowing software to store encryption keys, where usually they are placed in a file on a generic storage device. Even if such a file is encrypted, that encryption key has to be stored somewhere in plaintext. Thus, there is usually a means to gain access to any software-stored secrets.

Hardware encryption devices often have reduced instruction sets or dedicated processor elements that are only able to execute authorized code. Additionally, most of these devices do not support add-on software, nor do they allow other code to run. This effectively prevents malware or other unauthorized code from gaining a foothold in the device. Again, this is much more protection than can be provided by a typical computer, which can run any software brought to the platform by a user.

There are many examples of hardware-based encryption devices. In the following sections, TPM, HSM, USB, and hard-disk encryption devices are discussed. But these are just a few of the many options available.

EXAM TIP

The CompTIA Security+ exam does not seem to contain a significant amount of detail on hardware-based encryption devices. The emphasis seems to be on the knowledge that they exist and recognition of the benefits of their use. Just keep in mind the four types of devices mentioned specifically in the objectives list: TPM, HSM, USB, and hard drives.

One example of a hardware-based encryption device is a wireless access point or wireless base station. These devices support encryption services for the radio wave signal used to carry network protocol information. Additionally, wireless adapters on wireless clients support the same hardware encryption features in order to be able to decode and encode signals being exchanged with the base station.

Another example of a hardware-based encryption device is a credit card point-of sale-device. These devices, also known as credit card terminals, typically encrypt the information they read from swiped cards before transmitting them to a processing entity. This onboard encryption is essential due to recent large-scale credit card theft attacks against insecure point-of-sale devices. Encryption has also been a requirement of the PCI-DSS security standard since the 2.0 version of the standard released in October 2010.

Yet another form of hardware-based encryption device is a network bulk encryptor. This is a device that is installed inline along a network path in order to capture cleartext or standard network communications and encrypt them for the remainder of their transmission path. Network bulk encryptors are installed in pairs, one at each end of a communication segment. The benefit of a hardware solution for network encryption is to offload the effort and resource requirements to a dedicated device, separate the encryption functions from full-featured computers, and gain performance improvements through the use of dedicated cryptographic hardware.

A final example of a hardware-based encryption device is a modern CPU with an onboard encryption instruction set. CPU manufacturers Intel and AMD have been producing CPUs with Advanced Encryption Standard (AES) instruction for several years. These additional encryption-focused instruction sets assist with encryption and decryption performance. Rather than needing to code the AES algorithm into software, programmers can call upon those functions built into the CPU.

 Quick check

1. Name at least two benefits of hardware-based encryption devices.

2. Which is usually able to offer better encryption performance: hardware or software?

Quick check answers

1. Benefits include faster algorithm processing, tamper-proof or tamper-resistant key storage, and protection against unauthorized code.

2. Dedicated hardware is able to offer better encryption performance.

Trusted Platform Module

The *Trusted Platform Module (TPM)* is a formal specification as well as a cryptoprocessor found on some motherboards implementing this specification. Originally, TPM chips were found mainly in portable systems, such as notebook computers. Today, TPM chips are common components in a wide range of devices, including all forms of computers, mobile phones, and tablets.

The Trusted Platform Module provides for a form of secured hardware storage of encryption keys as well as some assistance with cryptographic operations. These assistance functions include limiting access to stored encryption keys, serving as a random number generator to increase the entropy of encryption calculations, crafting a non-forgeable identity reference of hardware and software, supplying an endorsement key unique to each TPM, and performing hardware authentication.

Many of these services and features are quite advanced technology, and most end users will never really recognize when these are in use. However, many amazing cryptography services are made possible with the presence of a TPM chip on a system's motherboard.

The most recognizable use or function of the TPM is its link to storage encryption. Storage devices that are encrypted by using software-based full-disk encryption might be able to store encryption keys in the TPM. Additionally, some software might be able to use the TPM's randomization function in the crafting of keys. Hard disk drives and SSDs (solid-state drives) that provide their own onboard hardware encryption can also use the TPM to store their encryption keys. In addition, hardware-based encryption can make broader use of the TPM's other cryptographic features.

EXAM TIP

The CompTIA Security+ exam is likely to mention TPM in conjunction with full-disk encryption rather than in any other context. Though this is a common use of the TPM chip, it is not its only use. Other uses for the TPM include verifying platform integrity, performing password storage, digital rights management, and software license protection.

 Quick check

1. What is a common purpose or use for a TPM chip?

2. If a TPM is considered a storage device, what is it designed to hold?

Quick check answers

1. TPM chips are most commonly used in storage device encryption.

2. Encryption keys.

Hardware security module

A *hardware security module (HSM)* is an add-on hardware device that can provide crypto-processing and other security features to a computer, device, or network connection that does not have these items natively. The use of an HSM can provide for faster encryption and decryption operations by offloading those intensive functions from the main CPU and limited system resources. HSMs provide for faster digital signatures, more efficient digital enveloping, and improved secure authentication services.

Most HSMs are add-on adapters. HSMs are designed as slide-in PCMCIA (Personal Computer Memory Card International Association) or PC cards, ExpressCards, or other specialty adapters supported by popular networking devices, such as switches, routers, multiplexors, concentrators, and firewalls. There are also HSM form factors of computer adapter cards, usually with a PCI interface, as well as inline network adapter HSMs.

HSMs provide for accelerated encryption computation, which is most recognizably beneficial when extremely long symmetric keys (longer than 256 bits) or extra long asymmetric keys (longer than 2,048 bits) are used. These longer key lengths often stress the typical computer CPU and system resource set but can be handled adeptly by dedicated cryptographic hardware such as an HSM.

HSMs are available in both generic or at least compatible form factors for use on typical off-the-shelf computing devices as well as in proprietary forms. The compatible forms can be used in any typical IT infrastructure because they are designed around standardized physical interfaces and software APIs. The proprietary forms of HSMs are used in specialty situations, such as ATMs, point-of-sale devices (credit card terminals), and smart card readers. These specialty implementations have proprietary physical interfaces as well as nonstandard (and unpublished) software interfaces. Thus, they are much more difficult to tamper with via external or unapproved connections.

An HSM is not dissimilar to a TPM. However, the primary distinction is that a TPM is usually a chip installed onto the motherboard by the manufacturer. Therefore, the TPM is a permanent component of a system. An HSM is usually an add-on component (although integrated versions for specialty equipment are available). This means that if you have a computer that does not come equipped with a TPM, the motherboard or even the entire system would need to be replaced in order to gain access to a TPM. If a system does not have an HSM from the vendor, often a variety of HSM products are available that can be installed into it, connected to it as a peripheral, or used in conjunction with the system (along a network segment, for example) in order to add the HSM product.

EXAM TIP

The CompTIA Security+ exam seems to include only cursory information in regard to HSMs. Generally, when you understand the basic definition of an HSM (that it is a hardware add-on module to provide cryptographic services to a computer or other device), then you know enough about this topic.

HSMs, like the TPMs, are able to store encryption keys in a tamper-resistant hardware/software storage system, provide randomization services, and perform encryption and decryption operations, as well as many other cryptographic services. Though not every HSM device provides all possible cryptographic services, there are so many varied HSM products that almost any set of specific cryptographic needs and requirements has an available HSM solution.

 Quick check

1. Is an HSM embedded in a typical motherboard?

2. What are typical features or capabilities of an HSM?

Quick check answers

1. No. A TPM might be embedded in a motherboard, but an HSM is usually an add-on device.

2. HSMs, like TPMs, are able to store encryption keys in a tamper-resistant hardware/software storage system, provide randomization services, and perform encryption and decryption operations, as well as many other cryptographic services.

USB encryption

 USB encryption is a phrase that usually refers to USB storage devices that provide onboard encryption services. Many vendors now offer onboard–encryption USB storage drives as part of their product lines. A device that provides additional features, especially onboard encryption, will likely be a more expensive product than the same device without that feature. However, the additional protection for the confidentiality and integrity of USB-stored data as well as a significant reduction in malware distribution over USB is often well worth the additional expense.

Most USB devices that provide onboard encryption are fully self-contained and rarely need any additional software or specialized hardware on the computers or systems where they are put to use, although, some of these devices might be able to take advantage of a TPM or HSM to store their master encryption key in the secured compartment provided by those mechanisms rather than storing it on the USB device itself. some USB devices might offer additional services or features through optional software that can be installed onto a target computer.

USB devices that provide hardware encryption either include an on-device credential system or rely upon software-based or hardware-based credentials from the connected computer. Those USB devices that offer onboard credential systems usually have either a keyboard or a fingerprint reader. Because the typical USB storage device is rather small, the keyboards on these devices are often just 10-digit number pads. Those USB devices supporting fingerprint readers usually employ the type of reader in which the finger is swiped across the thin slit of the reader rather than being pressed on a reader area. When these devices are plugged into a receiving USB port, the user provides the code or fingerprint to unlock the encryption. When the USB device is pulled out of the port, it automatically reverts to a locked state.

Some USB devices that provide onboard encryption rely upon a software interface to accept credentials when unlocking the storage. The software might be included on a plaintext partition on the USB device that can be read by any computer. The software might need to be formally installed, it might be able to run in place without being formally installed (this is known as a portable application), or it might auto-launch when the USB device is plugged into a computer. In any case, the software will need to be used to provide credentials. Software-based credentials for USB devices are mostly commonly passwords. A long and complex password should be defined to minimize the risk of password guessing or cracking if the device is ever lost, stolen, or otherwise accessed by an unauthorized individual.

Some USB devices that offer onboard encryption can be configured to only operate when connected to specific systems, rather than being usable on any system. This is usually most effective when TPM chips are present on the systems where use is desired. The USB device will perform a system call or hardware request in order to determine the identity of the system and/or TPM chip present. If the returned identity is not on its list of approved systems, it will disable itself for use on that system. This can be a very secure feature, but if only one system is defined as approved and that system becomes unavailable, the drive will be unusable and unrecoverable.

Some of these devices automatically time out when they are not in active use for a specified period of time. This increases the security of the device by compensating for a user who forgets about the USB drive while it is plugged into a computer. When the timeout setting disables the device, if the user needs access to the drive, he or she just needs to provide the credentials again. However, if the user is no longer near the computer and someone else attempts to access the drive contents, if the timeout is in force, the unauthorized user will be denied access.

USB devices that do not have onboard hardware–provided encryption can always be encrypted by using a software solution such as TrueCrypt, or an operating system–controlled file system solution such as Windows EFS and Linux's dm-crypt+LUKS. Either individual file encryption or full-disk encryption can be applied to any storage device.

EXAM TIP

Keep in mind that most USB drives are not encrypted and thus are a common vector of data loss, data leakage, and malware infection. Whenever possible, apply encryption to USB devices that don't offer native hardware support for encryption.

✔ **Quick check**

1. True or false: only USB drives that provide onboard hardware encryption can provide file protection for data stored on them.

2. What forms of credentials can a USB drive use to unlock its encrypted storage?

Quick check answers

1. False. Any USB drive can be used to host-encrypted data. Those with onboard encryption provide on-the-fly. hardware-controlled encryption, whereas those without onboard encryption need a software solution to provide encryption.

2. USB devices can use on-device keypads; fingerprint scanners; software credentials, usually passwords; or TPMs or HSMs.

Hard drive encryption

Hard drives can support a range of encryption options. As previously discussed, any hard drive can have individual file encryption or full-disk encryption applied to it by using a native operating system feature or through an add-on software product. However, there are many other options available to consider when it comes to *hard drive encryption*.

Some hard drives provide onboard encryption. This form of hardware-based encryption, like onboard USB drive encryption, is provided by dedicated cryptoprocessor chips built into the device. Encrypted hard drives of this type can be traditional spinning platter-based disks or solid-state drives (SSDs). The benefit of a self-encrypting hard drive is that the work of the encryption is offloaded from the system to the hard drive's dedicated processing elements.

EXAM TIP

The CompTIA Security+ exam focuses mostly on software solutions for full-disk encryption rather than encryption provided by a hardware solution.

Unlike USB-encrypted flash drives, a hardware-encrypted hard drive will not be able to use an on-device keyboard or fingerprint reader. A hardware-encrypted hard drive will need to use a TPM or an HSM, or it will need to have a software-only management interface to handle credentials for granting (or denying) access to the secured content.

A hardware-encrypted hard drive can be installed as an internal drive, like those found on typical computers or notebooks. However, a hard drive with onboard encryption can also be housed in an external casing. Using a hard drive enclosure allows the drive to be added to a system without any additional internal hard drive connection interfaces available, to a system that does not use the same connector as the drive, or to a system that uses a different physical size form factor than that of the drive. An external enclosure also allows the user to move the drive between systems. If a hard drive with onboard encryption is to be used externally so that it can be moved between systems, be sure to use a device that can be unlocked from other systems. Any encrypted drive linked to a TPM or an HSM will depend upon the presence of that specific cryptoprocessor to be accessible.

NOTE ENCRYPTING A DRIVE

Another option for hard drive encryption would be to use an enclosure or a drive controller that provides encryption services and then attach a standard hard drive.

Benefits of a hardware-encrypted hard drive include speed performance for the encryption and decryption processes, encryption that is not dependent upon platform or software, and a guarantee that all data on the device will be encrypted. With operating system–controlled or software-controlled encryption, there is a chance that only a portion of a hard drive will be encrypted, if a partition or volume that does not cover the entire surface is created, rather than a full and complete partition or volume. Partitioning (or volumes) would not be a concern with hard drives that use onboard encryption.

A final benefit of on-device encryption is that some devices provide an easy disposal mechanism. This is a special instruction that corrupts the data on the drive or that makes the drive physically unusable. This allows a hard drive to be rendered useless in a matter of seconds, rather than having to perform zeroization, degaussing, or even physical destruction of the device. These processes, when performed on standard hard drives, are either time consuming, unable to be verified as 100 percent effective, difficult, dangerous, or expensive.

Quick check

1. True or false: hard drives providing onboard encryption can only be used as internal drives.

2. What are some options for providing credentials to a hard drive that provides its own encryption services?

Quick check answers

1. False. A hard drive with onboard encryption can be used in an external enclosure. Such a drive could even be used between systems if it is not dependent upon a TPM.

2. Software-based credentials (including passwords), TPM, or HSM.

Cloud computing

Cloud computing (as well as virtualization) was discussed thoroughly in Chapter 3, "Secure network design and management." Refer to that chapter for information on this aspect of data security.

Chapter summary

- As a company policy, data loss prevention (DLP) focuses on implementing defenses against data loss and theft.

- As a product, DLP is a technology solution to assist with the fulfillment of a company's DLP policy.

- The goal of DLP is to focus on the potential for data to be lost or disclosed and to implement preventions, defenses, and detections to either eliminate the possibility or make the act more difficult to perform, and to detect any attempts to violate security in regard to data exposure.

- Any occurrence of data exfiltration is unwanted, and DLP attempts to thwart such events by using an approach based on monitoring, detection, and interruption of unwanted data activities.

- Data loss or leakage events can occur either by means of malicious intent or accidental mistake.

- DLP solutions are often an important part of maintaining compliance with government regulations, industry standards, or contractual obligations against data loss.

- One of the most important tools in the protection of data security is that of encryption. Data encryption is a key technology in preventing unauthorized disclosure of information, as well as preventing corruption or intentional integrity changes.

- Encryption is the technology that converts or transforms original data into a chaotic and seemingly random and thus unintelligible form.

- Data encryption provides protection for the confidentiality of data. Because only those in possession of the correct key and IV for a specific ciphertext can decrypt it into plaintext, the content of the data is protected against unauthorized disclosure—assuming a reasonably strong algorithm, a reasonably difficult key, and the use of reasonable security for key exchange.

- Hashing is used to detect violations of integrity—in other words, changes to data.

- After a hash value is calculated, it is not possible to decrypt or reverse the hash back into the original data.

- Consider only encryption products that offer modern or current algorithms.

- Select encryption products that indicate that they use secure storage of keys, credentials, and other elements of identification and access.

- Full-disk encryption is the application of data encryption technology to an entire storage device.

- Full-disk encryption operates transparently to the end user after it is properly installed and configured.

- Every file, all metadata, every temporary file, every swap file, everything on the storage device is protected with full-disk encryption.

- A drawback to full-disk encryption is that a single master encryption key is used to encrypt the contents of the disk. If that one key is ever lost, corrupted, or stolen, it could be disastrous.

- From the user's perspective, the potential means of unlocking a storage device hosting full-disk encryption can range from automatic and transparent to complex, multifactor, and multistep. These means include TPM only, user password with TPM, USB only, USB with TPM, and user password with USB and TPM.

- The TPM (Trusted Platform Module) is a special chip designed for use by encryption solutions as a secure and tamper-proof storage location for encryption keys.

- A recovery option gives you the ability to regain access to an encrypted disk in the event that you forget your master password or lose your master USB key.

- There are circumstances where full-disk encryption does not provide sufficient protection—specifically, if a hacker is able to access the physical system while the computer is active.

- Database encryption has quickly become an essential security issue as organizations realize how much damage and loss can occur due to a breach of a mission-critical database.

- For reliable database encryption, a centralized key management system is needed. This could be a software-only solution or it could involve various HSMs (Hardware Security Modules) to support large-scale key management.

- Encryption is not a substitute for backups.

- The main distinction between file encryption and full-disk encryption is that each individual file is encrypted by using its own unique encryption key.

- Individual file encryption does not protect metadata or temporary copies of open files.

- If the user's private key is ever lost or corrupted, individual file encryption would prevent the user from decrypting files.

- A key recovery agent is a trusted administrator or group of administrators who can be called upon to decrypt files when the user's private key is lost or corrupted.

- The two main risks related to removable and portable media are data leakage/loss and malware infection. USB flash drives seem to be the most prolific in terms of causing problems for organizations.

- The primary means by which this form of data loss or data leakage can be prevented is through on-device encryption.

- Though using encryption will not fully eliminate the risk of malware infection from a removable media device, it will significantly reduce it.

- Mobile device encryption is another important tool in the toolbox of the security manager in the effort to protect the organization against data loss and security breaches.

- One of the big issues with mobile devices of all types is that they can often be connected to computers over USB cables, via Bluetooth technology, or through wireless networks, and they appear on the computers as storage devices.

- It is important to not only select devices that support encryption but to actually implement the feature.

- For mobile phones that support encryption, the screen lock feature should be enabled with a password or other secure credential in combination with device encryption.

- Hardware-based encryption devices offer the security of strong encryption with the ease of minimal configuration and platform interoperability.

- When hardware-based encryption is implemented, the workload of cryptography computation is offloaded to dedicated hardware processors, which frees up the general system resources for other uses. This results in faster cryptographic processing as well as improved overall system performance.

- The TPM (Trusted Platform Module) is a formal specification as well as a cryptoprocessor found on some motherboards implementing this specification.

- The Trusted Platform Module provides for a form of secured hardware storage of encryption keys as well as some assistance with cryptographic operations.

- Storage devices that are encrypted by using software-based full-disk encryption might be able to store encryption keys in the TPM.

- An HSM (hardware security module) is an add-on hardware device that can provide cryptographic processing and other security features to a computer, device, or network connection that does not have these items natively.

- Many vendors now offer onboard encryption of USB storage drives as part of their product line.

- USB devices that do not have onboard, hardware-provided encryption can always be encrypted by using a software solution.

- Hard drives can support a range of encryption options. Any hard drive can have individual file encryption or full-disk encryption applied to it by using a native operating system feature or through an add-on software product.

- Some hard drives provide onboard encryption. This form of hardware-based encryption, like onboard USB drive encryption, is provided by dedicated cryptoprocessor chips built into the device.

- A hardware-encrypted hard drive will need to use a TPM or an HSM or have a software-only management interface to handle credentials for granting (or denying) access to the secured content.

Chapter review

Test your knowledge of the information in Chapter 10 by answering these questions. The answers to these questions, and the explanations of why each answer choice is correct or incorrect, are located in the "Answers" section at the end of this chapter.

1. Which of the following is the most common means of data loss or data leakage for organizations?

    A. Sending out digitally signed email messages

    B. Using social networks

    C. Misplacing a USB drive

    D. Working with open source software

2. What is the primary tool used to provide confidentiality protection for data on a storage device?

    A. Multifactor authentication

    B. Symmetric encryption

    C. Detailed logging

    D. Firewalls

3. What type of attack is designed to steal the master encryption key used by full-disk encryption directly from memory?

    A. Birthday attack

    B. Buffer overflow attack

    C. XSRF attack

    D. Cold boot attack

4. Which of the following is a true statement?

    A. Full-disk encryption requires a TPM be present on the system's motherboard.

    B. Only file encryption is transparent to the end user.

    C. Encryption is not a substitute for a backup.

    D. Disk encryption provides protection against all forms of data leakage attacks.

5. What is the purpose of implementing an HSM in support of database encryption?

    A. Performing centralized key management

    B. Managing time-stamp expiration

    C. Tracking user privileges and permissions

    D. Securing data destruction

6. Where or how are encryption keys stored or managed for individual file encryption?

    A. On a master per-user key ring

    B. In a hashing table

    C. By using a digital envelope on the encrypted file

    D. In a local database

7. Which of the following is not a valid means by which to have encrypted data stored on USB devices?

    A. Software-controlled file encryption

    B. Full-disk encryption

    C. Hardware-provided on-device encryption

    D. Session encryption

8. Which of the following statements is false?

   A. BYOD still requires organizations to establish mobile device security and use policies.

   B. A mobile device connected to a computer often can be used as an external or portable storage device.

   C. An organizational ban on mobile devices removes all threats and risks associated with those devices.

   D. A mobile phone can provide an unfiltered Internet link for company computers.

9. Which of the following is not a typical function of a TPM?

   A. Encryption key storage

   B. Revocation service

   C. Random number generation

   D. Crafting of a non-forgeable identity reference of hardware

10. Which of the following is not true in regard to an HSM?

   A. Some HSMs have PCI interfaces.

   B. HSMs provide for accelerated encryption computation.

   C. Proprietary forms of HSM are used in specialty situations, such as ATMs, point-of-sale devices (credit card terminals), and smart card readers.

   D. HSMs are commonly found as components on most off-the-shelf motherboards.

Answers

This section contains the answers to the questions for the "Chapter review" section in this chapter.

1. **Correct Answer: C**

   A. **Incorrect:** Though it is possible to have a data leakage or loss event over digitally signed email messages, it is not the most common means.

   B. **Incorrect:** Though it is possible to have a data leakage or loss event through social networks, it is not the most common means.

   C. **Correct:** According to CompTIA, the most common means of a data loss or leakage event is due to a misplaced USB drive.

   D. **Incorrect:** Open source software is not inherently a source, cause, or means of data leakage or data loss.

2. **Correct Answer: B**

   A. **Incorrect:** Multifactor authentication is a good security concept related to logons, but it does not provide confidentiality protection for stored data.

   B. **Correct:** Symmetric encryption is the primary tool for providing confidentiality protection for stored data.

   C. **Incorrect:** Detailed logging is a good security concept related to creating a historical record of events, but it does not provide confidentiality protection for stored data.

   D. **Incorrect:** Using firewalls is a good security concept related to controlling access to a network, but it does not directly provide confidentiality protection for stored data.

3. **Correct Answer: D**

   A. **Incorrect:** A birthday attack focuses on finding a hash collision or brute-force guessing an encryption key.

   B. **Incorrect:** A buffer overflow attack exploits software's lack of input sanitization in order to inject code into memory.

   C. **Incorrect:** XSRF (cross-site request forgery) attacks focus on taking advantage of a server's trust in an authentication client.

   D. **Correct:** A cold boot attack is designed to steal the master encryption key used by full-disk encryption directly from memory.

4. **Correct Answer: C**

   A. **Incorrect:** Full-disk encryption can use a TPM or can be configured to not use a TPM in favor of a password, a USB hosted file, or an HSM.

   B. **Incorrect:** All forms of encryption—file, database, and disk encryption—can be transparent to the end user.

   C. **Correct:** Encryption is not a substitute for a backup. In fact, the only substitute for a backup is another backup.

   D. **Incorrect:** Disk encryption provides protection against only some forms of data leakage attacks. Attacks or mistakes made while the disk unlock key is available will still be possible.

5. **Correct Answer: A**

   A. **Correct:** An HSM can be used to perform centralized key management for database encryption.

   B. **Incorrect:** An HSM is an encryption device; it does not manage time stamp expiration. It might set time stamps in order for objects to expire.

   C. **Incorrect:** An HSM is an encryption device; it does not perform authorization or accounting.

   D. **Incorrect:** An HSM is an encryption device and does not perform sanitization functions.

6. **Correct Answer: C**

   A. **Incorrect:** Individual file encryption does not use master key rings.

   B. **Incorrect:** Individual file encryption does not use hashing tables.

   C. **Correct:** Encryption keys are stored or managed by using a digital envelope on the encrypted file for individual file encryption.

   D. **Incorrect:** Individual file encryption does not use a local database.

7. **Correct Answer: D**

   A. **Incorrect:** Software-controlled file or full-disk encryption is a valid option for encrypted USB storage.

   B. **Incorrect:** Full-disk encryption is a valid option for encrypted USB storage.

   C. **Incorrect:** Hardware-provided file or full-disk encryption is a valid option for encrypted USB storage.

   D. **Correct:** Session encryption is used for real-time communications, not static storage on a USB device.

8. **Correct Answer: C**

   A. **Incorrect:** This is a true statement, because a BYOD does not itself resolve mobile device security concerns.

   B. **Incorrect:** This is a true statement, because data loss and leakage are serious threats even with nontraditional storage mechanisms,

   C. **Correct:** An organizational ban on mobile devices might reduce the risk, but it does not eliminate it. Workers and visitors might still accidentally or intentionally bring a mobile device into a restricted area and use it to violate company policy.

   D. **Incorrect:** This is a true statement. A mobile phone can provide tethering services.

9. **Correct Answer: B**

   A. **Incorrect:** Encryption key storage is a typical function of a TPM.

   B. **Correct:** A TPM does not perform revocation services; that is an operation of a certificate authority or certificate server.

   C. **Incorrect:** Random-number generation is a typical function of a TPM.

   D. **Incorrect:** Crafting of a non-forgeable identity reference of hardware is a typical function of a TPM.

10. **Correct Answer: D**

    A. **Incorrect:** This is a true statement. However, HSMs are not limited to PCI interfaces.

    B. **Incorrect:** This is a true statement. Offloading encryption computation to an HSM can provide for better overall system and security performance.

    C. **Incorrect:** This is a true statement. However, "proprietary" does not necessarily mean that the HSM is tamper-proof or provides better security than standard implementations.

    D. **Correct:** HSMs are add-on modules in most cases rather than native components of motherboards.

## CHAPTER 11

Identity and access control

Access controls are a key part of modern security systems. They ensure that the correct users have access to only the data and systems they are supposed to have access to. Identity management helps ensure that the users are who they claim to be, and that they are in the right groups and organizational structures to receive the privileges they should have.

This chapter explore the differences between identification, authentication, and authorization. We will delve into how authentication and authorization are accomplished by systems such as RADIUS (Remote Authentication Dial-In User Service), the Kerberos protocol, LDAP (Lightweight Directory Access Protocol), and Active Directory Domain Services. In addition, we will discuss the concepts common to identity and account management, access control practices and technologies, and the privileges they help control.

Exam objectives in this chapter:

Objective 5.1: Explain the function and purpose of authentication services

- RADIUS
- TACACS
- TACACS+
- Kerberos
- LDAP
- XTACACS

Objective 5.2: Explain the fundamental concepts and best practices related to authentication, authorization and access control

- Identification vs. authentication
- Authentication (single factor) and authorization
- Multifactor authentication
- Biometrics
- Tokens
- Common access card
- Personal identification verification card
- Smart card

- Least privilege
- Separation of duties
- Single sign on
- ACLs
- Access control
- Mandatory access control
- Discretionary access control
- Role/rule-based access control
- Implicit deny
- Time of day restrictions
- Trusted OS
- Mandatory vacations
- Job rotation

Objective 5.3: Implement appropriate security controls when performing account management

- Mitigate issues associated with users with multiple account/roles
- Account policy enforcement
  - Password complexity
  - Expiration
  - Recovery
  - Length
  - Disablement
  - Lockout
- Group based privileges
- User assigned privileges

Identification and authentication

 Identification and authentication are part of our everyday lives, and have been for longer than we have used computers. In fact, identification is likely almost as old as the human race. The basic act of *identification* occurs when you claim to be someone. For security purposes, identification usually involves a unique identifier such as a user name, a Social Security number, a driver's license number, or a national ID number, but your own name is also a form of identification.

In some cases, these identifiers are assigned by an employer, a vendor or service provider, the government, or another third party. In other cases, people create their own identifiers. In almost all cases, identifiers should be unique—duplicates can quickly cause confusion.

Social Security number confusion

In the United States, people often think of their Social Security numbers as unique identifiers, and many organizations treat them that way. Unfortunately, Social Security numbers weren't guaranteed to be unique, and that can cause problems!

The biggest case of Social Security number confusion of all time was due to an advertising campaign rather than an issue with how the numbers were issued. In 1938, a wallet manufacturer printed sample Social Security cards to demonstrate that the cards would fit in the wallets they produced. Unfortunately, the cards all displayed the Social Security number of a secretary working for the company.

This began almost four decades of the use of Mrs. Hilda Schrader Whitcher's Social Security number by people all over the country, as people adopted the number they found in their wallet as their own. In 1943, when use of the card peaked, 5,755 people used it. According to the Social Security Administration, over the years from 1938 to 1977, more than 40,000 people used her Social Security number as their own.

Obviously, making sure that we choose our identifiers well, and that we provide unique identifiers when we need them, is important. Though it's unlikely that you will be printing your user name on a card in every wallet sold at a major store, duplicate user IDs are a very real problem for organizations where there are many jsmiths!

Authentication

After you have an identifier, you need a way to prove that the person providing the identifier is actually the person he says he is. During a phone call with relatives, when one person says, "Hi, this is your brother John," you know who it is because you know your brother's voice and can tell it from the voice of other people who might call and greet you the same way.

 Authentication is the process of presenting an identifying piece or pieces of evidence of your identity to a system or individual. For most of us, that involves presenting a password along with a user ID, which we use as a form of identification.

Authentication and authorization

After you have authenticated yourself, you typically want to have permission to do something. That process is known as *authorization*, and it is also a familiar process that people handle quite often in their daily lives, such as when you answer a knock at your door. When the visitors identify themselves, you either allow them in or send them away if you don't want to provide access—thus authorizing them or denying them authorization to step inside.

> **MORE INFO**   **ROLE-BASED ACCESS CONTROL**
>
> Computers and networks use authorization to decide what roles and rights users receive. We'll dig into the concepts behind role-based access control later in this chapter.

User accounts

Users who provide their identity usually do so in the context of a user account. User accounts are usually maintained as part of a central account management system, although individual systems also provide their own user accounts.

One of the most common issues with identification occurs when users need to access resources on multiple systems, or to use the rights that they have in multiple roles in their organization. In some environments, this would require multiple accounts and could lead to confusion about where to log on with each ID. Fortunately, centralized authentication systems can be used to mitigate this issue by allowing a single account to be authenticated. After that central account has been authenticated, it can be authorized on each system that requires it. We will discuss some of the technologies that support this in the "Authentication services" section later in this chapter, when we discuss authentication services and single sign-on.

Single-factor vs. multifactor authentication

We are all used to using a password or passphrase to authenticate to computers, websites, and even our phones. Unfortunately, passwords are relatively easy to steal, and it is very difficult to ensure that a password is being used by the individual who should be using it. This means that greater security is needed, and that can be provided by *multifactor authentication*.

There are three types of authentication factors that can be used:

- Something you know, such as password or passphrase.
- Something you have, such as a smart card, a token, or some other physical item.
- Something you are, such as your fingerprint, voice print, or retina pattern. These are called biometric identifiers.

Why passwords?

Passwords are so common in our daily lives that we rarely question why we use them. Unfortunately, if you stop to think about it, they're not a very secure method of authentication. A password alone provides no proof that the person using it is who she says she is, only that she knows a user ID, and that she knows the password that is associated with that user ID. Worse, many users choose poor passwords—including the most common password in the world, "password."

Passwords are also a bad choice because they are often short. In the past, many computer systems required short passwords because they were not designed to work with passwords that had more than 8 or possibly up to 16 characters. Thus, we were taught to use a complex password with uppercase and lowercase letters, numbers, and punctuation, and to avoid dictionary words.

In modern computer systems, that advice tends to lead users to use a simple, short password with a capitalized letter or two, some numbers instead of letters, and punctuation at the end. Colleges and universities find that their users use common sports cheers or mottos with an exclamation point, and companies discover users using the company's name and a number.

So why do we use passwords if they have all of these issues? It is probably because we are used to them, and because they're easy to get into the hands of our users. Many modern authentication systems can support two-factor authentication or can use passphrases. The good news is that passphrases, which are sequences of words or phrases used instead of passwords, are generally more secure because they're longer, less likely to be quickly cracked, and are becoming more broadly useable. Even better news is that two-factor authentication is becoming more common, with tokens and smartphone-based applications, as well as SMS (short message service, which most of us know as texting) two-factor authentication, all appearing in more places.

> **MORE INFO**   **PASSWORD BEST PRACTICES**
>
> We discuss passwords and password best practices in more depth near the end of this chapter in the "Account management" section.

Two-factor authentication is common in environments in which there is a need for more security than that which a simple password provides. The second factor can be either an independent entry or something that is combined with an authenticator that the user knows.

For example, a push-button token, or one built as a smartphone application, might generate a 6-digit code, providing the "something you have," and the user provides a 4-digit PIN he created—thus providing the "something you know." Added together, this creates a 10-digit code, which would be very hard for an attacker to have access to, because the attacker would need both the token and the PIN that the user has memorized.

Organizations often deploy a token-based two-factor system for access to more secure areas or systems, such as a system administration VPN group or network or a payroll website.

Two-factor authentication is also becoming more broadly available as ways to provide factors become more readily available. In many organizations, almost all of the technical staff have smartphones, and those who don't often have the ability to send and receive SMS text messages. This makes an application-based token utility reasonably easy to adopt, with SMS tokens available for those who cannot run the application.

EXAM TIP

Know the differences between identification, authentication, and authorization.

 Quick check:

1. When a user provides her user name, she is providing a type of what?
2. When a system verifies that the user's password and user name match, it has provided what?

Quick check answers

1. Identification, a unique identifier for that user.
2. Authentication. Verifying a user name and password verifies that the user is who she claims to be, but it does not provide her with any specific access—for that, she needs authorization.

Biometrics

 Biometric technology takes advantage of the "something you are" factor and works with your unique physiology. We've all seen biometric technologies in movies, when the hero sneaks into a top-secret facility and needs a recording of an authorized user's voice, wears a contact lens to make his eye look like that of a user who is allowed in, or dons gloves that provide fake fingerprints to a scanner.

Biometric systems come in many flavors, and each has its own advantages and disadvantages. The most common biometric systems are fingerprint scanners, iris recognition scanners, and scanners that rely on hand geometry (shape) to determine who you are. Others look at a range of human characteristics and identifiers, from the ever-popular movie-style voice print to systems that map the veins in your hand or the distinctive shape of your face and its underlying bone structure. Some biometric systems even look at your behavior to help determine your identity.

When biometric data is captured from a user, that user is said to be enrolled. Enrollment methods vary and can range from a simple walk-up process that can be almost as simple as setting a password to a more complex process that requires multiple captures to develop a full profile of the person's unique features.

Common biometric technologies

There are several biometric technologies that are frequently found in use today. Some, like handprints, have been in use in some form for centuries, whereas others rely on modern technology to make them useful. They include:

- Hand geometry systems, which gather top and side views of the user's hand, measure them, and compare them to a stored pattern for the user.
- Fingerprint systems, which check the unique pattern of ridges and valleys on your fingertips.
- Facial recognition, which take two-dimensional or three-dimensional representations of the user's face to check them against a database that recognizes distinct points and lines in the face.
- Iris recognition, which uses near-infrared light to light up the user's eye, then compares the iris against a stored picture of the user's iris.
- Voice print systems, which take a sample of the user's voice to compare it to a prerecorded statement.
- Signature-based systems, which compare user signatures to a previously enrolled signature.

EXAM TIP

Pay attention to the types of biometric authentication and what they measure. The most common types are fingerprints, hand geometry, and iris scans.

In addition to these common choices, some systems look at the user's gait and verify that how he walks matches his profile. Others look at vein patterns, retina patterns, or even the pattern of heat and blood flow in the face, via a technique known as facial thermography.

Biometric system failure modes

Biometric systems have two failure modes, false acceptance and false rejection:

- ***Type I error*** This type of error occurs when an authorized person is incorrectly rejected.
- ***Type II error*** This type of error occurs when an unauthorized person is incorrectly identified an as authorized person.

If you have ever used a fingerprint scanner, you've probably experienced a Type I error. A smudge or a fingerprint that is hard to read can easily result in the fingerprint reader rejecting your attempt to get access. Type II errors are potentially worse, because rejecting unauthorized users is often more important than delaying authorized users from using a system, or even entirely preventing their access.

The rate of occurrence for Type I errors is known as the *false reject rate*, or FRR. The Type II error rate is called the *false acceptance rate* (FAR), or the false match rate (FMR). These are used to calculate the relative operating characteristic (ROC), which compares the FRR against the FAR. This is typically done in a simple graph, such as the one shown in Figure 11-1, that shows that as you decrease the likelihood of false rejection, you're also more likely to increase the number of users who are incorrectly accepted.

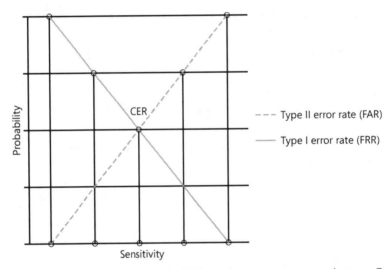

FIGURE 11-1 This graph shows a sample biometric crossover error rate between Type I and Type II errors for a biometric system. Note that as false acceptance goes down, the false rejection rate goes up.

Most organizations balance false acceptance and rejection based on the security requirements that drive their biometric implementation. The place where FAR and FRR cross over on a graph is called the *crossover error rate*. Organizations can use this point to determine how accurate different types of biometric devices are.

EXAM TIP

Know the difference between Type I and Type II errors. Remember that Type I is an incorrect rejection, and Type II is an incorrect acceptance.

Quick check

1. If a valid user is rejected when he attempts to authenticate by using a biometric system, what type of error is it?

2. What is the comparison graph of FRR and FAR called, and why is it important?

Quick check answers

1. Rejection of valid users is known as a Type I error.

2. A crossover error rate (CER) graph for the False Rejection Rate (FRR) and False Acceptance Rate (FAR) shows how accurate a biometric system is. Changing settings can adjust this rate, making false acceptance or false rejection lower or higher depending on the needs of the organization.

Deploying biometric authentication

When deploying a biometric solution, it is important to pay attention to several key factors beyond Type I and II errors, including:

- The location of the system and how users will interact with it.

- Whether the system will be used to identify a person or to verify identity—in other words, whether it is a single-factor system or part of a multifactor system.

- The number of users.

- Whether you have data about those users already or have to enroll every user to have everyone's data.

If we revisit Humongous Insurance, the example company from earlier chapters, we can look at their use of biometric systems. At Humongous Insurance, most employees have building access cards that allow them access to parts of the building they are allowed to be in. These cards don't require a PIN or other verification, and thus they provide only a low level of assurance that the user of the card is who he should be.

In higher security areas, a guard is used to look at the ID card. This helps, because the guard is likely to identify a person who doesn't match the picture on the ID card she is using. Unfortunately, humans also make mistakes or become used to a repetitive task. This is where a biometric solution comes in. At Humongous, certain areas like their data center use a biometric access system that checks the shape of the user's hand against a database of registered users, while requiring a PIN number. The hand scanner also checks to make sure the person using the scanner is alive by verifying that there is a pulse and warmth from the hand. For Humongous, this provides the security the company needs, without putting undue restrictions on most of their users.

Humongous also cares about how hard it is to enroll users, and how well their scanners capture data. This information is captured via the failure-to-enroll rate (FTE) and the failure-to-capture rate (FTC). Obviously, if Humongous chose a system that made it hard to enroll users, or worse, that regularly refused to capture users' biometric data when they needed access, the system would quickly be removed or worked around by its users.

Stealing biometric passwords and changing your biometric identity

One of the challenges of biometrics is exactly that which is exploited by those movie heroes: we can't easily change our physical features, and if they can be duplicated, this factor in our multifactor authentication system fails. This issue has been covered in popular TV shows, and many children know that you can duplicate fingerprints by using clear tape or glue.

This occasionally happens in the real world, too. Fingerprints and other biometric authenticators can be copied, or at times the user can be forced to use them.

In addition, it turns out that in some cases, your biometric identity itself can change. The authors of this book ran into exactly that issue with a hand geometry scanner that provided access to a secure area. In two separate instances, employees were unable to access the area. Further research showed that one employee had recently started wearing a ring, which caused her hand to show up on scans as being different. In the second case, the employee lost a significant amount of weight, resulting in his hand changing in size.

Thus, we know that although biometric systems can provide a useful layer of security, it isn't always sufficient to rely on them!

Tokens

An alternative to biometric authentication is token-based authentication. *Tokens* are "something you have," but to succeed as a token, the item needs to provide more security than something like a driver's license would provide. Thus, tokens typically include some form of code generation capability and use a matching software package on the authentication server that validates their code against its own internal logic.

Common token types include:

- USB-based tokens that plug in and provide authentication.
- Self-updating tokens that constantly provide a rolling code that changes every minute or every few minutes.
- Button press–based tokens that update their code every time a button is pressed.
- Smart card–based tokens that contain an embedded chip that is read by a reader when the token is used.

Smart cards

Smart cards are a frequently used authentication method, often combining an ID card with the user's picture and other information with the ability to serve as a token for access to buildings and systems. A smart card contains an embedded chip, allowing it to have internal storage, encryption, and other capabilities. Two common types of smart cards used in the United States are CACs and PIV cards.

Common Access Cards

The US military uses a smart card called the Common Access Card (CAC) for access. Members of the military, contractors, civilian employees, and others receive a CAC. A CAC contains an array of information about its holder, including a picture, details of the person's role, rank, and agency; the person's pay grade; and even the user's Geneva Convention category in case the holder is taken prisoner. More importantly, however, current CACs also embed an integrated chip used for identification, making them tokens that can be used for authentication when combined with a PIN that the user sets.

RFID tags vs. smart cards

Radio frequency ID (RFID) is a wireless technology used for a wide variety of purposes. One common use that many people are unaware of is its use in US passports, where an RFID chip allows the passport to be wirelessly read by a passport reader.

RFID is also widely used in systems that allow parking lot access via card readers, and for toll roads where an RFID transponder is read as a car passes through toll gates or arches on the road.

Unlike smart cards, RFID transponders typically provide a fixed response to queries. This fits their usage model, but it also means that they're vulnerable, because many implementations don't include a certificate or other means of validating that the RFID is actually the tag that it is supposed to be.

In the real world, this means that toll cards, passports, and other identifiers that use RFID could be cloned, copied, or simulated without the reader knowing it. Because RFID is often read at a distance or via an automated system, a human won't see that the RFID response is coming from a copy or a fake.

What can we learn from this? Perhaps the most important lesson is that we have to match the requirement for security with the technology in use. If a faked response doesn't create a significant issue, a low-security RFID tag might be acceptable. If you're admitting staff to a government high-security facility, a smart card with onboard encryption capabilities such as a CAC with a PIN and a picture of the legitimate owner makes a lot more sense.

Personal Identification Verification cards

The Personal Identification Verification (PIV) card is a card issued to US government employees to provide access to government buildings, systems, and resources. The requirements for the PIV card are defined by the National Institute of Standards and Technology (NIST) as part of FIPS (Federal Information Processing Standard) 201, a standard that describes the card, how it interfaces with systems, and how it securely stores credential information.

Chip and PIN

Smart cards are widely used in the United Kingdom for credit, debit, and ATM cards as part of the Chip and PIN standard that was adopted there. Unlike the United States, where we rely on the magnetic stripe on the card, Chip and PIN uses a smart card with a PIN. The system not only verifies that the card is legitimate by using its embedded chip, it also verifies that the user's PIN matches at the time it is entered.

The enhanced security of the Chip and PIN system has resulted in fraud moving to online purchases where the system isn't used. In addition, researchers have found a number of vulnerabilities in the systems that have been implemented, ranging from poor cryptographic protection due to weak random number generation to issues with how the PIN is verified.

EXAM TIP

CACs and PIV cards are both important concepts for US government identification and authentication. Make sure you know what both are, and what they are used for.

Quick check

1. What is the smart card commonly used by the US military called?

2. What type of authenticator is a token?

Quick check answers

1. The CAC is the type of smart card issued by the US military.

2. A token is considered "something you have." Other factors are "something you are" and "something you know": examples of these are biometric factors and passwords or PINs, respectively.

Authentication services

We've discussed a variety of methods that you can use to identify yourself to an authentication service. Each of these methods relies on a variety of underlying authentication services when they are deployed in an enterprise environment. Most organizations have one or more of these common authentication services, which check credentials such as user name, password, or another factor. After they have verified who you are, they provide access based on your role or the rights that you have, and then they log your access, providing an audit log.

In this section we take a deeper look at some of the most common authentication services: RADIUS, TACACS and TACACS+, the Kerberos protocol, LDAP, and Active Directory Domain Services. We'll also discuss single sign-on technologies such as OpenID, which is becoming increasingly common as companies adopt cloud services that they want to integrate with their central authentication services.

RADIUS

RADIUS, the Remote Authentication Dial-In User Service, has been in use for more than 20 years and is very commonly used in organizations to provide access to networks. RADIUS relies on a client/server model, as demonstrated in Figure 11-2, as well as realms.

> **NOTE** **RADIUS REALMS**
>
> A RADIUS realm is arbitrary text prepended or appended to a user name, much like the domain name in an email address. This realm information allows a RADIUS server to contact another RADIUS server for authentication, authorization, and access control services.

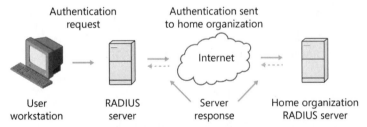

FIGURE 11-2 A RADIUS client (workstation) contacts the local RADIUS server to authenticate, and because the user is from another realm, the RADIUS server contacts the home server to verify the user.

As shown in the figure, the RADIUS server sends an authentication request to the user's home organization, as provided by realm information included with the user's credentials. The home organization's RADIUS server responds, providing authentication information for the user to the RADIUS server the user originally send the request to.

The three critical capabilities that RADIUS provides are:

- **Authentication** Checks the user's credentials to verify that they are correct. Typically the credentials are a user name and password. RADIUS can also integrate two-factor authentication, returning an access challenge requesting further authentication such as a PIN, token, smart card, or biometric scan.

- **Authorization attributes** These can include the IP address the user will receive, the allowed connection lifetime for the user, or even a list of access controls for the user, restricting what he can access.

- **Accounting data** This can include a start record for when the user's connection started, updates that track active connections, and stop records for when the session ends, with details such as the amount of time the user was connected, how much data was sent, and how the connection ended.

EXAM TIP

Know the three main capabilities that RADIUS provides—authentication, authorization, and accounting—and understand the concepts of roaming and realms.

As you can tell, RADIUS provides a wide array of features and capabilities, which make it a useful authentication protocol. It also enables users to roam, or travel between organizations or within very large organizations. In large organizations, roaming allows the company to use a central authentication system to allow global employees to log in at any site, worldwide. For groups that have agreed to work together, it allows users from other organizations to connect to an organization's network by using their home credentials. These home credentials are part of what is known as a realm, and users from multiple realms can be authenticated against their own realm's RADIUS server when roaming is allowed.

NOTE RADIUS PORTS

RADIUS uses UDP port 1812 for RADIUS authentication and 1813 for RADIUS accounting.

TACACS and TACACS+

TACACS (Terminal Access Controller Access-Control System) is a remote authentication proto-col. Cisco's proprietary implementation, which provided extensions and is known as *XTACACS* (eXtended TACACS), is a similar protocol used on their networking devices. TACACS, much like RADIUS, uses a client/server model where a client authenticates against a TACACS authentica-tion server via UDP port 49. The system that the user is attempting to authenticate to then allows or denies the connection to it based on the server's response.

Both TACACS and XTACACS are largely outdated, but a complete replacement of the protocol designed by Cisco, called *TACACS+*, has replaced them. TACACS+ is often paired with RADIUS for authentication for network devices. TACACS+, unlike TACACS, encrypts the entire packet of data it sends, protecting the entire authentication process instead of just the password, making it more secure than many comparable protocols. In addition, TACACS+ continues to use port 49, but switches to TCP traffic, making TACACS+ authentication more reliable than the UDP mode used by TACACS and XTACACS.

EXAM TIP

Know the differences between TACACS, XTACACS, and TACACS+. Remember that TACACS+ uses TCP and is encrypted, and has replaced TACACS and XTACACS.

The Kerberos protocol

The *Kerberos protocol* is a client/server authentication protocol that uses the concept of a ticket issued to systems or nodes on a network to allow them to authenticate and then communicate with each other. The Kerberos protocol authenticates both the client and the server, unlike the authentication protocols we have previously explored. This allows both ends in the communication to verify that the system they are connected to is the correct system and can be trusted. The Kerberos protocol commonly operates on TCP port 88, making it easy to recognize on the network.

In addition to mutual authentication, the Kerberos protocol uses encryption to protect its messaging, which helps prevent reading capture of Kerberos traffic. This means that attackers cannot read the content of the packets or replay them to attempt to gain access by using a system's ticket.

Kerberos authentication involves six steps in its authentication model, which the client works with to authenticate, as shown in Figure 11-3. The process for authentication is:

1. The client authenticates itself to the authentication server (AS).

2. The AS responds with an encrypted message by using the user's password and sends the user name to the key distribution center (KDC)

3. The KDC issues a ticket granting ticket (TGT) with a timestamp. This is encrypted by using the user's password and sent back to the user.

4. The user's client then sends the TGT to the ticket granting service (TGS), which is the server shown in the figure, when it needs to contact another system. The TGT is verified, and the TGS issues a ticket and session keys to the client.

5. The client then sends the ticket to the system it wants to communicate with, known as the service server (SS) along with the request it wants to have that service handle.

6. The client receives a response from the system allowing it access if it was granted.

EXAM TIP

Know the major parts of Kerberos authentication: the AS, KDC, TGT, TGS, and SS. Understand that clients must have a valid ticket and session key to connect to a service, and that the entire Kerberos process is designed to get the keys and ticket to the user's client.

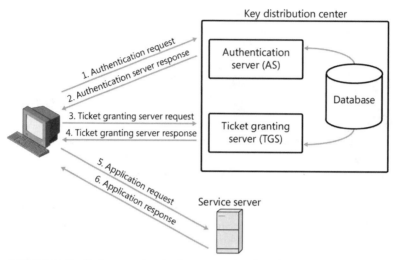

FIGURE 11-3 The Kerberos authentication process involves six steps, with an authentication request to the Authentication Server, a ticket granting request to the TGS, and finally an application request to a Service Server.

The Kerberos protocol does have potential issues. Because it is a client/server protocol, if the Kerberos server is unavailable, the client will not be able to authenticate. Worse, if the Kerberos server is compromised, attackers could give themselves access to any resource that any user could use. The most common issue with Kerberos is actually due to its requirement for accurate time settings between clients and servers. Often, systems will not have accurate time, either due to lack of access to network time servers or due to a local system issue such as a dying BIOS battery. When a client attempts to connect to a Kerberos server by using a timestamp that doesn't closely match the time the server expects, it will be rejected.

LDAP

The Lightweight Directory Access Protocol (*LDAP*) is a protocol designed to provide directory services and access to those services on a network. LDAP is often used for providing access to email or phone directories, but it also includes authentication capabilities, which means that LDAP can be used for a broad array of purposes.

LDAP traffic is usually sent over TCP 389, and secure LDAP traffic that is protected by a TLS or SSL tunnel is usually sent via TCP 636. However, LDAP does provide support for STARTTLS , which allows switching from unencrypted to encrypted channels over port 389 when required. LDAP is a client/server protocol like the other authentication protocols we have looked at in this chapter, but it provides an array of capabilities that go beyond simple authentication. These include:

- LDAP bind, which allows authentication.
- Searches against an LDAP directory.
- Comparisons to check entries.
- Addition, deletion, and modification of directory entries.
- The ability to request a secure TLS connection.
- Other capabilities that support directory connections and maintenance.

> **MORE INFO** **TLS AND LDAP**
>
> We discussed TLS in Chapter 3, "Secure network design and management." Remember that it is a wrapper protocol that can secure many types of traffic.

Figure 11-4 shows an LDAP hierarchy, starting at its root with the domain component (dc) set as dc=com, because this is a .com organization, then moving downward in the hierarchy through each level, including dc=humongousinsurance, then entries below with ou=staff and ou=departments. The final level includes uid=briangroth and cn=hr, as well as other examples.

FIGURE 11-4 LDAP data is stored in a hierarchical structure.

An LDAP entry has a set of attributes, each of which has a name, such as *phonenumber* or *givenname*. In addition, each entry has a unique identifier known as its distinguished name (DN). The DN is built from a relative distinguished name (RDN), which contains attributes from the entry combined with the entry's parent's DN. Thus, in the figure, you can see that Brian Groth's RDN is composed of his common name, *Brian Groth*, his dc, *HumongousInsurance*, and Humongous Insurance's dc, which is *com*. Figure 11-5 shows an example LDAP entry for Brian Groth. LDAP can provide various pieces of information about Brian depending on the viewing rights a particular user has on the corporate LDAP directory.

```
txt
dn: cn=Brian Groth,dc=humongousinsurance,dc=com
cn: Brian Groth
givenName: Brian
sn: Groth
telephoneNumber: +1 800 555 1234
mail: brian@humongousinsurance.com
manager: cn=Karin Zimprich,dc=humongousinsurance,dc=com
objectClass: inetOrgPerson
objectClass: organizationalPerson
objectClass: person
objectClass: top
```

FIGURE 11-5 Brian Groth's LDAP entry shows his RDN, his dc, and his personal information that is stored in Humongous Insurance's LDAP directory.

EXAM TIP

Remember that LDAP operates on TCP port 389 and LDAPS, the secure version of LDAP, operates on TCP 636. LDAP can both authenticate users and provide directory information.

Active Directory Domain Services

Active Directory Domain Services, often called *AD DS*, is the Windows directory service for Windows domains. The central control for AD DS is managed by systems called domain controllers. Domain controllers provide authentication and authorization services for domains. In addition, domain controllers provide the ability to create, deploy, and enforce policy on domain systems and to provide reporting and auditing of member systems.

AD DS uses a hierarchical design much like LDAP does; however, AD DS breaks groups into forests, trees, and domains. A forest is a collection of trees, which contain domains. A forest is the container that provides trust between users, computers, groups, and other objects in trees and domains.

Groups of objects in a domain are broken into organizational units, or OUs. As shown in Figure 11-6, an OU can contain other OUs, allowing administrators to sort groups of systems or users into functional groups. This can then be used to determine which users and systems receive specific policies, and to group users and systems differently than they would otherwise appear in the organizational hierarchy. An example is the Windows_7_Workstations OU, which Humongous Insurance uses to contain all Windows 7–based workstations in their North American organization for deploying policies, even though there are various groups that those workstations belong to.

AD DS also supports its own flavor of LDAP, allowing organizations that implement AD DS to use LDAP in addition to native Active Directory Domain Services authentication. This is often used to integrate AD DS with applications, servers, and services that are designed to use LDAP for their authentication.

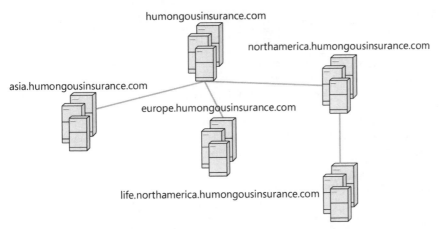

humongousinsurance.com

northamerica.humongousinsurance.com

asia.humongousinsurance.com

europe.humongousinsurance.com

life.northamerica.humongousinsurance.com

FIGURE 11-6 Humongous Insurance uses a single forest for its Active Directory Domain Services deployment. Each regional group has its own tree, with a domain set up for different units in that area.

Single sign-on

Single sign-on (SSO) is the capability provided by access control systems that allows a user to log on once and then continue to authenticate to multiple systems without having to log on again. Single sign-on is popular in enterprise environments because it reduces effort on the part of users, reduces the number of passwords used by those users, and can help cut support costs because users have fewer forgotten password calls.

The Kerberos protocol is often used for single sign-on systems because its ticket granting capability makes it relatively easy to continue to issue tickets for the user. Alternate options for SSO systems include token and smart card systems that automatically use the token or smart card to authenticate further sessions, and other tools that use SAML (the Security Assertion Markup Language) to handle web-based SSO.

Single sign-on is often also accompanied by single sign-out capabilities where logging off of the SSO service results in all services that were logged on being logged off.

OpenID

OpenID is an open standard for decentralized authentication of user identities designed to allow users of websites to consolidate their accounts through a trusted website. A users creates his or her OpenID on a site, which acts as an identity provider to other OpenID sites that act as OpenID acceptors, known as *relying parties*. Figure 11-7 demonstrates how single sign-on via OpenID works.

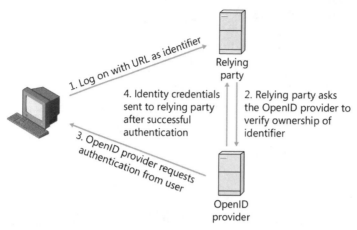

FIGURE 11-7 OpenID authentication requires a web browser, a relying party, and an identity provider to authenticate users without exposing the user's credentials to the web application. The identity provider acts as a notary, signing the certificate sent and certifying the user's identity.

OpenID doesn't specify a central authority for user accounts, nor does it have specific authentication method requirements. It does allow users to use a single sign-on for many sites by using a certificate-based system that is somewhat similar to Kerberos tickets that certify that users are who they say they are.

SAML

SAML (Security Assertion Markup Language) is another common technology used for single sign-on. SAML itself isn't only used for SSO, but it is a technology that can be used to make SSO work. In fact, Central Authentication Service (CAS), a single sign-on protocol commonly used on Internet 2, the Internet backbone maintained by higher education institutions, frequently relies on SAML as its underlying technology. SAML is used to allow identity providers to have users redirected to their site to authenticate, then to send SAML responses to the web browser, which provides the response to the service provider.

Fighting the risks of single sign-on

Single sign-on is a very attractive capability for most organizations. It reduces user complaints and allows users to work across a variety of services and systems without having to constantly interrupt their work to type in a password. In organizations whose employees move between a large number of systems that require different passwords, this can also reduce the amount of password reuse and bad password practices.

Unfortunately, single sign-on also brings risks with it. If every system can be accessed with a single password, and that password only has to be entered once during a session, attackers can take advantage of that access. Single sign-on shouldn't be used when higher security levels are required, because it can act as an easy in for an attacker with access to a user's machine or password.

Two-factor authentication using a token or a biometric factor can help stop attackers from taking advantage of a single sign-on system. Adding an additional authentication step for high-security systems provides a layer of defense that attackers won't be able to make it past without that extra factor.

 Quick check

1. What specific property of the Kerberos protocol makes it different from RADIUS and TACACS+?

2. What other authentication system does Active Directory Domain Services implement?

Quick check answers

1. Mutual authentication: the Kerberos protocol authenticates both the client and the server.

2. Active Directory has integrated support for LDAP.

Access control concepts and models

Now that we have identified our users, authenticated them, and authorized them, we need to figure out how to control their access to systems and services. This is where access control comes into play. Security professionals use three major models to describe access control systems:

- **Mandatory access control (MAC)** Enforces access control at the underlying operating system level. In technical terms, this means that MAC controls the access of subjects, such as users to objects such as files and programs, based on a defined policy.

- **Discretionary access control** Permits users to grant access to files and object, and to and change access rights to objects they control.

- **Role-based access control** Provides access based on a user's job or tasks the user is required to perform.

In addition to these models, we will also take a look at two critical concepts in all access controls: least privilege and separation of duties.

When used together, these models and ideas provide a strong foundation for security practitioners to use when architecting user rights and access.

Trusted operating systems

As you might imagine, implementing access control models such as those listed in the previous sections can be complex, and ensuring that they are properly applying their security model is difficult. Government organizations, government contractors, and other groups that require high levels of operating system security have established testing methodologies for operating systems that provide guidelines and procedures for testing the implementation of these capabilities. The criteria test for proper support for both multilevel security (the ability to provide both security clearance levels and to prevent access between levels) and the ability to provide evidence that that support meets government requirements. Operating systems that meet these criteria are called *trusted operating systems*.

The Common Criteria

One way to certify the ability of systems to provide multilevel security is to certify to the Common Criteria. The Common Criteria for Information Technology Security Evaluation, often simply called the Common Criteria or CC, is an international standard for computer security certification. The Common Criteria sets seven Evaluation Assurance Levels (EALs), EAL 1 through EAL 7, which match how deep the testing for that level goes. Each EAL has a series of security assurance requirements or (SARs) for that level. One key thing to bear in mind is that EAL levels don't guarantee better security! Instead, they certify that the product has been tested to that level of certification. Many systems are certified at an EAL level in a specific configuration, and variations on that configuration may might not meet that EAL level.

Current uses of CC testing include devices like firewalls, operating systems, and other security devices. Much like TCSEC, CC ratings are required by government organizations that are purchasing new solutions, and thus EAL levels may might show up in procurement requirements.

Least privilege

One of the most critical concepts used in information security management is called *least privilege*. The idea behind least privilege is that users and services that receive rights should only be given the minimum set of rights required to perform the operations that they need to perform. The concept of *implicit deny* exists here too, and much like the use of implicit deny in firewalls, in permission-based systems an implicit denial of rights is often enforced for any user or action that isn't explicitly permitted.

This means that if a user needs to create and read files in the user's own directory to do his or her job, that user should not receive rights that allow him or her to create and read files outside of that directory. This frequently breaks down in organizations that rely on least privilege when groups are assigned rights that individuals should have, or when members enter and leave groups and the privileges they need are assigned to the entire group. Over time, this means that individuals can gain more rights simply be being added to a group.

In many organizations, the most visible implementation of the concept of least privilege is the user account that users use to log on to their workstations. A frequent best practice is to provide users with a user-level account, rather than an administrative account such as administrator on a Windows-based PC, or root on a Linux system. This prevents users from causing chaos as they perform actions with full rights, and it limits what they can access, change, or delete.

The least privilege required to perform a job is also challenging to determine and maintain, and organizations often find themselves using the concept but not fully implementing it. A user account designed with reasonable rights for a large number of users probably doesn't provide the least privilege each would need but provides a lower level of privilege than an administrator or other account with expanded privileges would provide.

Least privilege is also used in areas other than user accounts. The concept remains the same when used in firewall rule design. A well-designed firewall rule intended to permit access to a web server that uses the concept of least privilege might only allow systems from a specific network to access the web server. This prevents users who aren't allowed to access the web server from getting to it via an overly broad rule, preserving the leave privilege concept.

EXAM TIP

Remember that least privilege allows users or programs to only access the data and resources necessary to do their intended functions.

Separation of duties

Another important access control concept is *separation of duties*. This is the policy in many banks, where tellers can cash checks and provide cash out of their drawer but don't have access to the vault. The bank separates the elements of this task into the individual actions taken to make a deposit work. When each element is assigned separately, multiple employees review the work and make sure that one employee isn't exploiting ownership of the entire process. By separating these duties, a bank ensures that a single person can't fake a deposit, withdraw money, or otherwise cheat the bank.

Some tasks can't be easily separated, and one individual has to perform all of the actions required to accomplish it. When this happens, organizations look to other solutions to ensure that employees aren't exploiting their positions, such as job rotation and mandatory vacation.

Job rotation

One of the most common solutions to the challenge of detecting fraud is job rotation. In this model, multiple employees move through the positions required to accomplish a task that might be a likely target for abuse. If one employee, or even multiple employees, are taking advantage of their position, the rotation is likely to result in an honest employee noticing that something is amiss.

Time-of-day restrictions

Organizations use *time-of-day restrictions* to limit when employees can access buildings, secure areas, workstations, and applications. This is common in companies with employees who are not required to provide off-hours support, and can help prevent employees from accessing data without the knowledge of their employer by coming in after their normal work hours. Time-of-day restrictions can also help provide greater physical security by preventing access to a vault or other area when there are no other employees in the area.

Mandatory vacation

Another common solution to the problem of detecting fraud is to require employees to take a mandatory vacation. In theory, requiring employees to take vacations long enough for their tasks to have to be performed fully without them will allow the employees who fill in for them to notice any problems. Most organizations require employees who must take a mandatory vacation to be gone for at least two weeks to ensure that enough time passes between their departure and when they return to prove that the process hasn't been bypassed.

EXAM TIP

Remember that mandatory vacations should be at least two weeks long. This might seem arbitrary, but it provides enough time to for replacement employees to complete tasks that might be delayed if an employee is only gone for a week.

By now you're likely pondering complex schemes to bypass separation of duties, job rotation, and mandatory vacation. Companies find these techniques to be effective, but they're not foolproof. What they do provide is the ability to significantly reduce the appeal of abusing privileges in an organization. If employees know that they're being monitored, and that other employees are likely to catch them if they try to abuse the system, they're far less prone to being tempted to cheat the company.

Access control models

Most organizations use multiple access control models to keep their data and systems safe. The three most common access control models are mandatory access control (MAC), discretionary access control (DAC), and role-based access control (RBAC). These models can be implemented in combination or independently.

When combined with the concepts of least privilege and separation of duties, these three access control models provide a way to design effective controls that prevent users and applications from performing actions they shouldn't be allowed to while ensuring that they have the rights they need to accomplish their jobs.

Evaluating control models: TCSEC

The Trusted Computer System Evaluation Criteria (TCSEC), often known as the Orange Book, was one of the Rainbow books published by the United States Department of Defense in the early 1980s. TCSEC provided a range of requirements around security policy and processes. The Orange Book was used by the US government as the core of its assessment and evaluation criteria for computer systems and software for almost two decades.

TCSEC provided four major classifications for security: A,B,C, and D, with levels under each of those specifying criteria required for each. Level A was the most secure, but common operating systems of the time such as Windows NT were frequently classified as low as level C2, because although they provided discretionary access control, they didn't provide any of the strict controls needed for higher levels. Level A1 systems required highly formal design and testing processes, extremely strong administrative controls, and both discretionary and mandatory access controls. Very few operating systems were ever certified to A1.

TCSEC was replaced in 2005 by the Common Criteria, but many security professionals still refer to the Rainbow books and the Orange Book when discussing access control models.

Mandatory access control

Mandatory access control (MAC) requires an operating system that can limit subjects such as programs or processes from performing actions on objects or targets such as files or system resources. The administrator of the system sets limits on what subjects can do and specifically controls their access.

Mandatory access control was originally specified for military computer systems where confidentiality of data was the most important concern. On those systems, MAC was expected to provide an absolute level of control, preventing mistakes from occurring that would allow subjects to gain access beyond what they were supposed to have, thus compromising the confidentiality of secure data.

The first design for a system like this is known as the Bell-LaPadula model. Bell-LaPadula is a formal model that focuses on confidentiality of data. It was designed to control access to classified information for the US military and government.

Bell-LaPadula categorizes systems as either subjects and objects. Subjects access objects, each of which has a classification and a compartment, which in combination make up that system's security level.

Bell-LaPadula has two security properties that relate to mandatory access control:

- **The Simple Security Property**   States that a subject at any specified security level can't read objects at a higher security level. This is usually summarized as "no read up."
- **The Star Property**   Prevents subjects from writing objects to a lower security level. This is stated as "no write down."

By using these two properties, you can easily see how the military could ensure confidentiality in a mandatory access control system. A user couldn't read things he or she wasn't allowed to because they existed at a higher level of security, and the same user couldn't leak information downward because they couldn't write down to a lower security level.

Of course, this only works when the system is a closed system and users can't remove data from it. In a mandatory access control system the limits on user rights can often be avoided by simply writing down information or printing it, taking it out of the operating system's ability to control where the data goes.

In normal practice, many of us run into a form of mandatory access control on a frequent basis when using databases. In a database management system (DBMS), the subjects, such as database connections from web servers, have controls enforced on them as they access objects such as tables or stored procedures.

EXAM TIP

Bell-LaPadula is easy to remember if you keep in mind the phrase "No read up, no write down." The two security principles are also easy to remember: Simple is first, Star is second.

Discretionary access control

Discretionary access control, sometimes called DAC, is an access control system that allows owners of objects such as files, directories, or services to grant rights on those objects to others. Most modern operating systems implement a form of DAC to allow users to grant access to other users on the system by using access control lists (ACLs). Much like the ACLs we discussed earlier in the book, these provide a set of rules about what can and cannot be done to an object. If you have used system with a Windows, Linux, or Mac OS operating system, you have used a form of discretionary access control.

Linux implements discretionary access control as shown in Figure 11-8. Each of the four files shown has permissions set to match its name: all_permissions allows all of the file access rights possible, executable can be run by any user, and readable and writeable each match their name. Note that each file has user, group, and world rights recorded at the beginning of each line. Each of the three groups of letters includes an *r* if there is a read right, a *w* if there is write permission, and an *x* if the file can be executed. If no right exists, a – is shown.

```
total 28
drwxr-xr-x  2 root root 4096 2013-06-02 20:02 .
drwxr-xr-x 26 root root 4096 2013-06-02 20:02 ..
-rwxrwxrwx  1 root root   40 2013-06-02 20:01 all_permissions.txt
-rw-r--r--  1 root root   40 2013-06-02 20:01 default_permissions.txt
---x--x--x  1 root root   34 2013-06-02 20:01 executable.txt
-r--r--r--  1 root root   34 2013-06-02 20:01 readable.txt
--w--w--w-  1 root root   27 2013-06-02 20:01 writeable.txt
```

FIGURE 11-8 This Linux sample file listing shows read, write, and execute permissions. File rights can be set at the level of users, groups, or world access; and read, write, and execute rights can be set for each of those groupings.

Discretionary access control is intended to allow users to control what they have ownership rights to, while allowing owners to specify who has access to their resources and what those rights are. It also prevents non-owners from taking control of the objects that they don't own.

Role-based access control

Role-based access control (RBAC) is frequently implemented in parallel with mandatory or discretionary access control systems. Role-based access control restricts access to users who have a specific job function or role in the organization, which is matched with permissions that grant access rights or the ability to perform actions.

Role-based access control has three rules that it enforces:

1. Subjects must be assigned a role to use the permissions that role provides. Thus, users who don't have that role can't use the permissions the role provides.

2. Subjects can only use roles that they are authorized to use. This means that their role is verified when they try to use it.

3. Subjects can only use permissions that their role authorizes. If they try to use a permission that their role doesn't have, they will be rejected.

This makes the most sense when you look at it in terms of the identification, authentication, and authorization process we looked at earlier in this chapter. If Alan Shen, a system administrator, logs onto a Humongous Insurance system, his logon is checked to verify what role he has. If another user tried to use an administrator role, that user would be rejected, whereas Alan's role as an administrator allows him to perform actions that administrators have permission to do. When he uses that role, his permissions as an administrator are verified. Even as an administrator, Alan might not be allowed to change certain files or enter specific directories. In short, when RBAC identifies a user, it checks that the user has that role. Then it makes sure that user is authorized to use the role, and finally it verifies that the role allows the user to take the action that they want to perform.

To be secure, role-based access control assignment requires that users not be given rights that allow them to control the system that controls their own access. If Alan's administrator role allows him to audit his own access and to control his own rights, he can hide evidence of inappropriate actions or grant himself abilities beyond those that he is supposed to have. Role-based access control is an area where separation of duties is critical.

One common issue with RBAC systems is known as role explosion. In a large organization, hundreds or possibly thousands of roles might exist, depending on the permissions that users need to accomplish their jobs. As more and more roles are created, they become harder to maintain and harder to audit, and eventually the system becomes so complex that it can be unusable. In addition, role-based access control also has issues when it is used in organizations that need more granular controls than simple role definitions can provide. Fortunately, modern access control systems are adding capabilities that allow individual users to receive specific capabilities in addition to role-based permissions.

EXAM TIP

Keep in mind that RBAC is based on the role that an individual has in the organization. Roles are based on organizational policies and shouldn't allow the user to have the ability to audit his or her own role.

 Quick check

1. What access control model allows users to make decisions about granting acces rights?

2. What access control concepts can help catch staff who are abusing their position?

Quick check answers

1. Discretionary access control allows users to make their own decisions about which users should have access to objects they control and what type of access they should receive.

2. Job rotation and mandatory vacation can both help by having other employees review work that is being done. This can help catch employees who are exploiting their access or rights.

Account management

Account management involves maintaining user information, including users' credentials and privileges. In most large organizations, account management is handled by a central account management team that handles passwords, user details, and rights management via a central system such as Active Directory Domain Services. Two critical parts of that management role are password management and privilege management.

Passwords

Passwords are the most commonly used authenticator for computer systems and fit in the category of "something you know." Passwords rely on secrecy for their security, which means that they are often the target of attack by attackers who try to acquire them by using malware, phishing, or other attacks that capture a password or trick the user into revealing it. Passwords are also often targeted by attackers who attempt to guess them through knowledge of the user or via brute-force attempts.

> **MORE INFO** **PASSWORD ATTACKS**
>
> You can find more about password attacks in Chapter 5, "Threats and attacks."

There are several key password concepts and processes that are used when passwords are implemented as part of authentication. These include *password resets* and *password recovery*, password expiration, and strong passwords.

Because passwords are something that users know, they're also something that users often forget, either because they haven't been used in a long time or because they were recently reset and the user didn't remember what he or she set the password to. When users forget their passwords, they will need their passwords reset or recovered. Password resets or recovery usually involve one of three methods:

- Reset via user self-service, with a password reset sent to the user via email or another method.

- Reset via authorized user, such as a helpdesk or other support person. This requires human intervention but can provide an additional layer of protection to keep attackers from resetting users' passwords.

- Recovery via an automated system that sends the forgotten password to the user.

Password recovery and user self-service password resets both can allow attackers to access passwords if they have access to the email account where the recovery or reset is sent. In many cases, organizations do not allow users to reset or recover their passwords by using methods like these for higher security accounts.

Password expiration occurs when the end of a password's lifespan has been reached. Many systems set a maximum password life for user and system passwords and then prompt for a password change as that time approaches.

Password expiration is intended to limit the damage that a compromised password can create. If a user loses his or her password or shares it, or if it is compromised by an attacker, that password will no longer be useful if the password expires and the legitimate user changes it.

Password expiration also has its own set of drawbacks. If users see the organization's password expiration policies as a problem, they might opt to create easily remembered passwords that they change slightly every time they are required to change their passwords. Other users might write their passwords down or simply re-share their passwords, thus negating the security advantages of password expiration..

Many systems monitor whether attempts to authenticate with a password succeed or fail. A common security measure is to lock the account, prohibiting further attempts to log on when a number of authentication failures set by policy is reached. This is known as *account lockout*. Locked out accounts can be automatically re-enabled after a set period of time, or they might require an administrator to reset them, depending on settings and security policies adopted by the organization.

Password strength is usually measured by complexity. The complexity of a password can be gauged in several ways:

- The number of different character types that it contains, including uppercase and lowercase letters, numbers, punctuation, and special characters.
- Whether the password uses dictionary words.
- Whether the password uses sequences that are meaningful to the user, such as a pet's name, a birth date, or other details of the user or the user's family. This can also include whether the password uses information that is easily known about the user.
- The length of the password.
- How hard the password is to crack by using a password cracking tool.

All of this complexity can leave users with a password like "kJx0hgTB," which most users would find difficult to remember. In addition, new tools that allow almost every potential shorter password to be tested when attacking systems have led to the need for longer passwords. Thus, *passphrases* have become increasingly common. A passphrase is typically a phrase or set of words that the user can easily remember. The increased length of a passphrase makes it much harder for attackers to use brute force, whereas the fact that it is a phrase means that a user will probably recall it more easily.

Passphrases can still be stolen, just like passwords, but they help provide a defense against automated attacks.

EXAM TIP

Password complexity rules and concepts are a key part of password-based security. Make sure you have a good understanding of why complex passwords are important and how to create them.

Preventing password-based attacks

Passwords are the most commonly attacked authentication mechanism. On a daily basis, systems connected to the Internet experience thousands of attempts to authenticate to them by using common user names and passwords. Amazingly enough, this still works at times, as users set up new systems that have poor passwords on common accounts, or as they install services that use default passwords when they are set up.

Figure 11-9 shows a short sample of log data from a single Linux system. Note the repeated attacks against user root, the Linux administrator user. In this case, the attack was conducted against the local system, but in the real world attacks often come from a variety of IP addresses scattered across the Internet. We discuss logs in more depth in Chapter 6, "Monitoring, detection, and defense."

```
May 19 18:18:55 bt sshd[21425]: Failed password for invalid user admin from 127.0.0.1 port 37032 ssh2
May 19 18:18:55 bt sshd[21431]: Failed password for invalid user temp from 127.0.0.1 port 37033 ssh2
May 19 18:18:55 bt sshd[21429]: Failed password for invalid user michelle from 127.0.0.1 port 37037 ssh2
May 19 18:18:55 bt sshd[21437]: Failed password for invalid user sam from 127.0.0.1 port 37039 ssh2
May 19 18:18:55 bt sshd[21441]: Failed password for invalid user brian from 127.0.0.1 port 37040 ssh2
May 19 18:18:55 bt sshd[21427]: Failed password for root from 127.0.0.1 port 37035 ssh2
May 19 18:18:55 bt sshd[21428]: Failed password for root from 127.0.0.1 port 37036 ssh2
May 19 18:18:55 bt sshd[21426]: Failed password for root from 127.0.0.1 port 37034 ssh2
May 19 18:18:55 bt sshd[21430]: Failed password for root from 127.0.0.1 port 37038 ssh2
```

FIGURE 11-9 This sample password attack log shows a brute-force attack in which users are attempting to attack a variety of user accounts on a sample system.

Fortunately, there are several ways to help fight off password attacks. They include:

- Locking out accounts after a specific number of bad logons. This often has an associated timer, but it might also require an administrator to unlock the account.
- Rate limits on attempted logons, which can prevent high-speed brute-force guessing of passwords.
- Automated testing of passwords for easily cracked or guessed passwords.
- Password complexity standards, including preventing common passwords such as *password* from being used.
- Changing default passwords.

Implementing password attack mitigation techniques can help, but passwords will remain a popular target. Two-factor authentication such as the token, smart card, and biometric systems we discussed earlier in this chapter can significantly decrease the likelihood of a password attack allowing access to your organization's high-security systems.

Privileges

Thus far in this chapter you have learned how users identify themselves, how they authenticate to systems and networks, and how those systems authorize them to perform actions. One key part of user management that we haven't explored is how privileges are maintained for users and what rights users can have. This is the final element needed to properly manage users on both stand-alone systems and in complex, multiuser, multiserver networks.

Privileges in common operating systems usually provide rights such as:

- Creating, editing, and deleting files.
- Running programs and executing files.
- Accessing networks, websites, or other remote resources.
- Granting rights to files.
- Creating network file and printer shares.
- Adding, modifying, creating, and deleting users.

This broad range of possible permissions makes privilege management a major task for system administrators. In order to properly manage user rights, user management is typically performed in one of three ways: via user-based management, group-based management, or role-based management.

User-based privilege management

User-based management sets privileges for each user, allowing very granular settings. Unfortunately, user-based management is also quite time consuming because each user account must be modified when a change that effects multiple users needs to be made. User-based management is useful when individual users have very distinctive permissions requirements, or for very small, simple systems where group management doesn't make sense because the groups themselves would be very small.

Group-based privilege management

Group-based privilege management allows privilege management via groups of users. These groups can overlap; for example, a user who is part of a group called "second-floor users" can also be a member of the "Human Resources" group. Due to the overlap that can exist between groups, group-based management can end up suffering from permission creep, in which additional permissions are added to a group to serve the needs of a small subgroup of users. Permission creep can be very dangerous, because tracking the permissions that many groups have is a complex task, and it often appears simpler to just grant a needed right to a group rather than to build a new group or role.

Role-based privilege management

Much like role-based access control, role-based privilege management pairs users with privileges based on roles. Unlike group-based management, role-based privilege management typically requires users to only be in one role at a time. This prevents privilege creep from other roles, but it also requires much more care in constructing role and permission pairing.

Centralized and decentralized privilege management

The management of privileges in enterprises is typically done centrally by using a system such as Active Directory Domain Services or RADIUS. In some cases, privileges might be managed locally by using privileges management done on the local system via group-based or role-based privilege management. In either case, the individual or individuals who are responsible for privilege management need to create a system to design and assign privileges.

This can be reduced to a reasonably simple process:

1. Determine what rights users need to have.

2. Build groups of users based on either roles or logical groups that match the rights required for the roles or groups.

3. Assign users to their roles or groups.

In many cases, group-based management is more attractive than role-based management because of the ability to provide users with multiple group memberships.

Long-term privilege management can only succeed with a well-thought-out plan. If you haven't thought ahead, new privileges will get matched with new groups, and membership in old groups will be requested out of habit, resulting in *privilege creep*.

Privilege creep

One of the most common privilege requests that administrators receive is "make our new user like our old user, just match their permissions." This often happens over and over again, with multiple generations of new users copying permissions from previous holders of that role or members of that group.

What the request rarely takes into account is that most professionals move between roles and groups in their organizations over time. Even in the best managed organizations, this is likely to result in problems. For example, Patrick Hines from HR might have started off in a sales role, and he might eventually become a vice president of the company. If a security administrator copies his permissions at some point in his career, an auditor or security analyst will probably find out that he has some rights he was granted to make his job in sales possible, others that let him perform his HR duties, and eventually, the reviewer might find out that his role as a vice president grants him an entirely new set of privileges. Thus, if Colleen Bracy replaces him as a vice president, she might find out that she can print to printers in the sales department, view human resources file shares, and access a system that was available to Patrick early in his tenure as a VP.

The most effective way to avoid this privilege creep is to require that requests actually specify the rights required. Denying requests such as, "give Colleen all the rights that Patrick had" can go a long way toward making sure that you're not cleaning up a rights management disaster a few years into a group's existence.

User-assigned privileges

The last type of privilege management is *user-assigned privilege* management. In this type of management, users typically have control over the files that they create and own as part of discretionary access control systems such as those used in Windows, Mac, and Linux operating systems.

User-assigned privileges aren't part of a central rights and privilege management system. This means that users can allow other users broader rights than your central system might allow, and that you might not have direct visibility into those rights. This is particularly true in systems that aren't part of your central privilege management structure, such as a cloud service.

User-assigned privileges are common despite this risk, because they allow users to make choices about who can access the files and applications that support their ability to complete their jobs. This type of privilege management relies on users doing their jobs responsibly, and usually points back to team standards and organizational policy.

The total damage that a user can create can also be limited by restricting the user's ability to grant privileges. If a user can only provide access to the files he or she creates or owns, and can only grant that access to members of the user's own group, department, or organization, your risk can be limited. At the same time, users can make reasonable decisions that allow them to be more effective in their jobs.

Chapter summary

- Identification involves who you are, authentication verifies that you are that person, and authorization allows a person with that identity to use privileges.

- Authentication can involve multiple factors, including something you have, something you are, or something you know. Something you have includes tokens and smart cards, something you know is often a password, and something you are is gathered by using biometric data collection.

- Biometric systems have both false accept (Type II) and false reject (Type I) rates. Companies use their crossover error rate (CER) to measure relative effectiveness.

- RADIUS is an authentication, authorization, and auditing service that is frequently used for remote access. It provides the ability for roaming users to authenticate across realms.

- TACACS and XTACACS are old protocols used for authentication, primarily for network equipment. TACACS+ is frequently implemented along with RADIUS for authentication to more modern devices.

- The Kerberos protocol, OpenID, and CAS are often used for single sign-on systems, which allow users to sign on once and then continue to be authenticated to a variety of systems.

- Access control systems include mandatory access control, in which only an administrator can set or change the rules; discretionary access control, which allows users to change access rights to objects they own; and role-based access control, which sets access rights based on the role of the employee.

- Password strength is gauged by its complexity, or by its length when used in a passphrase. Poor password habits include using dictionary words or information specific to the user.

- Group-based privileges rely on membership in a specific group. User-assigned privileges are set by the user, allowing the user to determine who accesses resources that user controls.

- Privileges are managed via user-based, group-based, or role-based privilege management schemes.

Chapter review

Test your knowledge of the information in Chapter 11 by answering these questions. The answers to these questions, and the explanations of why each answer choice is correct or incorrect, are located in the "Answers" section at the end of this chapter.

1. A token is what type of authenticator?

    A. Something you are

    B. Something you know

    C. Biometric

    D. Something you have

2. An access control system that relies on users to set rights uses what model?

    A. MAC

    B. DAC

    C. RBAC

    D. ABAC

3. Mandatory vacations help detect what?

    A. Least privilege

    B. Mandatory access control

    C. Inappropriate privileges

    D. Fraud

4. Privilege management that provides privileges based on a person's job role and responsibilities in the organization is known as what?

   A. User-based privilege management

   B. Group-based privilege management

   C. Role-based privilege management

   D. Mandatory privilege management

5. Which authentication protocol uses the concept of a ticket that is issued to a user's workstation?

   A. Active Directory Domain Services

   B. The Kerberos protocol

   C. TACACS+

   D. LDAP

6. The US government uses what type of token to identify its employees?

   A. A biometric token

   B. A CAC

   C. A PIV card

   D. A USB token

Answers

This section contains the answers to the questions for the "Chapter review" section in this chapter.

1. **Correct Answer: D**

   A. **Incorrect:** Something you are is a biometric identifier.

   B. **Incorrect:** Something you know is typically a password, PIN, or passphrase.

   C. **Incorrect:** Biometric information is something you are, such as a fingerprint, retina scan, or voice print.

   D. **Correct:** A token is something you have.

2. **Correct Answer: B**

   A. **Incorrect:** Mandatory access control (MAC) systems allow only the administrator to set or modify privileges.

   B. **Correct:** Discretionary access control (DAC) allows users to set rights and permissions on objects they control.

   C. **Incorrect:** Role-based access control (RBAC) systems determine access rights for users based on their jobs or assigned duties within the organization.

   D. **Incorrect:** Attribute-based access controls (ABAC), often used as part of an LDAP system, use the users' attributes such as organizational unit or job title to determine what rights they should have.

3. **Correct Answer: D**

   A. **Incorrect:** Least privilege is a best practice that provides a staff member with only the minimum rights required to perform a job.

   B. **Incorrect:** Mandatory access control is a type of operating system enforced access control, and mandatory vacations will not help with it.

   C. **Incorrect:** Inappropriate privileges can be granted, resulting in broader capabilities than desired, but mandatory vacations will not help detect them.

   D. **Correct:** Mandatory vacations help ensure that staff can't abuse their position. Vacations provide an opportunity for another staff member to handle duties normally assigned to the person on vacation, potentially revealing abuse.

4. **Correct Answer: C**

   A. **Incorrect:** User-based privilege management assigns privileges based on the needs of individual users and often creates issues due to the number of changes needed to support multiple users.

   B. **Incorrect:** Group-based privilege management focuses on groups that require similar types of privileges.

   C. **Correct:** Role-based privilege management manages privileges based on the job function or role of the user in the organization.

   D. **Incorrect:** Mandatory privilege management is a made-up concept and isn't a privilege management technique.

5. **Correct Answer: B**

   A. **Incorrect:** Active Directory Domain Services is the authentication and directory system used by Windows, which uses the Kerberos protocol for authentication, but is not itself an authentication protocol that deals with tickets..

   B. **Correct:** The Kerberos protocol uses a ticket-based system to allow systems to authenticate to various resources in a Kerberos realm.

   C. **Incorrect:** TACACS+ is an authentication system often used for network devices.

   D. **Incorrect:** LDAP is a directory services and authentication system. Active Directory Domain Services supports a version of LDAP as part of its capabilities.

6. **Correct Answer: C**

   A. **Incorrect:** Biometric identifiers are not tokens.

   B. **Incorrect:** CACs are issued to the US military but are not for general government use.

   C. **Correct:** PIV cards are the US government's personal identification card.

   D. **Incorrect:** USB tokens are used for many systems, but they are not the US government's standard identification method.

CHAPTER 12

Cryptography

 Cryptography is the art and science of transmitting information securely in the presence of untrusted individuals. Information security professionals rely upon cryptographic algorithms, or ciphers, to add security to communications that would otherwise be susceptible to eavesdropping and other attacks. In this chapter, you will learn how various cryptographic algorithms work to fulfill the four goals of confidentiality, integrity, authentication and nonrepudiation.

Exam objectives in this chapter:

Objective 6.1: Summarize general cryptography concepts

- Symmetric vs. asymmetric
- Fundamental differences and encryption methods
  - Block vs. stream
- Transport encryption
- Non-repudiation
- Hashing
- Key escrow
- Steganography
- Digital signatures
- Use of proven technologies
- Elliptic curve and quantum cryptography

Objective 6.2: Use and apply appropriate cryptographic tools and products

- WEP vs. WPA/WPA2 and preshared key
- MD5
- SHA
- RIPEMD
- AES
- DES
- 3DES

449

- HMAC
- RSA
- RC4
- One-time pads
- CHAP
- PAP
- NTLM
- NTLMv2
- Blowfish
- PGP/GPG
- Whole disk encryption
- TwoFish
- Comparative strengths of algorithms
- Use of algorithms with transport encryption
  - SSL
  - TLS
  - IPSec
  - SSH
  - HTTPS

Objective 6.3: Explain the core concepts of public key infrastructure

- Certificate authorities and digital certificates
  - CA
  - CRLs
- PKI
- Recovery agent
- Public key
- Private key
- Registration
- Key escrow
- Trust models

Objective 6.4: Implement PKI, certificate management and associated components

- Certificate authorities and digital certificates
  - CA
  - CRLs
- PKI

- Recovery agent
- Public key
- Private keys
- Registration
- Key escrow
- Trust models

Goals of cryptography

Information security professionals use the CIA triad to describe the profession's three main information protection goals: confidentiality, integrity, and availability. Cryptography, the practice of using encryption and decryption algorithms to obscure information in a reversible manner, is one of the main tools used to support two of these goals: confidentiality and integrity. In addition to supporting those major goals, some cryptographic algorithms can also be used to provide authentication and nonrepudiation functions.

> **MORE INFO CIA TRIAD**
>
> For more information on the three goals of information security: confidentiality, integrity, and availability, see the discussion of the CIA triad in Chapter 1, "Risk management and incident response."

The major goals of cryptography include:

- **Confidentiality**   Ensuring that sensitive information is not readable by unauthorized recipients. This is the most common use of cryptographic algorithms: encrypting sensitive information for transmission over an insecure channel, such as the Internet.
- **Integrity**   Ensuring that information is not modified in an unauthorized fashion. Some cryptographic algorithms can be used to create digital signatures that ensure that unauthorized changes have not been made to transmitted information.

- **Authentication**   Providing the ability to confirm the claimed identity of an individual or system. Public key cryptography can be used to create digital certificates that provide authentication capabilities.

- **Nonrepudiation**   Allowing the recipient of a message to undeniably prove to a third party that the message came from the purported sender. Digital signatures provide nonrepudiation and, when they are used, prevent the sender of a message from later denying that he or she originated the message.

Cryptographic algorithms have a long history, dating back thousands of years. Julius Caesar was one of the earliest users of cryptography,; he used a simple shift cipher to transmit secret military information between his commanders. This cipher, now known as the Caesar Cipher, simply shifted each character of a message by three letters. For example, the sender of a message would change all of the As in the message to Ds, the Bs to Es , and so on. The recipient of the message would know that the shift cipher was used and simply reverse the process to retrieve the original message.

Of course, the Caesar Cipher is now so simple that schoolchildren easily crack messages encrypted with it in classroom exercises. In the remainder of this chapter, we will explore modern technologies used to achieve the four goals of confidentiality, integrity, authentication, and nonrepudiation.

 Quick check

1. What are the four main goals of cryptography?

2. What goal of cryptography prevents an unauthorized recipient from reading the contents of a message?

Quick check answers

1. Confidentiality, integrity, authentication, and nonrepudiation

2. Confidentiality

Cryptographic concepts

The core building block of cryptography is the cryptographic algorithm: the mathematical process used to transform messages from their plaintext form to an encrypted form and vice-versa. *Encryption* is the operation of using a cryptographic algorithm to transform a plaintext message into a ciphertext message, as shown in Figure 12-1. Imagine the case of an email message being sent by Alice Ciccu to her colleague in another state, Bob Kelly. Alice knows that the message must travel over the Internet to reach Bob and that the Internet is inherently insecure. Unless she takes steps to protect the confidentiality of her message, other people might be able to read it while it is in transit. Therefore, Alice will encrypt the message, transforming it from plaintext to ciphertext, before she sends it on its way.

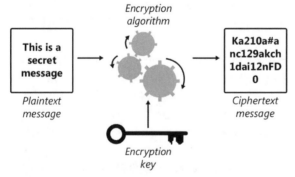

FIGURE 12-1 The encryption process converts a plaintext message into a ciphertext message by using an encryption algorithm and encryption key.

Decryption performs the reverse operation, returning a ciphertext message to the original plaintext. When Bob receives the message that Alice sent, it will initially be in the ciphertext form that resulted from Alice's encryption operation. Bob will not be able to read it any more than an eavesdropper on the Internet would have been able to read it. He must use the correct decryption key to decrypt the message from ciphertext, which will return the message to its plaintext form, as shown in Figure 12-2.

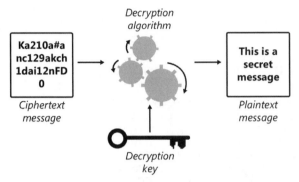

FIGURE 12-2 The decryption process converts a ciphertext message into a plaintext message by using a decryption algorithm and decryption key.

These operations are facilitated by the use of encryption and decryption *keys* possessed only by authorized individuals. You might think of an encryption key as the "password" that enables the encryption or decryption process to proceed.

> **NOTE** **SECURITY THROUGH OBSCURITY**
>
> One of the basic principles of cryptography is that the security of a cryptographic algorithm should never rely upon the secrecy of the algorithm itself. The practice of relying upon the secrecy of the algorithm, known as "security through obscurity," prevents the mathematical community from scrutinizing the security of an algorithm and discovering potentially fatal flaws in the algorithm. Instead, security professionals should use widely accepted algorithms that achieve security by relying upon the secrecy of the keys used to power the algorithm.
>
> For this same reason, security professionals should always make use of proven cryptographic technology. It is simply too mathematically complex to design your own secure encryption and decryption algorithms. Instead, you should choose proven technologies that have been widely accepted by the cryptographic community.

The encryption and decryption keys used in these operations are nothing more than long binary strings: collections of 1s and 0s. Each 0 or 1 in the string is called a bit, and the total number of 1s and 0s in the key is the *key length*, which is measured in bits. Examples of some common key lengths appear in Figure 12-3. The longer an encryption key is, the more security the cryptographic algorithm provides, because the longer key is less susceptible to a brute-force attack that simply guesses every possible key until the correct one is identified. Here are the approximate numbers of possible keys for each of the key lengths shown in Figure 12-3:

- 40-bit key: 1,099,511,627,776
- 128-bit key: 3.40 x 1038
- 1,024-bit key: 1.80 x 10308

```
01010111 00001010 10110111 00000011 00101011
```
40-bit key

```
01100010 01110011 10110000 10100001 01011010 00011000 01001011 11110100
00110111 01101100 00011111 11110100 01111100 00101110 11000010 10111110
```
128-bit key

```
10110010 01100111 01010000 00101110 00011101 10101001 11111000 00010111
10100011 00010100 10110101 01100011 01010011 01111100 10110011 11010101
01000101 11110010 11010000 00000000 01110111 10101110 10111110
01000101 11110010 11010000 11000000 01110111 10101110 10111110
11000101 00001001 01101001 11001010 11000001 10001001 10000001 01010010
01010001 11111000 00100101 00100011 10101111 01111111 00011011 11011011
01111100 00100000 01011010 11011010 11110000 01100100 00111010 00000100
11010000 01110011 10110111 00001110 11001001 00000100 01100010 00010001
11011111 11011111 11110000 11110001 10001010 10000111 00010100 01011101
01110000 01001111 11001110 11000111 01101001 01100000 00110111 10101000
10111101 11000101 11100111 01111100 00111010 00101011 10110000 10111111
01100101 01111100 11000101 00010110 10110100 01100010 10011110 11101010
10110011 00000001 00011000 11110011 10000010 10010010 11100111 11001110
10100100 11101101 10110000 10011000 01100110 11010011 11011100 10011110
11000001 10100101 11010101 01011100 11110101 11100010 01001011 10011001
10010000 00100101 01111000 10000111 10101011 01110000 10001100 01001010
11001110 11001101 01111110 01111101 00100110 11010110 00011001 11101010
```
1,024-bit key

FIGURE 12-3 Key length is a critical factor in determining the strength of an encryption operation.

You can compute the number of possible keys for a given key length *n* by using the simple formula:

2^n

Though these numbers might seem astronomical, 40-bit keys are now cryptographically insecure and vulnerable to brute-force attacks that use advanced computing hardware.

Symmetric vs. asymmetric cryptography

Cryptographic algorithms can be assigned to one of two categories based upon the keys used by the sender and recipient. In *symmetric cryptography*, both the sender and the recipient use the same key to encrypt and decrypt the message. This key, known as a shared secret key, must be securely exchanged in advance of the communication. The symmetric encryption and decryption process is shown in Figure 12-4.

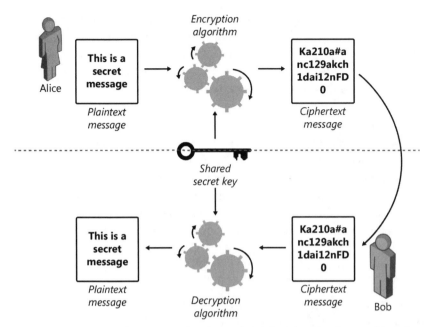

FIGURE 12-4 In symmetric cryptography, the sender and receiver use the same shared secret key.

Notice that Alice encrypts a message by using the encryption algorithm with the shared secret key to transform it into the ciphertext. When Bob receives the message, he uses the decryption algorithm, along with the same shared secret key used by Alice, to decrypt the message.

Real world

Protecting cryptographic keys

Preserving the secrecy of cryptographic keys is of paramount concern to security professionals. Anyone who gains unauthorized access to a key might be able to eavesdrop upon communications encrypted with that key and might even be able to impersonate a user of the cryptosystem. This was demonstrated clearly in 1985 when John Anthony Walker, a military cryptographer, was arrested and charged with providing cryptographic keys to the Soviet Union. Government officials believe that Walker gave the Soviets access to critical military communications that put many American lives at risk.

In *asymmetric cryptography*, on the other hand, the sender and receiver use different, but mathematically related, keys to encrypt and decrypt the message. Each participant in an asymmetric cryptosystem has a pair of mathematically related keys: a public key and a private key. The private key is preserved as a secret known only to the individual who owns the keypair. The public key is freely distributed to anyone the individual wants to communicate with. The public and private keys are related in such a fashion that anything encrypted with one key from a pair can be decrypted with the corresponding key *from the same pair*.

For example, if Alice wanted to use asymmetric cryptography to send a message to Bob, she encrypts the message with Bob's public key (see Figure 12-5). Due to the nature of asymmetric cryptography, this message can then only be decrypted with the other key from that same keypair—Bob's private key. Bob is the only person with access to that key, so the message can only be decrypted by Bob. In fact, Alice, who encrypted the message, does not have the ability to decrypt it herself because she does not have access to Bob's private key.

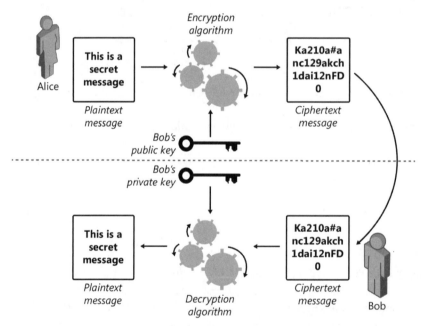

FIGURE 12-5 In asymmetric cryptography, the sender and receiver use different keys.

EXAM TIP

Students preparing for the exam are often confused by public and private keys. When you encounter a scenario like this, it might be helpful to make a quick diagram showing the keys possessed by each user. Remember, each user has only one private key (his or her own) and the public keys of every other user. You can't use a key that you don't have! Also, remember that the encryption and decryption operations must take place with different keys from the same pair (for example, Alice's public key and Alice's private key). You can't mix keys from different pairs (for example, Alice's public key and Bob's private key).

Computational complexity

Symmetric cryptography performs encryption and decryption faster than asymmetric cryptography. It takes more computing power to perform asymmetric cryptography, mainly because asymmetric cryptography requires longer key lengths to provide the same degree of security as symmetric cryptography. For this reason, in applications where speed is paramount, designers often opt for symmetric cryptography.

Scalability

Although symmetric cryptography operates faster than asymmetric cryptography, it suffers from a scalability problem. Because both the sender and recipient of a message use the same shared secret key in symmetric cryptography, providing secure communications capability between any two parties in a group requires that each pair of users have a shared secret key. As shown in Figure 12-6, the number of required keys quickly grows as the size of the group increases. Adding a new user to a group requires generating unique keys for that user to share with each existing member of the group. This isn't hard for the 4th member of a group, who only needs 3 keys, but becomes quite difficult for the 10,000th member of a group, who would need 9,999 new keys!

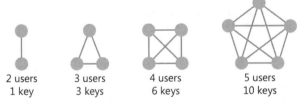

2 users   3 users   4 users   5 users
1 key   3 keys   6 keys   10 keys

FIGURE 12-6 The scalability challenge in symmetric cryptography increases with the number of users.

The number of keys required for symmetric cryptography in a group of size *n* is given by the formula:

$$\frac{n\,(n\text{-}1)}{2}$$

Asymmetric cryptography, on the other hand, only requires two keys for each group member. Adding a new member to the group requires only that you generate a public and private key for that new member. The number of keys required for asymmetric cryptography in a group of size *n* is given by the formula:

2n

Table 12-1 provides the number of keys needed for each type of algorithm with groups of various sizes. It quickly becomes apparent that symmetric cryptography is simply not scalable enough to support communication among large groups of users.

TABLE 12-1 Keys needed for different group sizes

Group size (n)	Symmetric keys needed	Asymmetric keys needed
2	1	4
3	3	6
5	10	10
10	45	20
1,000	499,500	2,000
10,000	49,995,000	20,000
100,000	4,999,950,000	200,000

> **MORE INFO**   **COMBINING SYMMETRIC AND ASYMMETRIC CRYPTOGRAPHY**
>
> Secure Sockets Layer (SSL) combines the scalability benefits of asymmetric cryptography with the speed benefits of symmetric cryptography. You'll learn more about this in the "Protecting data with encryption" section later in this chapter.

Stream and block ciphers

Cryptographic algorithms, or ciphers, can also be described by the way they operate on plaintext to convert it into ciphertext and vice-versa. Some algorithms, such as the Caesar Cipher discussed earlier in this chapter, encrypt data by operating on one unit of plaintext at a time, using mathematics to transform that unit into ciphertext. These ciphers, known as *stream ciphers*, typically operate on a single character or even a single bit at a time.

Most modern cryptographic algorithms operate on large blocks of text at a time, processing that entire block while encrypting it from plaintext into ciphertext. These algorithms are known as *block ciphers*.

One-time pads

One-time pads are a special type of cryptographic algorithm that present a unique benefit—they are the only unbreakable cipher known to exist. One-time pads function by using an extremely long shared secret key—in fact, the key must be as long as the message itself. Both the sender and recipient use this key to exchange a message.

For one-time pads to remain effective, it is critical that they only be used once. If a one-time pad is used more than once, it becomes possible to apply cryptanalytic techniques to reverse-engineer the key by identifying patterns in the encrypted text.

> **NOTE ESPIONAGE AND THE ONE-TIME PAD**.
>
> One-time pads appear often in spy novels and in real-world tales of espionage and spycraft. They are uniquely suited to this environment, where a spy might be at his or her home base, able to exchange large amounts of keying material with the spy's handler in advance. The spy can then go out into the field for long periods of time and continue operating until the key material eventually runs out.

One-time pads are clearly effective, but you might find yourself wondering, "If they are unbreakable, why doesn't everybody use them?" The answer is that it is very difficult to securely exchange one-time pad key material. After all, if you had a secure trusted channel that you could use to exchange the one-time pad, why wouldn't you just use that channel to exchange the actual messages that you wanted to send? This limits the usefulness of one-time pads to cases in which you might have physical access to your communications partner for a limited period of time when you can exchange key material that will be used for communication at a later date.

 Quick check

1. True or false: security professionals often design their own proprietary encryption algorithms and do not disclose the details of those algorithms to others to ensure the algorithm's security.

2. If Bob receives a message from Alice that she encrypted using asymmetric cryptography, what key should he use to decrypt the message into its plaintext form?

Quick check answers

1. False. This practice, known as security through obscurity, is shunned by the security community because it can prevent the discovery of fundamental flaws in the complex mathematics behind a cryptographic algorithm.

2. Bob should use his own private key to decrypt the message. If Alice encrypted it properly, she used Bob's public key to encrypt it.

Symmetric encryption algorithms

Information security professionals make use of a variety of symmetric encryption algorithms to protect the confidentiality of information both while it is in transit over insecure networks and while it is at rest in a potentially untrusted location. Users of these algorithms must select a shared secret key and find a method to share the key with both the sender and receiver of the message.

Data Encryption Standard

One of the most well-known symmetric encryption algorithms, the *Data Encryption Standard (DES)* was selected by the US Government in 1976 as the standard encryption algorithm for government applications. DES is a symmetric block cipher that uses 56-bit encryption keys to operate on 64-bit blocks of data. Though it was widely used for decades in both the public and private sectors, the cryptographic community now considers DES insecure, due to the possibility of modern computers successfully conducting a brute-force attack against the short encryption keys used by DES. The algorithm is no longer approved for use by the US government, and private-sector cryptographers should consider using a different symmetric cipher.

EXAM TIP

You might see DES referred to as having either a 56-bit or 64-bit encryption key. Both are correct. The encryption operation itself only uses 56 bits of the key, but there are an additional 8 bits used only for parity operations. Therefore, DES uses a 64-bit key, but only uses 56 bits of that key for encryption, giving it an *effective* key length of 56 bits. Watch out for this trickiness on the exam!

DES operation

DES transforms plaintext into ciphertext by performing a variety of cryptographic operations on 64-bit blocks of data. The core building block of DES is the Feistel function, shown in Figure 12-7, which operates on half-blocks of data that are 32 bits long.

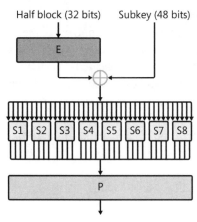

FIGURE 12-7 The DES Feistel function uses expansion, substitution, and permutation.

There are four steps taken during the Feistel function:

1. The expansion step (noted by the E-box in Figure 12-7) increases the size of the block to assist with encryption. It divides the 32-bit half-block into eight pieces of 4 bits each and then expands them by padding the left side of each block with a copy of the rightmost bit from the previous block and padding the right side of each block with a copy of the leftmost bit from the next block. For purposes of this expansion, block 8 is considered the block to the "left" of block 1, and block 1 is considered the block to the "right" of block 8. This results in an output of eight 6-bit blocks, or 48 total bits of data.

2. The second step, the XOR operation, is denoted by the $\oplus$ symbol in Figure 12-7. During this step, the 48 bits generated during the expansion step are XORed with a 48-bit subkey that is generated from the full DES encryption key. The first bit of the plaintext and the first bit of the subkey are XORed, followed by the second bits of each input, and so on until all 48 bits have been XORed. This produces a 48-bit output.

> **NOTE THE EXCLUSIVE OR (XOR) OPERATION**
>
> The Exclusive OR (XOR) operation used by the Feistel function is a common building block of cryptography. It is a binary operation, meaning that it operates on two single bits of data at a time. The output of the operation is 1 (true) if one and only one of the input bits is 1 (true). If both of the bits have the same value, either 0 (false) or 1 (true), the XOR operation's output is 0. In the key mixing stage of the Feistel function, the XOR operation takes the 48-bit subkey and the 48-bit expanded half-block of plaintext and transforms it bit by bit.

3. During the substitution phase, represented by the eight S-boxes in Figure 12-7, the XO-Red input is once again divided, into eight blocks of 6 bits each. The contents of these blocks are then changed based upon a lookup table. There are eight predefined tables, corresponding to each of the 8 S-boxes in the Feistel function. An example, the lookup table for S-box 1 (S1), appears in Figure 12-8. If the input to S1 was 100110, the lookup table removes the first and last bits (10) and uses them to find the correct row in the lookup table. The middle four bits (0011) are then used to identify the correct column. The contents of the cell at the intersection of that row and column (0100) are the 4 bits of output from that S-box. When this is repeated across the eight S-boxes, the 48 bits of input to the S-boxes shrinks to 32 bits of output.

S-Box 1 (S1)

First and Last Bit of Input	0000	0001	0010	0011	0100
00	1110	0100	1101	0001	0010
01	0000	1111	0111	0010	1110
10	0100	0001	1110	0100	1101
11	1111	1100	0100	0010	0100

First and Last Bit of Input	Middle Four Bits of Input										
	0101	0110	0111	1000	1001	1010	1011	1100	1101	1110	1111
	1111	1011	0100	0011	1010	0110	1100	0011	1001	0000	0111
	0010	1101	0001	1010	0110	1100	1011	0101	0101	0011	1000
	0110	0010	1011	1111	1100	1001	0111	0011	1010	0101	0000
	1001	0001	0111	0101	1011	0011	1110	10	0000	0110	1101

FIGURE 12-8 The S- Box 1 (S1) table used by DES provides the substitution result for all possible inputs.

4. The final operation of the Feistel function is the permutation (or rearrangement) of the bits, represented by the P-box in Figure 12-7. During this step, the bits of the S-box output are rearranged in a predefined fashion, as shown in Figure 12-9. The first bit is moved to the ninth position, the second bit is moved to the seventeenth position, and so on.

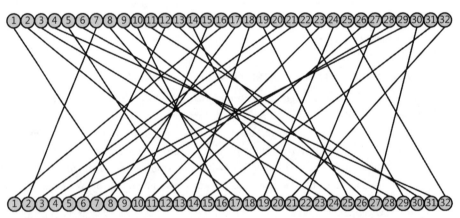

FIGURE 12-9 The permutation performed by the Feistel function is quite complex.

As you can see, the Feistel function is fairly complex, altering the input text in many ways by using the defined algorithms of DES. This function is only the building block of DES, however. As illustrated in Figure 12-10, the Feistel function is used sixteen times within a single

DES operation! Each 64-bit block of plaintext (remember, DES is a 64-bit block cipher) is divided into two half-blocks of 32 bits each. Those half blocks are then subjected to 16 rounds that consist of XORing half of the block with the output of the Feistel function applied to the other half.

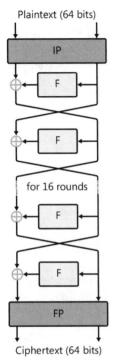

Plaintext (64 bits)

Ciphertext (64 bits)

FIGURE 12-10 The Data Encryption Standard (DES) uses the Feistel function sixteen times.

> **NOTE THE COMPLEXITY OF DES**
>
> You might want to take a moment to compare the complexity of DES to that of the Caesar Cipher discussed earlier in this chapter. The Caesar Cipher is a simple substitution cipher with only 25 possible keys, roughly equivalent in strength to a 5-bit encryption key. The eight S boxes of the Feistel function each perform substitution operations sixteen times during the execution of DES. That doesn't even consider the other operations of the Feistel function—and DES is an algorithm that isn't considered sufficiently strong today! Cryptography has certainly come a long way over the past two millennia!

The process of decryption by using DES follows exactly the same steps used for encryption. The only difference lies in the way that the subkeys are generated from the main DES key. True to the nature of a symmetric algorithm, the DES key used for encryption must be identical to the DES key used for decryption. The encryptor and decryptor of a message must have exchanged this key in advance.

Triple DES (3DES)

When cryptographers began to realize that DES was becoming cryptographically insecure, they were left in a quandary. Organizations in both government and the private sector had invested millions of dollars in hardware and software designed to work specifically with DES, and that investment was now facing obsolescence. Fortunately, cryptographers discovered that they could continue to use existing DES implementations in a secure manner by simply running data through the algorithm three times with different keys. This process became known as *Triple DES (3DES)*. Because 3DES simply uses DES multiple times, it remains a 64-bit symmetric block cipher.

Users of 3DES choose three 56-bit encryption keys, called K_1, K_2, and K_3. They then perform three steps:

1. Encrypt the plaintext by using DES with K_1.

2. Decrypt the result of step 1 by using DES with K_2.

3. Encrypt the result of step 2 by using DES with K_3.

   The output of step 3 is the ciphertext output of the 3DES algorithm.

> **NOTE DECRYPTION IN AN ENCRYPTION PROCESS?**
>
> If you looked at step 2 of the 3DES encryption process and scratched your head, don't worry! Remember that the encryption and decryption processes of DES are essentially identical. 3DES must use this decryption step to preserve backward compatibility with DES.

When the recipient of a 3DES-encrypted message wants to transform the ciphertext back into plaintext, the following process is used:

1. Decrypt the plaintext by using DES with K_3.

2. Encrypt the result of step 1 by using DES with K_2.

3. Decrypt the result of step 2 by using DES with K_1.

The user of 3DES can select the keys by using one of three approaches, each of which provides a different effective key length:

- In the most common approach, the keys are independent. K_1, K_2, and K_3 are unrelated, randomly generated 56-bit keys. This is the strongest approach, providing a key length of 168 bits (three keys of 56 bits each) that is actually reduced to an effective key strength of 112 bits due to the existence of attacks on this approach.

- In the second option, K_1 and K_2 are independent, but $K_1 = K_3$. This approach provides a key length of 112 bits (two keys of 56 bits each) that is reduced to an effective key strength of 80 bits due to existing attacks.

- In the final option, all three keys are the same: $K_1 = K_2 = K_3$. This is functionally equivalent to DES and provides the same (insecure) key length of 56 bits. It is preserved to provide backward compatibility with systems that are not able to perform 3DES.

The use of 3DES is still considered secure today by the National Institute of Standards and Technology (NIST), and it remains certified for US federal government use.

Advanced Encryption Standard

When the US federal government began to realize that DES's days were numbered, NIST announced a competition to replace it with a new encryption algorithm that would be called the *Advanced Encryption Standard (AES)*. The AES competition was open to developers around the world and, after a five-year selection process, NIST announced that the Rijndael cipher, developed by the Belgian cryptographers Vincent Rijmen and Joan Daemen, was the winner of the competition and would be the government standard moving forward.

Like DES, AES is also a symmetric block cipher that uses multiple rounds of substitution and permutation to transform plaintext into ciphertext. The major differences between DES and AES are the facts that AES uses 128-bit blocks (compared to the 64-bit blocks of DES) and allows the use of 128-bit, 192-bit, and 256-bit keys (compared to the 56-bit keys of DES).

AES is a widely used algorithm. The US federal government approves the use of any key length of AES for unclassified data and classified information at or below the Secret level. The 192-bit and 256-bit variants of AES are also approved for information classified at the Top Secret level.

Blowfish

Blowfish is a symmetric block cipher developed by Bruce Schneier that uses any key length between 32 and 448 bits to operate on 64-bit blocks of data. Like DES, Blowfish uses a 16-round Feistel function structure to perform multiple rounds of substitution by using S-boxes. Although DES uses the Feistel function shown earlier in Figure 12-7, Blowfish uses the Feistel function shown in Figure 12-11. This function relies upon four S-boxes. Unlike the DES S-boxes, the Blowfish S-boxes do not contain predefined values. Instead, the S-boxes are loaded for each encryption or decryption operation based upon the contents of the cryptographic key.

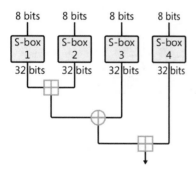

FIGURE 12-11 The Blowfish Feistel function uses four S-boxes.

Blowfish is still considered secure today, despite some known weaknesses when specific cryptographic keys are used. However, it is not as widely used as the more popular AES algorithm.

Twofish

Bruce Schneier, creator of Blowfish, later created the related *Twofish* algorithm. Like Rijndael, Twofish is a symmetric block cipher that operates on 128-bit blocks of data with either a 128-bit, 192-bit, or 256-bit key. There is a reason for this similarity, because Twofish was one of the algorithms that lost to Rijndael during NIST's AES competition. The algorithm used by Twofish, shown in Figure 12-12, bears similarities to Blowfish in that it uses S-boxes derived from the encryption key and a 16-round Feistel structure.

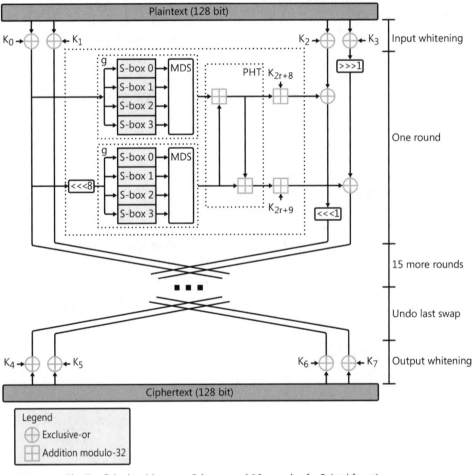

FIGURE 12-12 The Twofish algorithm uses S-boxes and 16 rounds of a Feistel function.

RC4

RC4 is a symmetric stream cipher developed by Ron Rivest of RSA Security. The name is believed to refer to the creator, representing either "Rivest Cipher 4" or "Ron's Code 4." RC4 uses a key length ranging between 40 and 256 bits and uses that key to create a pseudorandom keystream of unlimited length. The keystream is then XORed with the plaintext input to create RC4's ciphertext output.

RC4 is widely used in many network-based cryptographic implementations because of the fact that it is a stream cipher and is able to operate quickly and with continuous variable-length data segments. RC4 forms the basis of the Wired Equivalent Privacy (WEP) wireless encryption protocol (now considered insecure), as well as one form of the more secure Wi-Fi Protected Access (WPA) wireless security algorithm. RC4 is also used in the Transport Layer Security (TLS) algorithm used to protect web traffic and other network communications.

> **MORE INFO**   **APPLICATIONS OF RC4**
>
> For more information on the use of WEP and WPA encryption to secure wireless networks, see Chapter 3, "Secure network design and management." A discussion of TLS (and its predecessor, SSL) appears in the "Protecting data with encryption" section later in this chapter.

 Quick check

1. What modification to the DES algorithm allows for the reuse of DES implementations in a secure fashion?

2. What algorithm won the AES competition and replaced DES as the government encryption standard?

Quick check answers

1. DES can be used three times with different encryption keys, in a modification known as Triple DES (3DES).

2. NIST selected the Rijndael algorithm as the Advanced Encryption Standard.

Asymmetric encryption algorithms

Though symmetric algorithms offer high-speed confidentiality, they have several shortcomings, including the requirement for advance distribution of preshared keys, a lack of scalability, and a failure to provide nonrepudiation benefits. The more computationally expensive asymmetric algorithms step in to fill these gaps, providing enhanced security benefits, albeit at a greater cost.

Rivest, Shamir, and Adelman (RSA)

The first, and most well-known, asymmetric algorithm was invented by Ron Rivest (the same Rivest who invented RC4), Adi Shamir, and Leonard Adleman at the Massachusetts Institute of Technology in 1977. The algorithm, named *RSA* after its creators, uses a key length ranging from 1,024 to 4,096 bits.

> **IMPORTANT   COMPARING KEY LENGTHS**
>
> Though you may be tempted to compare the massive 1,024-bit minimum key length of RSA to the smaller 256-bit maximum of AES, resist the urge. Remember that asymmetric algorithms require much longer keys to achieve the same level of security provided by symmetric algorithms. It is not meaningful to directly compare key lengths when different algorithms are used.

As with any asymmetric algorithm, the complexity of RSA lies in finding an appropriate method to generate mathematically related, but secure, public and private keypairs. RSA does this by relying upon the difficulty of factoring the products of large prime numbers. The algorithm itself is still considered secure today.

Pretty Good Privacy (PGP)

The *Pretty Good Privacy (PGP)* algorithm combines the use of symmetric and asymmetric cryptography. The process used to encrypt a message by using PGP, as illustrated in Figure 12-13, uses the following steps:

1. The sender of the message chooses a randomly generated symmetric encryption key.

2. The sender encrypts the message by using the symmetric encryption key and a symmetric algorithm of the sender's choice.

3. The sender encrypts the randomly generated symmetric encryption key with the recipient's public key, using an asymmetric algorithm of the sender's choice.

4. The sender transmits the encrypted message from step 2 and the encrypted key from step 3 to the recipient.

When the recipient receives the message, he or she follows the process shown in Figure 12-14 to decrypt the message:

1. The recipient decrypts the encrypted key by using the recipient's private key. The recipient now has the randomly generated symmetric encryption key chosen by the sender.

2. The recipient decrypts the message by using the symmetric key.

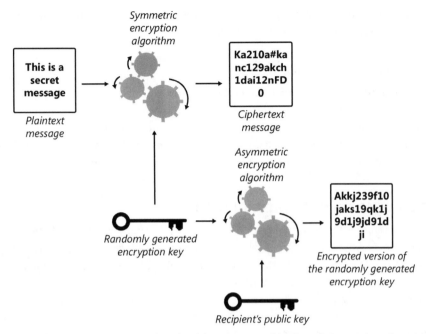

FIGURE 12-13 The PGP encryption algorithm uses a combination of symmetric and asymmetric cryptography.

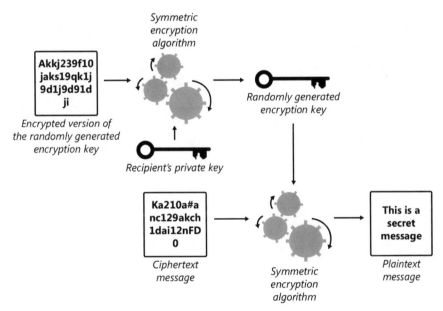

FIGURE 12-14 The PGP decryption algorithm also uses a combination of symmetric and asymmetric cryptography.

The GNU Privacy Guard (GPG) package is an open-source implementation of the PGP algorithm that is released to the public under the GNU Public License.

> **NOTE   QUANTUM CRYPTOGRAPHY**
>
> Another solution to the key distribution problem addressed by asymmetric cryptography is the use of quantum mechanics. In a technique known as Quantum Key Distribution (QKD), quantum mechanics can be used by two parties to exchange a symmetric encryption key. Cryptographers also believe that quantum computing might have other uses in cryptography, but no such applications have yet been made commercially available.

Elliptic curve cryptography (ECC)

In 1985, cryptographers Neal Koblitz and Victor Miller each independently published papers describing a new asymmetric cryptography technique known as *elliptic curve cryptography (ECC)*. Whereas RSA depends upon the difficulty of factoring the products of large prime numbers to create mathematically related keypairs, ECC depends upon the difficulty of finding the discrete logarithm of an elliptic curve. ECC-based algorithms are available for use in SSL, TLS, Secure Shell (SSH), and other cryptographic applications. ECC has low power requirements and is therefore commonly found in wireless devices.

 Quick check

1. What is the minimum key length used by the RSA asymmetric cryptographic algorithm?

2. True or false: PGP uses both symmetric and asymmetric cryptography.

Quick check answers

1. The minimum key length for RSA encryption is 1,024 bits.

2. True. PGP uses both symmetric and asymmetric encryption algorithms.

Digital signatures

Digital signatures provide an electronic alternative to the manual process of affixing a signature to a document. The sender of a message can digitally sign it to provide the recipient with the following assurances:

- The message came from the purported sender.

- The message has not been altered since the sender signed it.

- The recipient will be able to prove the above two facts to any arbitrary third party (nonrepudiation).

Digital signatures depend on asymmetric cryptography and, in practice, hash functions to create signed message digests.

Cryptographic hashes

 A *hash* function is a mathematical function that takes a variable-length input and translates it into a fixed-length output in a manner that is collision-resistant. The hash function should be constructed so that it meets several criteria:

- Any change in the input, no matter how minor, produces a completely different output.

- It is computationally infeasible to retrieve the message that was fed into a hash function from the output. That is, the hash function is irreversible.

- It is computationally infeasible to find two different inputs that produce the same hash output.

An example of applying the Message Digest 5 (MD5) hash function to three slightly different messages appears in Figure 12-15. Notice that even minor changes in punctuation result in completely different hash values.

> **MORE INFO   COMPUTING MESSAGE DIGESTS**
>
> You can try your own hand at computing hash values. As an example, try using the MD5 hash generator found at *http://www.md5.net*. You can type in the same input values shown in Figure 12-15, and you will receive the same output values. Be sure to type the input messages exactly the way they appear in Figure 12-15!

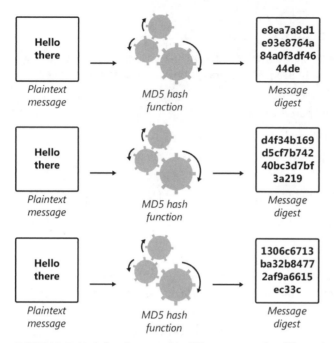

FIGURE 12-15 Hash functions provide different output for different inputs.

There are many hash functions available that produce a message digest from a variable-length input. Some common hash functions include:

- **Message Digest 5 (MD5)** A cryptographic hash function developed by Ronald Rivest that produces a 128-bit message digest. Although it is widely used, MD5 is considered cryptographically insecure and should no longer be used.

- **RACE Integrity Primitives Evaluation Message Digest (RIPEMD)** A cryptographic hash function available in different versions that produce 128-bit, 160-bit, 256-bit, and 320-bit message digests.

- **Secure Hash Algorithm v1 (SHA-1)** A cryptographic hash function designed by the US National Security Agency that produces a 160-bit message digest. SHA-1 is now considered insecure and should no longer be used.

- **Secure Hash Algorithm v2 (SHA-2)** A cryptographic hash function designed by the US National Security Agency and published in 1995 as a replacement for SHA-1. SHA-2 can produce hashes of 224, 256, 384 or 512 bits. SHA-2 is still considered secure.

- **Secure Hash Algorithm v3 (SHA-3)** A cryptographic hash function that was selected as the winner of a 2012 NIST competition to create a new hash function. As of this writing in April 2013, the SHA-3 standard was still in draft form.

- **Hash-based message authentication code (HMAC)** Technology that combines the use of hash functions and a symmetric key to provide the recipient of a message with assurance that the message came from the purported sender and was not altered in transit.

> **IMPORTANT** **HMAC VS. DIGITAL SIGNATURES**
>
> Though HMAC uses cryptography and hash functions to ensure integrity and authentication, it is important to recognize that it does *not* provide nonrepudiation, because it depends upon symmetric cryptography. The purported recipient of a message could forge the message because both the sender and recipient have access to the shared secret key. To provide nonrepudiation, the sender must apply a digital signature, as described in the next section.

Creating digital signatures

 Digital signatures depend upon one of the properties of asymmetric algorithms—that anything encrypted with one key from a keypair can be decrypted with the other key from that pair.

Earlier in this chapter, when we discussed the use of asymmetric cryptography for confidentiality, the sender of the message used the recipient's public key to encrypt the message so that it required the recipient's private key (known only to the recipient) to decrypt. With digital signatures, there is a different objective—you want to create something that only you could create and that anybody can verify. This requires using the sender's *private* key to create the digital signature, which anybody can then verify with the sender's public key.

Here's the process for creating a digital signature:

1. The sender and receiver agree upon a hash function that they will use to create a message digest.

2. The sender of the message uses the agreed-upon hash function to create a message digest of the message.

3. The sender of the message encrypts the message digest with the sender's private key to create a digital signature.

4. The sender attaches the digital signature to the message and sends it to the recipient.

> **IMPORTANT** **DIGITAL SIGNATURES *DON'T* PROVIDE CONFIDENTIALITY**
>
> Remember, digital signatures provide authentication, integrity, and nonrepudiation, but they do *not* provide confidentiality. If you also want a message to remain secret, you must also encrypt it by using the process described earlier in this chapter.

The process of creating a digital signature is illustrated in Figure 12-16.

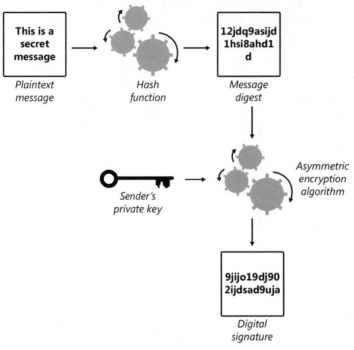

FIGURE 12-16 The creation of a digital signature uses asymmetric encryption and a hash function.

When the recipient of the message (or anyone else) wants to verify the digital signature, the recipient follows this process:

1. Using the same hash function selected by the sender, the recipient creates a message digest from the plaintext message.

2. The recipient decrypts the digital signature by using the sender's public key to obtain the message digest computed by the sender.

3. The recipient compares the message digests generated by steps 1 and 2. If they match, the message is authentic.

The process used to verify a digital signature is illustrated in Figure 12-17.

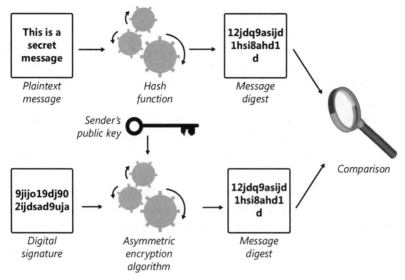

FIGURE 12-17 Verifying a digital signature requires two iterations of hashing.

It is very important to note that the only real conclusion you can draw from the digital signature process is that a message is authentic if the two digests match. If the digests do not match, you don't know what has gone wrong. The digital signature might be forged, the message might have been intentionally tampered with, or the message might have been inadvertently altered in transit. You also can't tell how "close" the message is to the authentic message because of the properties of hash functions illustrated earlier in Figure 12-15.

 Quick check

1. True or false: messages processed through the hash-based message authentication code (HMAC) algorithm provide the recipient with nonrepudiation.

2. What key does the sender of a message use to encrypt the message digest and create a digital signature?

Quick check answers

1. False

2. The sender's private key

Public-key infrastructure

Asymmetric cryptography removes some of the burden of key management by reducing the number of keys needed for a group of people to communicate. Further, it allows the free distribution of public keys by removing any sensitive information from the public key. However, one problem remains: if I don't know you personally, how can I be sure that the public key you are presenting to me is actually yours? In other words, how can I verify that you are who you claim to be? An imposter could easily create a public/private keypair and send it to me purporting to be you, and I would have no way to differentiate your legitimate public key from that of the imposter.

Digital certificates solve this problem by introducing the use of certificate authorities. In this trust model, users rely upon trusted third parties, known as certificate authorities (CAs), to verify the identity of individuals and servers before issuing them a signed copy of their public key, known as a digital certificate.

Digital certificates

Digital certificates serve as a secure method to exchange public encryption keys between individuals and entities previously unknown to each other through the use of a trusted third party known as a certificate authority (CA). If both parties trust the CA, they can rely upon the CA's assertion that the public key belongs to the other party. The main purpose of a digital certificate is to transmit a copy of a public key that has been digitally signed by a certificate authority.

You might liken the online use of a digital certificate to the offline use of a driver's license to verify identity. When two people want to assure each other of their identities in person, they might examine each others driver's licenses. By verifying that the photo on the license matches the person in front of them, they have a reasonable degree of assurance that the motor vehicles department has verified the person's identity as the individual whose name appears on the license.

Digital certificates are governed by the International Telecommunication Union (ITU) X.509 standard and contain the following standard fields:

- **Certificate subject**   The identity of the person or entity associated with the public key contained within the certificate.

- **Certificate issuer**   The identity of the certificate authority that issued the certificate to the subject.

- **Serial number**   A unique identification number assigned to the digital certificate by the CA.

- **Public key**   The public encryption key corresponding to the certificate subject. This is the main payload of the digital certificate.

- **Validity period**   The start date and end date of the certificate's useful life.

- **Signature algorithm**   The identity of the asymmetric encryption algorithm used by the CA to sign the digital certificate.

- **Digital signature**   The digital signature of the CA.

By signing a digital certificate, the certificate authority is attesting that, to the best of its knowledge, the subject is indeed associated with the public key contained within the certificate. The CA might rely upon the services of a registration authority (RA) to actually perform the identity verification and authorize the issuance of the digital certificate to the subject.

Figure 12-18 shows an example of a digital certificate used to secure a portion of a Microsoft website. The portion of the certificate shown in the figure includes the public key of the Microsoft web server and the digital signature of VeriSign, the certificate authority that issued the certificate to Microsoft after verifying that the requester was a legitimate, authorized representative of Microsoft Corporation.

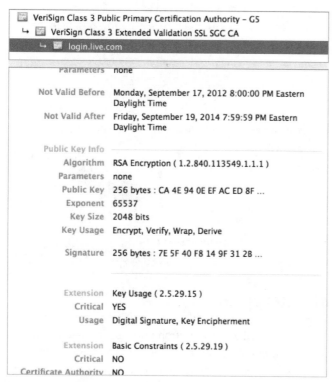

FIGURE 12-18 Web browsers allow users to display the contents of a digital certificate.

Certificate revocation lists

In some circumstances, a CA must revoke a digital certificate prior to its expiration. This might occur if a digital certificate is issued in error, if the private key corresponding to the certificate is compromised, or if similar circumstances occur. When the CA wants to revoke a certificate, it places the certificate's serial number on the CA's certificate revocation list (CRL). All users of digital certificates should check a certificate's serial number against the CRL before accepting the certificate as valid.

Key recovery and key escrow

Encryption is a powerful tool used to protect information from prying eyes. However, in the event that the decryption key is lost, it can also render the data inaccessible to authorized users—clearly an undesirable state! For this reason, cryptosystems should include provisions for key recovery by authorized recovery agents. In those cases, copies of the keys are backed up to an organization's centralized server and administrators have the ability to use the recovery agent to retrieve a key when necessary.

Key escrow uses similar technology to provide third parties with access to encrypted information. Although key recovery is a standard business practice, key escrow has been the subject of much controversy because of the desire of law enforcement and other government officials to use this technology to gain access to encrypted communications.

 Quick check

1. What key is used by a certificate authority to create the digital signature that appears within a digital certificate?

2. What is the main purpose of a digital certificate?

Quick check answers

1. The CA's private key

2. To securely exchange a user's public key with other parties.

Protecting data with encryption

The preceding sections of this chapter provided you with a strong base of knowledge about cryptographic technology and the application of encryption to messages. In this section, we examine the use of encryption technology to protect data stored on computer systems (data "at rest") and data being transmitted over a network (data "in motion").

Encrypting data at rest

Sensitive data should be encrypted while it is stored on a computer system and not in use, toprotect it from prying eyes. Unauthorized access might result when an individual gains access to data without the necessary permission. This might occur when a device is discovered in a recycling bin, a mobile device is lost or stolen, or any of a number of other circumstances. There are two ways in which security professionals can protect data at rest: by encrypting individual files or encrypting entire disk volumes.

File encryption

File encryption applies the same principles discussed in this chapter to protecting individual files stored on a computer system. File encryption normally (but not necessarily) uses a symmetric encryption algorithm, such as 3DES or AES, and encrypts files with a shared secret key. One of the main benefits of file encryption is that it survives moves of the file. If the file is copied to another drive, attached to an email message, or transmitted in any other fashion, the encryption remains in place, making the move from data at rest to data in motion.

Users can take advantage of many different encryption programs to provide file encryption. Figure 12-19 shows an example of using WinZIP to add an encrypted file to a ZIP archive.

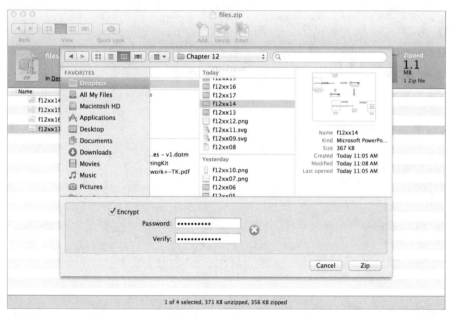

FIGURE 12-19 WinZIP can be used to implement file encryption.

Whole-disk encryption

Whole-disk encryption applies encryption technology to entire disk volumes. When a user logs onto a computer, the operating system gains access to the encryption key and provides the user with access to files on the encrypted volume transparently. However, if an unauthorized user tries to access the contents of the disk, that user will not be able to view the encrypted data. This technology is especially useful to protect the hard drives of laptops and other devices that are susceptible to loss or theft. When a file is copied from a volume encrypted with whole-disk encryption to another location that is not similarly protected, the encryption is lost.

Whole-disk encryption technology is built in to many modern operating systems. Windows users have access to Microsoft's BitLocker technology, and Macintosh users can take advantage of the FileVault technology of Mac OS X. Figure 12-20 shows an example of a user turning on FileVault encryption for a Mac disk volume.

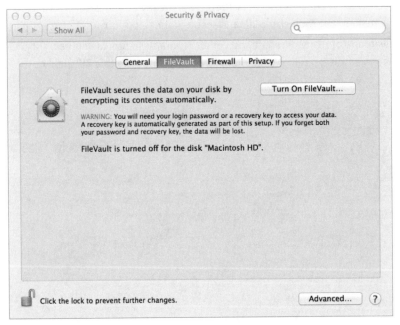

FIGURE 12-20 Mac users can use FileVault to implement whole-disk encryption.

> **NOTE STEGANOGRAPHY**
>
> Steganography is an alternative method of hiding data by storing it within the contents of another file. Steganography is often used to hide data within images that can then be posted to websites and other open forums without disclosing that they contain hidden information. Steganography is commonly thought to be a tool used by many unethical individuals, such as terrorists and child pornographers.

Encrypting data in motion

Transport encryption technology applies the principles of encryption to data that is in motion on a network. Security professionals have a variety of protocols at their disposal to assist in enhancing commonly used applications with the benefits of symmetric and asymmetric encryption technologies.

SSL and TLS

Secure Sockets Layer (SSL) is the most well-known application of encryption technology to transport-layer protocols. It uses a combination of symmetric and asymmetric encryption to provide confidentiality, integrity, and authentication. SSL is now outdated and has been replaced with a newer protocol called *Transport Layer Security (TLS)*, but both protocols are still commonly referred to as "SSL" by many IT professionals.

SSL and TLS can be used to protect any type of network communications, but they are best known for their application to web traffic through the use of Hypertext Transfer Protocol Secure (HTTPS), which applies SSL/TLS to the HTTP protocol.

When a user wants to establish a secure connection to a website by using HTTPS, the web browser initiates the following process:

1. The web browser initiates a connection request to the web server, noting that a secure connection is desired.

2. The web server responds with a copy of the server's digital certificate.

3. The client uses the public key of the certificate's issuing CA to verify that the digital certificate is authentic.

4. The client creates a symmetric encryption key that will be used for the remainder of the session. This key is known as the session key.

5. The client encrypts the session key with the public key of the server found in the digital certificate.

6. The client sends the encrypted session key to the server.

7. The server decrypts the encrypted session key with the server's private key.

8. The client and the server use the session key to continue the communication by using symmetric cryptography.

This process ensures that all of the communications between the client and server are encrypted and protected from eavesdropping while in transit over the Internet.

SSH

The Secure Shell protocol (SSH) provides administrators with the ability to establish an en-crypted terminal connection to a remote system. Unlike SSL, the SSH protocol usually uses public/private keypairs generated by the users of SSH instead of digital certificates. This means that users must trust the identity of the server based upon some other means, such as manually receiving a copy of the server key.

IPsec

The *Internet Protocol Security (IPsec)* suite of protocols uses cryptography to secure IP-based network communications. It consists of three major components:

- **Authentication Headers (AHs)**   These ensure that the origin of packets is authenti-cated and that the packets themselves have not been modified.
- **Encapsulating Security Payloads (ESPs)**   These provide confidentiality, integrity, and verification of the origin of packets.
- **Security Associations (SAs)**   These provide the key exchange and encryption al-gorithm pairings necessary for systems to negotiate a common set of protocols to be used during encrypted communication.

> **MORE INFO   IPSEC**
>
> More information on the implementation of IPsec can be found in Chapter 3.

IPsec is commonly used to establish virtual private network (VPN) connections between remote networks. It is application-agnostic, meaning that it can carry the network traffic as-sociated with any application without the application's knowledge or cooperation.

 Quick check

1. What are the three main components that make up IPsec?
2. What does the server provide to the client to convey its public key during TLS communication?

Quick check answers

1. The three major components of IPsec are Authentication Headers, Encapsulating Security Payloads, and Security Associations.
2. Digital certificates are used to provide authenticated copies of a server's public key.

Authentication

Cryptography can also be used to secure the password-based authentication process used by many systems. Over the years, IT professionals have designed (and sometimes abandoned!) several protocols that serve this purpose:

- The *Password Authentication Protocol (PAP)* was the earliest attempt to provide password-based authentication over a network. The main issue with PAP is that it uses *no* encryption! Anyone eavesdropping on a PAP-based authentication session is able to see the password sent in the clear!

- The *Challenge Handshake Authentication Protocol (CHAP)* addresses the weaknesses of PAP by introducing the use of encryption through a three-way handshake. When a client attempts to connect to a server, the server sends the client a challenge message. The client then computes a hash value for the challenge and password combined, and sends this hash to the server. The server evaluates the client's response and, if it matches the password in the database, the user is authenticated. This protocol is still considered secure.

- The *Microsoft Challenge Handshake Authentication Protocol (MS-CHAP)* is a proprietary version of the CHAP protocol that is no longer considered secure and should not be used because there are multiple known attacks against it.

- Microsoft also developed the *NT LAN Manager (NTLM)* protocol, which used a 128-bit MD4 hash value to protect the password. NTLM was upgraded to the use of a HMAC-MD5 hash containing the user name and server identity with the release of NTLMv2.

Users should be aware that Microsoft no longer recommends the use of MS-CHAP or NTLM to secure authentication sessions.

 Quick check

1. What is the major issue with the use of the PAP protocol?

2. Which protocol is more secure: CHAP or MS-CHAP?

Quick check answers

1. Passwords are sent in unencrypted form.

2. CHAP is more secure than MS-CHAP because there are multiple known attacks that undermine MS-CHAP's security.

Chapter summary

- The four main goals of cryptography are confidentiality, integrity, authentication, and nonrepudiation.

- Encryption is the process of converting plaintext into ciphertext so that it cannot be read by unauthorized individuals. Decryption performs the reverse process of converting ciphertext back into the original plaintext.

- The key length used with an encryption algorithm is a critical determiner of the level of security. The longer the encryption key, the more secure the encryption will be.

- In symmetric encryption algorithms, both the sender and recipient use the same shared secret key for encryption and decryption. Examples of symmetric encryption algorithms include 3DES, AES, Blowfish, and Twofish.

- In asymmetric cryptography, each participant has a public and private key. Messages encrypted with one key from a pair can be decrypted with the other key from that pair. RSA and ECC are commonly used asymmetric encryption techniques.

- Digital signatures combine hash functions with asymmetric cryptography to provide the recipient of a message with nonrepudiation: the ability to prove that a message originated with the purported sender.

- Digital certificates are digitally signed copies of public keys issued by certificate authorities (CAs) to individuals and entities. CAs maintain a list of revoked certificates known as the certificate revocation list (CRL).

- File encryption technology is used to protect the contents of individual files and applies even when a file is copied or transmitted via email. Whole-disk encryption protects the entire contents of a disk volume, but the encryption does not survive the file being copied off the encrypted volume.

- Transport Layer Security (TLS) and the older Secure Sockets Layer (SSL) can be used to add encryption to application-layer protocols. SSL and TLS combine the use of asymmetric cryptography, facilitated by digital certificates, with symmetric cryptography.

- The Internet Protocol Security (IPsec) protocol suite adds cryptographic capability to any IP-based network communication. IPsec consists of three components: authentication headers (AHs), encapsulating security payloads (ESPs) and security associations (SAs).

Chapter review

Test your knowledge of the information in Chapter 12 by answering these questions. The answers to these questions, and the explanations of why each answer choice is correct or incorrect, are located in the "Answers" section at the end of this chapter.

1. Matthew is preparing a purchase order system for his company and wants to use cryptographic technology that would allow the company to prove in court that the originator of a purchase order actually created the order and that it was not forged. What goal of cryptography is Matthew trying to achieve?

    A. Nonrepudiation

    B. Confidentiality

    C. Authentication

    D. Integrity

2. Alice would like to send a message to Bob by using asymmetric cryptography. She wants to ensure that only Bob is able to decrypt the message. What key should she use for the encryption?

    A. Alice's public key

    B. Bob's public key

    C. Alice's private key

    D. Bob's private key

3. Jim is planning an encryption system to protect sensitive data in his organization. He would like to use the Advanced Encryption Standard (AES) and is considering the best key length to use. Which one of the following is *not* an acceptable key length supported by AES?

    A. 128 bits

    B. 192 bits

    C. 256 bits

    D. 512 bits

4. Christopher received a message from Richard that contains a digital signature. When Christopher wants to verify the digital signature, what key should he use to decrypt it?

    A. Christopher's public key

    B. Christopher's private key

    C. Richard's public key

    D. Richard's private key

5. Darcy would like to create a digital certificate to enable TLS encryption on her website. What type of organization must she contact to obtain a valid digital certificate that will be automatically accepted by the web browsers of her users?

   A. SSH

   B. ESP

   C. CRL

   D. CA

6. Ryan is selecting an authentication protocol to secure client/server communications on his network. Which one of the following protocols is best suited to provide this security?

   A. MS-CHAP

   B. PAP

   C. CHAP

   D. NTLMv1

Answers

This section contains the answers to the questions for the "Chapter review" section in this chapter.

1. **Correct Answer: A**

   A. **Correct:** Nonrepudiation, which can be achieved through the use of digital signatures, would allow Matthew to prove to a third party that the originator of a purchase order actually created the order.

   B. **Incorrect:** Confidentiality can be used to protect the contents of a message from view, but it would not prevent the sender from later denying that he or she created it.

   C. **Incorrect:** Integrity can be used to ensure that the message sent by the sender was correctly received, but it would not prevent the sender from later denying that he or she created it.

   D. **Incorrect:** Authentication can be used to prove the identity of the sender to the recipient, but it does not allow the recipient to prove the sender's identity to a third party.

2. **Correct Answer: B**

   A. **Incorrect:** If Alice encrypts the message with her own public key, it could only be decrypted with Alice's private key, which only Alice knows.

   B. **Correct:** If Alice encrypts the message with Bob's public key, it could only be decrypted with Bob's private key, which only Bob knows.

   C. **Incorrect:** If Alice encrypts the message with her own private key, it can be decrypted with her public key, which is generally known.

   D. **Incorrect:** If Alice encrypts the message with Bob's private key, it can be decrypted with his public key, which is generally known.

3. **Correct Answer: D**

   A. **Incorrect:** AES supports the use of a 128-bit key. Users can also choose a 192-bit or 256-bit key.

   B. **Incorrect:** AES supports the use of a 192-bit key. Users can also choose a 128-bit or 256-bit key.

   C. **Incorrect:** AES supports the use of a 256-bit key. Users can also choose a 128-bit or 192-bit key.

   D. **Correct:** AES does not support the use of a 512-bit key. The maximum key length for AES is 256 bits.

4. **Correct Answer: C**

   A. **Incorrect:** To verify a digital signature, the recipient of a message must use the sender's public key. Christopher's public key would be used by individuals seeking to send Christopher an encrypted message.

   B. **Incorrect:** To verify a digital signature, the recipient of a message must use the sender's public key. Christopher would use his private key to decrypt a message sent privately to him.

   C. **Correct:** To verify a digital signature, the recipient of a message must use the sender's public key. In this case, Christopher would use Richard's public key to verify Richard's signature.

   D. **Incorrect:** To verify a digital signature, the recipient of a message must use the sender's public key. Richard would use his own private key to create the signature, but Christopher would use Richard's public key to verify it.

5. **Correct Answer: D**

   A. **Incorrect:** The Secure Shell (SSH) protocol allows encrypted administrative connections to servers.

   B. **Incorrect:** The Encapsulating Security Payload (ESP) is a protocol used to encrypt the contents of packets in IPsec communications.

   C. **Incorrect:** The certificate revocation list (CRL) is a list of certificates issued by a CA that are no longer valid.

   D. **Correct:** Certificate authorities (CAs) are responsible for issuing digital certificates to individuals and organizations.

6. **Correct Answer: C**

   A. **Incorrect:** The Microsoft Challenge Handshake Authentication Protocol (MS-CHAP) is an authentication protocol developed by Microsoft that is no longer considered secure.

   B. **Incorrect:** The Password Authentication Protocol (PAP) sends passwords via cleartext and should never be used.

   C. **Correct:** The Challenge Handshake Authentication Protocol (CHAP) provides a secure means for password authentication.

   D. **Incorrect:** The NT LAN Manager (NTLM v1) protocol is no longer considered secure.

Glossary

Numbers

802.1x A standard for port-based network access control that authenticates users before allowing them access to the network.

A

access control list A list of which IP addresses and networks are allowed to send data via specific ports. Often deployed on routers, gateways, and sometimes on switches.

access list A list of allowed users for an area or facility.

access log A log file that tracks access to systems, directories, files, or resources.

Active Directory Domain Services A directory service used by Windows domains that provides authentication and authorization services as well as security policy enforcement.

address space layout randomization (ASLR) A mechanism used to randomize the memory locations of core system components during their initial loading phase at startup.

Advanced Encryption Standard (AES) The symmetric block cipher approved by the US government as a replacement for DES. AES uses 128-bit, 192-bit, and 256-bit keys to operate on 128-bit blocks of data.

advanced persistent threat (APT) A term used to describe a new type of threat created by long-term, talented attackers who specifically target organizations. Often characterized by their deployment of increasingly sophisticated malware to retain access to their target.

adware A type of malware that displays ads.

alarm A warning that a dangerous condition exists. An alarm is more important than an alert.

alert A signal that draws attention to something. Alerts might indicate a trend, an issue, or simply provide notice that a condition has been met.

all-in-one security appliance Sometimes called a unified threat management (UTM) device, an appliance that combines firewall, IDS or IPS, antimalware, anti-spam, and other security tools into a single device.

annualized loss expectancy (ALE) A quantitative measure of a risk that identifies the expected financial loss from a risk each year.

annualized rate of occurrence (ARO) The number of times per year that a risk is expected to materialize.

anti-malware product Any technology used to detect and remote malicious code as well as prevent initial infection; this includes anti-virus, anti-spam, and anti-spyware products; pop-up blockers, and host-based firewalls.

anti-spam product A security filter focusing on unwanted messages.

anti-spyware product A security scanner similar to an anti-virus product but that focuses on tracking, keystroke logging, or other forms of data-gathering types of software.

anti-virus product A software technology that aims at detecting, removing, and blocking a wide range of malicious software.

application-layer firewall A type of firewall that is able to process application data, filtering traffic based on protocols and application-specific requirements.

architecture review A review of the layout and design of a system, network, or service to determine if it has vulnerabilities.

asset value (AV) The value (normally in dollars) assigned to an asset by the organization.

asymmetric cryptography Cryptography that uses an algorithm in which the sender and receiver use different, but mathematically related, keys for the encryption and decryption operations.

attack surface The sum of the exposure of an organization, system, or application to attack.

audit log A log that contains audit information such as user access to files. Audit logs can be collected for any event or action that has an audit requirement.

authentication A process that provides the ability to confirm the claimed identity of an individual or system by presenting evidence of that identity.

authorization The process of providing access rights to resources on a system.

availability The ability of authorized users to gain legitimate access to information.

B

backdoor Malware that provides access to a system or application. Some backdoors are created by the legitimate organization that builds the software or application to provide access to themselves or for emergencies.

baseline A security tool used to ensure consistency in deployment across an organization. Every new system must be constructed and configured in compliance with the baseline before it is installed into production

baseline reporting A report that compares the current state of an asset to the baseline security configuration that it is expected to have.

biometrics A method that identifies users by their physical traits, such as fingerprints, iris or retina patterns, voice print, or hand geometry. This is often referred to as "something you are."

BIOS The firmware of a motherboard.

black box penetration testing Also known as a zero-knowledge penetration test, a test that provides no information about the subject of the test to the penetration tester.

block cipher A cryptographic algorithm that operates on large blocks of text, a block at a time.

Blowfish A symmetric block cipher developed by Bruce Schneier that operates on 64-bit blocks with a key size between 32 and 448 bits.

bot An infected, remote-controlled system. Often called a zombie, and typically part of a botnet.

botnet A group of malware-infected, remote-controlled systems with a shared command and control system.

bottleneck A limiting factor to gaining greater throughput or production work accomplished.

buffer overflow A specific type of exploit that takes advantage of poor input management on the part of a software application's programmers. Because the programmers failed to limit how much input is accepted and stored into memory, hackers are able to inject sufficient data to exploit execution functions, allowing them to arbitrarily run their own code.

business continuity The practice of designing systems and business processes so that they can continue uninterrupted in the face of a human-made or natural disaster.

business impact assessment (BIA) A risk assessment designed to identify the risks that might disrupt business operations and prioritize those risks based upon their likelihood of occurrence and potential impact.

BYOD (bring your own device) A company policy that allows workers to bring in their own mobile devices and use them to connect into the company's network. Some BYOD policies specify the minimum security feature requirements that users must follow in order to use their own devices on or with the company's IT infrastructure.

C

cable lock A locking mechanism on the end of a reinforced tethering cable used to secure portable devices and other equipment.

canonicalization An attack that uses how characters and data are encoded to avoid filters.

chain of custody A documented paper trail containing details surrounding the collection of a piece of evidence, identifying every individual who came into contact with the evidence after collection and documenting evidence storage locations.

Challenge Handshake Authentication Protocol (CHAP) A secure cryptographic protocol used for password authentication over a network.

Classless Inter-Domain Routing (CIDR) A method used to allocate IP addresses; allows any bit boundary to be used, rather than the 8-bit boundaries used in classful network design.

clustered server Two or more servers performing the same function. In the event that one server fails, the other server or servers in the cluster simply carry the load that would normally be carried by the failed server.

code review A vulnerability assessment methodology that requires analysis of the source code of a program or application. Such reviews can identify both vulnerabilities in the code and logic errors.

cold boot attack An attack in which the RAM chips are supercooled to slow down the rate of data decay in order to facilitate the capture of an encryption key.

command injection An attack that attempts to insert system commands into applications and scripts.

confidentiality The protection of sensitive information against unauthorized access.

configuration baseline A basic set of settings required for systems.

content inspection A network filtering capability that inspects network traffic. Deep content inspection allows inspection of entire files and network traffic streams.

continuous security monitoring The process of using tools and human intelligence to watch over a secure environment on an ongoing basis.

cookie A file left by a website that contains user and application data.

crossover error rate A biometric concept, the CER is the point on a graph at which the false acceptance rate (FAR) and false rejection rate (FRR) are equal. This is often used to compare biometric devices. The system with a lower CER is typically more desirable.

cross-site request forgery (XSRF) An attack that takes advantage of a server's trust in an authenticated user account or user's system.

cross-site scripting An attack that exploits a user's trust in a website by using client-side scripts inserted into webpages viewed by users who browse to the page where the script resides to perform arbitrary actions.

cryptography The art and science of transmitting information securely in the presence of untrusted individuals.

D

data encryption A key technology in preventing unauthorized disclosure of information, as well as preventing corruption or intentional integrity changes.

Data Encryption Standard (DES) A symmetric block cipher formerly used by the US government that uses 56-bit encryption keys to operate on 64-bit blocks of data. DES is no longer considered secure.

data execution prevention (DEP) A security mechanism used to protect against arbitrary code being executed from random locations in memory.

data exfiltration A form of data leakage or data loss in which data is moved to a location outside of the protected and authorized environment.

data loss prevention (DLP) Both a company policy as well as products available in the technology market. As a company policy, DLP focuses on implementing defenses against data loss and theft. As a product, DLP is a technology solution that assists with the fulfillment of a company's DLP policy.

database encryption An encryption concept applied to DMBS-stored data, which can range from individual cell encryption to full table encryption as well as any other intermediary division (such as rows or columns).

decommissioning (of encryption) Converting data in place from an encrypted form into its original plaintext form.

decryption The operation of using a cryptographic algorithm to restore a ciphertext message to its original plaintext.

defense in depth A security concept that emphasizes the importance of layers of security to provide stronger protection.

demilitarized zone (DMZ) An intentionally exposed portion of a network that is typically used to host services provided to outside systems or users.

denial of service (DoS) attack An attack that attempts to prevent access to a service or system, often by disabling the system or exhausting its resources.

design review Similar to an architecture review, a review that analyzes the design of a system or service to identify vulnerabilities and other issues.

differential backup A backup type that copies every file that has changed on the source disk since the most recent full backup to the backup media.

digital certificate A cryptographic device used to verify that a public key belongs to an individual or server.

digital signature A cryptographic technique used to provide the recipient of a message with authentication, integrity, and nonrepudiation.

directory traversal An attack that attempts to access directories that are not intended to be accessible to users.

disaster recovery The practice of contingency planning for the actual disruption of business operations by a natural or human-made disaster.

discretionary access control (DAC) An access control system that grants users the ability to decide what rights they will grant to other users on objects they control.

distributed denial of service (DDoS) attack A denial of service attack typically involving a large number of systems in many locations that attack a system or network, usually causing an outage due to the traffic load or load on an application or service.

DNS changer A form of malware that alters a domain name to an IP resolution requested by a system. DNS changers might hard-code false resolutions into the local DNS cache (by poisoning the HOSTS file that is read into memory upon startup). Some DNS changers alter the DNS server addresses in the IP configuration so queries are sent to a hacker-controlled DNS server, in order to feed you false IP addresses and redirect your traffic to unintended, often malicious locations.

Domain Name System (DNS) The system that translates IP addresses to human readable names such as www.humongousinsurance.com.

Dumpster diving Theft of items from an organization's or individual's trash to gain information about the person or organization.

E

EICAR A standardized test for anti-virus products.

electromagnetic interference (EMI) Radio emanations generated by an electronic device.

elliptic curve cryptography (ECC) An asymmetric cryptographic approach that relies upon the difficulty of finding the discrete logarithm of an elliptic curve.

encryption The operation of using a cryptographic algorithm to transform a plaintext message into a ciphertext message.

escaping metacharacters The use of an escape character, often the backslash (\), just before the metacharacter, which causes the string or statement to avoid, disable, or "escape" from the meaning or function of the metacharacter that follows.

event log A log that tracks system events.

evil twin A wireless network set up by an attacker that appears to be a legitimate wireless network belonging to the organization or individual.

exploit Any software code written to take advantage of a vulnerability, flaw, or weakness in software or hardware.

exposure factor (EF) A quantitative measure of the proportion of an asset that will be damaged if a risk materializes.

Extensible Authentication Protocol (EAP) An authentication framework used for wireless networks.

F

false acceptance rate (FAR) The rate at which a biometric system incorrectly allows unauthorized users access to a system.

false positive A positive result when a negative result should have resulted.

false rejection rate (FRR) The rate at which a biometric system incorrectly rejects authorized users.

File Transfer Protocol (FTP) A network protocol used to transfer files between hosts.

firewall A network security device designed to block or allow network traffic based on a set of rules.

firewall rules The rules that a firewall uses to decide what traffic to allow or deny passage.

firmware On-device–stored software providing the basic low-level intelligence for device operation.

flood guard A technique used to prevent network attacks or problems that result in very high network traffic levels. Intrusion prevention systems can provide flood guard capabilities, as can some switch-based protection tools.

FTPS A secure version of the File Transfer Protocol that adds support for transport layer security (TLS) or Secure Sockets Layer (SSL) encryption.

full backup A backup type that copies every file stored on the source disk to the backup media.

full-disk encryption The application of data encryption technology to an entire storage device.

fuzz testing A software evaluation technique that attempts to uncover errors in coding through stressing the input processing of a targeted application.

G

GPS tracking If a mobile device is lost or stolen, the device can report its GPS coordinates back to a centralized monitoring service for recovery.

gray box penetration testing A middle ground between white box and black box penetration testing. The testers are equipped with partial knowledge of the environment but must gather any other needed information on their own.

guideline A recommendation of controls that should be implemented as best practices within an organization.

H

hardening A security management process that attempts to reduce the attack surface of a system, network, or organization. It includes two primary steps or phases: removing unnecessary components and securing that which is a necessary component.

hardware lock A physical lock, which can be either a preset, cipher, biometric, or multifactor lock.

hardware security The security effort of an organization that focuses on hardware, its use, and its onboard firmware.

hardware security module (HSM) An add-on hardware device that can provide cryptoprocessing and other security features to a computer, device, or network connection that does not have these items natively.

hash A fixed-length value created by a hash function from variable-length input, such as a message, file, or disk image. Also known as a *message digest*.

header manipulation An attack against web browsers and servers that changes the HTTP headers sent between them. This is often aimed at co-opting a user's session.

honeynet A network of intentionally vulnerable systems that are exposed to attackers to gather information about their attack methods, tools, and behavior.

honeypot A single intentionally vulnerable system that is exposed to attack to gain information about attack methods against the system type or service it appears to expose.

host-based firewall A software firewall installed into an operating system in order to provide local firewall benefits of inbound and outbound filtering.

HTTPS Secure HTTP with support for TLS or SSL encryption.

Hypertext Transfer Protocol (HTTP) An application protocol that is the foundation of the web as we know it.

I

identification The process of claiming to be someone. In most cases for this book, identification is associated with a user name.

impersonation A social engineering attempt where an attacker pretends to be someone else to gain access or information.

implicit deny In firewalls and access control lists, a default deny that exists at the end of rulesets. In permissions-based systems such as firewalls, an implicit deny exists when no explicit permission is set, thus the default final rule for firewalls blocks any traffic not otherwise permitted.

incremental backup A backup type that copies every file that has changed on the source disk since the most recent full or incremental backup to the backup media.

individual file encryption File encryption performed on a file-by-file basis where each file can be encrypted by a unique encryption key, which is then enveloped with the user's public key and stored on the encrypted file.

infrastructure as a service (IaaS) A cloud service model that provides either physical or virtual hardware and other resources, duplicating a typical infrastructure that might otherwise be built and maintained physically by an organization.

input limit check A filter that verifies that received input is within an expected valid range or length of data.

input validation The inspection, analysis, parsing, and filtering of data before it is accepted into memory.

integrity The protection of information against unauthorized modification or deletion.

interference A situation that often results from rogue access points, which cause wireless disruption for legitimate access points.

Internet Control Message Protocol (ICMP) A protocol that provides diagnostic, control, and error messaging for networked devices.

Internet Protocol (IP) The underlying communication protocol for the Internet. It provides routing between networks based on IP addresses, thus creating internetworks.

intrusion detection system (IDS) A system that detects network attacks based on signatures or behavior patterns but cannot block attacks.

intrusion prevention system (IPS) A system that can block attack traffic and that must be placed inline with traffic to do so.

IPsec A protocol suite that provides capabilities intended to secure IP communications. IPsec provides authentication and encryption capabilities.

IPv4 The fourth version of IP, currently the primary version in use around the world. IPv4 uses a 32-bit addressing scheme and faces issues with address exhaustion.

IPv6 The latest version of IP. The intended replacement for IPv4, IPv6 provides support for larger addresses spaces as well as additional capabilities including auto- mated configuration, additional security, and larger packet sizes.

K

Kerberos protocol An authentication system that re- lies on tickets and that provides mutual authentication of the client and server. The Kerberos protocol is widely used for single sign-on in organizations.

key A binary string used to provide secrecy in any cryptographic operation.

key exchange Any mechanism that supports the transaction of keys between communication partners, preferably performed in such a way as to prevent eaves- dropping or interception.

key length The number of bits contained within a cryptographic key.

key recovery agent A trusted administrator or group of administrators who can be called upon to decrypt files when the user's private key is lost or corrupted.

keylogger A program that can be classified as a form of spyware, but is usually much more specific and focused. A keylogger collects the keystrokes from the local keyboard. This log of typed material can be saved to a file for later retrieval or uploaded to an Internet service (FTP or email).

L

LDAP injection An injection attack against an LDAP directory server, typically to gain information or rights.

least privilege The concept that users and programs should only have the minimum set of privileges required to accomplish their role or purpose.

Lightweight Directory Access Protocol (LDAP) A directory protocol that provides authentication services as well as directory management tools.

Lightweight Extensible Authentication Protocol (LEAP) A proprietary authentication method created by Cisco and primarily used for wireless networks.

load balancer A system that distributes traffic be- tween multiple servers.

load balancing The practice of spreading requests across multiple servers with the same capabilities.

log rotation The replacement of logs as they are filled, after a set duration of time, or as other measures are met. Log rotation ensures that logging does not ex- haust system resources such as drive space or memory.

logic bomb Malware that performs an action or ac- tions when a specific condition is reached.

loop protection A network control concept that is typically implemented using spanning tree protocol, a protocol that detects when a network loop has been created and shuts down the loop.

lossy mathematical operation A calculation function that discards or drops data as it performs calculations.

M

MAC filter Filtering based on the hardware address of network devices. MAC filtering is sometimes used to help restrict the systems allowed on a wireless or wired network.

malicious add-on Typically a browser plug-in that is actually malware. Often poses as a useful utility or as a plugin required to view a website.

malware A catch-all name for malicious software such as viruses, spyware, and trojans.

malware inspection A type of content inspection that focuses on detecting malware like viruses, trojans, and similar threats.

management controls Controls that ensure that the risk management process is running effectively. These have an indirect impact on the security of an organization's information assets.

mandatory access control (MAC) An access control system in which policies are set by the administrator, not by users.

mandatory vacation The concept that users must take a vacation (typically at least two weeks) to allow their substitutes to find any malfeasance on their part.

man-in-the-middle An attack that places the attacker between the source and destination of traffic or communications.

mantrap A physical security device that uses two doors on either side of a room that cannot both be open at the same time. Mantraps are useful for keeping unauthorized individuals from accessing secure spaces by following authorized users.

mean time between failures (MTBF) The average amount of time that passes between failures for a particular piece of equipment.

mean time to recovery (MTTR) The average amount of time required to repair a defective piece of equipment or otherwise restore it to operation.

message digest See *hash*.

metacharacter Any character that has been assigned a special programmatic meaning by a programming language or execution environment.

multifactor authentication Authentication that requires more than one factor, such as a password, biometric identifier, or token. The factors are usually from different classes: something you have, something you are, and something you know.

N

NetBIOS A system that provides a network name service, as well as the ability to connect to other PCs on a local area network.

Network Address Translation (NAT) The process of modifying IP address information between networks. This can allow multiple systems to use a single external address, to change addresses between networks, or to map addresses on a one-to-one basis. NAT can also handle port changes and other modifications to IP traffic traversing a NAT system.

nonrepudiation A goal of cryptography that allows the recipient of a message to undeniably prove to a third party that the message came from the purported sender.

NT LAN Manager (NTLM) A password authentication protocol developed by Microsoft for use in the Windows NT operating system.

O

offline scanning A feature of some malware scanners that restarts a system off of a bootable USB drive and then runs a malware scan with the installed operating system not active.

operational controls Controls that protect information systems and that are carried out primarily by individuals, rather than technology.

P

packet filter firewall A type of firewall that filters packets based on the source or destination IP address, port, or protocol.

passphrase A phrase or set of words used as a password. These are often preferable to passwords because they can be longer but easier to remember, making them harder to crack by using brute-force methods.

Password Authentication Protocol (PAP) An insecure network-based password authentication protocol that sends passwords in cleartext form.

patch A software fix intended to solve problems or to remediate a security vulnerability. Often used interchangeably with *update*.

penetration test An attack-based test that attempts to exploit vulnerabilities and weaknesses in an organization's defenses.

personally identifying information (PII) Information about an individual that can be used to distinguish or trace an individual's identity, or that is otherwise linked or linkable to an individual.

pharming Phishing attacks that are intended to cause recipients to visit websites to get ad commissions, personal information, or credentials. Pharming is distinguished from traditional phishing attacks due to its use of fake websites, which users are directed to as part of the pharming attack.

phishing attack An attack that attempts to acquire sensitive information, such as passwords, financial account numbers and Social Security numbers, by posing as a legitimate requestor in an email message.

platform as a service (PaaS) A cloud service model that provides underlying computing platforms and tools such as application delivery or development environments.

policy A formal, written statement that outlines, normally in broad terms, the objectives of an organization's management.

pop-up blocker A product that prevents websites from opening additional browser windows in order to reduce the annoyance of advertising or the possibility of a social engineering or malware attack.

port scanner A tool used to survey networked systems to identify what services they expose by connecting to ports open on that system. Some port scanners have additional capabilities such as operating system identification and firewall bypass techniques.

port security A network security capability that limits the hardware addresses that can connect to a port.

power level controls Controls of wireless network devices that provide the ability to limit their network broadcast power, limiting the range that the device can be accessed from.

Pretty Good Privacy (PGP) A cryptographic algorithm that combines the use of symmetric and asymmetric cryptography.

privilege creep A frequent issue over time for permission sets as users receive permissions based on their predecessors, or when users have permissions accumulated over years of service that aren't related to their current role.

privilege escalation The process of using an exploit or vulnerability to perform actions as a more trusted user.

procedure Specific, step-by-step directions for implementing a control.

Protected Extensible Authentication Protocol (PEAP) An encapsulation protocol for EAP that provides an encrypted and authenticated TLS tunnel. PEAP helps to correct problems with EAP's security model, which presumes that communications cannot be monitored, resulting in exposed communications.

protocol analyzer A packet capture tool used to look at and analyze network traffic content. Also known as a sniffer.

proximity card A smart card that can be read remotely via RFID or other wireless technology.

proximity reader A device designed to read proximity cards.

proxy An appliance, server, or application that acts as an intermediary for requests between systems. Used to filter traffic or to restrict or provide access to resources.

R

RADIUS A widely used authentication and accounting service used for centralized authentication.

ransomware An attack that locks, freezes, or encrypts data or an entire computer, then displays messages that attempt to extort the victim into paying money to have the system released.

RC4 A symmetric stream cipher developed by Ron Rivest and widely used in network security applications.

recovery point objective (RPO) The amount of data that is considered an acceptable loss by the organization.

recovery time objective (RTO) The organization's desired recovery time for a particular service in the event of a disaster.

redundant array of independent disks (RAID) The use of either mirroring or parity with multiple disks to protect against the failure of a single disk.

reflected XSS Also known as nonpersistent cross-site scripting, a cross-site scripting attack that is typically passed via HTML form submission or as HTML query parameters that are used immediately, rather than being stored and redisplayed to future users.

remote administration tool (RAT) Software with both legitimate and malicious purposes.

remote wipe The ability to trigger a deletion of on-device data after a device is no longer in your possession. Also known as *remote sanitization*.

removable media A wide range of storage technologies and devices, including USB flash drives; portable hard drives; optical discs, such as CDs, DVDs, and Blu-ray Disks; tapes; memory cards, such as SD cards; and floppy disks.

replay attack An attack that resends captured network traffic, usually to attempt to authenticate by using previously used logins.

risk The intersection of a threat and a vulnerability, such as an event that might cause harm to the assets or operation of an organization.

risk acceptance A strategy where the organization decides that the most prudent course of action is to simply monitor the evolution of a risk.

risk avoidance A risk management strategy that alters business activities to remove the possibility of a risk materializing.

risk deterrence A risk management strategy that uses measures designed to reduce the likelihood that a threat will surface.

risk equation A calculation of risk reached by multiplying likelihood and impact, in the equation $R = L \times I$.

risk mitigation A risk management strategy that uses controls designed to reduce the likelihood that a risk will affect an organization and/or the impact that a risk will have on the organization if it materializes.

risk transference A risk management strategy that moves the liability for a risk from one entity to another.

rogue access point An access point added to a network that it is not supposed to be on.

role-based access control (RBAC) An access controls system that controls access to objects such as files and programs based on the roles of subjects (users). Roles are typically assigned based on job duties, position, or responsibilities in the organization.

rootkit A malware tool that is intended to help attackers preserve access to and control of a machine.

router A network device used to connect networks and direct traffic between them.

RSA An asymmetric encryption algorithm that uses keys between 1,024 and 4,096 bits long based upon the difficulty of factoring the products of large prime numbers, named for its inventors Ron Rivest, Adi Shamir, and Leonard Adleman.

ruleset A set of rules applied to a firewall or other device that define what it will take action on.

S

screen lock A security feature on a mobile device similar to a password-protected lock screen or screen saver on a typical computer.

secure coding practices Efforts to include defensive and security elements in programming code.

Secure Shell Protocol (SSH) An encrypted network protocol used to provide remote command-line (shell) access, as well as other secure network traffic services.

Secure Sockets Layer (SSL) A protocol that combines the use of symmetric and asymmetric cryptography to provide authentication, encryption, and message integrity checking for application protocols. SSL has been replaced by TLS, although many people use the term *SSL* to refer to TLS.

security information and event management (SIEM) system Devices and software that centralize logging, event monitoring, and other network and system monitoring capabilities, along with reporting and alerting services, into a single system. SEIM systems have largely replaced earlier security information management (SIM) and security event management (SEM) tools.

security log In general use, a log that contains log entries related to the security of a system or application. For Windows systems, a Windows system log that tracks logons and other security-related information.

security management The focus on governance of the security controls, countermeasures, and configuration of an operating system (or any hardware or software product) with the goal of tuning and improving security over time.

separation of duties The concept that staff members must have their tasks separated so that a single staff member cannot perform a function entirely on his or her own. This prevents that single staff member from exploiting his or her privileges.

service set identifier (SSID) broadcast A broadcast that provides the public name of a wireless network to systems wanting to connect. SSID broadcast is disabled as a security precaution for some networks because it requires connecting users to know the SSID of the network before they can connect.

sheep dip A stand-alone anti-malware scanning system that is intended to be used as a precleaning tool against removable media devices before they are connected to the production environment.

shoulder surfing A social engineering attack that involves looking over a person's shoulder or at his or her screen or keyboard as the victim performs work or types in a password.

signature A fingerprint for attacks or malware.

Simple Mail Transfer Protocol (SMTP) A protocol for email transmission across IP networks.

single point of failure A system or process component that, if it fails, can cause an entire business function to fail in a cascading manner.

single sign-on An authentication system that allows a single authentication to be used for a variety of diverse services without requiring the user to re-enter a password.

single loss expectancy (SLE) The amount of financial loss expected each time that a risk materializes.

smart card A type of token that can be used in an authentication system. Smart cards often have cryptographic modules that help ensure secure authentication.

smurf attack A denial of service attack that sends huge numbers of ICMP packets from a faked source IP to a broadcast address, resulting in massive return traffic.

sniffer See *protocol analyzer*.

sniffing Capturing data from a network connection.

social engineering Hacking people. Involves exploiting human factors to gather data or to gain access to systems, information, and physical locations.

software as a service (SaaS) A cloud service model that provides software as a service, rather than the underlying hardware or operating system.

software development life cycle (SDLC) A framework for the planning, oversight, and control of the programming process with a focus on secure coding practices. Also known as *systems development life cycle*.

source code review The process of reading and interpreting source code line by line.

spam filter A content inspection system that specifically targets spam email.

spambot A botnet that is used to transmit spam.

spear phishing Phishing attacks targeted at a specific organization or group of users.

SPIM Spam via instant message.

spoofing Falsifying information. In network attacks, spoofing often involves presenting a fake IP address.

spyware Malware that spies on the users of the system it is installed on. Typically spyware gathers information about browsing habits, but it can also gather personal information, bank accounts, or other high-value data.

SQL injection Injection of SQL code to be run against a database, usually via a vulnerable web application.

standard A written description of the specific controls that must be used to achieve an organization's policies.

stateful packet inspection A type of firewall filtering that tracks whether connections are open between systems and allowed by a ruleset, rather than checking each packet as it traverses the firewall as required by packet filter firewalls.

stored XSS Also known as persistent cross-site scripting, these attacks typically work by submitting script code into improperly secured input forms that are later displayed to users who access the data stored by the web application. This causes the user's browser to execute the script, performing the actions scripted by the attacker.

stream cipher A cryptographic algorithm that operates on a single unit of text at a time, normally a character or a bit.

subnet A division of an IP network.

supernet A combination of one or more IP networks.

switch A network device that sends traffic to systems based on their IP address and MAC address by using a CAM table, which matches IP addresses to hardware addresses.

symmetric cryptography Cryptography that uses a cryptographic algorithm where both the sender and receiver make use of a shared secret key for both the encryption and decryption operations.

T

TACACS The Terminal Access Controller Access-Control System, an authentication protocol primarily used for network devices.

TACACS+ A replacement for TACACS that provides separate authentication, authorization, and accounting services. TACACS+ has replaced TACACS and XTACACS in most organizations that used them.

tailgating Following a person with legitimate access rights into a secure area.

technical controls Controls that leverage technology to reduce the likelihood or impact of a risk on an organization.

Telnet A network protocol used for remote command-line access, largely replaced by SSH due to security issues, because Telnet has no provision for encryption of data.

template In the context of information security, a set of security settings that can be applied to a system to make it meet a hardening standard.

Temporal Key Integrity Protocol (TKIP) A wireless network security protocol used to protect network traffic.

threat A possible danger that might exploit a vulnerability, resulting in harm to the organization.

time-of-day restriction Restrictions on user rights or privileges based on the time of day. Often used to prevent employees from accessing systems after hours.

token A hardware device that is used for authentication. Typically tokens either plug in via a USB port, display a code, or have an embedded chip that provides the "something you have" factor of multifactor authentication.

Transmission Control Protocol (TCP) One of the core protocols of the IP suite. TCP is a connection-oriented protocol that provides reliable delivery of traffic between hosts.

Transport Layer Security (TLS) A method that uses symmetric and asymmetric cryptography to provide authentication, encryption, and message integrity checking for application protocols. TLS prevents eavesdropping and modification of traffic it protects, and was designed as a replacement for Secure Sockets Layer (SSL).

trend A general direction of movement for something that is being monitored. Trends often indicate issues before they become evident.

Triple DES (3DES) A security enhancement to the DES algorithm that applies the standard DES algorithm three times and can increase the key length to up to 168 bits.

trojan Malware that pretends to be desirable software in order to get victims to download or run it.

trusted operating system An operating system that provides multilevel security and evidence of correctness. The Common Criteria is one example of a standard for trusted operating systems.

Trusted Platform Module (TPM) A special chip designed for use by encryption solutions as a secure and tamper-proof storage location for encryption keys.

Twofish A symmetric block cipher developed by Bruce Schneier as an entry into the AES competition. Twofish operates on 128-bit blocks of data with a 128-bit, 192-bit, or 256-bit encryption key.

Type I error See *false rejection rate (FRR)*.

Type II error See *false acceptance rate (FAR)*.

U

update A new version of software intended to fix a problem or to add functionality. Often used interchangeably with *patch*.

URL filtering A type of content inspection and filtering that focuses on web traffic.

URL injector An attack that changes the link a user clicked to an alternate URL. This might be performed by adware/spyware-like tools in order to track activity or redirect users to marketing materials, or this might

be performed to hijack a website and direct users to a hacker-controlled version of a website.

user behavior modification Training users to avoid risky activities. These include blindly opening email attachments, downloading files from the Internet, following hyperlinks from social networking, using P2P file sharing services, and using portable storage devices (especially between secure and insecure, company and personal, or private and external environments).

User Datagram Protocol (UDP) A protocol that, unlike TCP, is not connection-oriented and does not provide guarantees of reliability, but does provide checksums to ensure data integrity.

V

video surveillance Monitoring a physical location by using video cameras. Many current deployments use a combination of network-based and traditional hard-wired cameras, allowing live monitoring and recording of the area where the cameras are deployed.

virtual LAN (VLAN) A technique that allows segmentation of networks through use of VLAN tags. This allows logical separation of networks on the same physical hardware.

virtual private network (VPN) A network that uses encrypted tunnels to connect sites or systems through public networks. VPNs are often used for remote access or to connect sites via a secure connection across the public Internet.

virtualization The concept of creating a virtual, rather than actual, version of a system, application, network, or hardware. Virtualization allows systems to be abstracted, providing the ability to assign resources dynamically, to more easily move systems, and a variety of other advantages.

virus Malware that spreads by copying itself into files and drives.

virus hoax A false or misleading message that attempts to trick people into taking actions that damage their computers or reduce the network's security.

vishing Voice phishing, usually conducted via VoIP phones.

Voice over IP (VoIP) A replacement for traditional telephony over data networks.

VPN concentrator A device that provides virtual private network services, providing secure network connections for remote users.

vulnerability A weakness in an organization's security controls that might allow a breach of confidentiality, integrity, or availability.

vulnerability scanner A tool used to find weaknesses in systems and devices, typically by using a list of predefined known issues. Vulnerability scanners connect to services and use testing techniques, including version number identification and tests of how the service or system responds to traffic or connections, to identify vulnerabilities.

W

web application firewall A firewall specifically designed to understand and handle web-based attacks like SQL injection and cross-site scripting attacks.

web application vulnerability scanner A vulnerability scanner specifically designed to target web applications. Web application vulnerability scanners require additional specialized capabilities to simulate user input and to test for attacks such as SQL injection, cross-site scripting, and other web application–specific attacks.

web security gateway A network security appliance designed to filter web user traffic to prevent attacks, malware, and undesired web browsing.

whaling A type of phishing that targets high-profile targets.

white box penetration testing Sometimes also called clear box, crystal box, or transparent box testing, provides complete knowledge of the asset or assets that are being tested during a penetration test.

whitelisting A security filtering concept where all input is rejected by default unless it satisfies the filter requirements of items, software, or rules on the allowed list.

Wi-Fi Protected Access (WPA) A security protocol for wireless networks that replaced WEP and uses TKIP to provide per-packet keys, making attacks much harder than those against WEP.

Wi-Fi Protected Access II (WPA2) The wireless security protocol that replaced WPA, adding additional encryption capabilities and certification by the Wi-Fi Alliance.

Wired Equivalent Privacy (WEP) A now-outmoded security protocol for wireless networks. WEP has numerous security issues which resulted in its replacement by WPA.

worm A self-spreading malware program that spreads via a network, typically exploiting vulnerable services or operating systems.

X

Xmas attack A network attack that sends TCP packets to a victim with all possible TCP flags set.

XML injection Injection of information into an XML file or transaction, often to seize rights or permissions.

XSRF See *cross-site request forgery*.

XSS See *cross-site scripting*.

XTACACS An extended version of TACACS created by Cisco.

Z

zero-day attack An attack against a vulnerability that has not yet been announced or patched, thus it is exploited at "day zero" of the vulnerability/patch cycle.

zombie A remotely controlled compromised system, typically part of a botnet.

Index

Symbols & Numbers

A

D

H

U

About the authors

DAVID SEIDL is the Director of Information Security at the University of Notre Dame, where he leads the university's dedicated information security team. He also serves as a concurrent instructor for the Mendoza College of Business, where he teaches a popular networking and security course. David has been recognized as a leader in the security industry, receiving Network Computing's Security Seven award in 2013 for his contributions to higher education information security. David holds the CISSP, GCIH, and GPEN certifications, as well as a master's degree in Information Security.

MIKE CHAPPLE, Ph.D., is Senior Director for Enterprise Support Services at the University of Notre Dame. In this role, he oversees the information security, IT architecture, project management, strategic planning, and communications functions for the Office of Information Technologies. Mike also serves as a concurrent assistant professor in the university's Computer Applications Department, where he teaches an undergraduate course on information security. He is a technical editor for *Information Security* magazine and has written several books, including *Information Security Illuminated* (Jones and Bartlett, 2004), *SQL Server 2008 for Dummies* (Wiley, 2008), and the *CISSP Study Guide 6th Edition* (Sybex, 2012). Mike earned both his bachelor's and doctoral degrees from Notre Dame in computer science and engineering. He also holds an MS in computer science from the University of Idaho and an MBA from Auburn University. You can reach Mike by email at *mike@chapple.org*.

JAMES MICHAEL STEWART has been working with computers and technology for nearly 30 years. His work focuses on security, certification, and various operating systems. Recently, Michael has been teaching job skill and certification courses, such as CISSP, ethical hacking/penetration testing, computer forensics, and CompTIA Security+. He is the primary author of the *CISSP Study Guide 6th Edition* (Sybex, 2012), the *Security+ Review Guide 2nd Edition (SY0-301)* (Sybex, 2011), and *Network Security, Firewalls, and VPNs* (Jones & Bartlett Learning, 2010). Michael has also contributed to many other security-focused materials, including exam preparation guides, practice exams, DVD video instruction, and courseware. In addition, Michael has co-authored numerous books on other security, certification, and administration topics. He has developed certification courseware and training materials as well as presented these materials in the classroom. Michael holds a variety of certifications, including CISSP, CEH, CHFI, and CompTIA Security+. Michael graduated in 1992 from the University of Texas at Austin with a bachelor's degree in philosophy. Despite his degree, his computer knowledge is self-acquired, based on seat-of-the-pants, hands-on, "street smarts" experience. You can reach Michael by email at *michael@impactonline.com*.

How to download your ebook

Thank you for purchasing this Microsoft Press title. Your companion PDF eBook is ready to download from our official distributor's site on oreilly.com.

To download your eBook, go to http://aka.ms/PressEbook
and follow the instructions.

Please note: You will be asked to create a free online account and enter the access code below.

ACCESS CODE:

LRHMJZN

CompTIA Security+ Training Kit (Exam SY0-301)

Your PDF eBook allows you to:

- search the full text
- print
- copy and paste

Best yet, you will be notified about free updates to your eBook.

If you ever lose your eBook file, you can download it again just by logging in to your account.

Need help? Please contact:
mspbooksupport@oreilly.com
or call 800-889-8969.

Now that you've read the book...

Tell us what you think!

Was it useful?
Did it teach you what you wanted to learn?
Was there room for improvement?

Let us know at http://aka.ms/tellpress

Your feedback goes directly to the staff at Microsoft Press,
and we read every one of your responses. Thanks in advance!